Journal of the Early Book Society
for the Study of Manuscripts and Printing History

Edited by Martha W. Driver
Volume 18, 2015

Copyright © 2015
Pace University Press
41 Park Row
New York, NY 10038

All rights reserved
Printed in the United States of America

ISBN: 978-0-9619518-2-5
ISSN: 1525-6790

Member

Council of Editors of Learned Journals

♾ ™ The paper used in this publication meets the minimum requirements of American National Standard for information Sciences—Permanence of Paper for printed Library Materials,
ANSI Z39.48—1984.

The *Journal of the Early Book Society* is published annually. *JEBS* invites longer articles on manuscripts and/or printed books produced between 1350 and 1550. Special consideration will be given to essays exploring the period of transition from manuscript to print. Authors are asked to follow *The Chicago Manual of Style*. A Works Cited list at the end of the text should include city, publisher, and date. Manuscripts are to be sent, in triplicate, along with an abstract of up to 150 words, to Martha Driver, Early Book Society, Department of English, Pace University, 41 Park Row, New York, New York 10038. Only materials accompanied by a self-addressed, stamped envelope (or international reply coupon) will be returned. Members of the Early Book Society who are recent authors may send review books for consideration to Susan Powell, Reviews Editor, 7 Woodbine Terrace, Headingley, Leeds LS6 4AF, England. Brief notes on recent discoveries, highlighting little-known or recently uncovered texts and/or images, may be sent to Daniel Wakelin, Faculty of English, University of Oxford, St. Cross Building, Manor Road, Oxford, OX1 3UL, UK. Subscription information may be obtained from Martha Driver or from Pace University Press.

Those interested in joining the Early Book Society or with editorial inquiries may contact Martha Driver by post or e-mail (MDriver@Pace.edu). Information may also be found at <www.nyu.edu/projects/EBS>. For ordering information, call Pace University Press at 212-346-1405 or visit http://www.pace.edu/press. Institutions and libraries may purchase copies directly from Ingram Library Services (1-800-937-5300).

The editor wishes to thank Gill Kent, the Pace University Press Graduate Assistants Mary Katherine Cornfield and Angela Taldone, and Manuela Soares, Associate Director, Pace University Press, for their help and advice on this issue.

Journal of the Early Book Society
for the Study of Manuscripts and Printing History

Editor:
Martha W. Driver, *Pace University*

Associate Editors:
Susan Powell, *University of Salford*
Daniel Wakelin, *University of Oxford*

Editorial Board:

Matthew Balensuela, *DePauw University*
Julia Boffey, *Queen Mary, University of London*
Cynthia J. Brown, *University of California, Santa Barbara*
Richard F. M. Byrn, *University of Leeds*
James Carley, *York University*
Joyce Coleman, *University of Oklahoma*
Margaret Connolly, *University of St Andrews*
Susanna Fein, *Kent State University*
Alexandra Gillespie, *University of Toronto*
Vincent Gillespie, *Lady Margaret Hall, Oxford University*
Stanley S. Hussey, *Lancaster University*
Ann M. Hutchison, *Pontifical Institute of Mediaeval Studies and York University*
Michael Kuczynski, *Tulane University*
William Marx, *University of Wales, Lampeter*
Carol M. Meale, *Bristol University*
Linne R. Mooney, *University of York*
Charlotte C. Morse, *Virginia Commonwealth University*
Daniel W. Mosser, *Virginia Polytechnic Institute and State University*
Ann Eljenholm Nichols, *Winona State University*
Judy Oliver, *Colgate University*
Michael Orr, *Lawrence University*
Steven Partridge, *University of British Columbia*
Derek Pearsall, *Harvard University*
Pamela Sheingorn, *Baruch College and The City University of New York Graduate School and University Center*
Alison Smith, *Wagner College*
Toshiyuki Takamiya, *Keio University*
Andrew Taylor, *University of Ottawa*
John Thompson, *Queen's University, Belfast*
Ronald Waldron, *King's College, University of London*
Edward Wheatley, *Loyola University*
Mary Beth Winn, *SUNY Albany*

Contents

Articles

Making Miscellaneous Manuscripts in Fifteenth-Century England: 1
The Case of Sloane 2275
    RALPH HANNA

Kyng Alisaunder and Oxford, Bodleian Library, MS Laud Misc.   29
622
    NICOLE CLIFTON

Mirk's Festial and Theodoric Rood   50
    SUSAN POWELL

The Language of Identity: Henri Estienne's Anti-Italian Polemics   103
    NICHOLAS SHANGLER

Reading Chaucer in the Tower: The Person Behind the Pen in an   136
Early-Modern Copy of Chaucer's Works
    MIMI ENSLEY

Les Vies des Femmes Célèbres: Antoine Dufour, Jean Pichore, and a   158
Manuscript's Debt to an Italian Printed Book
    ANNELIESE P. RENCK

Nota Bene: Brief Notes on Manuscripts and Early Printed Books Highlighting Little-Known or Recently Uncovered Items or Related Issues

The Sizes of Middle English Books, ca.1390-1430   181
    RALPH HANNA

Oxford, Bodleian Library, MS Laud Misc. 740 and New York   192
Public Library, MS Spencer 19: A Common History?
    KATHRYN WALLS

A Previously Unrecognized French Alexander Romance   207
    J.R. MATTISON

A Previously Unidentified *Somniale Danielis* Text in Takamiya   213
MS 33 with an Updated Handlist of Latin *Somniale* Texts from
England
   ALEXANDRA REIDER

New Findings in a Late-Medieval Catechetic Prose Sequence   228
   MICHAEL MADRINKIAN

Tracing Neurological Disorders in the Handwriting of Medieval   241
Scribes: Using the Past to Inform the Future
   DEBORAH THORPE

Descriptive Reviews

Francisco Alonso Alemeida   249
A Middle English Medical Remedy Book: Edited from Glasgow
University Library MS Hunter 185
   CARRIE GRIFFIN

Joanna Bellis, ed.
John Page's The Siege of Rouen: *Edited from London,*   252
British Library MS Egerton 1995
   LIVIA VISSER-FUCHS

Peter W. M. Blayney   255
The Stationers' Company and The Printers Of London, 1501–1557
   ALEXANDRA GILLESPIE

Thomas A. Bredehoft   257
The Visible Text: Textual Production and Reproduction from
Beowulf *to* Maus
   OLIVER PICKERING

Laura Cleaver and Helen Conrad O'Briain   260
Latin Psalter Manuscripts in Trinity College Dublin and the Chester
Beatty Library
   MICHAEL P. KUCZYNSKI

Brenda Dunn-Lardeau, ed.   264
Catalogue des imprimés des XVe et XVIe siècles dans les collections
de l'Université de Québec à Montréal
   JOYCE BORO

Oton de Granson   267
Poems
   OLIVIA ROBINSON

Susanna Fein and Michael Johnston, eds.   269
Robert Thornton and His Books, Essays on the Lincoln and London Thornton Manuscripts
   JOHN J. THOMPSON

Simon Horobin and Linne R. Mooney, eds.   272
Middle English Texts in Transition: A Festschrift Dedicated to Toshiyuki Takamiya on his 70th Birthday
   JILL C. HAVENS

Michael Johnston   275
Romance and the Gentry in Late Medieval England
   DEREK A. PEARSALL

Kathryn Kerby-Fulton, John T. Thompson, and Sarah Baechle, eds.   278
New Directions in Medieval Manuscript Studies and Reading Practices: Essays in Honor of Derek Pearsall
   KEVIN GUSTAFSON

Kathleen E. Kennedy   282
The Courtly and Commercial Art of the Wycliffite Bible
   ANN ELJENHOLM NICHOLS

Peter J. Lucas and Angela M. Lucas   285
The Medieval Manuscripts at Maynooth: Explorations in the Unknown
   MARGARET CONNOLLY

William Marx, ed.   287
The Middle English Liber Aureus *and Gospel of Nicodemus*

Niamh Pattwell, ed.
Exornatorium Curatorum

Francisco Alonso Almeida, ed.
A Middle English Medical Remedy Book
   VERONICA O'MARA

Carol M. Meale and Derek Pearsall, eds.   291
Makers and Users of Medieval Books: Essays in Honour of A. S. G. Edwards
    HELEN PHILLIPS

Richard J. Moll, ed.   294
William Caxton: The Book of Ovyde Named Methamorphose
    TAKAKO KATO

Ed Potten and Satoko Tokunaga, eds.   298
Incunabula on the Move: The Production, Circulation and Collection of Early Printed Books
    SUSAN POWELL

Robert R. Raymo and Judith G. Raymo, compilers   302
Shari Perkins and Jared Camins-Esakov, eds.
The Chaucer Collection of Robert R. Raymo
    DEREK A. PEARSALL

Richard H. Rouse and Mary A. Rouse   305
Bound Fast with Letters: Medieval Writers, Readers, and Texts
    A.I. DOYLE

Fiona Somerset and Nicholas Watson, eds.   307
Truth and Tales: Cultural Mobility and Medieval Media
    LINNE R. MOONEY

John Scattergood   311
John Skelton: The Career of an Early Tudor Poet
    JULIA BOFFEY

Daniel Wakelin   314
Scribal Correction and Literary Craft: English Manuscripts 1375-1510
    SUSAN POWELL

About the Authors   321

Making Miscellaneous Manuscripts in Fifteenth-Century England: The Case of Sloane 2275

RALPH HANNA

I.

British Library, MS Sloane 2275, deserves attention for any variety of reasons. The book provides a major collection of Latin texts composed by the fourteenth-century hermit Richard Rolle "of Hampole" (West Riding, Yorkshire). In addition, the manuscript unusually brings an extensive piece of the central Middle English literary canon, the widely dispersed poem *The Prick of Conscience*, into contact with sophisticated Latin texts. Finally, as a production, Sloane 2275 is a thorough mess, indeed after Oxford, Magdalen College, MS lat. 93, probably the most difficult book to explain that I have ever run across.[1]

The mid-fifteenth-century Sloane manuscript might be described as having a triple focus. Its only extended English, *The Prick of Conscience*, appears near the book's center and involves, not a consecutive bout of copying, but fits and starts, in three of the eight units in which the book was produced. This segment is wedged between two more extensive endeavors in Latin. The Rolle anthology opens the volume. Excepting some brief filler texts at the end of constituent units, some of them (items 3 and 4) decidedly *post factum* additions, presentation of Rolle absorbs more than half the book, 150 folios and four of the production units.

The Rolle materials here rank among the seven or eight most extensive collections of the hermit's Latin.[2] Moreover, these materials are largely focused upon Rolle's larger and more challenging, nonexegetical texts, actually a minority of the works ascribed to the hermit. Besides Sloane 2275, only BodL, MS Bodley 861, and its probable grandchild Oxford, Corpus Christi College, MS 193, provide readers with the complete set of Rolle's four Latin "treatises." Among fullscale efforts at reproducing Rolle's works, BodL, MS Laud misc. 528; Oxford, Balliol College, MS 224A; Hereford Cathedral, MS O.viii.1 (probably the direct source of Corpus 193); and BNF, MS lat. 15700, all lack the difficult *Melos amoris*.[3]

In Sloane 2275, these materials have been presented – and read – with unusual care. The texts are equipped with extensive marginalia – finding notes, "nota" marks, textual corrections. But such extensive annotation occurs in Sloane only in portions dedicated to Rolle. The most extensive materials appear in about the first seventy folios, then through early portions of *Incendium amoris* (through fol. 85), and resume in Rolle's *Super novem lecciones*, before ceasing.[4] In those portions, this annotation is accompanied by a great deal of page-foot textual correction; such materials imply not only very thorough engagement with these texts, but an equally conscientious effort at "correction" through consultation of multiple exemplars, an activity evidenced elsewhere in the book.

At the end of Sloane 2275, two booklets present Latin devotional/instructional texts. Unlike the Rolle at the head, a collection with minimal parallels, these materials are utterly commonplace. They are texts so canonical in medieval Latin anthologies that they were familiar to, and frequently translated, in whole or in part, by medieval persons writing in English (and are even familiar to monolingual modern English scholars): the pseudo-Augustinian "Speculum peccatoris," Honorius's *Elucidarium*, Innocent III's *De miseria*, the pseudo-Bernardine *Meditationes* ("Multi multa sciunt..."), for example. I return to consider this Latin/vernacular overlap of textual interests at the conclusion of the essay.

Although one can divide the contents of the manuscript into more or less homogeneous chunks of material, their physical transmission is a thorough mess. The seventeen texts are disposed across what I would describe, probably a bit tendentiously, as eight production units, some certainly expansions of already standing copy, some breaking a single text into separate chunks. In addition, the volume evidences the activity of something like a dozen to fifteen scribes, although five hands are responsible for over 90 percent of the whole, the remainder appearing together to provide very short stints in two isolated segments of the book (fols. 153ra-65va, 215ra-17vb or 219rb). Such clearly communal production might be considered a major factor contributing to the disorder of the volume.

More than simply multiple hands is at issue. At least in part, the book's disarray reflects the fact that only two of the scribes here (those I call 2, who signs as "Merssh," and 5) appear to have had sophisticated professional training and are capable of writing carefully formal book hands. Further, on the basis of his hand, one of the untutored individuals, scribe 1, who identifies himself only as "M," clearly organized – if that is the proper term – the work into the form that now survives. Just to provide a sense of some of the difficulties, Sloane 2275 is the only manuscript I have ever examined (although I should not claim that it is unique, only "rare" in a late-medieval English context) where catchwords have been imposed regularly only on the first leaves of quires and thus "run backward." (That is, they connect the head of one quire to the end of the preceding, rather than the reverse.) The majority of these represent M's supply, all but one of the original copyists (scribe 3 is the exception) having not bothered.

As the overview of contents indicates, for both its Latin portions, the Sloane manuscript draws on, and augments, materials shared with another book, BNF lat. 15700. This volume, at least half a century older than Sloane, was copied by a single scribe in a consistent, yet current anglicana, s. xiv ex. Like the Sloane manuscript, BNF lat. 15700 is a fascicular book, in this case six or seven separate units.[5] Although the manuscript is now ordered with a set of consecutive quire signatures (+, a-y), these were clearly imposed, not during the copying, but in preparation for the book's binding. Throughout the whole there is sporadic evidence that quires were originally signed only by the leaf-number (sometimes in roman, at other times in arabic), the whole then retained, and only arranged in their current order as a final step. The Paris manuscript shares half its texts with Sloane, ten in all (out of Sloane's seventeen text items). Insofar as these shared texts have been studied, they plainly demonstrate both manuscripts' recourse to common exemplars; for example, the two manuscripts form part of a distinctive group of only four books among the 110 surviving copies of Rolle's *Emendatio vitae*.[6]

Yet neither book is a pallid copy of the other, testimony to the tailoring of both volumes from additional exemplars augmenting a common core. Sloane includes only the first ten main texts of the Paris manuscript and has no parallels to the concluding three or four booklets of the earlier volume. These present hardy standbys by English authors who chose to write in Latin, like Robert Grosseteste's *Templum Domini* and instructional works ascribed to Peter of Blois, archdeacon of Bath and London. Conversely, lat. 15700 lacks materials present in Sloane, such as Rolle's *Melos amoris* (which absorbs most of Sloane's Booklet 1) and Honorius's *Elucidarium* (the sole text in its Booklet 8). Of the first omission, one might note that *Melos, Kunstprosa* if there ever were such, is a true niche market item, absent, as I indicate above, from a number of larger Rolle "author anthologies" and apparently sought out by the Sloane team to fulfill, with unusual success, a desire for extensive presentation of the hermit's major works.

BNF lat. 15700 almost certainly represents an Oxford collection. For example, Sloane and Paris share a text known from no other source, Robert Allington's "sermo de decem mandatis et decem plagis." Allington was a suitably obscure Oxford don, associated with the University at least from 1379 to 1395 (when he demitted as Chancellor); he is known almost exclusively as a logician, and this is his only surviving sermon. The immediately following text in BNF, at the point when Sloane ceases to represent that book's materials, supports this provenance; another sermon (and unique survival), this is ascribed in BNF to one John Brenchley OESA. From his surname presumably a Kentishman, he was an Oxford Doctor of Theology and known otherwise only through records of two sermons preached before royalty, in 1393 and 1402.[7] Presenting texts by figures so obscure testifies to intense local knowledge, particularly so given the early date of this manuscript, contemporary with the activities of both men. A more detailed look at the production of Sloane 2275 will suggest that it emanates from a different situation.

II. Copying Sloane 2275

At least one reason for Sloane's particularly messy state is that the book represents a communal project constructed piecemeal, in the main by enthusiastic yet amateurish bookmen. The production required a considerable effort in gathering exemplars and their distribution among a range of contributors. However, I think the Sloane group's procedures can be narrowly described; this narrative will demonstrate that, leaving aside their comparison of received texts against additional sources, the producers compiled those portions shared with BNF lat. 15700 directly from that manuscript, not from any shared exemplar set. But given this primary source of material, communal copying necessarily produced some dislocation obscuring the exact relationship of the two books.

The items shared by the two codices all represent materials that comprise the first two booklets of the BNF manuscript and the opening eighteen leaves of the third. The dislocation of BNF contents items in Sloane probably depends upon one group of book producers having one separable part of that text for copying at that same time that their colleagues were engaged with other portions. This act of production efficiency, a substantial exemplar reproduced by several hands in a fraction of the time it should have taken a single scribe to do so, presumes an obvious point, although perhaps one easy to overlook. In such a communal situation, where copying proceeds simultaneously, one (set of) scribe(s) at work on one exemplar portion, another on a second, and so on, all the scribes are precluded from access to materials being copied at the same time. Only the director of the enterprise may know with certainty where any given piece of the exemplar might be found.

One may begin considering the problem by noticing one fact, rather submerged in Sloane 2275 as it now exists. Only one of the hands at work in the book, that of the putative director M, copied materials in more than one nonconsecutive textual unit. He appears at the head of the manuscript, opening Booklet 1,[8] and again much later near the conclusion, as the first and concluding hand in Booklet 7 and as the main hand in Booklet 8. M's copying in Booklet 1, *Melos amoris*, represents the single Rollean text the team cannot have acquired from BNF lat. 15700. And again, in both Booklets 7 and 8, M begins his copying with a text not from that source either. This observation may well imply that this book "began small," that M had begun producing for private consultation a sequence of loose quires with some texts of personal interest. Only belatedly, in seeking materials to extend these generically (works of Rolle, works of general devotional utility), may he have discovered the Paris manuscript and conceived a more extensive collection.

Leaving aside for a moment these alien materials, the disposition of texts in Sloane is entirely consonant with a single production decision. Having acquired BNF lat. 15700, M set about having its initial three booklets reproduced, to supplement those materials he had already copied. The disposition of these materials in Sloane implies that M simply took the obvious course, the path of least resistance. While retaining one segment of this exemplar for his own reproduction, he found two companions willing to undertake the work and gave each of them one of the remaining constituent booklets of lat. 15700 to reproduce. One can present this decision as follows:

M retained BNF Booklet 1, with a selection of commonplace devotional texts, and used it, somewhat capriciously,[9] to extend his book beyond the text he had already copied at the head of what is now Sloane Booklet 7.

He gave "Merssh"/scribe 2 BNF Booklet 3, beginning with Rolle's *Contra amatores mundi*, with instructions to use this to continue the Rolle materials M had already copied in Sloane Booklet 1.

He gave a third scribe/scribe 3 BNF Booklet 2, with Rolle's *Incendium amoris* and *Novem lecciones*, and instructed him to begin copying these in a new run of quires, now Sloane Booklet 3 (eventually to be extended as Booklet 4).

This was, or should have been, a perfectly sensible and straightforward procedure. However, it did not altogether account for decisions made by the scribe of BNF lat. 15700, or for the fact that his booklets were not as generically homogeneous as those M appears to have planned for his developing manuscript. As he had finally decided to dispose his book, the scribe who produced BNF had managed to arrange his separate units so that he had presented what M apparently was striving to reproduce, an extended sequence of Rolle texts, across separate runs of quires. However, this sequence, in the current BNF lat. 15700, folios 33 to 110, included the **end** of that scribe's first booklet (currently with M), all his second (currently with scribe 3), and the head of his third (currently with scribe 2/Merssh). Moreover, Merssh faced an additional problem; in the materials he had for reproduction, the main Rolle text was succeeded by a sequence of rather brief items, the first an anonymous selection from a preaching manual, its lack of marking and its attachment to a Rolle text perhaps indicating that it was an additional work by the hermit.[10] Yet the next item in his copying segment was clearly not Rolle's, but Allington's sermon, explicitly ascribed.

Whether initially or at some later point, M must have been aware of this situation, that the form of the split exemplar was not altogether congruent with the form of book he was planning to produce. On the one hand, he will have discovered that, given the disposition of the desired texts in BNF, he was holding, at the end of his stack of quires, Rolle's *Emendatio vitae*, which certainly needed to be joined with other Rolle materials, not copied with the miscellaneous devotional book he was engaged in producing. Merssh, on the other hand, will have been wondering whether he should copy the preaching manual with other Rollean materials and whether he should ignore Allington (and other texts) altogether. Scribe 3, engaged with Rolle's *Incendium*, seems, on the basis of his adjustment of quire size as his stint proceeded, to have decided to split his materials, BNF booklet 2, between two separate units, and his gradually more extensive quires allowed a few blank leaves at the end of his work with the *Incendium*.

M solved these difficulties quite economically. On the one hand, he appears to have decided that he had no interest in recopying the *pastoralia* that comprise most of BNF Booklet 3. He does seem, however, to have decided that the preaching manual deserved inclusion as a text potentially Rollean and that Allington's sermon was also worthy of reproduction. And given that much of his projected volume was to be "Rolle collected," it was easy to decide that *Emendatio vitae* should be removed from the materials which he was copying and placed somewhere in the developing book adjacent to the extensive run of other texts by the hermit.

Each of the texts was then disposed of differently. M elected to place Allington's sermon with the "general use" devotional materials on which he was at work. The obvious solution for the problem of *Emendatio vitae* was to pass it on to Scribe 3, to encourage him to continue his reproduction of BNF Booklet 2, and to place this text at the end, following the materials from BNF on which the scribe was already engaged. This scribe (number 3) was also given the ambiguous preaching manual; if this represented Rolle's work, it would serve as well at the conclusion of any Rolle text, in this case on the blank leaves at the end of Scribe 3's *Incendium* (rather than as a pendant to

Contra amatores, its position in the exemplar, BNF lat. 15700).

Having copied materials from the the redistributed booklets of BNF lat. 15700, all three major scribes seem to have withdrawn from the project, at least temporarily. M may have determined that Allington's sermon was to follow materials he had already included in Sloane's Booklet 7, but he did not copy this text (or the head of the following one). Similarly, although scribe 3 had filled blank leaves at the end of his stint with the head of the English *Prick of Conscience*, he did not continue the copying of this text.

Instead, copying proceeded through a series of brief adventitious stints provided by a variety of more or less informal hands. As already indicated, one such group of contributors supplied both Allington's sermon and the head of Innocent's *De miseria*, which succeeds it in Booklet 7 (fols. 215ra–$17^{vb}/19^{rb}$). A second congeries, again as opportunity allowed, extended *The Prick of Conscience* into a new run of quires (fols. 153ra–65va). Neither Merssh nor scribe 3 seems to have been further involved in the project, and M appears to have returned only after an interval, first to conclude Booklet 7 and then, once work was completed, to organize the steadily growing stack of quires into a bindable ordered collection.

However, as I indicate above, even leaving aside those two texts that constitute Sloane, Booklet 2, plainly *post factum* because inserted within the completed Booklet 1, and not readily to be aligned with any other activity in the volume, producing Sloane required a number of exemplars, in addition to the Oxonian BNF lat. 15700. I mention above two of these, which M appears to have had to hand and to have used before the bulk of the work began. These materials included a copy of Rolle's *Melos amoris* (its text closest, among extant copies, to that in Lincoln Cathedral, MS 209)[11] and a grouping of devotional texts. But in addition, producing the book required at least two further exemplars, one for Honorius's *Elucidarium* and another for the Middle English *Prick of Conscience*. Given the immense number of copies of the former text, tracing this source would be a protracted procedure;[12] I discuss the second of these exemplars in the next section of this essay.

One can, however, identify the source of M's devotional materials. Extraneous to texts derived from the Paris manuscript, Sloane includes two Anglo-Latin items of reasonably wide diffusion (so wide that both, again, are available in English), Edmund Rich's *Speculum ecclesie* and the pseudo-Bonaventuran – it is an Anglo-Latin confection – *Meditationes passionis Christi*. The first of these has a clear transmission history; Sloane's version is a textual twin of the copy in BL, MS Royal 5 C.iii. This complicated manuscript, joining together a variety of separate productions, includes, in the same textual portion, copies of Rolle's *Incendium amoris* and of the preaching manual also reproduced in Sloane and BNF lat. 15700.

The descent of the *Meditationes* is slightly murkier; the closest congener to the version in Sloane appears in Salisbury Cathedral, MS 113. This book might reflect the same Oxford background as BNF lat. 15700, since it was copied by and belonged to the former Oxonian and cathedral canon, Thomas Cyrcetur.[13] However, in both the Sloane and Royal copies, this text has not been derived from a single source; the exemplar available to both M and Cyrcetur had been subjected to conflation from another textual type, one also recorded, although in another unit of this composite book, in the Royal manuscript.

Royal 5 C.iii has a firm medieval provenance. It belonged to the well-known London figure, master of Whittington College, Thomas Eborall; his note of ownership states that he had purchased the book from someone equally well known, the London bookseller John Pye.[14] Another copy of the *Meditationes*, in BodL, MS Bodley 110, with a text closely resembling that conflated with Royal's in both the Sloane and Salisbury manuscripts, was also purchased from John Pye. In addition, the other two copies of this textual version appear in books copied by William Ebesham, a scribe who derived texts from the London booktrade. Thus, not only did M and his team acquire materials from Oxford, but they also drew on exemplars current in the metropolis. Moreover, the conflated *Meditationes* once again implies that the group may not have been simply passive receivers of any of their exemplars, but that a certain measure of textual comparison and intervention into received materials was characteristic of their work (cf. the discussion signaled in note 6).

These various activities raise the question of where the manuscript was produced. Sloane 2275 is utterly reticent on this score, and the only information that points toward the book's provenance is a late-fifteenth-century note in the upper margin of fol. 241^v, "Master demmer of feyfelde." Although the title might suggest a university graduate, there is no "Demmer" in Emden's biographical surveys of Oxford and Cambridge scholars. However, one can probably identify the place with which "Demmer" is associated as Fyfield in Wiltshire, about five miles south of Marlborough. Sometime in the period between 1533 and 1538, a William Walton sued a man named John Demmer for "detention of deeds."[15] This action formed part of a property dispute, which, on the basis of other documents in the Public Record Office, had been running for fifty years, concerning properties bequeathed by William Cannynges. These were in Bishop's Cannings, Wiltshire, seven-eight miles west of Fyfield.

Whoever "Master Demmer" was, it is difficult to believe that the exemplars I am describing, not to mention the numerous hands visible in the manuscript, can have been gathered in a rather obscure north Wiltshire village. However, the ecclesiastical arrangements of Fyfield turn out to be provocative in this regard. Although the village had a church, dedicated to St. Nicholas, this did not have parochial status, but was essentially a chapel, dependent upon an adjacent church, (West) Overton St. Michael's and All Angels. In turn, this church was an ecclesiastical property; although in Salisbury diocese, the manor of Overton and the advowson of St. Michael's belonged to St. Swithun, Winchester, that is, the monastic priory that served Winchester Cathedral.[16]

Such an institution would obviously provide a more promising locale for producing MS Sloane 2275 than would Fyfield. And indeed, information is forthcoming that would confirm that Winchester Cathedral priory was the place where the book was produced. Scribe 2 identifies himself as "Merssh," and priory records include a number of references to Nicholas Mersch, described as "*custos operum*" and a monk and priest. He participated in the election of William Waynflete as bishop of Winchester in 1447, and the account of the election records all the monks who voted on this occasion. These include other individuals with surnames beginning in M, most notably Richard Marlborough (a surname associable with the Fyfield area), who was prior of the house from 1451 to 1457.

When the chapter elected Marlborough to this post, Nicholas Mersch served as their proctor. He carried to bishop Waynflete the letters requesting permission to elect a new prior and subsequently reported the result of the election for Waynflete's approval. On the second occasion, his co-proctor was William Wroughton, described as "*professor sacre scripture*"; like Mersch, Wroughton was a monk of St. Swithun, but he was also an Oxford Bachelor and Doctor of Theology between 1444 and 1447, and almoner of St. Swithun from 1447 to 1457.[17]

Certainly, Wroughton indicates one kind of connection between Winchester Cathedral staff and the Oxonian origins of the Sloane team's primary exemplar, the manuscript now in Paris. But equally, it is worth considering the monks' superior, bishop William Waynflete. The Sloane manuscript was produced at a date roughly contemporary with those activities that over a thirty-year period produced the bishop's most enduring foundation, Magdalen College, Oxford. Waynflete can scarcely be described as lacking an interest in books, their collection, and their production; on one memorable day in the 1480s, he is alleged to have presented his College with eight hundred books.

Moreover, Waynflete was scarcely a stranger to the metropolis. His Oxford College was at least partly founded on certificates of mortmain that he arranged while serving as royal Chancellor in the early 1450s. Further, the medieval diocese of Winchester ran all the way to the Surrey bank of the Thames (where the bishop was in charge of policing the brothels of Southwark). And one of Waynflete's favored residences, his house in Esher (Surrey), was conveniently adjacent to the capital.[18] It is easy enough to envision channels by which exemplars both Oxonian and metropolitan might have reached St. Swithun to facilitate the production of Sloane 2275.

III. The *Prick of Conscience* and the Binding of Sloane 2275

The English poem at the center of Sloane 2275, *The Prick of Conscience*, is the *éminence grise* of Middle English studies – 150 years passed between the only modern efforts at presenting editions of the work. This neglect is not hard to understand, for the poem certainly does not provide what one would, at any point in the recent past, have considered stimulating reading. After a "contempt of the world" opening, its poet examines, at great and repetitious length, the traditional "Four Last Things," Death, Judgment, Hell (with Purgatory thrown in), and Heaven. Yet however forbidding it may be, the text was integral to Anglophone spiritual life for two centuries (even achieving early print). *The Prick of Conscience* exists, in one form or another, in more copies than any other piece of medieval English writing except the Wycliffite Bible, in at least 170 manuscripts.

As already indicated, most of the copying in Sloane 2275 appears to have been undertaken simultaneously, with work on an agreed sequence of texts shared among a variety of hands, some only lately and briefly engaged. But this is not true of one important part of the enterprise, namely *The Prick of Conscience*. Its initial appearance in the volume, on two folios that would have been blank at the end of Booklet 4, the conclusion of the Rolle materials (fols. 150ra-52va) looks as if the text might initially have appeared only in part and as filler, the supply of the poem's hortatory prologue alone; in this position, these nearly four hundred verse lines would then have eliminated a lacuna.

Moreover, the remainder of the poem's copying is decidedly disorganized and considerably less professional, even in the markedly unprofessional context provided by the Sloane manuscript. The extensive presentation of the Middle English, a version of the full text, rather than simply part of it as filler, begins with one of the manuscript's two patches of very short stints in a variety of hands. Further, the scribe who succeeds these (and who eventually copied most of the text) is the only major scribe in the Sloane manuscript who consistently copies in a document-based, rather than formal hand. The material support in this portion of the volume is decidedly below the standard elsewhere; the parchment is considerably thinner and less well finished, indeed not of the quality one expects to find used in a formally produced codex.

There are further oddities – and some insoluble mysteries – about the presentation of *The Prick of Conscience* here. First of all, the text is presented, like all others in the volume, as prose. Of course, traditionally, all English verse appears in this format; lineation came only with the extensive introduction of Latin and French models after the Conquest. And while unusual, one could cite a number of more or less contemporary analogues.[19]

Further, the form of the poem in the Sloane manuscript is decidedly unusual. The text has been very substantially reduced, to a degree unusual even among copies of this poem (routinely abridged and excerpted). Moreover, it is derived from a distinctly minority version of the transmission ('Type III'), attested completely in only about a dozen copies. The great students of *The Prick of Conscience*, Robert E. Lewis and Angus McIntosh, imply that the features here may simply be inherited. They identify Sloane's version of the poem as a twin of Chicago, Newberry Library, MS 39.2, similarly radically reduced (although not presented as prose).[20]

However, this identification introduces yet further problems. *The Prick* has a negligible circulation in areas associable with M's other sources of supply, London or Oxford. The twin Newberry manuscript is written in the language of the central East Midlands. Indeed, the bulk of Type III copies of the poem emerge from this area, the majority placeable in a narrow band running from eastern Warwickshire to the edges of East Anglia.[21]

Yet this odd set of origins, and thus potentially of exemplar supply, is not the only problem here. For the language of the Sloane *Prick of Conscience* does not represent the usage of the East Midlands at all, nor that of Hampshire or Wiltshire. The version offered here is written in the language the Middle English dialect atlas places most proximate to that of an absolutely central piece of the Middle English literary canon; it resembles more nearly than any surviving English book the language of BL, MS Cotton Nero A.x, with *Sir Gawain and the Green Knight* and *Pearl*. Both books share forms associable with the Cheshire/north Staffordshire border, the area around Macclesfield. This is obviously a very distant placement, one consonant neither with the localization of those copies with closely related texts nor with that of the scribal community I have identified.[22]

One thus faces insoluble difficulties in defining the descent of the Sloane copy of *The Prick*. However, there is a ready explanation for the display of alien language on offer here. When the editors of *Linguistic Atlas of Late Mediaeval English* surveyed the text, they analyzed the language of folios 150 to 160, in other words those portions of the text copied by at least half a dozen hands. There is thus, given the reported consistency of forms across this variety of hands, the likelihood that the language here represents *literatim* copying of the forms of the received exemplar. This is a particularly plausible scenario in a situation where the responsible scribes were more accustomed to Latin, and individuals with limited exposure to English might have made this decision in any variety of locales. But such a decision to practice an intense literalism of reproduction does provide a striking contrast with active textual intrusion elsewhere in the book with Latinate materials, particularly Rolle.

Along with the mysteries and production deviancies I outlined above, there is considerable further evidence that *The Prick of Conscience* was the last text copied for inclusion here and that its provision was neither entirely planned nor accommodated. In addition to the arguments already mounted, this conclusion is implicit in M's final activity with the volume, his arrangement for binding of all those dispersed portions. This activity is inscribed in one of the volume's messiest features; there are at least five separate efforts at affixing signatures to the constituent quires:

[1] Scribal signatures by the leaf in the first halves of each quire
        quires 1-6 (Booklet 1) signed "a-f"
        quires 7-10 (Booklet 3) signed "a-d"
        quires 11-14 (Booklet 4) signed "e-h"
        the remaining quires unsigned
[2] Added signatures in red ink by the leaf in the first halves of each quire, probably M, supplementing those provided by the original scribe
        quires 7-14 (Booklets 3 and 4) signed "g-o"
        the remaining quires unsigned
[3] Signatures in red ink on the final verso of each quire
        quires 15 and 16 (Booklet 5) signed "p," "q"
        quires 19-24 (Booklets 7-8) signed "r-y"
        the remaining quires (1-14, 17-18) unsigned
[4] Signatures in crayon on the final verso of each quire, a fragmentary set
        quire 15 = "xv," quire 19 = <"xvij"?> (rubbed and cut off), quire 20 = "xviij," quire 23 = "xxj"
[5] Signatures in crayon on the final verso of each quire
        quires 19-24 signed "s-z," together with a crayon notation on fol. 168^v (the end of quire 16): "*hic R erit cum quaternis ven*" (too rubbed to read, the last word perhaps "*venientibus*" or "*venturis*")

These systems, imposed, cancelled, reimposed, imply that the English text was being copied simultaneously with the organization of the bulk of materials for binding. The concluding portions of *The Prick of Conscience* (Booklet 6) were never signed, and they are not accounted for in the final signature system imposed on the whole book by the director M. Moreover, M, in affixing these directions, knew neither how large *The Prick* was nor how many quires it might absorb, another sign of the dispersed production that marks this book. On folio 168^v, where he supplied the (accurate) quire signature "q" in red ink, he added a note in crayon, roughly translatable, "R will sit here, along with the quires to come." M was uncertain exactly what would appear, and counted on a single placeholding signature to accommodate an indeterminate group of quires, while adjusting the signatures later in the projected book to accord with this decision. The English poem, in its fullest extent, formed the final text copied for this volume and was in progress, even as the remainder was being organized for a binding.

Thus, the manuscript's second Latin block, Booklets 7 to 8, although bound last in the finished whole, certainly preexisted this note (even if it was not, as I argue above, begun in one of the earliest stages in the book's production). Indeed, these units bear three sets of signatures, all of them accurate ones, were one to assume the absence of booklet 6 with its conclusion to *The Prick of Conscience*. These portions of Sloane 2275 are heavily weighted, as I have noted, toward devotional texts.

But as Sloane 2275 is now bound, these texts are expansively repetitious. For these Latin materials, those associated with both the Paris manuscript and the *Elucidarium*, display a single focus. As indicated, none of them is either recondite or obscure. It is thus perhaps not surprising that the majority are extensively utilized in *The Prick of Conscience*. They are the sources that that Yorkshire poet chose to communicate in English.[23] Thus, the manuscript, insofar as it is not substantial Rolle, provides complementary materials, English and fuller Latin, that underlay and inspired it.

IV. Making "English" Miscellanies

From this situation, I infer that the received bilingualism of this volume represents an afterthought. Its English text, rather than central, as its position in the organized whole might imply, has been dragged into this particular combination as a secondary reflection of the Latin that originally formed its poet's sources. If the goal of texts in both languages were instructional (one of several potential "use-values" for the Sloane manuscript), the team responsible for the book appears to have discovered that Latinate materials, which they might have intended for reference use, for example, in the production of vernacular sermons, already existed in a prepared English version (and one that included Latin prompts that could direct further recourse to the already copied *originalia*).

This reading of the Sloane production seems to me almost parable-like in identifying a general cultural milieu. The book challenges recent efforts at associating complex miscellaneous manuscripts produced in fifteenth-century England with the English vernacular.[24] In contrast to these opinions, the Sloane manuscript rebuffs the notion that, for this book's producers, there was a selfsubstantial "vernacular." At best, the English texts appear here as a belated form of entrée to more sophisticated Latinate ones, and the volume's production history implies their always secondary status. In addition, as this superficial introduction to a complex manuscript implies, the Latinate materials communicated in Sloane 2275 frequently display considerably greater intellectual sophistication than the English, and the book conveying them shows a more varied and interesting sequence of motives and resulting compilational problems than many vernacular books.

By way of instantiating that contention, I offer an informal survey of fifteenth-century miscellaneity, using as my sample books in the collection "Bodley" in that Oxford library. This is a thoroughly unscientific exercise and merely my uncritical reading of Bodleian *Summary Catalogue* descriptions.[25] On that basis, I find eighty to eighty-five fifteenth-century Bodley manuscripts of English manufacture that I would describe as miscellaneous, that is, containing three or more texts.

Of these, fifty-nine, something like 70 percent of the sample, are entirely Latinate and another twelve present various combinations of Latin and other languages.[26] On that basis, associating "miscellaneity" and "vernacularity" attends to only 15 percent of the available relevant archive. Equally, such narrowed attentiveness is written all over published accounts of Bodley manuscripts. Most of the ten miscellanies completely in English have attracted scholarly attention and are well known in published accounts – the Chaucerian Bodley 638 and 686, and the religious miscellanies Bodley 423 and 938, for example. Typically, printed studies of a deviant scribal rendition of *Piers Plowman* in Bodley 851, the so-called "Z Text," overwhelm what has been said about this book's more important Latin texts composed by Englishmen, the unique full copy of Walter Map's *De nugis curialium* and an extensive anthology of Latin verse.[27]

In a more historicist vein, the statistics imply, just as does the Sloane *Prick of Conscience*, that vernacular texts are not only derivatives of Latin, but always sit within a much larger and more fully developed tradition of Latin book production. Behind this stretch centuries of development and consequently, of conventions of presentation. Professional scribes compiling fifteenth-century English books are likely to have been aware of these and to have seen them as models for emulation. One might well argue that emphasizing "vernacular miscellaneity" reverses the usual medieval "state of things." Prioritizing English/ness as a normative literary medium ("the literature of the nation") speaks, not to any medieval situation at all, but to concerns more overtly prominent in the Elizabethan period. Equally, it is difficult to see how one might intelligently address "vernacular miscellanies" without some immersion in those Latin books that provided both their translated texts and their production models.

The concept of "author" or "authorial anthology" would offer one example. This is an important motive in the opening three fifths of Sloane 2275, with its very unusual effort at "anthologizing" Rolle.[28] But such an interest is more widely attested in my sample, for example in MSS Bodley 281, 426, and 438, anthologies presenting William of Auvergne, Peter of Blois, and Roger Bacon, respectively. "Miscellaneity" certainly answers the relative rarity of medieval writing in English and the attendant difficulties of meeting growing demand for such materials. However, "miscellaneity" remains very far from an exclusively vernacular project, and treating it as such ignores enormous swathes of book-historical evidence, much of it, as Sloane 2275 exemplifies, of considerable interest.

Keble College, Oxford

APPENDIX: MANUSCRIPT DESCRIPTIONS

BL, MS Sloane 2275[29]

s. xv med. Parchment. Fols. ii + 244 + ii. Overall 250 mm x 180 mm. 50-54 lines to the page (at the head; considerable variation throughout), in double columns. There are probably a dozen to fifteen hands at work here, the majority offering very short stints in two patches, fols. 153ra-165va and 215ra-219rb (parts of texts 9 and 15-16, in Booklets 5 and 7, respectively). Five hands may be identified as primary contributors:

scribe 1 (who signs "quod M," fol. 52rb): rough textura rotunda with anglicana-like r; he copied all of texts 1, 4, 10-14, and most of 16-17 (Booklets 1-2, 7-8), as well as all catchwords outside Booklet 4, and probably red and crayon signatures and notes at quire ends (a prima facie indication that he is the director).

scribe 2 (who signs as "Merssh" and says the text has been corrected, fol. 61vb): mixed anglicana/secretary; he copied texts 2-3 (Booklets 1-2), as well as considerable marginalia, some again signed.

scribe 3: large and clumsy textura rotunda; he copied texts 5-8 and three folios of text 9 (Booklets 3-4).

scribe 4: loose anglicana; he copied about the last half of text 9 (fols. 165va-83rb, Booklets 5-6).

scribe 5: neat anglicana-based fere textura; he copied fols 239ra-44vb, the conclusion of text 17 (Booklet 8).

Contents:
Booklet 1 = fols. 1-61, 66-67, 72, then expanded
1. Fols. 1ra-52rb: RICHARD ROLLE, *Melos amoris*, ed. E. J. F. Arnould (Oxford: Blackwell, 1957). In his discussion of this book (lxxii-iii, lxxxiii), Arnould identifies the text as forming a pair with Lincoln Cathedral, MS 209.

2. Fols. 52va-61vb: RICHARD ROLLE, *Contra amatores mundi*, ed. Paul F. Theiner (Berkeley: University of California Press, 1968). In his discussion of this book (54, 57, 59), Theiner identifies the text as most closely linked to BNF lat. 15700, and more distantly to Lincoln 209, perhaps another indicator of the production team's activities at deriving texts from more than one source.

Collation: 1-5^{12} 6^{4} (subsequently expanded with eight folios of smaller parchment, in which state these original leaves are now 1, 6, 7, 12), signed "a-f."

Booklet 2 = fols. 62-65, 68-71, an extension of the preceding
3. Fols. 62ra-64ra: ANSELM OF BEC, "Meditatio 11," ed. PL 158: 762-769.
4. Fols. 64ra-72vb: PSEUDO-AUGUSTINE, "Meditationes de spiritu sancto," here ascribed to Augustine, inc. "Domine deus spiritus sancte timeo et desidero loqui"; on the text, see A. Wilmart, *Auteurs spirituels et textes dévots du moyen âge latin* (Paris: Bloud et Guy, 1932), 415-456.
   Collation: The expanded 6^{12}, with the inserted eight folios, fols. 62-65, 68-71, of smaller parchment, signed "f."

Booklet 3 = fols. 73-110, then extended
5. Fols. 73ra-108va: RICHARD ROLLE, *Incendium amoris*, long version, ed. Margaret Deanesly (Manchester: University of Manchester Press, 1915). Deanesly presents a "best-text" edition and offers only a brief description of this book (p. 3).
6. Fols. 108va-109va: JOHN OF WALES, an except from his *Ars praedicandi*, inc. "Predicatio est thematis assumptio"; see Harry Caplan, *Medieval* Artes Praedicandi: *A Hand-List*, 2 vols., Cornell Studies in Classical Philology 24-25 (Ithaca NY: Cornell University Press, 1934-1936), no. 121 (24:22), an extract from Caplan's no. 62 (24:13-14).
   Collation: 7-8^8 9^{10} 10^{12}, signed "a-d," with later red-ink signatures "g-k."

Booklet 4 = fols. 111-152, extending the preceding, starting with its concluding blank leaves
7. Fols. 109va-140ra: RICHARD ROLLE, *Super novem lectiones mortuorum*, ed. Malcolm R. Moyes, 2 vols., Elizabethan & Renaissance Studies 92/12 (Salzburg: Universität Salzburg, 1988). Moyes provides a "best-text" edition, and his discussions of this book at 2:65-68, 122; and in his "The Manuscripts and Early Printed Editions of Richard Rolle's Expositio super Novem Lecciones Mortuorum," *The Medieval Mystical Tradition in England [III]...*, ed. Marion Glasscoe (Cambridge: D. S. Brewer, 1984), 81-95, at 88, offer conflicting information about the quality and nature of its text.
8. Fols. 140ra-150ra: RICHARD ROLLE, *Emendatio vitae*, ed. Rüdiger Spahl, Super alta perennis 6 (Bonn: Bonn University Press, 2009) (discussion of this book at 56). Spahl places this copy in his Group G, which contains only four books, including BNF lat. 15700, suggestive

of a tight circulation (114-115). He also demonstrates that Sloane has conflated its text with another of the group, MS Bodley 122 (the fourth copy, Sloane's twin, is Champaign, University of Illinois, MS 144/Moyes 102-03, ibid. 93-96 for BNF).

9. Fols. 150ra-183rb: *The Prick of Conscience*, ed. Hanna-Wood (full citation in n.23). For discussion of this book, see Lewis-McIntosh, 70-71 (MV 38) (full citation in n.20); the edition includes a list of manuscripts supplementing those Lewis-McIntosh describe (378-383).

Collation: 11-12^{12} 13^{10} 14^{8}, signed "e-h," with later red-ink signatures "l-o."

Booklet 5 = fols. 153-168, following the preceding and then extended

9b. *The Prick of Conscience* extended, initially in plain fere textura, but this individual writes only a folio and six lines, and there is a bewildering series of shifts among hands until fol. 165va. From that point to the end, i.e. the extension forming the remainder, a single hand on particularly thin parchment.

Collation: 15-16^{8}, unsigned, with later red-ink signatures "p-q"; in addition, the first quire is numbered "xv" in crayon, and at the end of the second, fol. 168^{v}, there is a note in crayon "***hic R erit cum quaternis ven***" (? too rubbed to read, last word perhaps "***venientibus***"/"***venturis***").

Booklet 6 = fols. 169-83, an extension of the previous

9c. *The Prick of Conscience* concluded, with fol. 183^{v} blank.

Collation: 17^{8+1} (+9) 18^{6}, both unsigned (and not included in the crayon or numerical counts in subsequent sections).

Booklet 7 = fols. 184-229

10. Fols. 184ra-191rb: EDMUND RICH, *Speculum ecclesie*, ed. Helen P. Forshaw, *Speculum Religiosorum...*, Auctores Britannici Medii Aevi 3 (London: Oxford University Press for the British Academy, 1973). In her discussion of this manuscript (8), Forshaw identifies the text as forming a pair with BL, MS Royal 5 C.iii.

11. Fols. 191rb-198vb: PSEUDO.-AUGUSTINE, "Speculum peccatoris", ed. PL 40:983-92.[30] This text, in both Latin and English versions, is so widespread in Rolle manuscripts that Allen devotes a page to dismissing the hermit's authorship, *Writings Ascribed*, 317-18.

12. Fols. 198vb-205rb: PSEUDO.-BERNARD OF CLAIRVAUX, *Meditationes*, ed. PL 184:485-508.

13. Fols. 205rb-207ra: (PSEUDO-)BASIL OF CAESAREA, "Admonitio," ed. PL 103:685-700.

14. Fols. 207ra-214vb: PSEUDO-BONAVENTURA, *Meditationes*

de Passione Christi, ed. M. Jordan Stallings (Washington: Catholic University of America Press, 1965). Actually a text produced in England. In her discussion of this manuscript (44, 68-79), Stallings shows that this copy belongs to a group of five, including most proximately, Salisbury Cathedral, MS 113, as well as BodL, MS Bodley 110 (like Royal 5 C.iii, purchased from John Pye), and two books copied by William Ebesham (Oxford, St. John's College, MS 147; Manchester, John Rylands University Library, MS lat. 395). Sloane and Salisbury differ from the remainder of this group in having been conflated with a book from a different family of manuscripts, in part represented by Royal 5 C.iii; in the Royal copy, the *Meditationes* appear in a fascicle separate from that with other texts related to Sloane 2275.

15. Fols. 215ra-218rb: ROBERT ALLINGTON, "Sermo de decem mandatis et decem plagis"; cf. Sharpe, *Handlist* 522, noting the only other known copy, in BNF, lat. 15700, fols. 111-114.

16. Fols. 218va-229vb: INNOCENT III, *De miseria humanae conditionis (De contemptu mundi)*, ed. Michele Maccarrone (Lucca: Thesaurus Mundi, 1955), with an extensive list of copies.

Collation: 19-20^{12} 21^{10} 22^{12}, unsigned, with later red-ink signatures "r-u," as well as crayon ones "s-x." In addition, the first two quires are numbered <"xvij"?> (rubbed and cut off) and "xviij" in crayon.

Booklet 8 = fols. 230-244

17. Fols. 230ra-244vb: HONORIUS OF REGENSBURG, *Elucidarium*, ed. Yves Lefevre, *L'Elucidarium et les Lucidaires: contribution, par l'histoire d'un texte, à l'histoire des croyances religieuses en France au moyen âge* (Paris: Boccard, 1954).

Collation: 23^8 24^8 (lacks 8), unsigned, with later red-ink signatures "x-y," as well as crayon ones "y-z." In addition, the first quire is numbered "xxj" in crayon.

BNF, MS lat. 15700

This is a somewhat summary account. Between them, Spahl, *Emendatio*, 75-76; and Moyes, *Super novem*, 2:93-96 (full citations at Sloane texts 7 and 8 above) provide a generally accurate description; a few items capable of refinement or further detail are mentioned in the notes here.

s. xiv ex. Parchment. Overall 265 mm x 190 mm. 42 long lines to the page. Written in a single current anglicana (some brief patches in a different ductus early in Booklet 3).

Contents:
Booklet 1 = fols. 1-40
1. Fols. 1-9: PSEUDO-BERNARD, *Meditationes* = Sloane 2275, text 12.
2. Fols. 9-11: PSEUDO-BASIL, "Monita" = Sloane 2275, text 13.
3. Fols. 11-20^v: PSEUDO-AUGUSTINE, "Speculum peccatoris" = Sloane 2275, text 11, and in the same expanded form
4. Fols. 20^v-33: INNOCENT III, *De Miseria* = Sloane 2275, text 16.
5. Fols. 33-40^v: ROLLE, *Emendatio vitae* = Sloane 2275, text 8.

Collation: 1-5^8, signed "+, a-d"; regular catchwords except at the end. A hand of s. xv has added in the blank foot of fol. 40v a heading to join with the following quire and text of *Incendium amoris*.

Booklet 2 = fols. 41-96
6. Fols. 41-70: ROLLE, *Incendium amoris*, long version = Sloane 2275, text 5 (half the last page blank, with another heading, supplied s. xv, to join to the next).
7. Fols. 70^v-94: ROLLE, *Novem lecciones* = Sloane 2275, text 7.[31]

Collation: 6-12^8, signed "e-l"; the catchwords at fols. 64^v and 72^v appear later additions; at the end, fol. 96^{rv} is blank, and there is no catchword.

Booklet 3a = fols. 97-112+
8. Fols. 97-110: ROLLE, *Contra amatores mundi* = Sloane 2275, text 2.
9. Fols. 110-111: JOHN OF WALES, "Predicacio est" = Sloane 2275, text 6.
10. Fols. 111-114: ALLINGTON's sermon = Sloane 2275, text 15 (**running into the head of the next quire**), at its end a two-line mnemonic for the plagues of Egypt, "Sanguis, rana, culex" (Walther 17276).

Collation: 13-14^8, signed "M-N"; the catchword at fol. 104^v, uniquely in this book, is centered, rather than in the gutter, and in a scroll.

(At this point, Sloane ceases its recourse to BNF materials.)

Booklet 3b (the previous continued) = fols. 113-135
11. Fols. 114^v-115^v: JOHN BRENCHLEY OESA, sermon (Sharpe, *Handlist* 219).
12. Fols. 115^v-117^v: PETER OF BLOIS, "De amicitia christiana" excerpts (Bloomfield 404), ed. *PL* 207:871-958.[32]
13. Fols. 118-123: PSEUDO-AUGUSTINE (actually AMBROSE OF AUTPERT), "De conflictu virtutum et viciorum," ed. *PL*

41:1091-1103, with half a page blank at the end.

14. Fols. 123ᵛ-135: (PSEUDO-)AUGUSTINE, "Exhortationes ad Julianum comitem," ed. *PL* 40:1047-1078.

Collation: 14-16⁸ 17⁸ (lacks 8), signed "o-q." At the end, fol. 135ᵛ is blank and without catchword; the final, presumably blank leaf of the quire has been excised.

Booklet 4 = fols. 136-142

15. Fols. 136-142ᵛ: ALCUIN, "De virtutibus et vitiis ad Guidonem," ed. *PL* 101:613-638.

Collation: 18⁸ (lacks 8), signed "r." Again, at the end, missing a final blank leaf now excised.

Booklet 5 = fols. 143-154

16. Fols. 143-151: ROBERT GROSSETESTE, *Templum Domini* (Bloomfield 5982, but see further S. Harrison Thomson, *The Writings of Robert Grosseteste, Bishop of Lincoln, 1235-1253* [Cambridge: Cambridge University Press, 1940], 138-140), ed. as *Templum Dei*, ed. Joseph Goering and F. A. C. Mantello, Toronto Medieval Latin Texts 14 (Toronto: Pontifical Institute, 1984).

17. Fols. 152-153: "De penitencia," i.e. PETER OF BLOIS, "De penitentia vel satisfactione a sacerdote iniugenda" (Bloomfield 3308, excerpt only), the incipit at *PL* 207:1092.

18. Fols. 153-154ᵛ: "De confessione," i.e. PETER OF BLOIS, "De confessione sacramentali" (Bloomfield 5210, a fragment only), ed. PL 207:1077-1092.[33]

Collation: 19⁸ 20⁴, signed "s-t"; there is a catchword at fol. 154ᵛ to join to the following separately produced materials.

Booklet 6 = fols. 155-73

19. Fols. 155-171ᵛ: "De beneficiis Dei homini graciose impensis," inc. "Tractatum hunc quem vobis pater carissime caritatis affectu transmitto quem eciam in capitula diuersa," apparently unique.[34]

20. Fols. 172-173ᵛ: "Libellus ANSELMI," identified by Moyes with *PL* 158:667-686, from the homilies ascribed to him, breaking off incomplete, with a number of following excised stubs.

Collation: 21⁸ 22⁸ (lacks 6) 23⁸ (lacks 5 to 8), signed "v-y."

NOTES

1. See "Producing Magdalen College MS lat. 93," *Yearbook of English Studies* 33 (2003):142-155, a study that probably rendered a confusing book yet more so. I offer a full description of Sloane 2275, with further detail on the specific texts, in the Appendix, an effort to reduce distracting annotation of the arguments here presented. Throughout I abbreviate large collection titles: BL = The British Library, London; BodL = The Bodleian Library, Oxford; BNF = Bibliothèque nationale de France, Paris.
2. See "The Transmission of Richard Rolle's Latin Works," *The Library* 7th ser. 14 (2013):313-33, at 326. Douai, Bibliothèque municipale, MS 367 (originally from Sheen OCart), not there included, has seven texts, mainly excerpted materials; see the the grand bibliographical study, Hope E. Allen, *Writings Ascribed to Richard Rolle Hermit of Hampole and Materials for his Biography* (New York: Modern Language Association, 1927), 37-39.
3. Cambridge, Emmanuel College, MS 35 also has three of the texts, in this case lacking, rather surprisingly, given the text's enormous circulation, a copy of *Emendatio vitae* – although that is incomplete (and mainly a later supply) in the extensive Bodley 861. For these texts, see Allen, *Writings*, 113-29, 198-245.
4. For *Novem lecciones*, the second most widely disseminated piece of Rolle's Latin, see Allen, *Writings*, 130-144.
5. Again, I provide a description (abbreviated, because the book has previously been described with considerable accuracy) in the Appendix.
6. See the references to Rüdiger Spahl's discussion at text item 8 in the Appendix description of Sloane 2275.
7. For these two figures, see Richard Sharpe, *A Handlist of Latin Writers of Great Britain and Ireland before 1540*, Publications of the Journal of Medieval Latin 1 (Turnhout: Brepols, 1997), 522 and 219, respectively; and A. B. Emden, *A Biographical Register of the University of Oxford to A.D. 1500*, 3 vols. (Oxford: Clarendon Press, 1957-1959), 30-31 and 2156, respectively. For further inferential connections of BNF lat. 15700 with Oxford, see note 34 below, on the manuscript's text 19.
8. He appears at the head twice, in fact, on the second occasion engaged in the manifestly *post factum* additions that comprise part of what I designate Booklet 2.
9. He did not respect the text order provided by the exemplar; BNF texts 1-3 are presented in Sloane in the order 3-1-2. Further, just as he had begun this unit with a text he had found in an exemplar other than BNF, he inserted into the BNF sequence a further text from that alien source (Sloane item 14, following which there is a break in his copying).
10. Cf. Pitts's misadventures with this text, discussed Allen, *Writings*, 426.

11. For this book, dated, like BNF lat. 15700, s. xiv ex., see R. M. Thomson, *Catalogue of the Manuscripts of Lincoln Cathedral Chapter Library* (Woodbridge: Boydell and Brewer, 1989), 169-70.
12. For the fullest list of copies, about 330, of which fifty-five to sixty are in British collections, see Dagmar Gottschall, *Das 'Elucidarium' des Honorius Augustodunensis: Untersuchungen zu seiner Überlieferungs- und Rezeptionsgeschichte* (Tübingen: Niemeyer, 1992), 297-306.
13. For him, see R. M. Ball, "Thomas Cyrcetur, a Fifteenth-Century Theologian and Preacher," *Journal of Ecclesiastical History* 37 (1986):205-39.
14. For Eborall, see Emden, *Biographical Register*, 622-23; and Wendy Scase, "Reginald Pecock, John Carpenter and John Colop's 'Common Profit' Books: Aspects of Book Ownership and Circulation in Fifteenth-Century London," *Medium Ævum* 61 (1992), 261-274, passim. For John Pye, see C. Paul Christianson, "Evidence for the study of London's late medieval manuscript-book trade," *Book Production and Publishing in Britain 1375-1475*, ed. Jeremy Griffiths and Derek Pearsall (Cambridge: Cambridge University Press, 1988), 87-108, at 101 and 107 n.42. For William Ebesham, to whom I refer in the next sentence, see A. I. Doyle, "The Work of a Late Fifteenth-Century English Scribe, William Ebesham," *Bulletin of the John Rylands Library* 39 (1957):298-325.
15. Kew, Public Record Office, The National Archives, C 1/927/4.
16. See D. A. Crowley et al., eds, *A History of the County of Wiltshire: Volume 11: Downton Hundred; Elstub and Everleigh Hundred*, The Victoria County History (London: Oxford University Press for the Institute of Historical Research, 1980), 181-203 passim. It may be worth noting that the vicar of St. Michael's and All Angels (and thus of its dependency Fyfield St. Nicholas) was in 1489-1494 a Matthew Delamer, a form that might potentially be rendered "Demmer." This may be a distinctively local surname; cf. Fisherton Delamere (although more frequently in the Middle Ages referred to as "Fisherton iuxta Wylye"), about five miles southeast of Warminster. That Winchester Priory held a church in Salisbury diocese certainly required negotiations from time to time with the bishop there, a possible conduit by which a text owned by the Salisbury canon Thomas Cyrcetur could have passed to Winchester.
17. See Jane Greatrex, ed., *The Register of the Common Seal of the Priory of St Swithun, Winchester 1395-1497*, Hampshire Record Society 2 ([Winchester]: Hampshire County Council, 1978), here especially nos 316, 332-333, 336-337 (100-101, 110-112). For Wroughton, see Emden, *Biographical Register*, 2096 (although lacking any reference to the title accorded him in the Winchester documents).
18. See the biography, Virginia Davis, *William Waynflete Bishop and Educationalist* (Woodbridge: Boydell, 1993), passim.

19. For example, BodL, MS Digby 102, mainly a copy of *Piers Plowman* C, in Worcestershire language but probably produced in London in the 1420s.
20. See *A Descriptive Guide to the Manuscripts of the* Prick of Conscience, Medium Ævum Monographs n.s. 12 (Oxford: Society for the Study of Medieval Languages and Literature, 1982), 49, 70-71; and the map of the poem's transmission at 170-73.
21. The discussions in Lewis and McIntosh's *Guide* have subsequently been slightly revised in Angus McIntosh, M. L. Samuels, and Michael Benskin, *A Linguistic Atlas of Late Mediaeval English*, 4 vols (Aberdeen: Aberdeen University Press, 1986) (*LALME*). For the relevant examples, see Lewis and McIntosh's MV16 (also *LALME*, 3:510-511), the "twin" Newberry MV17 (Huntingdonshire, *LALME*, 1:73), MV26 ("SLincs, but mixed," *LALME*, 1:105), MV32, MV66 (*LALME*, 3:122-123), MV67 (*LALME*, 3:417 and 535), MV75 (*LALME*, 3:24), and MV91 (*LALME*, 3:324-325). One "Type III" manuscript does display language proximate to Winchester, that of central Wiltshire, MV15 (*LALME*, 3:548).
22. For the language here see *LALME*, 3:42-43.
23. See Sarah Wood's summary account and her extensive discussion of the poem's sources, *Richard Morris's* Prick of Conscience, ed. Ralph Hanna and Wood, Early English Text Society 342 (Oxford: Oxford University Press, 2013), lii-lxi, 287-366.
24. This interest was manifested in a June 2013 conference at the British Academy, London. Much of it seems to have been stimulated by uncritical appropriations of "Miscellaneity and Vernacularity: Conditions of Literary Production in Late Medieval England," *The Whole Book: Cultural Perspectives on the Medieval Miscellany*, ed. Stephen G. Nichols and Siegfried Wenzel, Recentiores: Later Latin Texts and Contexts (Ann Arbor: University of Michigan Press, 1996), 37-51. But see Armando Petrucci, ed. and tr. Charles M. Radding, *Writers and Readers in Medieval Italy: Studies in the History of Written Culture* (New Haven: Yale University Press, 1995), 1-18, where Petrucci identifies the "miscellany" as the typical medieval book.
25. R. W. Hunt et al., *A Summary Catalogue of Western Manuscripts in the Bodleian Library at Oxford*, 7 vols. in 8 (Oxford: Clarendon Press, 1895-1953), here 2, i:78-590 (entries 1840-3116).
26. Anglo-Norman appears with Latin in MSS Bodley 57, 82, 90, 233, 399 (the Latin an addition) and 761; MS Bodley 9 is trilingual.
27. For further detail, see A. G. Rigg, "Medieval Latin Poetic Anthologies (II)," *Mediaeval Studies* 40 (1978):387-407, reprinted in Charlotte Brewer and Rigg eds., *Piers Plowman: A Facsimile of the Z-Text in Bodleian Library, Oxford, MS Bodley 851* (Cambridge: D. S. Brewer, 1994), 23-42.
28. Paralleled in the uniquely extensive (but similarly understudied) MS Bodley 861, a book that contains notes on the difficulties underlying its own

manufacture; see Allen's not always pointed description, *Writings*, 22-34.
29. In the descriptions and notes to them, I use the following brief references to standard bibliographical guides: Bloomfield = Morton W. Bloomfield et al., *Incipits of Latin Works on the Virtues and Vices, 1100-1500 A.D...* (Cambridge MA: Medieval Academy, 1979); Bloomfield Supp. = Richard Newhauser and István Bejczy, *A Supplement to Morton W. Bloomfield et al. Incipits of Latin Works...* (Turnhout: Brepols, 2008); Römer = Franz Römer, *Die handschriftliche Überlieferung der Werke des heiligen Augustinus*, Band II/1, Österreichische Akademie der Wissenschaften Philosophisch-historische Klasse Sitzungsberichte 281 (Vienna: Böhlau, 1972); Walther = Hans Walther, *Initia carminum ac versuum Medii Aevi posterioris Latinorum*, 2nd edn (Göttingen: Vandenhoeck und Ruprecht, 1969). PL, of course, indicates the *Patrologia Latina*.
30. In fact, a text known variously as "*sermo de divino iudicio*," "*liber de miseria hominis*," or the like, its incipit "*Fratres*" (fol. 191rb = BNF fol. 11) derived from (pseudo)-Augustine, sermo 251 (*PL* 39:2210) with considerable expansion (Bloomfield Supp. no. 2176, Römer 378), followed by a section with incipit "*Homo*" (fol. 195ra = BNF fol. 15^v, Römer 379), and eventually by the "*Speculum*" proper (fol. 196va = BNF fol. 17^v, Römer 173-75). The three texts also appear, joined in this order, in at least Cambridge, Emmanuel College, MS 243; Peterhouse, MS 218; and BL, MS Egerton 673, as well as in various other combinations, e.g. in BL, MS Additional 6718; BodL, MS Canon. Pat. Lat. 13; and the books described N. R. Ker, *Medieval Manuscripts in British Libraries*, 4 vols. (Oxford: Clarendon Press, 1969-92), 4:402, 548.
31. Moyes's account here requires some supplementation, since fols. 94^v-95^v have three extensive theological notes: [7a] a single paragraph, "*Commendatio castitatis*. Cum enim secundum beatum Ierominum in carne preter carnem viuere*," cited and discussed from this manuscript, Allen, *Writings*, 427; she identifies the text as part of CONRAD OF SAXONY (PS.-BONAVENTURA), "*Speculum beate virginis Marie*"; see Bloomfield Supp, no. 1093a. The other longer notes are likely further excerpts from same source: [7b] fol. 94^v "*Diffinicio virginitatis*. Quidam sapiens quem recitat quidam Apostillatorum*," also at Uppsala, Universitetsbiblioteket, MS C.17, fol. 46^v (a Vadstena book with Rolle materials, perhaps derived from Syon); [7c] fols. 94^v-95^v "*Detestacio fornicacionis*. De contrario dicte virtutis videlicet incontinencia beatus Bernardus ita*." At the conclusion of this last segment are three further short notes, fol. 95^v: [7d] "Tanta est virtus sedule recordacionis passionis Ihesu Christi," including the full text of the Latin Passion-lyric "*Candet nudatum pectus*" (not in Walther) and an additional verse, "Christi passionem si bene recolis, | leue requitabis (?) quicquid pacieris"; [7e] "Femina est confusio hominis," 'SECUNDUS

THE PHILOSOPHER"s definition, with added phrases at the end; [7f] "Obediencia est pio studio proprie voluntatis abnegacio."
32. With a further excerpt at the end [12a] fol. 117^v from ARNULFUS DE BOERIIS (PSEUDO-BERNARD), "Documentum vitae religiosae," ed. PL 184:1177-1182.
33. In the lower margin, fol. 154^v, [18a] four very brief theological notes, "Diabolus miseram animam aggreditur per cognicionem," etc.
34. The only other copy I know of appears in a description of a Lichfield Cathedral folio destroyed in the Civil War; see N. R. Ker, "Patrick Young's Catalogue of the Manuscripts of Lichfield Cathedral," *Mediaeval and Renaissance Studies* 2 (1950):151-168, at 155-156, 160. This volume, Young's MS 22, contained in order: [1] the sermons of John Felton (vicar of St. Mary Magdalen, Oxford), [2] this text (Young cites a full incipit), [3] BNF text 18 (Peter of Blois), [4] Rolle's *Incendium amoris* (a lost copy heretofore unnoticed), and [5-7] three brief tracts by Thomas of Ireland. For these last, which have virtually no English circulation, see Richard H. and Mary A. Rouse, *Preachers, Florilegia and Sermons: Studies on the Manipulus Florum of Thomas of Ireland*, Studies and Texts 47 (Toronto: Pontifical Institute, 1979), 246-50. This lost volume sounds like the kind of book that should have emanated from same Oxonian surroundings as BNF lat. 15700, although, if a single production, given Felton's obit (1434), this was clearly later and contemporary with Sloane 2275. A copy of one of the Thomas of Ireland texts appears in a book produced for a graduate and donated to the College in the 1460s, Oxford, Merton College, MS 68.

WORKS CITED
(does not include those in the descriptions)

Manuscripts
Cambridge, Emmanuel College, MS 35
Chicago, Newberry Library, MS 39.2
Douai, Bibliothèque municipale, MS 367
Hereford Cathedral, MS O.viii.1
Kew, Public Record Office, The National Archives, C 1/927/4
Lincoln Cathedral, MS 209
London, BL, MS Cotton Nero A.x
London, BL, MS Royal 5 C.iii
London, BL, MS Sloane 2275
Oxford, BodL, MSS Bodley 9, 57, 82, 90, 110, 233, 281, 399, 423, 426, 438, 638, 686, 761, 938 (passing references only)
Oxford, BodL, MS Bodley 851
Oxford, BodL, MS Bodley 861

Oxford, BodL, MS Digby 102
Oxford, BodL, MS Laud misc. 528
Oxford, Balliol College, MS 224A
Oxford, Corpus Christi College, MS 193
BNF, MS lat. 15700
Salisbury Cathedral, MS 113

Studies and Editions

Allen, Hope E. *Writings Ascribed to Richard Rolle Hermit of Hampole and Materials for his Biography*. New York: Modern Language Association, 1927.

Ball, R. M. "Thomas Cyrcetur, a Fifteenth-Century Theologian and Preacher." *Journal of Ecclesiastical History* 37 (1986):205-239.

Bloomfield, Morton W. et al. *Incipits of Latin Works on the Virtues and Vices, 1100-1500 A.D.*... Cambridge: Medieval Academy of America, 1979.

Brewer, Charlotte, and A. G. Rigg, eds. *Piers Plowman: A Facsimile of the Z-Text in Bodleian Library, Oxford, MS Bodley 851*. Cambridge: D. S. Brewer, 1994.

Christianson, C. Paul. "Evidence for the study of London's late medieval manuscript-book trade." In *Book Production and Publishing in Britain 1375-1475*, ed. Jeremy Griffiths and Derek Pearsall, 87-108. Cambridge: Cambridge University Press, 1988.

Crowley, D. A. et al., eds. *A History of the County of Wiltshire: Volume 11: Downton Hundred; Elstub and Everleigh Hundred. The Victoria County History*. London: Oxford University Press for the Institute of Historical Research, 1980.

Davis, Virginia. *William Waynflete Bishop and Educationalist*. Woodbridge: Boydell and Brewer, 1993.

Doyle, A. I. "The Work of a Late Fifteenth-Century English Scribe, William Ebesham." *Bulletin of the John Rylands Library* 39 (1957):298-325.

Emden, A. B. *A Biographical Register of the University of Oxford to A.D. 1500*. 3 vols. Oxford: Clarendon Press, 1957-59.

Gottschall, Dagmar. *Das 'Elucidarium' des Honorius Augustodunensis: Untersuchungen zu seiner Überlieferungs- und Rezeptionsgeschichte*. Tübingen: Niemeyer, 1992.

Greatrex, Jane, ed. *The Register of the Common Seal of the Priory of St Swithun, Winchester 1395-1497*. Hampshire Record Society 2. [Winchester]: Hampshire County Council, 1978.

Hanna, Ralph. "Miscellaneity and Vernacularity: Conditions of Literary Production in Late Medieval England." In *The Whole Book: Cultural Perspectives on the Medieval Miscellany*, ed. Stephen G. Nichols and Siegfried Wenzel, 37-51. Recentiores: Later Latin Texts and Contexts.

Ann Arbor: University of Michigan Press, 1996.
———. "Producing Magdalen College MS lat. 93." *Yearbook of English Studies* 33 (2003):142-155.
———. "The Transmission of Richard Rolle's Latin Works." *The Library* 7th ser. 14 (2013):313-333.
———, and Sarah Wood, eds. *Richard Morris's* Prick of Conscience. Early English Text Society 342. Oxford: Oxford University Press, 2013.
Hunt, R. W., et al. *A Summary Catalogue of Western Manuscripts in the Bodleian Library at Oxford*. 7 vols. in 8. Oxford: Clarendon Press, 1895-1953.
Lewis, Robert E. and Angus McIntosh. *A Descriptive Guide to the Manuscripts of the* Prick of Conscience. Medium Ævum Monographs n.s. 12. Oxford: Society for the Study of Medieval Languages and Literature, 1982.
McIntosh, Angus, M. L. Samuels, and Michael Benskin. *A Linguistic Atlas of Late Mediaeval English*. 4 vols. Aberdeen: Aberdeen University Press, 1986.
Moyes, Malcolm R., ed. *Richard Rolle's Expositio super novem lectiones mortuorum*. 2 vols. Elizabethan & Renaissance Studies 92/12. Salzburg: Universität Salzburg, 1988.
———. "The Manuscripts and Early Printed Editions of Richard Rolle's Expositio super Novem Lecciones Mortuorum." In *The Medieval Mystical Tradition in England [III]...*, ed. Marion Glasscoe, 81-95. Cambridge: D. S. Brewer, 1984.
Newhauser, Richard, and István Bejczy. *A Supplement to Morton W. Bloomfield et al. Incipits of Latin Works on the Virtues and Vices, 1100-1500 A.D...*. Turnhout: Brepols, 2008.
Petrucci, Armando. *Writers and Readers in Medieval Italy: Studies in the History of Written Culture*, edited and translated by Charles M. Radding. New Haven: Yale University Press, 1995.
Rigg, A. G. "Medieval Latin Poetic Anthologies (II)." *Mediaeval Studies* 40 (1978):387-407.
Römer, Franz. *Die handschriftliche Überlieferung der Werke des heiligen Augustinus, Band II/1*. Österreichische Akademie der Wissenschaften Philosophisch-historische Klasse Sitzungsberichte 281. Vienna: Böhlau, 1972.
Scase, Wendy. "Reginald Pecock, John Carpenter and John Colop's 'Common Profit' Books: Aspects of Book Ownership and Circulation in Fifteenth-Century London." *Medium Ævum* 61 (1992):261-274.
Sharpe, Richard. *A Handlist of Latin Writers of Great Britain and Ireland before 1540*. Publications of the Journal of Medieval Latin 1. Turnhout: Brepols, 1997.
Spahl, Rüdiger, ed. *De emendatione vitae. Eine kritische Ausgabe...* Super alta perennis 6. Bonn: Bonn University Press, 2009.

Thomson, R. M. *Catalogue of the Manuscripts of Lincoln Cathedral Chapter Library*. Woodbridge: Boydell and Brewer, 1989.

Walther, Hans. *Initia carminum ac versuum Medii Aevi posterioris Latinorum*. 2nd edn. Göttingen: Vandenhoeck und Ruprecht, 1969.

Kyng Alisaunder and Oxford, Bodleian Library, MS Laud Misc. 622

NICOLE CLIFTON

Introduction

An archeology of the book requires attention to all the historical layers of an individual volume, from its original composition to the later hands that annotate its margins. Manuscript study often focuses on the moment of origin, with scant attention to the later layers of occupation and disturbances of the original site. Oxford, Bodleian Library, MS Laud Misc. 622, though a ruined remnant of a once-larger manuscript, offers a rich site in which to study late-medieval reactions to two Middle English romances, *Kyng Alisaunder* and *Titus and Vespasian*.[1] In contrast to the other surviving manuscripts of *Kyng Alisaunder*, which include multiple romances, Laud Misc. 622 contains mainly texts that focus on the history and geography of the Middle East. It thus places the Alexandrian material in a specialist context. The manuscript covers the classical period via *Kyng Alisaunder*; continues into early Christian times with *Titus and Vespasian* and the *Life of St. Alexius*; and concludes with a short text about the sights of the Holy Land in the era of the manuscript's creation, around 1400.

The selection of texts argues that the compiler of this manuscript saw it as a collection focusing on history. Most significantly, for my purposes, the interactions of two fifteenth-century readers with its contents confirm that late-medieval readers also perceived the couplet versions of *Kyng Alisaunder* and *Titus* as historical accounts, just as much as the alliterative versions, *The Wars of Alexander* and *The Siege of Jerusalem*, which have received more critical attention. Joyce Boro has demonstrated that readers of sixteenth-century manuscript romances likewise read these texts as history; my research extends hers to show that the roots of such reactions lie further in the past.[2] Furthermore, Laud Misc. 622 appears to be a vernacular analogue to compilations of Latin historiography, such as that in London, British Library MS Royal 13.A.1, an English-made collection focusing on Alexander the Great, recently analyzed by Charles Russell Stone.[3]

Stone argues that the texts of Royal 13.A.1 represent a range of attitudes toward Alexander, from admiring to unflattering, historical to fantastic; that its "conflicting traditions of Alexander's legacy" respond "both to the conqueror's reputation and the era in which the codex was produced";[4] and that the later history of the manuscript reflects the efforts of early modern historiographers and book collectors to find a version of Alexander that could serve the needs of subsequent generations of readers, scholars, and students. By the fifteenth century, copies of Plutarch's *Lives* were coming into England,[5] and new English texts such as Lydgate's *Fall of Princes* presented an Alexander who "straddles the border of monasticism and humanism."[6] In such a transitional environment, the marginal responses in Laud Misc. 622 indicate the areas of Alexander's life that hold the most interest for fifteenth-century vernacular readers, and thus add significant details to our understanding both of the tastes of vernacular readers in this period and of the early-modern development of the legend.

Two readers of the Laud manuscript actively respond to *Kyng Alisaunder* and, to a lesser extent, to *Titus and Vespasian* and the short text about the Holy Land. Although many Middle English romance manuscripts contain names and other marginalia indicating that their texts were available to and valued by their readers, few include direct interactions with the text.[7] Thus, these two readers offer valuable insights into late-medieval perceptions of romance. In this essay, I first describe the manuscript, then outline the interactions of the two readers—whom I call "the Corrector" and "the Sketcher"—with its main texts, which are Middle English adaptations of well-known Latin histories. I compare Laud Misc. 622 to the other extant manuscripts of *Kyng Alisaunder* and of *Titus and Vespasian*, concluding that at least this surviving section of Laud Misc. 622 was both planned and read as a guide to Middle Eastern history and geography. Since medieval and early modern English readers considered Alexander a model for both kings and explorers, I focus primarily on *Kyng Alisaunder*, with a secondary emphasis on *Titus*.[8]

The couplet *Kyng Alisaunder* deals with the whole life of Alexander, beginning somewhat before his conception, and following the romance tradition of making the hero's biological father a foreign sorcerer, Neptanabus. Other fantastic elements include prophecies, talking trees, and Alexander's affair with Candace, queen of Ethiopia. The romance stresses Alexander's battles, especially his long campaign against the Persian emperor, Darius. It relates daring exploits such as Alexander's going disguised into the enemy camp, and gives details of letters and inspiring speeches by both Alexander and his opponents. It ends with his death and division of his empire. The fifteenth-century readers' interest in details of history and geography shows them reading against the grain of the fantastical, romance elements in this version of Alexander's life.

Description

Laud Misc. 622 is now a remnant of a once-larger manuscript: "from the page dimensions clearly once a very large book of which only the conclusion survives."[9] Since just eight items remain, we can only speculate about its original composition. It could have been a miniature library, with a variety of genres represented, or it could have been unified thematically or by some other criterion.[10] Laud Misc. 622 is best known for containing the most complete extant text of *Kyng Alisaunder*, including over a thousand lines about Alexander's travels in India omitted from the other surviving manuscripts. Written on vellum, the Laud manuscript dates to around 1400 and measures 378 by 264 millimeters, with red and blue initials. Seven of its eight items were certainly written by the same late-fourteenth-century scribe: verses on Old Testament history, related to the *South English Legendary*; *Fifteen Tokens before the Day of Judgment*; an Advent song, also from the *South English Legendary*; *Titus and Vespasian* (also known as the *Bataile of Ierusalem*); *The Vision of St Alexius*; Adam Davy's *Five Dreams about Edward II*; and *Kyng Alisaunder*. There is some controversy about the eighth item, a note about pilgrimages in the Holy Land. Gisela Guddat-Figge indicates that it is a later addition,[11] but the editor of *Kyng Alisaunder*, G. V. Smithers, says that despite the differences in some letter forms and an overall "smaller and more compressed" style, this hand "is probably identical with that in which KA is written."[12] After close examination, I agree with Smithers's identification. Most letter forms are identical in *Kyng Alisaunder* and the note on pilgrimages. The exceptions are a markedly different thorn, and minor differences in "a" and final "e." The compressed format of this item suggests that it was an afterthought, and changes in letter-form might be due to compression of the hand.[13]

All the items of Laud Misc. 622 are written in two columns per page, approximately fifty-five lines per column. Smithers dates *Kyng Alisaunder* to between 1250 and 1327;[14] its early date may explain some of the Corrector's efforts to make the language more accessible. *Titus*, dating to around the mid-fourteenth-century, required less modification to be comprehensible for later readers.[15] The provenance of this manuscript is unknown before its acquisition by Archbishop Laud. Names in the margins have so far resisted inquiry, though they do indicate a readership in the fifteenth century.[16]

The Readers

The medieval readers of a particular manuscript had to read what was in front of them, not an editor's attempt to restore the authorial readings. This is why we now find value in "bad" texts: they represent the text as it was known to actual readers.[17] At the same time, medieval scribes and readers were able to recognize a "bad" (in their own terms) text; we can see them struggle with archaic or corrupt texts, making their own efforts to improve passages they found difficult.[18] The editor of *Kyng Alisaunder*, G. V. Smithers, privileges the Bodleian version of the romance partly because it includes the extended section on India, partly because he finds London, Lincoln's Inn MS 150, "very corrupt."[19] The scribe of Lincoln's Inn 150 alters "problematic words and phrases,"[20] such as *galpeþ* [bells], which becomes *galopeþ*,[21] and *jouaunt* [merry fellow], which he turns into *geaunt*.[22] Most of these changes do not affect the readability of the lines. Whether the deer bell from the woods or gallop through them, the hunters can still pursue their prey without loss of sense. These changes appear to indicate either scribal incomprehension of uncommon vocabulary or a deliberate practice of simplification for an audience that would have trouble with unusual words. Joyce Boro notes that Nicholas Grimald, a sixteenth-century copyist of the alliterative *Romance of Alisaunder* (*Alexander A*) underlined and glossed words that gave him trouble, and was sometimes "impatient" due to "linguistic difficulty."[23] The vocabulary of alliterative poetry is generally more obscure than that of other contemporary verse, but Grimald provides a useful point of comparison, as a reader who, though educated and interested in Alexander, struggled with the language of his text.

The Corrector of Laud Misc. 622 is another reader who had difficulty with the vocabulary, spellings, omissions, and other idiosyncrasies of a text that already appeared archaic some 150 years after its creation. He takes matters into his own hands, working hard to update the text, though his additions rarely improve it. Smithers characterizes many of his interventions as "self-evidently inept or fatuous," or damaging to "the syntax or the meaning of a line,"[24] suggesting that the Corrector was not a careful reader. Although he may indeed have misunderstood these lines,[25] I argue that the presence of unnecessary corrections shows that the Corrector did read attentively. The scribe was accurate, and at times corrected his own work, so the Corrector did not face a corrupt text. Indeed, the scribe's self-corrections may have given the Corrector the idea that he could likewise alter the text. The Corrector of Laud Misc. 622 is an alert, interested reader, who notices and corrects minor errors, and struggles to make sense of other lines. When he intervenes at the expense of a passage's syntax, he may have found the sentence structure as well as the vocabulary of *Kyng Alisaunder* archaic. Thus he may have thought that his corrections could at least improve locally what he found, as a whole, still awkward.

The patterns to his corrections show attentive reading. He makes more interventions at certain points in the text, as if he skimmed passages of less interest and spent more time on other pages. The number of scribal corrections per page is highly variable, but usually low, and less frequent than those made by the Corrector (see Fig. 1: Scribal and Corrector Interventions on p. 21). The Corrector intervenes steadily, with one to four corrections per page being most common (see Fig. 2: Corrector's Interventions only on p. 21). The passages receiving the highest number of corrections correspond to the areas that receive the most comments in Lincoln's Inn MS 150, suggesting that multiple later readers of this romance were interested in the same material, especially the exotic peoples and animals encountered by Alexander in his travels in Africa and the Middle East.

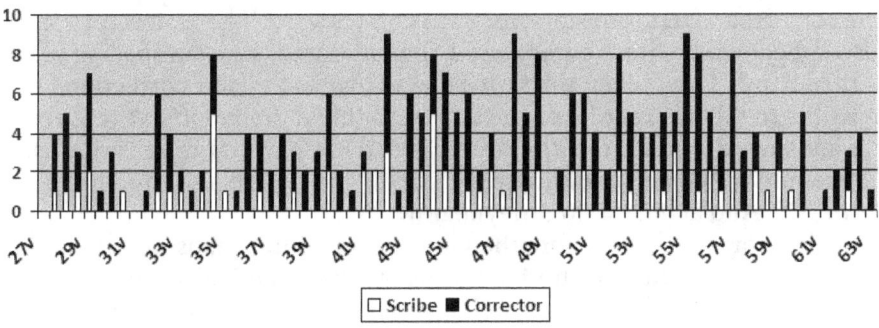

Figure 1. Scribal and Corrector Interventions

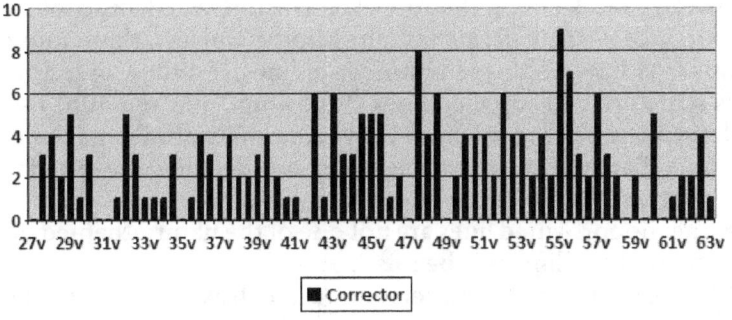

Figure 2. Corrector Interventions only

In Laud Misc. 622, the Corrector focuses his efforts on *Kyng Alisaunder*, with a few similar additions made to *Titus and Vespasian* and to the additional short text about the holy land. The Corrector made more changes to *Kyng Alisaunder* because this text is the oldest in the manuscript, and its language is therefore more difficult for a fifteenth-century reader. Smithers' notations of corrections as scribal or by a later hand first drew my attention to the number of changes that the Corrector made. Since the Corrector often enters changes over gaps that may be scribal, it is not always immediately obvious which hand entered the alterations. However, certain letters in the Corrector's hand are distinctive. Where the scribal *w* is a multicompartment Anglicana *w*, the Corrector's *w* is more like a *v* with an extra center stroke. The scribe consistently uses long *s* initially as well as medially, and round *s* at the end of words, whereas the Corrector uses a sigma-shaped *s* both initially and finally, as well as long s medially and finally. The scribal *l* is upright, while the corrector's *l* tends to slope forward or backward. The Corrector's hand also appears to be more compressed, in contrast to the even spacing of the scribal hand. Thus, when the scribe leaves blanks for later corrections, it is possible to tell whether he or the Corrector filled them. Often the Corrector adds words omitted by the scribe: "Myd her *men* waren so vertuous,"[26] "Fyue hundreþ *þowsynde* kniȝttes saun fail,"[27] "Kniȝth and *squyer* wiþ her lorde,"[28] "And al þin *ost* do ordeyne now."[29]

The Corrector does more than just fill convenient gaps; he also makes corrections and additions both interlinearly and marginally, showing a determination to produce a corrected text. He does not comment on the narrative, unlike one reader of *Kyng Alisaunder* in the Lincoln's Inn manuscript, who summarized the story, indicated speakers, and sometimes added comments such as "pretty saying."[30] The Corrector adds three entire lines to the text. Two of these additions are to "headnotes," monorhymed sections of the narrative modeled on the Anglo-Norman rhymed *laisses* of the source, the *Roman de Toute Chevalerie*.[31] In Middle English, these monorhymed sections may have an uneven number of lines, but the Corrector objected to this structure and supplied lines (following 3693 and 4062) so that the couplet structure of the romance could continue unbroken. He also adds an entire line, "Berus, notys, rotys and oþer þing," detailing the diet of vegetarian teetotalers who "ne eteþ non oþere þing / Þan þe erþe ȝeueþ."[32] The three preceding monorhymed lines are not one of the nature-themed headers, so it does seem that a line may be missing.

A few of the Corrector's interventions, such as supplying missing words, suggest that he was checking the Laud MS against another text. Others, such as anticipating the appearance of exotic animals by changing the word "mone" to "monoceros" argue rather that he was working on his own, trying to make sense of the text by thinking about elements elsewhere in the story.[33]

He cares about having the "right" number of lines in a text made up of couplets, but he does not worry about meter, often inserting words that render the line hypermetric. Smithers points out that many of the interventions "disagree with one or more of the other MSS.... Some of these sound like guesses," and adds, "The evidence as a whole suggests that he had no authority but his own for the great majority, and perhaps for all, of his alterations."[34]

The Corrector's adjustments reveal a reader struggling with a text. Unfamiliar with certain archaic or dialect words, he substitutes words he knows. Disturbed by missing pronouns, articles, conjunctions and prepositions (though such omissions are acceptable in Middle English), he adds them. To clarify the text, he adds (or changes) twenty-nine pronouns, adds sixteen prepositions, adds a conjunction to seven lines, and adds "al" or another intensifier to five lines. He also adds final –s in several instances to make a word plural or possessive. This last type of change indicates that he was unaware of the s-less genitive in some Middle English words, and that he did not understand some of the more unusual Middle English plurals, such as *childer*, which he changes to *childryn*. In all, he intervenes in 192 lines (out of 8021): two percent of the total number of lines. To be sure, this number might seem negligible, but to put it another way, the Corrector intervenes on all but seven of the seventy-two pages of *Kyng Alisaunder*. He shows sustained attention to the text, from beginning to end.

Some of his changes to vocabulary are as pointless as Smithers claims, but others have implications for the Corrector's identity and the provenance of the manuscript. An example of a pointless change is the addition of a titulus to "vilely" so that it expands to "vilenly;" either word works for both sense and grammar in the line, "þan in seruage vile(n)ly serue."[35] However, sometimes the Corrector substitutes words that are in wider usage in the fifteenth century than earlier. For example, he changes "fonge" to "fonde" in "Corne and drynk and metes fonge."[36] "Fonde" is a more common word, though the *Middle English Dictionary* shows that "fonge," after about 1400, appears mostly in northern works, suggesting that the Corrector is not from the north.[37] In the line "Chaumpe bataile to wenden to," he adds letters to create "chaumpayne" out of "chaumpe."[38] The MED's earliest citation for *chaumpe*, in this sense, is *Kyng Alisaunder*; other citations are mostly fifteenth century, and the heraldic sense appears to be more common. "Chaumpayne" enters the language in the fifteenth century, and its use is more wide-spread.[39]

The Corrector does not always simplify. He chooses an unusual word, "gynful," to replace "gilful."[40] "Guileful" remains in use into the modern period, and the MED gives citations from various parts of England for it. "Ginful," on the other hand, gets citations only from the *South English Legendary*, *Piers Plowman*, the *Siege of Jerusalem*, and *Saint Erkenwald*.[41] These works, using the vocabulary of alliterative poetry, tend to associate "ginful" with pagans, Jews, and the Devil. Making this change gives a stronger negative cast to the astrologer Neptanabus (Alexander's biological father, in the romance account); it also serves as another indication that the Corrector is from the middle section of the country. He adds *ch* to *bisette* in three lines, producing *bischette*.[42] This might be a dialectal change, but it seems more likely to be an alteration to vocabulary. Alexander "bisette" [enclosed] foreign peoples, including Turks, dwarves, and wolflings; but the Corrector may imagine that Alexander shot them.

Some of the Corrector's changes help to indicate his origins. His plural *-us* ending occurs in the south and east.[43] He spells "about" as *abowte*, a preference appearing in the East Midlands and Yorkshire.[44] He adds letters to an erasure to create the word "sekynde";[45] the *-ynde* ending for the present participle is associated with East Anglia.[46] He spells "thousand" as "þowsynde,"[47] which LALME maps to Huntingdonshire and Hertfordshire.[48] He turns *he* into *ȝhe* in five lines.[49] This spelling for "ye" occurs in the East Midlands and Yorkshire. He uses three different forms of IT: *yt*,[50] *hyt*,[51] and *jt*.[52] Though *yt* and *hyt* occur in many areas, LALME localizes *jt* to Cambridgeshire.[53] His verbal choices, *doth* for "do" and present indicative ending in *-ȝth*, also suggest the East Midlands.[54] Conclusions must be tentative, since the sample size is small and many of the items on LALME's questionnaire do not appear in the Corrector's entries, but it seems likely that he came from somewhere near Cambridge.

The Corrector's interventions in *Titus and Vespasian* are far less extensive but similar to those he makes in *Kyng Alisaunder*, both in type and in placement. Most of his additions are concentrated on the spread of folios 13v and 14r, where the narrative presents the besieged Jews resorting to cannibalism. Some of these are the sort of minor clarifications seen in *Kyng Alisaunder*. More significantly, the Corrector changes two lines to make them more detailed and dramatic. I show his changes in italics:

> And then þe Jewes þider ronne,
> Upon his erand they bygonne,
> And her liflode bare hem froo.
> Þan þese wymmen had mych woo,
> And bilefte in mychel drede,
> For noo more store þei ne had at nede.
> (Herbert, Titus, 3477–3482)

> And ____ þe jewes þat þider ^ rome [*dede*]
> *Þe womans chyld* þer *hem be* nome
> Þe wymen *hadde sorwe + meche* woo
> For her lyflode þai beren hem froo

And for þis siȝht þai weren in drede
Þat þai duden þat wicked dede
(Laud Misc. 622, fol. 13v)

The Laud version differs notably from other manuscripts, even before the Corrector's alterations. The Laud scribe left a blank in line 3477 and reversed lines 3479 and 3480. The corrector added *dede* in the margin, with a caret in the line. The *rome/nome* rhyme appears to be scribal. The next two lines in Laud are heavily altered by the Corrector (changes in italics), to the point where it is not possible to discern many of the original letters. The scribal version in the Laud manuscript already gives a more dramatic and disapproving reading of this scene, referring to the women's "wicked dede" rather than to their "nede," as in other manuscripts.[55] The Corrector's changes intensify both pathos and criticism, stressing that the "liflode" is in fact a "chyld," and multiplying descriptors of the women's distress: not just "woo" but "sorwe" as well.

Other changes on these pages are significant less for their content than because there are more such interventions here than in the rest of *Titus*. As in *Kyng Alisaunder*, the Corrector seems to become more attentive at dramatic points. Another alteration that intensifies emotion occurs on folio 5v in the line corresponding to Herbert's line 1629, where the Corrector changes a past tense to a present. In place of "Here may we seen god was our freende," the addition reads "Here mowe we seen god *ys howre* frende," with the change in very dark ink that stands out on the page. The original text is not legible, but there is space enough for it to have read "their" rather than "our," prompting the correction.

The Corrector's changes to *Titus*, then, seem didactic, meant to stress religious and moral themes, emphasizing both the crimes of the Jews and the present availability of God to Christians.[56] Finally, the Corrector adds a handful of missing words to the short text about sites in the Holy Land—a pronoun, a verb, a conjunction—drawing boxes around them as he does with many of his additions to *Kyng Alisaunder* and *Titus and Vespasian*. The vertical compression of this text means that corrections are made in the margins, not between lines. Overall, it appears that the Corrector takes a particular interest in Middle Eastern geography and exotica; though he alters *Titus* to bring out the drama of a gruesome scene, he reads *Kyng Alisaunder* with attention to Alexander's life, battles, and explorations, with the primary goal of clarifying the text, not increasing its drama or emphasizing a moral message.

The other attentive reader of Laud Misc. 622 is the Sketcher; the delicacy of his lines suggests that he is not the same reader as the more heavy-handed Corrector. The Sketcher adds two simple *bas-de-page* sketches, each involving two figures, one in *Kyng Alisaunder* and the other in *Titus and Vespasian*.

Although neither is elaborate, both show that the Sketcher was not just doodling but deliberately illustrating the action in the text. The drawing in *Kyng Alisaunder* accompanies a description of an attack on Alexander's army by adders, scorpions, and dragons. Dragons "of diuers coloure" come flying at Alexander's men; they "fouȝtten aȝein wiþ grete vigoure" and kill more than 110 of Alexander's troops.[57] A second wave of dragons follows, some with two or three heads. At the foot of folio 51v is a line drawing of a man throwing stones at a dragon. Smithers characterizes this drawing as "a rough ink sketch",[58] but the lines are controlled and deliberate. The head of the dragon is clearly drawn, with horns, while the body is suggested by a series of curving, sinuous lines, possibly indicating rapidly beating wings.[59] The man has curly hair and a rough growth of beard, and holds stones gathered up in the lap of his robe. His right arm is drawn back, the hand holding a stone ready to throw. A tree stands in the background. While not a major plot event like Darius's death, the fight with dragons is vivid, memorable, and recognizable as a trial of a knight's worth, like Guy of Warwick's two battles with dragons.[60] Alexander, as a hero of the ancient world, takes on an epic-sized version of Guy's individual battle, with armies of men and dragons ranged against each other. For any one soldier, of course, the combat would be individual, so the Sketcher depicts a single man's encounter with the devilish enemy.

The other sketch appears on folio 15r, toward the end of *Titus and Vespasian*, depicting a man doffing his hat to show respect to another. The second man turns away and points to his backside, a gesture widely used to indicate scorn. Renditions of similar scenes appear in British Library MS Additional 62925, known as the Rutland Psalter, folio 67r, and The Hague, Koninklijke Bibliotheek, MS D.40 folio 124r.[61] The sketch in Laud Misc. 622 illustrates a scene in which the leaders of the Jews go to Emperor Vespasian and plead for mercy, but the emperor brusquely refuses to show any forgiveness to those who killed Jesus. The style of the sketch so closely resembles that of the illustration in *Kyng Alisaunder* that I am convinced they are by the same reader. Whatever he thought of the other items in Laud Misc. 622, he read the two romances attentively enough to give each an appropriate illustration at a dramatic moment.

The Sketcher may also be responsible for some *nota* marks in *Kyng Alisaunder*; the delicacy of line, at any rate, more closely resembles the Sketcher's entries than the Corrector's hand. These marks appear next to striking lines and proverbs on folios 39r, 40r, and 41r. The first marks "Out of inde from prestre john."[62] Prester John was a figure of great interest to medieval readers; he might be considered variously as an exotic king, as the ruler of an Eastern Christian realm, as a historical figure, or as a mythic anachronism, depending on the interests, education and attitude of the reader.⁶³ Another *nota* appears alongside the first line of a comparative couplet: "He hem to hiwe by fyue by sex / So þe bocher dooþ þe oxe."⁶⁴ Medieval and early-modern readers sometimes mark such similes, perhaps for their own later use, or simply in admiration; the most prolific commenter in the Lincoln's Inn 150 copy of *Kyng Alisaunder* writes out two such lines from another area of the story: "mo knightes then/ sterres and mo/ men then in the sea/stones."⁶⁵ In Laud Misc. 622, the final lines of two proverbs receive marks: "Þe peny is of riche mounde / Þat ysaueþ þe hole pounde"⁶⁶ and "Hij ben worþi to habben care / Þat nylleþ be by oþere yware."⁶⁷ Educators from Erasmus to English schoolmasters recommended such reading practices to build their students' own rhetorical arsenals: have students mark "all such words or things, as either are hard to them in the learning of them, or which are of some speciall excellency, or use, worthy the noting," urged John Brinsley in 1612.⁶⁸

Comparisons

Comparison of the Laud Misc. 622 *Kyng Alisaunder* to the other extant manuscripts of this text is instructive. The oldest text, that in the Auchinleck Manuscript, is fragmentary, with only a few leaves surviving.⁶⁹ The only marginalia are late accounts on a damaged page now held at the University of London; these were probably added after dismemberment. If we ignore short texts added to fill out gatherings, *Kyng Alisaunder* appears among a group of texts dealing with historical topics: *Guy of Warwick*, *Bevis of Hampton*, *Of Arthour and of Merlin*, two Charlemagne romances, *Kyng Alisaunder*, *The Anonymous Short English Metrical Chronicle*, *Horn Childe and Maiden Rimnild*, and *King Richard*. Except for the chronicle, all of these qualify as "romances," and most of them relate English history, even if some of the English heroes are mythical. Charlemagne and Alexander stand out from the others, and even they have a role to play in English history: they represent the classical and continental *imperium* that moves west in the *translationem studii et imperii*. In this respect, the Auchinleck manuscript offers a model for one version of what the Laud manuscript might have been: a collection of varied texts including a section on Middle Eastern history, which survives perhaps because it was of particular interest to some reader.

Lincoln's Inn MS 150 offers a different view of *Kyng Alisaunder*. The manuscript includes two Arthurian texts, one an abbreviated version of Auchinleck's *Of Arthour and of Merlin*, the other *Lybeaus Desconnus*; the anonymous *Seege or Bataile of Troye*; and then, shifting genres to religious dream-vision, a copy of the A-version of *Piers Plowman*. The romances present a trio of characters belonging to the Nine Worthies: Hector, Alexander, Arthur. The manuscript focuses less on history than on admirable characters from history. *Piers Plowman*, then, might encourage the individual reader to focus on his own soul rather than on historical worthies. Alternatively, it could offer Piers as an answer to secular worthies. It is also possible that the manuscript is simply a miscellany, copying a few pieces that its compiler liked or had at hand. Whatever its origins, one sixteenth-century reader interacted with it in ways that support my contention that the Corrector of Laud Misc. 622 increases his corrections in areas he finds most interesting. This reader of Lincoln's Inn MS 150 comments more prolifically in the same areas where the Corrector of Laud Misc. 622 concentrates his entries. It appears that readers in the fifteenth and sixteenth century reacted to the story of *Kyng Alisaunder* in similar ways, focusing on battles, letters and speeches, *sententia*, and above all, exotic travels.

The manuscript context for *Titus and Vespasian* is didactic, on a continuum from the religious to the historical. Most of the manuscripts that include *Titus* are religious or moralizing miscellanies. In this category are British Library Additional MS 10036 (early 15th century); BL Additional MS 36983 (ca. 1442); BL MS Harley 4733 (ca. 1460); Oxford, Bodleian Library, MS Douce 78 (third quarter of the fifteenth century); and MS Douce 126 (first half of the fifteenth century). However, the remaining two manuscripts have a more historical slant and also associate *Titus* with the works of one or more major poets. Oxford, Bodleian Library MS Digby 230 precedes *Titus* with Lydgate's *The Siege of Thebes* and *The Siege of Troy*, suggesting that this collection, like the Laud manuscript, has a historical theme. Coventry, City Record Office MS 325/1 includes assorted works of Hoccleve, Lydgate, and Chaucer, as well as *Mandeville's Travels*. Guddat-Figge calls the manuscript an "anthology of works by the most outstanding Middle English poets, and two very popular anonymous poems"—that is, *Titus* and *Mandeville's Travels*.[70] Texts include Lydgate's *Siege of Thebes* and Hoccleve's *Tale of the Emperour Gereslaus*, which lend a historical flavor to a manuscript whose other contents skew towards morality and didacticism.[71] The historical emphasis of Laud Misc. 622, then, is not unique, but the diachronic variety of its perspectives on Middle Eastern geography is striking.

At the same time, the main focus of both the book and its fifteenth-century readers lies firmly in the distant past. The only item dealing with contemporary issues is Adam Davy's dreams about Edward II; the manuscript as it has come down to us contains no chronicle connecting the ancient world to the scribe's present day. In this it contrasts with well-known manuscript books compiled in the fifteenth and sixteenth centuries. Robert Thornton's interests included recent English kings as well as the ancient and mythic past; he copied a prose *Life of Alexander* in Lincoln, Cathedral Library MS 91 and in British Library MS Additional 31042, *The Siege of Jerusalem*, Lydgate's "Verses on the Kings of England," and *Richard Coer de Lion*.[72] Similarly, London, Lambeth Palace MS 491, a fifteenth-century manuscript, associates a chronicle of England with the *Siege of Jerusalem* and *The Awntyrs of Arthure at the Terne Wathelyne*. John Colyns concentrated on current events in his book, British Library, Harley MS 2252, which is distinctive for "its engagement with the political and mercantile world of Henry VIII's Tudor London."[73] The focus on the ancient world might imply that the Sketcher and the Corrector shared a scholarly interest in history, or it could suggest that these readers coded their political commentary as reactions to fiction, as Lois Potter argues for the seventeenth century.[74] The Corrector's concern for accessibility certainly argues that he found the romance worth updating for a contemporary audience, whatever the reasons for its appeal.

Conclusion

The later layers of Laud Misc. 622—the additions by known readers and by doodlers whose access to the manuscript makes them potential readers—show that the manuscript had an active afterlife well after its point of creation. Assorted doodles and pen trials in the margins, such as the six attempts at "alleluya" on folio 30v, and *"ego sum bonus puer quem deus amat"* on folio 47v, indicate that the manuscript was at least available for reading, while the interventions of the Corrector and the Sketcher show that two readers gave the main texts close attention. The Corrector's systematic alterations and additions to the text of *Kyng Alisaunder* indicate a determined effort to understand and make accessible a text whose language had become old-fashioned. The original coordinator of Laud Misc. 622 seems to have wanted a range of texts relating Middle Eastern history over time, covering the classical and biblical eras as well as his own. Although *Kyng Alisaunder* is in many ways the product of the late thirteenth century,[75] its margins show a shift toward a different Alexander: no longer the medieval exemplum of kingship yet not quite the explorer prototype seen by the sixteenth-century reader of the Lincoln's Inn *Kyng Alisaunder*. Later readers approach *Kyng Alisaunder* as history rather than as romance, and annotate its margins accordingly.

Northern Illinois University

NOTES

1. G. V. Smithers, ed., *Kyng Alisaunder*, 2 vols., EETS o.s. 227, 237 (London: Oxford University Press, 1952-1957); J. A. Herbert, ed., *Titus and Vespasian, or The Destruction of Jerusalem* (London: Roxburghe Club, 1905).
2. Boro, "Miscellaneity and History: Reading Sixteenth-Century Romance Manuscripts," *English Manuscript Studies 1100-1700* 15 (2009): 123-151.
3. Charles Russell Stone, *From Tyrant to Philosopher-King: A Literary History*

of Alexander the Great in Medieval and Early Modern England (Turnhout: Brepols, 2013).
4. Ibid., 43.
5. Ibid., 185, citing Roberto Weiss, *Humanism in England During the Fifteenth Century* (Oxford: Blackwell, 1941), 123.
6. Stone, *From Tyrant*, 168.
7. Gisela Guddat-Figge reports marginalia that comment directly on the text in only seven of the ninety-nine manuscripts in Gisela Guddat-Figge, *Catalogue of Manuscripts Containing Middle English Romances* (Munich, Germany: Wilhelm Fink, 1976), although the list of names inscribed in romance manuscripts is extensive. Guddat-Figge's Index III, 320-323, includes scribes and owners as well as other signatures. Boro, "Miscellaneity," comments on the political reading of Troy in Cambridge, CUL MS Kk.5.30, where one reader used the margins of Troy romances to "praise and repeatedly name King James" (129).
8. Treatments of the medieval Alexander are extensive, and include essays in W. J. Aerts, ed., *Alexander the Great in the Middle Ages: Ten Studies on the Last Days of Alexander in Literary and Historical Writing* (Nijmegen, The Netherlands: Alfa, 1978); Gerrit H. V. Bunt, *Alexander the Great in the Literature of Medieval Britain* (Groningen, The Netherlands: Egbert Forsten, 1994); George Cary, *The Medieval Alexander*, ed. D. J. A. Ross (Cambridge, UK: Cambridge University Press, 1956); Stone, *From Tyrant to Philosopher-King*; Richard Stoneman, "The Latin Alexander," in *Latin Fiction: The Latin Novel* in Context, ed. Heinz Hofmann (London: Routledge, 1999), 167-186. More attention has been given to the Anglo-Norman Alexander, especially the beautifully illustrated version of Oxford, Bodleian Library, Bodley MS 264, and to the alliterative *Wars of Alexander*, than specifically to *Kyng Alisaunder* in couplets. Works concentrating on *Kyng Alisaunder* include Gerrit H. V. Bunt, "Alexander's Last Days in the Middle English *Kyng Alisaunder*," in *Alexander the Great in the Middle Ages: Ten Studies on the Last Days of Alexander in Literary and Historical Writing*, ed. W. J. Aerts, et al. (Nijmegen, The Netherlands: Alfa, 1978), 202-229; Gerrit H. V. Bunt, "An Exemplary Hero: Alexander the Great," in *Companion to Middle English Romance*, ed. H. Aertsen and A. A. MacDonald (Amsterdam: VU University Press, 1990), 29-55; Martin Camargo, "The Metamorphosis of Candace and the Earliest English Love Epistle," in *Court and Poet: Selected Proceedings of the Third Congress of the International Courtly Literature Society* (Liverpool, 1980), ed. Glyn S. Burgess et al. (Liverpool, UK: Cairns, 1981), 101-111; John Scattergood, "Validating the High Life in Of Arthour and of Merlin and Kyng Alisaunder," *Essays in Criticism* 54 (2004): 323-350. The couplet version of *Titus and Vespasian* has been seriously neglected, with scholars tending to focus instead on the

alliterative version, Ralph Hanna and David A. Lawton, eds., *The Siege of Jerusalem*, EETS 320 (Oxford: Oxford University Press, 2003). One recent essay on the couplet romance has appeared: Maija Birenbaum, "Affective Vengeance in *Titus and Vespasian*," *Chaucer Review* 43/3 (2009): 330-344.
9. Ralph Hanna, *London Literature, 1300-1380* (Cambridge, UK: Cambridge University Press, 2005), 105.
10. For influential discussions of manuscript miscellanies, see Phillipa Hardman, "A Medieval 'Library *In Parvo*,'" *Medium Aevum* 47 (1978): 262-273; Derek Pearsall, "The Whole Book: Late Medieval English Manuscript Miscellanies and their Modern Interpreters," in *Imagining the Book*, ed. Stephen Kelly and John J. Thompson (Turnhout, Belgium: Brepols, 2005), 17-29; Stephen G. Nichols and Siegfried Wenzel, eds., *The Whole Book* (Ann Arbor: University of Michigan Press, 1996); Michael Johnston, *Romance and the Gentry in Late Medieval England* (Oxford: Oxford University Press, 2014), esp. chap. 3, "Gentry Romances: The Manuscript Evidence," 90-127.
11. Guddat-Figge, *Catalogue*, 285.
12. Smithers, *Kyng Alisaunder*, 2:2.
13. Ibid., 2:2–3.
14. Ibid., 2:44.
15. Herbert, *Titus*, 47; the earliest manuscripts are from around the turn of the fifteenth century.
16. The names are Honorius Gonereid, fol. 71a, dry point or very faint pencil; Joh. Downe, fol. 64b. See Guddat-Figge, *Catalogue*, 286.
17. See, e.g., Jessica Brantley, "The Prehistory of the Book," *PMLA* 124/2 (2009): 632-639; Jacqueline Cerquiglini-Toulet, "L'Echappée belle: stratégies d'écriture et de lecture dans la littérature de la fin du moyen âge," *Littérature* 99 (Oct. 1995): 33-52; Kate Harris, "John Gower's *Confessio Amantis*: The Virtue of Bad Texts," *Manuscripts and Readers in Fifteenth-Century England*, ed. Derek Pearsall (Cambridge, UK: Brewer, 1983), 27-40; George Kane, "Good and Bad Manuscripts: Texts and Critics," in *Chaucer and Langland: Historical and Textual Approaches* (Berkeley: University of California Press, 1989), 206-213; Daniel Wakelin, *Scribal correction and literary craft: English manuscripts 1375-1510* (Cambridge, UK: Cambridge University Press, 2014).
18. See Ralph Hanna, "Problems of 'best text' editing," in *Manuscripts and Texts: Editorial Problems in Later Middle English Literature*, ed. Derek Pearsall (Cambridge, UK: Brewer, 1987), 87-94, particularly 88-89; Daniel Wakelin, "When Scribes Won't Write: Gaps in Middle English Books," *Studies in the Age of Chaucer* 36 (2014): 249-278; Barry Windeatt, "The Scribes as Chaucer's Early Critics," *Studies in the Age of Chaucer* 1 (1979): 119-141.
19. Smithers, *Kyng Alisaunder*, 2:8.
20. Smithers, *Kyng Alisaunder*, 2:9.

21. *Kyng Alisaunder*, Laud Misc 622, l. 462; Lincoln's Inn 150, l. 459.
22. *Kyng Alisaunder*, Laud Misc 622, l. 3201; Lincoln's Inn MS 150, l. 3186.
23. Boro, "Miscellaneity," 132; see also 134.
24. Smithers, *Kyng Alisaunder*, 2:9.
25. Smithers, *Kyng Alisaunder*, 2:10.
26. *Kyng Alisaunder*, Laud Misc 622, l. 2372, fol. 38r.
27. Ibid., l. 1913, fol. 36r.
28. Ibid., l. 2836, fol. 40v.
29. Ibid., l. 2024, fol. 36v.
30. Lincoln's Inn MS 150, fol. 56v. I analyze this reader's responses in an essay in preparation.
31. Brian Foster, ed., *The Anglo-Norman Alexander*, 2 vols, ANTS 29–33 (London: Anglo-Norman Text Society, 1976, 1977). On the headnotes, see Scattergood, "Validating the High Life," and Smithers, 2:35–40.
32. *Kyng Alisaunder*, ll. 5922–5293, fol. 54v.
33. Ibid., l. 5712, fol. 53v; "monoceros" does not appear in the text until l. 6529, fol. 57r.
34. Smithers, *Kyng Alisaunder*, 2:9, 2:11.
35. *Kyng Alisaunder*, l. 3066, fol. 41v.
36. *Kyng Alisaunder*, l. 6141, fol. 55v.
37. *The Middle English Dictionary*, s.v. "fongen," University of Michigan, http://quod.lib.umich.edu/m/med/, accessed 9 June 2015.
38. *Kyng Alisaunder*, l. 1237, fol. 33r.
39. *The Middle English Dictionary*, s.v. "chaump(e)" and "champain(e)," University of Michigan, http://quod.lib.umich.edu/m/med/, accessed 9 June 2015.
40. *Kyng Alisaunder*, l. 444, fol. 29v.
41. *The Middle English Dictionary*, s.v. "ginful," University of Michigan, http://quod.lib.umich.edu/m/med/, accessed 9 June 2015.
42. *Kyng Alisaunder*, ll. 6252, 6256, 6262, all fol. 56r.
43. Angus McIntosh, M. L. Samuels, and Michael Benskin, eds., *A Linguistic Atlas of Late Mediaeval English*, 4 vols. (Aberdeen, UK: Aberdeen University Press, 1986), 4:105. Hereafter *LALME*.
44. Ibid., 4:116.
45. *Kyng Alisaunder*, l. 5707, fol. 53v.
46. *LALME* 2: map 57, Present part. (6); 4:106.
47. Ibid., l. 1913, fol. 36r.
48. *LALME* 2: map 236 THOUSAND (6); 4:265-266.
49. *Kyng Alisaunder*, ll. 5708, 5931, 6143, 6156, 6748; fol. 53v, fol. 54v, fol. 55v, and fol. 58r.
50. Ibid., ll. 4022, 7024; fol. 45v, fol. 59v.
51. Ibid., l. 4967, fol. 50r (altered from he).

52. Ibid., l. 209, fol. 28v.
53. *LALME* 4:10.
54. Ibid., 4:109–110.
55. *Titus*, Laud Misc. 622, fol. 13v.
56. Birenbaum argues in "Affective Vengeance" that *Titus and Vespasian* emphasizes God's love for his creation, including the Jews.
57. *Kyng Alisaunder*, ll. 5313-5314.
58. Smithers, *Kyng Alisaunder*, 1:283n.
59. The horns may have been suggested by the characterization of "deuelen" (l. 5348) for the defeated enemy.
60. *Guy of Warwick*, ll. 3758–3766 and 6763–6914, in David Burnley and Alison Wiggins, *The Auchinleck Manuscript* (Edinburgh, UK: National Library of Scotland, 2003), http://auchinleck.nls.uk/mss/guy_cp.html.
61. Both of these are reproduced in Michael Camille, *Image on the Edge* (Cambridge, MA: Harvard University Press, 1992), 45 and 25, respectively.
62. *Kyng Alisaunder*, l. 2585.
63. References to Prester John first appear in the twelfth century in Otto of Freising's Chronicle, Charles Christopher Mierow, trans., *The two cities: a chronicle of universal history to the year 1146 A.D.*, (New York: Octagon Books, 1966), 443–444). They spread widely in the thirteenth century, when confused reports of Genghis Khan's exploits reached Western Europe. By the fourteenth century, it was clear that the Mongols would not help to re-take Jerusalem, and the realm of Prester John was pushed farther east, into India. John Andrew Boyle shows that despite the apparent anachronism, Alexander the Great was associated with Prester John through Alexander's link to the land of Gog and Magog (*Kyng Alisaunder* ll. 6126–6127): John Andrew Boyle, "Alexander and the Mongols," *Journal of the Royal Asiatic Society of Great Britain and Ireland* 2 (1979): 123–136.
64. *Kyng Alisaunder*, ll. 2827–2828, fol. 40r.
65. *Kyng Alisaunder*, Lincoln's Inn MS 150, l. 1731, fol. 44v.
66. *Kyng Alisaunder*, MS Laud Misc. 622, ll. 3023–3024, fol. 41r.
67. Ibid., ll. 3025–3026, fol. 41r.
68. John Brinsley, *Ludus Literarius*, ed. E. T. Campagnac (Liverpool, UK: Liverpool University Press, 1917), 46; for Erasmus, see Desiderius Erasmus, "De Ratione Studii," ed. Jean-Claude Margolin, in *Opera Omnia Desiderii Erasmi Roterodami* (Amsterdam: North Holland Publishing Co., 1971), 2:79–151, at 117. For further discussion of annotation techniques, see Heidi Brayman Hackel, *Reading Material in Early Modern England* (Cambridge, UK: Cambridge University Press, 2005); Heather Jackson, *Marginalia: readers writing in books* (New Haven, CT: Yale University Press, 2001); Fred Schurink, "Manuscript Commonplace Books, Literature, and Reading in Early Modern England," *Huntington Library Quarterly* 73/3 (2010):

453–469, especially 460–464; William H. Sherman, *John Dee: The Politics of Reading and Writing in the English Renaissance* (Amherst: University of Massachusetts Press, 1995); Margo Todd, *Christian Humanism and the Puritan Social Order* (Cambridge, UK: Cambridge University Press, 1987).
69. In the Auchinleck itself, two folios of *Kyng Alisaunder* remain, fols. 278–279. The University of London has two fragments (London University Library MS 593), and the University of St Andrews has two more (St Andrews University Library MS PR.2065 A.15); see Derek Pearsall and I. C. Cunningham, eds., *The Auchinleck Manuscript* (London: Scolar Press, 1977), and Burnley and Wiggins, *Auchinleck*.
70. Guddat-Figge, *Catalogue*, 111.
71. The seventeen items in this manuscript include Hoccleve's "Learn to Die," Lydgate's "Danse macabre," and Chaucer's "Lak of Stedfastnesse." *Mandeville's Travels, Titus and Vespasian*, and Lydgate's *Siege of Thebes* are items 14, 15, and 16, suggesting a shift in emphasis after the first seventy-seven folios. A single scribe is responsible for the first ninety-five folios, with a second scribe taking over for items 15–17 (Guddat-Figge, *Catalogue*, 110–111).
72. Guddat-Figge, *Catalogue*, 135–142 and 159–163; Johnston, *Romance and the Gentry*, esp. chap. 4, 159–205.
73. Carol Meale, "London, British Library, Harley MS 2252, John Colyns' 'Boke': Structure and Content," *English Manuscript Studies* 15 (2009): 65–122, at 65; see also Carol Meale, "The Compiler at Work: John Colyns and BL MS Harley 2253," in *Manuscripts and Readers in Fifteenth-Century England*, ed. Derek Pearsall (Cambridge, UK: Brewer, 1983), 82–103; and Boro, "Miscellaneity," 136–138.
74. Lois Potter, *Secret Rites and Secret Writing: Royalist Literature 1641–1660* (Cambridge, UK: Cambridge University Press, 1989).
75. See Bunt, "Exemplary Hero," 29–55; Camargo, "Metamorphosis," 101–111.

WORKS CITED

Primary Sources

London, Lincoln's Inn MS 150
Oxford, Bodleian Library, MS Laud. Misc. 622

Secondary Sources

Aerts, W. J. *Alexander the Great in the Middle Ages: Ten Studies on the Last Days of Alexander in Literary and Historical Writing*. Nijmegen, The Netherlands: Alfa, 1978.
Birenbaum, Maija. "Affective Vengeance in *Titus and Vespasian*." *Chaucer Review* 43.3 (2009): 330–344.

Boro, Joyce. "Miscellaneity and History: Reading Sixteenth-Century Romance Manuscripts." *English Manuscript Studies 1100–1700* 15 (2009): 123–151.

Boyle, John Andrew. "Alexander and the Mongols." *Journal of the Royal Asiatic Society of Great Britain and Ireland* 2 (1979): 123–136.

Brantley, Jessica. "The Prehistory of the Book." *PMLA* 124.2 (2009): 632–639.

Brayman Hackel, Heidi. *Reading Material in Early Modern England.* Cambridge, UK: Cambridge University Press, 2005.

Brinsley, John. *Ludus literarius*, ed. E. T. Campagnac. Liverpool, UK: Liverpool University Press, 1917.

Bunt, Gerrit H. V. "Alexander's Last Days in the Middle English Kyng Alisaunder." In *Alexander the Great in the Middle Ages: Ten Studies on the Last Days of Alexander in Literary and Historical Writing*, ed. W. J. Aerts, et al., 202–229. Nijmegen, The Netherlands: Alfa, 1978.

———. "An Exemplary Hero: Alexander the Great." In *Companion to Middle English Romance*, ed. H. Aertsen and A. A. MacDonald. Amsterdam: VU University Press, 1990, 29–55.

———. *Alexander the Great in the Literature of Medieval Britain*. Groningen, The Netherlands: Egbert Forsten, 1994.

Burnley, David, and Alison Wiggins, eds. *The Auchinleck Manuscript.* Edinburgh, UK: National Library of Scotland, 2003. http://auchinleck.nls.uk.

Camargo, Martin. "The Metamorphosis of Candace and the Earliest English Love Epistle." In *Court and Poet: Selected Proceedings of the Third Congress of the International Courtly Literature Society (Liverpool, 1980)*, ed. Glyn S. Burgess, et al., 101–111. Liverpool, UK: Cairns, 1981.

Camille, Michael. *Image on the Edge.* Cambridge, MA: Harvard University Press, 1992.

Cary, George. *The Medieval Alexander*, ed. D.J.A. Ross. Cambridge, UK: Cambridge University Press, 1956.

Cerquiglini-Toulet, Jacqueline. "L'Echappée belle: Stratégies d'écriture et de lecture dans la littérature de la fin du moyen âge." *Littérature* 99 (1995): 33–52.

Erasmus, Desiderius. "De ratione studii," ed. Jean-Claude Margolin. In *Opera omnia Desiderii Erasmi Roterodami*. Vol. 2, 79–151. Amsterdam: North Holland Publishing Co., 1971.

Foster, Brian, ed. *The Anglo-Norman Alexander.* 2 vols. ANTS 29–33. London: Anglo-Norman Text Society, 1976, 1977.

Guddat-Figge, Gisela. *Catalogue of Manuscripts Containing Middle English Romances.* Munich, Germany: Wilhelm Fink, 1976.

Hanna, Ralph. *London Literature, 1300–1380.* Cambridge, UK: Cambridge University Press, 2005.

———. "Problems of 'Best Text' Editing." In *Manuscripts and Texts: Editorial Problems in Later Middle English Literature*, ed. Derek Pearsall, 87-94. Cambridge, UK: Brewer, 1987.

———, and David A. Lawton, eds. *The Siege of Jerusalem.* EETS 320. Oxford: Oxford University Press, 2003.

Hardman, Phillipa. "A Medieval 'Library In Parvo.'" *Medium Aevum* 47 (1978): 262–273.

Harris, Kate. "John Gower's *Confessio Amantis*: The Virtue of Bad Texts." In *Manuscripts and Readers in Fifteenth-Century England*, ed. Derek Pearsall, 27–40. Cambridge, UK: Brewer, 1983.

Herbert, J. A., ed. *Titus and Vespasian,* or *The Destruction of Jerusalem.* London: Roxburghe Club, 1905.

Jackson, Heather. *Marginalia: Readers Writing in Books.* New Haven, CT: Yale University Press, 2001.

Johnston, Michael. *Romance and the Gentry in Late Medieval England.* Oxford: Oxford University Press, 2014.

Kane, George. "Good and Bad Manuscripts: Texts and Critics." In *Chaucer and Langland: Historical and Textual Approaches*, 206–213. Berkeley: University of California Press, 1989.

McIntosh, Angus, M. L. Samuels, and Michael Benskin, eds. *A Linguistic Atlas of Late Mediaeval English.* 4 vols. Aberdeen, UK: Aberdeen University Press, 1986.

Meale, Carol. "London, British Library, Harley MS 2252, John Colyns' 'Boke': Structure and Content." *English Manuscript Studies* 15 (2009): 65–122.

———. "The Compiler at Work: John Colyns and BL MS Harley 2253." In *Manuscripts and Readers in Fifteenth-Century England*, ed. Derek Pearsall, 82–103. Cambridge, UK: Brewer, 1983.

The Middle English Dictionary. Ann Arbor: University of Michigan, 2007. http://quod.lib.umich.edu/m/med/.

Nichols, Stephen G., and Siegfried Wenzel, eds. *The Whole Book.* Ann Arbor: University of Michigan Press, 1996.

Otto of Freising. *The Two Cities: A Chronicle of Universal History to the Year 1146 A.D.*, trans. Charles Christopher Mierow. New York: Octagon Books, 1966.

Pearsall, Derek. "The Whole Book: Late Medieval English Manuscript Miscellanies and Their Modern Interpreters." In *Imagining the Book*, ed. Stephen Kelly and John J. Thompson, 17–29. Turnhout, Belgium: Brepols, 2005.

———, and I. C. Cunningham, eds. *The Auchinleck Manuscript.* London: Scolar Press, 1977.

Potter, Lois. *Secret Rites and Secret Writing: Royalist Literature 1641–1660.* Cambridge, UK: Cambridge University Press, 1989.
Scattergood, John. "Validating the High Life in Of Arthour and of Merlin and Kyng Alisaunder." *Essays in Criticism* 54 (2004): 323–350.
Schurink, Fred. "Manuscript Commonplace Books, Literature, and Reading in Early Modern England." *Huntington Library Quarterly* 73.3 (2010): 453–469.
Sherman, William H. *John Dee: The Politics of Reading and Writing in the English Renaissance.* Amherst: University of Massachusetts Press, 1995.
Smithers, G. V., ed. *Kyng Alisaunder.* 2 vols. EETS o.s. 227, 237. London: Oxford University Press, 1952, 1957.
Stone, Charles Russell. *From Tyrant to Philosopher-King: A Literary History of Alexander the Great in Medieval and Early Modern England.* Turnhout, Belgium: Brepols, 2013.
Stoneman, Richard. "The Latin Alexander." In *Latin Fiction: The Latin Novel in Context*, ed. Heinz Hofmann, 167–186. London: Routledge, 1999.
Todd, Margo. *Christian Humanism and the Puritan Social Order.* Cambridge, UK: Cambridge University Press, 1987.
Wakelin, Daniel. *Scribal Correction and Literary Craft: English Manuscripts 1375–1510.* Cambridge, UK: Cambridge University Press, 2014.
———. "When Scribes Won't Write: Gaps in Middle English Books." *Studies in the Age of Chaucer* 36 (2014): 249–278.
Windeatt, Barry. "The Scribes as Chaucer's Early Critics." *Studies in the Age of Chaucer* 1 (1979): 119–141.

Mirk's *Festial* and Theodoric Rood

SUSAN POWELL

Until the publication in 2007 of Part XI of the *Catalogue of Books Printed in the XVth Century now in the British Library* (BMC XI),[1] the second edition (1486) of John Mirk's sermon collection, the *Festial*, was conventionally ascribed to the short-lived Oxford press of Theodoric Rood.[2] In BMC XI, however, the lack of evidence for Rood as printer of the *Festial* led to the 1486 edition being ascribed to the "Printer of Mirk." This essay seeks to interrogate the arguments against "Rood" and for "Printer of Mirk" and to argue that the evidence is too slight to assert that Rood was not the printer of Mirk. The first part of the essay assesses the evidence presented in BMC XI in relation to the fifteenth-century Oxford presses, especially the thirteen editions still ascribed to Rood. The second part of the essay reviews the BMC XI arguments against Rood as printer of the *Festial* (summarized as type, paper, language, and time). In particular, the essay highlights the importance of considering the 1486 edition in relation to its distinctive text, an area (language) that BMC XI does not investigate.[3]

Caxton printed the collection of sermons known as the *Festial* on June 30, 1483 (STC 17957).[4] It was printed again three years later in an edition traditionally ascribed to Rood (STC 17958), and then again by Caxton, using Rood's edition, in 1491 (STC 17959). There is no mention of Rood in the 1486 edition, nor of Oxford—the colophon reads: "Here endith the boke that is callid festiuall. the yere of oure lord M cccc. lxxxvi. the day aftir seint Edward the kyng." This is the first of the numerous uncertainties about the Oxford presses. St. Edward the King might be King Edward the Confessor, who was celebrated on October 13; it might be King Edward the Martyr who was celebrated on March 18 and June 20. Since the more likely of the two is Edward the Confessor, for the purpose of this essay I take the date of the end of the printing process as October 14, 1486.[5]

BMC XI succinctly explains why the nomenclature "Printer of Mirk" is used in preference to "Rood:"

> The Printer of Mirk's *Liber Festivalis* cannot be identified as Theodericus Rood. There is not only a gap of at least three years between Rood's last assumed printing of Latin works and the printing of this work in English, but the paper stocks are not connected with those used earlier on in Oxford. The type is a crude adaptation of two founts used by Rood. The book is therefore here ranged with Oxford printing, although its place of printing should be considered as uncertain.[6]

First, there is a three-year gap. Second (implicit in the second sentence), Rood printed in Latin—the *Festial* is in English. Third, the paper stocks are different from ones "used earlier." Fourth, the type is adapted from two used by Rood ("crude" seeming to imply that it was not done by Rood himself). So "Printer of Mirk" is a safe title—the reasons to link the 1486 edition with Rood and Oxford are not secure. On the other hand, we must bear in mind from the start that there are no reasons to link it with anyone else, or anywhere else.

Why did earlier scholars link this second edition of the *Festial* with Rood and Oxford? There were a number of publications in Oxford between 1478 and the *Festial* of 1486. Since there was no other printing in Oxford before or after these dates until John Scolar (1517–1528), it was natural to assume that all the works were by the same printer, and Rood was the only name cited in any of these works. Any problematization of the issue was confined to brief articles in bibliographical journals, and one cannot emphasize enough the indebtedness of scholars working with incunables to the editors of BMC XI (principally Lotte Hellinga, with important work by Paul Needham) for their painstaking and scholarly presentation of the facts. As explained above, their conclusion (principally that of Hellinga, working on printing types) is that there is not enough evidence to link Rood with the *Festial*. The intention of this essay is to unpick these facts, but with a different conclusion: while it is possible that Rood had little or no active part in the printing of the *Festial*, his lack of involvement cannot be proved, and it is entirely likely that the 1486 edition was Rood's own project.

BMC XI divides the "Oxford" productions of 1478 to 1486 into three printers, the Printer of Rufinus (1478–1479), Rood (1481–1483/1484), and the Printer of Mirk (1486).[7] There is a strong connection with Cologne—Rood says he is from Cologne, and the Printer of Rufinus uses Cologne types.[8] None of these (perhaps) three printers appears to have stayed in England for long, and of all their publications, only two have a name attached: Theodoricus Rood. There are no names attached to the output of the Printer of Rufinus (three books) and the Printer of Mirk (the *Festial*), and of the twelve works (thirteen editions) assigned to Rood, only two are signed.[9] This in itself might make us ask why we should be so careful to say "Printer of" in two cases but assign eleven unsigned works to Rood. Certain reasons for doing so exist and are analyzed below.

Rood

Theodoric Rood was from Cologne, as he himself says in two editions, the *Expositio super libros Aristotelis: De anima* (1) and the *Epistolae* of Phalaris (2) (STC 314 and 19827).[10] However, not one of the eleven other editions attached to his name (3-12) mentions either Rood or Oxford—yet they are all editions by Rood, according to BMC XI. Nine editions use the same typefaces as the two editions that are clearly by him—only two, Richard Rolle's *Explanationes in Iob* (10) (better known as the *Expositio*) and the *Logica* attributed to Richard Swineshede (11), use different types but in combination with his known types. The paper stocks are related (but, given the nature of their distribution by the importers, so are numerous paper stocks used by different printers).[11] All the works attributed to Rood are in Latin, and all are appropriate for an Oxford school and/or university market. That is the evidence for attributing ten unsigned works to Rood. Given there is so little evidence for "Rood" as printer of these editions, one would expect there to be much less evidence for Rood as "Printer of Rufinus" and "Printer of Mirk."

The name of Rood is usually associated with that of Thomas Hunt. Hunt (who had died by 1498) was the authorized book dealer (*stationarius*) of the University of Oxford and an importer and retailer of books.[12] At the end of the *Epistolae* of Phalaris (2), a Latin verse links the German (*Sanguine germanus*) Theodoric Rood, whom Cologne sent (*quem collonia misit*), with his English companion (*socius ... anglicus*) Thomas Hunt, and includes the optimistic line, "Dii dent vt venetos exuperare queant" [may the gods grant that they [Rood and Hunt] may be able to overcome the Venetians], that is, prove superior to the Venetians, who were foremost in the craft of printing.[13] Rood and Hunt have been commonly linked with all the Oxford editions, but in fact, although Hunt was very likely involved with their distribution (and certainly with the distribution of one edition mentioned below), he is specifically referred to only here.

The colophon to the *Expositio* of Aristotle (1) dates the work to October 11, 1481, but the *Epistolae* of Phalaris (2) is not so clearly dated. In both, Rood says that he has printed the texts not just in Oxford but "in alma vniuersitate Oxonie," in the University of Oxford which nourishes scholars ("alma" being a traditional epithet, as in *alma mater*), and this is the important fact about Rood's press: that it was a fledgling university press, printing texts for and sometimes by Oxford fellows.[14] The *Expositio* (which I refer to below as the Alexander, since it was by an Alexander then assumed to be Alexander of Hales) was on the three books of Aristotle concerning the soul, Aristotle being fundamental to university scholarship.[15] It had never been printed before, and (as discussed below) five copies were purchased by Magdalen College Oxford as soon as Rood printed them.[16] The Phalaris was a humanist text used at the university. It had already been published in the same translation from the Greek (by Francesco Griffolino) in Rome in 1468/1469, again in 1470/1471, in Treviso in 1471, and later (GW M32838, M32878, M32894, and more).

These two are the only editions to name Rood, Cologne, and the University of Oxford. Only the Alexander is dated, as is the third edition ascribed to Rood by BMC XI, John Lathbury's *Liber moralium* (3) (STC 15297), dated in its colophon to the last day of July 1482. After this no date is given in any edition ascribed to Rood,[17] just as there is no mention of Rood in any edition.[18] Lathbury was a fourteenth-century English friar who spent most of his career in Oxford, and his work is a commentary on the Lamentations of Jeremiah, remarkable for its exegesis of scripture through classical *exempla*.[19] Like the Aristotle, it had not previously been published and was not published again during the incunable period.[20] Margaret Lane Ford was responsible for investigating incunable owners in BMC XI. For the Aristotle and Lathbury there are twenty-one names before 1600, of whom thirteen can be identified; half of them are fellows of Oxford colleges (Brasenose, Lincoln, Queen's, St. John's, and All Souls) and half as many again of Cambridge colleges; there is an Austin canon who is the earliest owner of a vellum Alexander, some Durham monks, probably at Durham College Oxford, a secular priest (perhaps a bishop), and Thomas Cranmer (a late owner of an Alexander).[21]

If we pause at these three works, we can see that they were scholarly texts that were read in the colleges of both universities and by the higher clergy and that two of them were unobtainable in print elsewhere. There is an Oxford focus in that two at least appear to have been printed for that university, or at least with fellows of Oxford in mind, and the third had been written (first as lectures) by an Oxford friar of the previous century. All three were folio volumes, the Aristotle and Lathbury of 240 and 292 leaves respectively, and the Phalaris of 88 leaves.

Other works in the BMC XI Rood list are in the same category, most obviously the enormous folio edition (350 leaves) of William Lyndewode's *Constituciones prouinciales* (9). Again, the background was Oxford: Lyndewode had usefully met Archbishop Chichele at Oxford, where he incepted

Doctor of Common Law and Doctor of Civil Law in 1407 before embarking on a highly successful judicial, administrative, and diplomatic career.[22] His *Constituciones* provided details of the constitutions of the province of Canterbury from the Council of Oxford in 1222 to Chichele's episcopate (1414–1442), together with a glossed commentary of the whole work. It was an invaluable practical tool for canon lawyers and academics, as well as the clergy in general. No English-printed Lyndewode apart from Rood's ever had the commentary, although it was taken up and used in later Continental editions.[23] There was also a *tabula*, or index, leading the reader not just to chapters but also sections within chapters, and an index of the councils in chronological order.[24] This was, therefore, an important academic publication and a boon for the study of English canon law at the university.

None of the other books mentioned so far is recorded in the day-book of John Dorne, the Oxford bookseller whose accounts survive for 1520. However, four copies of Lyndewode are there, any one of which, or none, might be Rood's Lyndewode, which had gone through another nine editions since Rood's edition.[25] Some of the fourteen names in extant copies have been identified—two belonged to clergy (one of them a dean of Hereford, who probably bought it new, since he died in 1490); two copies are still in Durham and Hereford cathedral libraries; one was owned by a Syon sister, Cristina Waytt.[26]

These works of Rood must have required capital to print, and the question of sponsorship should be considered now, before we look at the rest of the editions ascribed to Rood in BMC XI. In order to consider sponsorship, we need first to go back in time to the earliest Oxford publications. As noted above, BMC XI distinguishes three printers, Rood, "Printer of Mirk," and—chronologically earlier than these—"Printer of Rufinus." Again the name indicates that little is known about this man. (It will be worth bearing in mind that almost everything to do with printing in Oxford is in some doubt.)

The Printer of Rufinus

The Rufinus is the *Expositio sancti Ieronomi* (STC 21443), then attributed to St. Jerome, as the title says, but now known to be the work of Tyrannius Rufinus.[27] This is dated December 17, 1468, which would appear to be an error for 1478, for the reason that the other two works clearly by the same printer, Aegidius de Columna's *Tractatus . . . de peccato originali* (STC 158) and Aristotle's *Ethica Nichomachea* (STC 752), use the same type and are both dated 1479.[28] The Printer of Rufinus may therefore have been active for only a year or less. That he is not Rood has been argued from the fact that the Alexander is the first work named and dated by Rood: had he been responsible for the earlier editions, surely he would have indicated the fact?

Moreover, a gap exists between the works of 1478 and 1479 and the Rood Alexander of 1481. However, what is most conclusive is that the type used by the Rufinus printer is very different from that used by Rood.[29]

The Printer of Rufinus (whoever he was) seems to have come to Oxford (probably from Cologne) specifically to print the Rufinus from a certain small manuscript in the possession of the man who must have been his sponsor, James Goldwell, bishop of Norwich. The evidence for the link is clear-cut and was brilliantly uncovered by Albinia de la Mare in an article written in collaboration with Lotte Hellinga:[30] a miniature of St. Jerome in British Library MS Sloane 1579 had been closely copied in a printed edition now in Cambridge University Library; the manuscript had been delicately cast off (i.e., marked up for printing), the manuscript had an erased coat of arms, and the printed edition had the Goldwell coat-of-arms.[31] Goldwell is a man extremely well-known to bibliophiles. As far as is known, he was the first Englishman ever to buy a printed book, the *Rationale divinorum officiorum*, printed in Mainz in 1459.[32]

The Rufinus is still in the library of Goldwell's college, All Souls Oxford, to which he gave ten manuscripts and thirty printed books.[33] He owned at least eleven books printed in Rome between 1467 and 1473, presumably bought when he was King's Proctor at the Papal Curia. Before that he had been in Germany (Hamburg) as early as 1465 on diplomatic service, where he might have met the printer of his Rufinus/Jerome. The Rufinus is forty-two leaves, the Aegidius only twenty-four (but a smart book with a red colophon, the only example of red printing in England before Caxton ca. 1484).[34] However, the *Ethica* is a huge 174 leaves, although still a quarto format. The printer may have had university sponsorship for it, as the work was on the Oxford syllabus.[35] Extant copies are largely in the Bodleian and Oxford college libraries: two are still in contemporary Oxford binding, and one of them is closely associated with All Souls.[36] It may be that Goldwell sponsored the press as well as the printer. It was a very tiny one, "not much more than a table-top toy," as Hellinga says, just able to print one small page at a time—for the Aristotle he got a slightly better press that could do two pages at a time.[37]

Rood and his Sponsors

The Printer of Rufinus clearly had a rather ad hoc and short-lived establishment, having come to Oxford from Cologne specifically to print the Rufinus and having picked up a couple more commissions while he was in Oxford. When Rood came from Cologne, did he, too, depend on sponsorship, and was it the same sponsorship as the Printer of Rufinus enjoyed? Three of the four works of Rood so far considered, the Alexander, the Lathbury, and the Lyndewode (1, 3, 9), were 240, 292, and 350 leaves respectively, and the Phalaris (2) was not small at eighty-eight leaves.[38] Rood did not come from Cologne to print these works as a speculative venture. They are large items, involving some financial outlay, and he must have been assured of a market and of support in preparing his books for that market. It must be remembered that Europe could supply as many Latin books as the English market wanted. To try to rival this market in England required some assurance of at least preliminary success.[39]

Rood must therefore have had a sponsor or sponsors, like the Printer of Rufinus. He is the only Oxford printer to use vellum, in fact the first printer in England to issue deluxe versions of his books. This required money. The Alexander survives in one vellum copy, the Lathbury in four complete copies and a fragment, and the Lyndewode in one copy.[40] Some copies of the Alexander and the Lathbury are also decorated with woodcut borders.[41] The Lyndewode has a frontispiece woodcut showing a priest in a biretta. As already noted, the Phalaris has a Latin verse (written by the Italian humanist poet Pietro Carmeliano, who also supplied verse for Caxton), as does another work to be mentioned later, the *Compendium totius grammaticae* of John Anwykyll (4, 4a). Carmeliano's poems and encomia were directed at the highest in the land, and by 1490 he was Latin secretary to Henry VII.[42] All this suggests deliberate display and financial outlay on Rood's part or on behalf of Rood.

Rood's sponsors certainly included fellows of the university, the *alma universitas* that nourished him. Three of the four complete Lathburys and one sheet of the fragment are particularly interesting, in that (as Neil Ker discussed in 1947) the lower right margins of the first halves of the quires in all three copies have the names of Oxford fellows, and many leaves have the sign-manual of Thomas Hunt, showing that he was involved in the commission.[43] Of the eight names, five were fellows of All Souls at this time, and two were fellows of University College.[44] The eighth name is that of All Souls College itself, and the bursars' accounts for 1480/1481 actually record twenty shillings paid out for the printing and parchment of a Lathbury.[45] All Souls was a large college at the time,[46] and it was, of course, Goldwell's college. Perhaps Goldwell had transferred his patronage to Rood, and it was through his influence that the Lathbury was printed by subscription.

Rood is, however, connected not only with All Souls but also with Magdalen College Oxford and not so much (if at all) with Goldwell as with another bishop, William Waynflete.[47] All the rest of the works associated with Rood (4-8, 10-12) are quartos, some extant only in a few leaves, ranging in size from eight leaves (Augustine, *Excitacio fidelis ad elemosinam faciendam* (12)) to 164 (*Logica* (11)). They are all texts that would be used at grammar schools in preparing young men for university and professional careers in Church or State. St. Paul's School, founded by John Colet in 1509, used both the *Excitatio* (12) and another of these quarto editions, the *Vulgaria* of Terence (5).[48]

Some editions would also be used in the Bachelor of Arts teaching at university, and a fragment of the *Longe Parvula* (7) in the British Library records ownership by a fellow of All Souls.[49] Latin grammar and Latin composition (rhetoric) formed two of the three elements of the most basic level of university education, the trivium.[50] The *Compendium* (4, 4a) (STC 695, 696) and the *Doctrinale puerorum* (8) (STC 315) are grammar textbooks; the Terence (5) and Cicero (6) (*Vulgaria Terentii* and *Oratio pro T. Milone*, STC 23904 and 5312) teach composition through classical examples, while the *Longe Parvula* (7) (STC 23163.13) does it in a more didactic format. They are all complementary—a Walter Slugg who graduated with a civil law degree in 1508 owned a *Compendium* and a Terence bound together with the *Doctrinale* (but in a later Antwerp edition).[51] In fact, one of the two editions of the *Compendium* (4a) shares consecutive quiring signatures with the Terence (5), showing that they were printed together (though not always issued together).[52]

As textbooks, these editions were much used—for example, the *Longe Parvula* (7) is known from only two leaves, b2 and [b5], and the *Doctrinale* (8) from the same, c2 and [c3]. When discarded, they would be used for binding and endpapers, and fragments of the Rolle (10), the *Compendium* (4, 4a), the *Longe Parvula* (7), and the *Logica* (11) are extant, all from the same sixteenth-century Oxford binding.[53] Similarly, discarded leaves of Rood's Alexander (1), Phalaris (2), and Lyndewode (9) (perhaps from Westminster School) were used as binders' waste at Westminster Abbey.[54]

Logic was the third element of the trivium, and the *Logica* (11) (STC 16693) is the only textbook that appears to have been printed specifically for the Oxford curriculum. It consisted of nineteen treatises (of which only the seventeenth was by Richard Swineshede, to whom the whole volume was conventionally ascribed) compiled as a single book, also a quarto (so not a display book), but a very lengthy tome of 164 leaves. Swineshede himself was a fellow of Merton College Oxford, and the extant copy there contains several names, perhaps of Merton and Corpus Christi scholars.[55] The work was newly compiled by and for the university, undoubtedly by a university man,[56] and is the only other of Rood's works in Dorne's list of 1520. Ten copies were sold in that year (and here it must be Rood's work, since it was unique), so it was still selling well in Oxford nearly forty years after its publication.[57]

Magdalen College Oxford

Mention is made above of Rood's connections with Oxford and with the Oxford college All Souls, and it is stated that five copies of the *Expositio super libros Aristotelis* attributed to Alexander of Hales were purchased by Magdalen College Oxford as soon as Rood printed them.[58] The schoolbooks discussed above, which appear to be later in time than the Alexander (1), Phalaris (2), and Lathbury (3), are likely to have been printed for Magdalen College, as perhaps the Alexander was, and at this point the second bishop enters the scene. William Waynflete already had seventeen years' experience in Winchester and Eton (the feeder schools for New College Oxford and King's College Cambridge, respectively) when he became bishop of Winchester, the richest see in England.[59] By 1458 he had established his own foundation of Magdalen College Oxford, and by 1480 a school was attached to the college.[60]

The emphasis in Winchester, Eton, and Magdalen was on a sound grounding in Latin as a precursor to all other studies (which would, of course, be in Latin), and it was Magdalen College School that acquired a reputation as the foremost school in England for its teaching of grammar through humanist texts, that is, through classical authors.[61] Several notable grammarians came from the Magdalen stable.[62] The first master of the school was John Anwykyll, whose grammar book, *Compendium totius grammaticae* (4, 4a), is discussed further below.[63] John Stanbridge, Anwykyll's usher (second master) from 1486, succeeded him at his death in 1487. Stanbridge published several grammar books after he had left Oxford for a new post in Banbury; one of these, the *Paruulorum institutio* (STC 23164.6), has links with the *Longe Parvula* (7), printed by Rood in the early 1480s, but, given the early (assumed) date of publication, Stanbridge would at this time still have been a junior member of New College Oxford, so his authorship may be unlikely.[64]

John Holt was a junior fellow of Magdalen College who became usher at the school in the mid-1490s, whence he was appointed master to the boys in Archbishop John Morton's household at Lambeth, where he wrote his Latin grammar book (written in English), *Lac puerorum* [the milk of children].[65] On Morton's death in 1500, he became master of the cathedral school in his home town of Chichester, and by late 1502 he was master to the young Henry, duke of York (the future Henry VIII).[66] One of Stanbridge's pupils at Magdalen College School became perhaps the most famous schoolmaster and grammarian of the next generation, William Lily, first High Master of Dean Colet's new foundation of St. Paul's School (ca. 1510), and author of several grammar books, epigrams, and the like, with such wide circulation that "Lily's grammar" or the "Royal grammar" (1548–1549) was still in revised use in the late seventeenth century.[67]

Of these, it was only Anwykyll who was almost certainly published by Rood. As noted above, the *Compendium* (4, 4a) has prefatory dedicatory verses by Pietro Carmeliano. The first is addressed to "you tender young boys" [*Vos teneri iuuenes*], that is, the pupils of Magdalen College School, who are urged to celebrate "your John who taught you well to speak words in Latin" [*vestrum . . . ioannem / Qui bene vos docuit verba latine loqui*]. This firmly links the work (published in two editions, STC 695, 696) to Anwykyll and Magdalen College School, while the second poem, below the first, praises the bishop of Winchester, William Waynflete: "for the author John composed this work at your persuasion" [*hoc opus auctor enim te persuadente ioannes. / Edidit*].[68] Here Waynflete is named as the patron of a grammar book written for his school by one of his masters and published by Theodoric Rood. I think it is fair to suggest, at least, that Rood printed not only this for Magdalen and its founder but other schoolbooks, and perhaps even some of his works which are not obviously schoolbooks.

It seems significant that Waynflete barely visited his foundation before the last five years of his life, when he made two lengthy formal visits, each coinciding with a royal inspection of Magdalen (by Edward IV in September 1481 and Richard III in July 1483).[69] October 11, 1481, is the date of Rood's only dated printed edition (1) and may mark his appearance in Oxford. If Waynflete encouraged Anwykyll to write the *Compendium* (4, 4a) (printed "not after 1483"),[70] then perhaps he encouraged others at Magdalen (College and/or School), and perhaps he encouraged Rood himself. Margaret Lane Ford suggests that the Lyndewode (9) (printed "c. 1483–4") was "printed at the instigation of a high-placed ecclesiastic who would have influenced, possibly even guaranteed, distribution in a different, perhaps much wider circle [than Rood's schoolbooks]."[71] A copy of the Lyndewode was recorded in the Royal Library in 1542. It is extant and has no distinguishing marks other than some early-sixteenth-century annotations, but might Waynflete have presented it to Richard III on his 1483 visit?[72] Like Goldwell, Waynflete's enthusiasm for books is recorded, although, unlike Goldwell, no list of his books is extant.[73] The Magdalen College records credit him with donating around eight hundred books for the "new library,"[74] of which only three manuscripts appear to be extant, and no printed books.[75]

Certainly these years saw a concerted effort to establish the library at Magdalen as well as to generate books for it. As Dennis Rhodes says, "It can scarcely be mere coincidence that the only college founded at Oxford in the second half of the fifteenth century gives evidence of a more direct contact with the book trade than any other."[76] The "*custos librarie*" was buying books, including five copies of Rood's Alexander in 1481 (as noted above), and in 1482 payment was made to two bookbinders, Thomas Uffington and John Bray, Uffington being employed for six days and using two skins of parchment, perhaps on four of the Alexanders (1), which he was paid four shillings for binding. In 1483/1484, twelve pence was paid for binding in parchment what must have been Rood's edition of Lathbury (3), and in

1484/1485 payments were made for binding books and supplying chains for them. After Waynflete's death in 1486, John Cornish was employed as both scribe and bookbinder for the chapel books, and more chains were acquired for the library books. Payments for chapel books were numerous.[77] Allowances made in 1481 to readers in theology, moral philosophy, natural philosophy, and logic and a teacher of grammar reinforce the importance to Magdalen College and its school of subjects such as those printed by Rood.[78]

The focused nature of Rood's output and his essential relationship to the academic life of Oxford indicate that he was not a speculative printer. Instead, he developed a relatively secure clientele, with contacts perhaps throughout the university, certainly at All Souls (perhaps through Goldwell) and at Magdalen (through Waynflete). His middleman was the university bookdealer Thomas Hunt, who was in an official position to distribute his books to the university and to network for him. Fellows of the university must have been responsible for the authorship, adaptation, and compilation of texts he printed.

In light of these observations, I would dispute the standard view of Rood as a struggling jobbing printer—inevitably, the comparison is with Caxton and has both the benefit and the disadvantage of hindsight. BMC XI has not overturned this traditional view: the Printer of Rufinus is "a rather unambitious jobbing printer," as is Rood, who is linked with the St. Albans Printer and some London printers as "jobbing printers, who settled for only a few years, to produce such works as and when they were commissioned by patrons." There is disparagement, too, in the statement that "In the few years Rood worked in Oxford, he appears to have hedged his bets, not relying entirely on a single set of clients within the university."[79] It may be that Rood is bracketed with other "failed" printers because of his short stint in Oxford, whereas an assessment of his actual achievements in print (without the benefit of hindsight) would produce a different verdict.

The Printer of Mirk

We turn now to the BMC XI arguments against the *Festial* being by Rood. As noted above, they are fourfold: the gap in years between Rood's last known (i.e., assumed) work; the language of the *Festial*; the paper stocks; the types. The main arguments relate to paper and type: "the paper stocks are not connected with those used earlier on in Oxford," and "the type is a crude adaptation of two founts used by Rood."[80] This is a summary of arguments elsewhere in BMC XI, which are worth looking at.

Type

The *Festial* uses Type 4: 115G for its text and Type 6: 115G for the display of quotations in the text and for headings.[81] Type 4: 115G is used on its own as a text type in Rood's Phalaris (2); it is the title type in Rood's *Excitatio* of Augustine (12).[82] In other works of Rood, it is used together with other types.[83] Type 6 is not used elsewhere in the works attributed to Rood (it is "new"), but it was created by recasting Rood's Type 5, keeping the capitals and adding a new lowercase.[84] Hence the type is "a crude adaptation of two founts used by Rood."

In fact, therefore, it appears to be only Type 6 that is "a crude adaptation," whereas Type 4 is pure Rood, "in use by Rood from *c.* 1483-4 and by the Printer of Mirk in 1486 or 1487."[85] Indeed, the Printer of Mirk is at one point called "the recipient of a final version of Rood's text types."[86] If Type 4 is Rood, and Type 6 is crudely adapted from Rood, is it the crudeness that suggests that it cannot be by Rood? I notice elsewhere in BMC XI the comment that Rood's Lyndewode has "crude headlines."[87] Is it not possible that Rood's workmanship was a little crude? One piece of evidence brought to light long ago is that Rood was paid for repairing and gilding a university bedel's silver mace.[88] This suggests a recognized skill in metalwork, but perhaps not such expertise as other type-makers might have—perhaps Rood was responsible for the crudely adapted Type 6 of the *Festial* (and so for the *Festial* itself). After all, it has been suggested (rather dismissively) that he cut his own Types 3, 4, and 5.[89]

If the *Festial* type does actually have Rood connections, then so, too, do the woodcuts. The *Festial* has a number of woodcuts: two full-page, nine half-page (cut down from a larger size), and five tiny woodcuts just one column wide.[90] The different sizes and odd distribution are unusual, and one wonders in what circumstances they were chosen and inserted in this random way into the text. Well over a century ago, Henry Bradshaw suggested that the larger ones might have been made for a folio *Golden Legend* (like Caxton's) and the smaller for a Book of Hours. Neither of these has been found—the woodcuts appear to have been unused, perhaps the series unfinished, and then they were adapted for the *Festial*. But not just for the *Festial*—it was mentioned earlier that Rood's Lyndewode (9) has a woodcut, and this woodcut is from the same series as the *Festial* woodcuts.[91] The *Festial* is therefore linked to Rood by the Lyndewode. If we accept the date "*c.* 1483-4" for the Lyndewode, then the woodcuts were ready then.[92] Perhaps Rood already knew at this time that the woodcuts would not be needed for a *Golden Legend* and inserted one into his Lyndewode; perhaps he used others later in the *Festial*. (This seems likely because Caxton completed his own *Golden legende* [STC 248760] in November 1483.[93] One might speculate that he preempted Rood's plans.)

Paper

It seems, therefore, that the argument from type is not entirely unassailable, although it is sufficient for Hellinga to prefer "Printer of Mirk." On the matter of paper stocks, the BMC XI research was conducted by Paul Needham, who, interestingly, does not use the "Printer of Mirk" attribution but places the *Festial* in his study of Rood's paper stocks.[94] It has already been seen that the *Festial*'s paper stocks "are not connected with those used earlier on in Oxford."[95] Elsewhere in BMC XI it is said that they are "exceptionally numerous and mixed" and "have nothing in common with the stocks used by Rood."[96] There appear to be thirty-three different paper stocks used in the *Festial*—a large number. However, Caxton's *Royal Book* of the same date (1486) has twenty-six paper stocks in an edition of 162 leaves,[97] and Rood's own Lathbury (3) (July 1482) has twenty-two (some only on a sheet or two) in an edition of 292 leaves, so thirty-three in an edition of 174 leaves is not entirely anomalous.[98] As for the fact that these paper stocks "have nothing in common with the stocks used by Rood," Rood's paper stock 55 with the watermark Banner is a variant of Rood's paper stock 2, which was used in the Alexander (1) and the Phalaris (2), the only two books unquestionably by Rood.[99] But that is a variant and not the original paper, and the *Festial* is indisputably printed entirely on paper stock that Rood had not used before. But perhaps that is not so strange. As Needham notes, Rood's nine quarto volumes have twenty-one paper stocks in all, "many of them making only a single appearance."[100] Perhaps Rood never kept large stocks and just acquired small quantities of paper where he could. Perhaps the printing of the *Festial* was not a continuous enterprise but stopped and started as opportunity arose.

Language

A third argument against Rood as printer of Mirk is implicit, rather than emphasized, in the BMC XI statement: "There is not only a gap of at least three years between Rood's last assumed printing *of Latin works* and the printing of this work *in English*" (emphasis added).[101] Many years ago, Norman Blake speculated on Rood's output in a characteristically robust few pages.[102] He had no reason to suppose that the *Festial* was not by Rood, although he was aware of the time lapse and the lack of anything beyond a date of printing: "The question naturally arises as to why Rood should have turned to an English work for his final printed edition since he had been content to produce Latin religious and educational material until then."[103] Blake was not afraid to speculate, and he always looked at things from the printer's point of view. He saw Rood hunting for a market from the time of his arrival in England and considered his printing of the *Festial* a last-ditch attempt:

> The Oxford printer could see that Caxton was active in Westminster and that his press was flourishing. The bulk of the books produced by him were in English, and the

publication of the *Liber festivalis* looks like a desperate attempt to change direction to prevent bankruptcy by imitating a policy that was already well established elsewhere.[104]

Is it likely, however, that Rood produced the *Festial* as a last-ditch attempt at solvency? After establishing an academic market at Oxford in Latin, to produce a folio edition, with 174 leaves and several woodcuts, of an English work published only a few years earlier by Caxton would not seem to be the way to avoid bankruptcy. It is Latin that must have been Rood's advantage over Caxton—no Latin was published at Westminster in the 1480s, only at Oxford, St. Albans, and London.[105] It is, therefore, important to consider "why Rood should have turned to an English work."

It is certainly true that publication in English was new at Oxford—the *Festial* remains the only English work printed there (if it was). However, there is no real reason Rood should not have turned to printing English, only "that it does not prima facie seem plausible."[106] This is hardly a sound argument, and it must be remembered that Rood made something of a niche market for himself in publishing English writers, if not in English. His very first work was thought then to be by Alexander of Hales; Lathbury, Anwykyll, Stanbridge, Lyndewode, and Rolle were all English,[107] as was Roger Swineshede and perhaps others of those who wrote tracts of the *Logica*. And Rood published these English writers of Latin texts for a niche English market.

But there is more to the "Englishness" of his works than this. Two of his Latin texts, the *Vulgaria* of Terence (5) and the *Compendium* (4, 4a), include English. The Terence is as much English as Latin, since that is the nature of *vulgaria*—they are commonplace sentences of conversational English paired with their Latin equivalents, a radical new pedagogic method of the time.[108] The book begins simply: "gOdd spede you. saue ȝou or rest mery. Saluete. Salue. Saluus sis chri[s]to" and proceeds with gradually more taxing (and didactic) sentences to the last entries: "Recommaund me to my maistere & grete wele all my fellawys & frendys I pray the. Preceptori meo commendatum dicas vel facias. Cunctosque sodales & amicos meos nomine meo salutes oro. Vel iube saluere," and "Fare wele and godd be wyth ȝowe Vobiscum deus. Dominus tecum. Vale. Valete. Ad deum."[109] The *Compendium* also occasionally introduces *vulgaria* when they may help to explain a point of Latin grammar (the actual grammar is taught in Latin). For example, in dealing with an unspecified agent, when English would prefer the active and Latin the passive voice, Anwykyll provides examples "vt in his uulgaribus They labour in te felde Laboratur in agro They fight in the playne Pugnatur in plano vel in campo. They synghe in te quere Cantatur in choro," and so on.[110]

The relevance of these educational textbooks to Rood's edition of the *Festial* is that it also mixes English and Latin. The most striking example is a macaronic *narratio* in the Corpus Christi sermon (Figs. 1-5), where Rood's edition inserts new material with English and Latin quotations from the scriptures and from St. Augustine, followed by a *narratio* (an excerpt from which is below), which reads much like a *vulgaria* text:

> Narracio We rede that there was a Jewe that went with a cristen man a felowe of his in to a churche of cristen people and herde masse *Et post missa*m *dixit iudeus* And aftyr whan masse was don | the iewe seyde to the cristen man *Si ego tantum edissem quantum tu comedisti non esuriem ut puto in tribus diebus*. yf I hadde eton as moche as thou haste eton I shulde not be an hungered as I trowe in many dayes.[111]

Although so macaronic an insertion is unique, the edition consistently inserts Latin citations, both to support existing English authorities and within new passages. Many of Mirk's scriptural and patristic citations (which are almost invariably in English in the extant manuscripts) are translated into Latin. For example, Mirk's sermon for Pentecost has no Latin in any of the extant witnesses except Southwell Minster MS 7 (K), a late copy that regularly adds Latin scriptural and legend citations, appropriate Latin verse, and rubricated Latin marginalia.[112] In the Pentecost sermon the Southwell manuscript inserts five Latin citations, all scriptural.[113] Only one is replicated (not in the same position) in what I shall call for convenience Rood's edition, and its replication is hardly surprising, since it is from the Gospel of the day: "Et apparuerunt illis dispertite lingue tamquam ignis" (Acts 2:3).[114] Although the Southwell manuscript and the 1486 edition are entirely independent, the technique is to some extent the same (and it is a scholarly technique). Where Mirk cites scripture in English, the Southwell manuscript and Rood's edition often add the Latin of the Vulgate and sometimes other authorities. However, Rood's editor goes beyond the Southwell scribe in including entirely new material, substantiated by Latin quotation. There are eight Latin interventions in Rood's Pentecost sermon, and while all of them ostensibly supply the Latin text for scriptural quotations, their insertion is not merely to give authority to the English, since five of them are the result of revisions of the original text.[115]

The sermon begins with a discussion of wit and wisdom (in relation to "Whit Sunday," falsely etymologized), substantially paraphrased in the Rood edition. Mirk points out that "he þat hath wytte to gete goode he is holdyn a wyse man, but he þat hath wysdam to forsake goode and bene pore for Goddys sake he is holdyn a fole."[116] At this point Rood's edition adds:

> But loke what holy scripture seythe *Dominus recitauit nomen pauperis quia ipsum approbauit et nomen eius in libro scriptum fuit* Oure lord hathe receyued the name of the pore man for he hath preuyd huym in his pouerte and wretyn his name in the boke of lyffe *Sed nomen diuitis tacuit quia ipsum non approbauit* But he lefte the riche man for he hathe not preuyd hym[117]

After the Gospel narrative, the sermon explicates the tongues of fire that descended on the apostles at Pentecost (Acts 2:3), including a discussion of the unruliness of the tongue: "for a tong is þe best membur of a man whyl it is wel rewlyd ande þe werste whan it is oute of rewle."[118] Here the Rood edition adds: "*Venenum aspidum sub labiis eorum* Bitter veneme is vnder the tonges that speakithe euyll seythe Dauid in the sawter. And as seint Ieme seythe [...]'.."[119] This quotation from the Psalms is not found in any of the extant manuscripts: on the other hand, perhaps surprisingly, neither this edition nor the Southwell manuscript provides the Vulgate text for the quotation from James 3:6 that follows ("as seint Ieme seythe"). The next example involves more substantial paraphrase. Mirk writes that the unrepentant sinner will "go to þe fyre of helle, and he þat wil leuyn hys synne and amende hym, þagh he hadde syngyd neuer so greuoslyche beforen, he schal go to þe blessed fyre of hevn."[120] After "helle" Rood's text paraphrases the rest as:

> for thoughe thou shuldiste dye spare not to preche the worde of god and telle the trouthe *Item deus est misericors penitentibus peccata sua* Also god is mercyfull to theym that be sory for her synnes & woll leue hem. *Cum uero confessus fuerit et reliquerit ea misericordia consequatur.* For thoughe a man haue do neuer so moche [col. b] synne and he woll shreyue hym and forsake his synne mercy shall folowe hym and he shall haue foryeuenesse and so come to the bryghte fyre euer lastyng blysse [...]'.[121]

None of the extant manuscripts provides any of this material,[122] nor does the substantial revision of the *Festial* made some time after 1434, nor Caxton's first edition of the *Festial* (STC 17957, 1483), which rarely provides a Latin quotation at all.[123] Clearly a manuscript (not one used by Caxton, and certainly not Caxton's edition) was revised by an academic or one of the Latinate clergy, someone familiar with the scriptures and Fathers and to whom this quasi-macaronic use of English and Latin came easily.[124] Why might this not have been produced or planned by Rood? Oxford is a likely place of origin, and the academic preparation and subsequent printing of an English work is in line with Rood's publications. While an English work written in English is a departure from the Latin books of Rood's previous editions, it is not a departure in kind, since this second edition of the *Festial* makes copious use of Latin; moreover, it is only with the benefit of hindsight that one might see an English work as an anomaly in Rood's output. Might it not at the time of its conception have been a legitimate development of his printing ventures?

Time

The final BMC XI argument against Rood as "Printer of Mirk" is "the gap of at least three years between Rood's last assumed printing of Latin works and the printing of this work in English."[125] One should now note "assumed printing"; in fact, as we have seen, no date can be given to any "Rood" edition after the Lathbury (3) of July 31, 1482. In her revision of Duff, Hellinga dates the Phalaris (2) to 1481, the Anwykyll (4, 4a), and the Terence (5) "not after 1483," the Lyndewode (9) "c. 1483–4," and all the rest between 1481 and 1483.[126] In BMC XI (published only two years before Duff/Hellinga and with the same editor) the Rolle (10), *Logica* (11), and *Excitatio* (12) are dated rather later: "c. 1483–4" for all three, not "1481–3."[127] Since the arguments for dating are supplied in BMC XI (and not in Duff/Hellinga), it may be as well to follow BMC XI. [128]

The date of the Lyndewode is based on the fact that Caxton used some of the same paper stocks in these years,[129] and the dating of the other undated editions is based on overlaps of paper and type in all these works and the fact that one (the *Vulgaria*) was bought in 1483.[130] It would seem that nothing in the argument of paper stocks suggests a date earlier than 1483 for the undated editions. Indeed: "Interlinkages of paper stocks within this group of nine [undated] quartos suggest that they were printed more or less continuously, and all later than the Chancery folio Lathbury of 31 July 1482 (Duff 238)."[131] As for type, the use of Type 1: 100B in the two dated editions (1, 3) and in the Cicero (6) and *Longe Parvula* (7) might suggest an earlier date but do not confirm it.[132] Moreover, until BMC XI, the Phalaris was more generously dated to 1485. The consequences of the backdating of the Phalaris to 1481 would appear to clinch the "Printer of Mirk" (i.e., not Rood) argument. As Needham points out: "When the '1485' Oxford Phalaris is cancelled, the evidence for a continuous activity of Rood's shop from 1481 to the '1486/7' edition of Mirk, *Liber Festivalis*, disappears." He goes on to show the consequences of this: "as Lotte Hellinga notes (p. 15), we need not assume it was printed by Rood, nor even, necessarily, that it was printed in Oxford."[133]

However, even if we accept these dates, there is in fact a gap of perhaps only two years between the (probable) date of the Lyndewode and perhaps other Rood editions ("c. 1483–4") and the likely date of the completion of the printing of the *Festial* (October 14, 1486), and some of that time would be employed in printing the book. So there is not the "gap of at least three years" that BMC XI suggests, and indeed, elsewhere in BMC XI the gap is reduced to "an interval of at least two years."[134] With a good imagination, it is possible to hazard a number of guesses why a printer might pause in his work for two years (if indeed it was as long as that). The St. Albans Printer suspended printing for "at least a year or two" after 1481 or 1482,[135] and Caxton himself seems not to have been printing between 1486 and 1488.[136]

However, earlier scholarship provides a likely answer to the gap in time between Rood's editions and the *Festial*. In the year 1482/1483, Rood is known to have given up a house he rented from Magdalen College.[137] He may simply have moved elsewhere, but 1482/1483 has been suggested as when the Cologne printer Arnold ther Hoernen died.[138] Rood's Type 1, which he used for the Alexander, Lathbury, Cicero, and *Longe Parvula*, is related to types used by ther Hoernen.[139] Gertrud, ther Hoernen's widow, had a son, Diederich Molner. One volume of a four-volume work of Aristotle commentaries (by Johannes Versor) is dated November 29, 1485, and is signed "per Theodoricum impressorem Colonie" [by Theodoric printer of Cologne] at an address that had been that of ther Hoernen and using his Types 3 and 1.[140] No other editions are so explicitly ascribed to Theodoric, but Gertrud's next husband, Konrad Welker of Boppard, would appear to have used the same types and to have printed with or on behalf of Theodoric until June 1486, when Welker first issued an edition in his own name.[141] The evidence is complicated, but it seems likely that Theodoric Rood and Diederich Molner were the same man, Rood being merely a nickname,[142] and that he left Oxford at his stepfather's death to take over the printing shop in Cologne. When this happened is not certain; the only certain fact is that Rood (if he was the Cologne Theodoric) was printing in Cologne in the later months of 1485. If Rood left Oxford before 24 March 1483 (the latest date of the year in which he vacated the Magdalen lodgings), it seems likely that some at least of his quarto editions (if we use the BMC XI latest dates "*c.* 1483-4") were printed later, presumably by his assistant or assistants. (He would not have needed to take back his printing press and types, since his stepfather had left him his own.) However, if Rood was only certainly printing in Cologne late in 1485, it may be the case that he first completed his projects in hand and perhaps even started to print the *Festial*, a process which was finished, presumably by other hands, 13 October 1486.[143]

Rood as Printer of Mirk

Might the *Festial* have been in hand before Rood's return to Cologne? Had it perhaps been planned even before he knew that Caxton was to publish a *Festial*? Might Rood have been preempted in the *Festial* as I suggest above that he might have been in a *Golden Legend*? I find it an odd coincidence that Caxton produced both a *Festial* and a *Golden Legend* in the same year, 1483 (June 30 and November 20, respectively),[144] and yet Rood also produced a *Festial* and (it seems from the woodcut evidence) intended a *Golden Legend*. Might the *Festial* have been an early project of Rood, delayed by the circumstances of his commitments in Oxford and then in Cologne? Might its printing have been under way, or at least planned, when Rood left Oxford?

Scholars dislike speculation, but in dealing with a subject of such uncertainties—and indeed ignorance—speculation can be enlightening, if of necessity inconclusive. There are (at least) three possibilities: that Rood left Oxford in 1482/1483 and others completed the printing jobs he had in hand, that he left a year or two later after completing the editions he had in hand, or even that he left Oxford but returned at some point in 1486, having printed the Versor in Cologne at the end of 1485. In relation to all these is the possibility that Rood printed at least some of the *Festial* himself. There are signs that the work was stopped and started, probably by more than one compositor. Hellinga points out the incompetence of some of the printing and suggests that it was completed in batches: "Large gaps of several lines in the text suggest that this edition was not set seriatim, and the printers lacked expertise in casting-off."[145] The quiring is of several different sizes: (no sig.)^8, a–b^8, c^6, d^8, e^6, f^8, g^4, h^8, i^6, k–l^8, m^6, n–o^8, p^6, q^8, r^6, s^8, t–v^6, x^8, u^6, z^4.[146] The type is adapted from two used by Rood, but the letters are often badly cut and/or badly composed, particularly in the display type (Type 6).[147] As noted above, the thirty-three different paper stocks "are not connected with those used earlier on in Oxford," are "exceptionally numerous and mixed," and "have nothing in common with the stocks used by Rood."[148]

Henry Bradshaw was first to comment on the "odd assortment of woodcut illustrations."[149] The woodcuts are in three sizes, large (first quire, first folio, recto and verso), small (c4vb, e3ra, e5ra, f2va, h1ra, h1rb) and large cut to small (h5v, i5v, k7r, l2r, l6r, l8v, m5v, n6r, o7v). The cuts on signatures e3ra and e5ra are the same cut (used for the Eve of Pentecost and also for Pentecost); the small woodcuts occur only in the *Temporale*, apart from the first sermon of the *Sanctorale* (where two different woodcuts of St. Andrew awkwardly head each column of sig. h1r). Thereafter the use of the cuts is more professional, and nine woodcuts precede fourteen sermons up to and including the Annunciation sermon. However, from this point on there are no more cuts, despite there being another twenty-six sermons to the end of the edition.[150]

This appears very amateurish, but not all the *Festial* looks amateurish. In many ways it is a smart production, or intended as such—two columns, large type with a special display type, and woodcuts. (Caxton's earlier edition had none of those features, although he adopted the two-column layout and adapted one of Rood's woodcuts from the *Festial* for his second edition.)[151] Only a detailed investigation of type and paper in relation to text and woodcut would allow one to marshal arguments for a number of printers/compositors, of whom Rood might have been one.

If we include the *Festial*, the period of publication of the editions attributed to Rood coincides with the last five years of William Waynflete's life when he was most active in relation to his foundation of Magdalen College and during which period he was named as patron of Anwykyll's *Compendium totius grammaticae* (printed by Rood "not after 1483").[152] Might the *Festial* have been a project suggested by Waynflete to scholars of Magdalen and by them to Rood? Rood seems to have depended on support for his more substantial works, and the *Festial* was not insubstantial. At 174 leaves, it was shorter than its nearest comparative publication, the Lathbury (292 leaves), but, like the Lathbury was a folio edition in double columns, and with the addition of woodcuts, which the Lathbury did not have.

Waynflete not only had pedagogic interests (he had spent seventeen years of his life at Winchester and Eton), but was also a bishop with diocesan responsibilities. The *Festial* was explicitly written (as the Prologue says) as a preaching tool through which the parish priest might educate his people.[153] It was the best-known sermon collection of its date and was to be the only printed vernacular sermon collection of the pre-Reformation period. A version revised and latinized at the University of Oxford (perhaps at Magdalen College) was still worth printing, even after Caxton had printed his own *Festial*. Indeed, it was better, as Caxton himself must have thought, since his second edition of the *Festial* in 1491 used Rood's text rather than his own text of 1483.[154]

In 1481 Waynflete had transferred his books to Magdalen College. At the same time he had deposited all the documents to do with the college's foundation, but his transfer of property was slow and piecemeal. By 1480 only about a fifth of the college endowment had been handed over; between 1480 and 1483 a further two-fifths were transferred, but even at his death there was a shortfall of 17 percent, and the transfer was not finally settled until 1501, five years after his death.[155] In December 1485 he had retired to his episcopal palace at Bishop's Waltham, never to leave it. During the following months, in 1486, Magdalen College must have been very apprehensive, not to say expectant, of his death. Was the shortfall in his endowment of Magdalen a concern? Was the completion of the *Festial* important as an original commission of Waynflete or as an incentive for him to remember his foundation and complete his provision for it? Did Rood return to Oxford in 1486 to complete the *Festial* or to take back the printing from other, less competent men? If any of these speculations is true (and others are possible), it was too late anyway. Waynflete died at Bishop's Waltham on August 11, 1486, just two months before the *Festial* was completed on October 14. Its importance thereafter depended on Caxton, in whose 1491 edition imitation was the sincerest form of flattery. The *Festial* ran through twenty editions by Pynson, de Worde, Ravynell, Hopyl, Morin, and Julian Notary and was the only printed vernacular sermon collection before Cranmer's very different "Book of Homilies" of 1547 (STC 13638.5).[156] In all these editions, it was Rood's text which survived.

Conclusion

Speculation aside, if there is limited evidence to link Rood with the *Festial*, there is no evidence at all to link anyone else with the *Festial*. "Printer of Mirk" may well be a safe appellation, even if with less justification than the term "Printer of Rufinus." However, given that only two of the publications of the second Oxford press (so called despite the uncertainties) are acknowledged by Rood as his own, perhaps "Printer of Lathbury," "Printer of Anwykyll," "Printer of Terence," and so on throughout the other presumed Oxford editions might not be an entirely facetious suggestion.

I think it is probable that Rood was responsible for the second edition of the *Festial*, and I have attempted to show that the arguments of type, print, language, and gap in time used against "Rood" and for "Printer of Mirk" are not wholly sound. Indeed, it seems to me that the unarticulated clinching factor for "Printer of Mirk" has been the fact that the *Festial* is in English ("unarticulated" because, as noted at the start of this essay, it is merely implicit in the statement: "There is ... a gap of at least three years between Rood's last assumed printing of Latin works and the printing of this work in English."). I have argued above against this implied argument.

The suggestion that the *Festial* might have been printed, at least in part, by Rood cannot be refuted (nor can it be proved). The suggestion that it might have been an early commission of Waynflete is plausible, if perhaps tendentious. More generally, my contention is that the collapsing of "Rood" into "Rood" and "Printer of Mirk" may have been both a radical and an unnecessary step. Despite the wisdom and scholarship of BMC XI, long experience of the manuscript *Festial* and some knowledge of the early printed editions does not convince me that the 1486 edition could not have been Rood's own project, conceived at Oxford, revised at Oxford, and printed at Oxford. With or without Rood as printer, the 1486 edition of the *Festial* can reasonably still be attached to the name of Rood.

Emeritus, University of Salford

APPENDIX 1: PRINTER OF MIRK, THEODORICUS ROOD, PRINTER OF RUFINUS

Dates in square brackets at the end of an entry refer to the date of publication according to the revised dates (p. 210) in E. Gordon Duff, *Printing in England in the Fifteenth Century: E. Gordon Duff's Bibliography with Supplementary Descriptions, Chronologies and a Census of Copies by Lotte Hellinga* (London: Bibliographical Society and British Library, 2009) (Duff/Hellinga).

PRINTER OF MIRK
[John Mirk], [*Festial*] (folio; 174 leaves; Rood Type 4, 6) (STC 17958, Duff/Hellinga no. 300). sig. z3r "Here endith the boke that is callid festiuall. the yere of oure lord M cccc. lxxxvi. the day aftir seint Edward the kyng" [Edward the Confessor October 13, Edward the Martyr March 18/ June 20] ["14.10.1486 or 19.3.1486/7"]

THEODORICUS ROOD
1. Alexander de Alexandria (formerly attributed to Alexander of Hales), *Expositio super libros Aristotelis: De anima* (folio; 240 leaves; Type 1, 2; 1 vellum extant) (STC 314, Duff/Hellinga no. 21). fol. 240rb "Im/pressum per me Theodericum rood de / Colonia in alma vniuersitate Oxonie / Anno incarnacionis dominice. M.cccc.lxxxi. xi. die mensis Octobris" ["11.10.1481"]

2. Phalaris, *Epistolae* (folio; 88 leaves; Type 4) (STC 19827, Duff/ Hellinga no. 348). fol. 88r "Hoc opusculum in alma vniuersi/tate Oxonie. A Natali christiano/ Ducentesima & nonagesima septima./Olimpiade foeliciter impressum est. /Hoc Teodericus rood quem collo/nia misit/ Sanguine germanus nobile pressit opus/Atque sibi socius thomas fuit angli/cus hunte .Dii dent vt venetos exuperare queant." ["1481"]

3. John Lathbury, *Liber moralium super trenis iheremie prophete* (folio; 292 leaves; Type 1, 2; 6 vellum extant) (STC 15297, Duff/Hellinga no. 238). fol. 271vb "Anno domini M.cccc.lxxxij. vlti/ma die mensis Iulij" ["31.7.1482"]

4. John [Anwykyll], *Compendium totius grammaticae* (at least 13 quires, last extant n3; Type 4, 5) (STC 695, Duff/Hellinga no. 28). sig. a1v "Vos teneri iuuenes vestrum celebrate ioannem / Qui bene vos docuit verba latine loqui ... ', "Eiusdem in reuerendi domini /Gulielmi episcopi vintonie /Laudem carmen ...Te gulielme pater ...hoc opus auctor enim te persuadente ioannes. /Edidit vnde tibi fama perennis erit" (quoted from STC 696.1, Duff/Hellinga no. 30 (Deventer 1489)) ["not after 1483"]

4a. John [Anwykyll], *Compendium totius grammaticae* (84 leaves? 12 quires of 6/8, ending m8 (*Vulgaria Terentii* begins n); Type 4, 5) (STC 696, Duff/Hellinga no. 29) ["not after 1483"]

5. Terence, *Vulgaria Terentii* (32 leaves, beginning n1; Type 4, 3) (STC 23904, Duff/Hellinga no. 392) ["not after 1483"]

6. Cicero, *Oratio pro T. Milone* (at least 5 quires of 6; Type 1) (STC 5312, Duff/Hellinga no. 104) ["1481–3"]

7. [John Stanbridge?], *Longe Parvula* (only 2 leaves extant; Type 1) (STC 23163.13, Duff/Hellinga no. 239) ["1481–3"]

8. Alexander de Villa Dei, *Doctrinale puerorum* (at least 3 quires; Type 4, 3) (STC 315, Duff/Hellinga no. 22) ["1481–3"]

9. William Lyndewode, *Constituciones prouinciales* (folio; 350 leaves; Type 4, 3, 5, 2) (STC 17102, Duff/Hellinga no. 278). fol. 339vb "Explicit tabula... completa In festo /co*n*uersacionis [*sic*] Sancti Pauli anno domini /Millesimo. CCCC. xxxiij." (January 25, 1433, i.e., Lyndewode date) ["*c.* 1483–4"]

10. Richard Rolle, *Explanationes in Iob* (better known as *Expositio.. . mortuorum*) + **Augustinus,** *Sermo de misericordia* (64 leaves; Type 5, 3) (STC 21261, Duff/Hellinga no. 363) ["1481–3"]

11. [Richard Swineshede], *Logica* (164 leaves; Type 3, 5) (STC 16693, Duff/Hellinga no. 277) ["1481–3"]

12. Augustinus, *Excitacio fidelis ad elemosinam faciendam* (8 leaves; Type 3, 4, 5) (STC 922, Duff/Hellinga no. 38) ["1481–3"]

PRINTER OF RUFINUS
1. Tyrannius Rufinus (formerly St. Jerome), *Expositio sancti Ieronomi in simbolum apostolorum ad papam Laurentium* (42 leaves) (STC 21443, Duff/Hellinga no. 234). sig. e[9]v "Explicit exposicio sancti Jeronimi... Impressa Oxonie et Finita An/no domini .M.cccc.lxviii. [1468 for 1478] xvii. die /decembris" ["17.12.1478"]

2. Aegidius de Columna, *Tractatus ... de peccato originali* (24 leaves) (STC 158, Duff/Hellinga no. 3). fol. c[8]v "Explicit tractatus breuis et vtilis de /originali peccato ... Impressa et finita Oxonie./A natiuitate domini .M.cccc.lxxix. xiiii. die /mensis marcij" ["14.3.1479"]

3. Aristotle, *Ethica Nichomachea* (174 leaves) (STC 752, Duff/Hellinga no. 32). sig. fol. y[6]r [for fol.] "Explicit textus ethicorum Aristotelis ... Impressus Oxoniis /Anno domini .M.cccc.lxxix." ["1479"]

APPENDIX 2: A COMPARISON OF PASSAGES FROM THREE SERMONS OF MIRK'S FESTIAL IN MANUSCRIPT AND PRINT

A. Corpus Christi Day Sermon
Powell, ed., *John Mirk's Festial*, **41/159–164** (London, BL, MS Cotton Claudius A.II., fol. 80v)
Þan he þat reseyith hit and beleuith he geteth hym grete merette, for he geteth hym þe kyngdam of heven. And he þat leueth not þus and reseyuit hytte he takyth hys dampnacion in þe peyne þat eure schal laston. Þan for to schapyn ȝoure beleve þe bettyr I telle þis ensaumpul. I rede þat in Seynte Gregory tyme [...]

Caxton 1483 (STC 17957, sig. f2v) (Figure 1)
than he that receyueth it & beleueth it / he getith hym the kyngdom of heuen and he that beleuyth not thus he receyueth his dampnacion in the payne that euer shal laste / than for to sharpe your beleue I telle you thys ensaumple I rede in saynt gregoryes tyme [...]

"Rood" 1486 (STC 17958, sig. g2ra–vb) (Figures 2 and 3)
(Square brackets mark quotations in Latin and English that are not found in the manuscripts and the 1483 printed edition; italics indicate a display type, with expansions in regular font.)
he that resceyuith it here and beleued verely ther vpon shall haue euer lastynge lyffe in [col. b] the kyngdome of heuen [as the gospell seythe. *Qui manducat hunc panem uiuet in eternum.*[157] who so etith of this brede shall leue euer and neuer be dede] and he that resceyuith hit and beleuith not thus [*Reus erit in iudicio*[158] at the day of dome] he shall be dampned in to euer lastyng payne. [*Augustinus in persona Christi. Manducas me non mutabis me in te sed tu mutabis in me.* Seynte Austyn seythe in the persone of criste Ete me but y shall not tourne and chaunce in to the but thou shalte tourne and chaunge in to me. *Narracio* We rede that there was a Jewe that went with a cristen man a felowe of his in to a churche of cristen people and herde masse *Et post missam dixit iudeus* And aftyr whan masse was

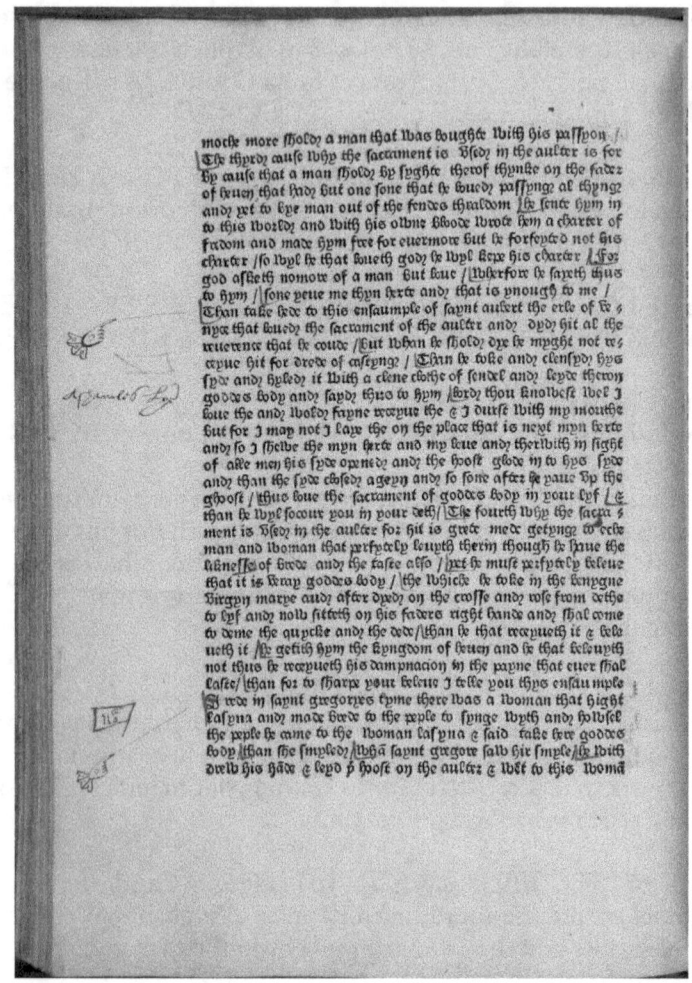

Figure 1. Caxton 1483 (STC 17957). Lambeth Palace Library ZZ 1483.6, sig. f2v. With the permission of Lambeth Palace Library.

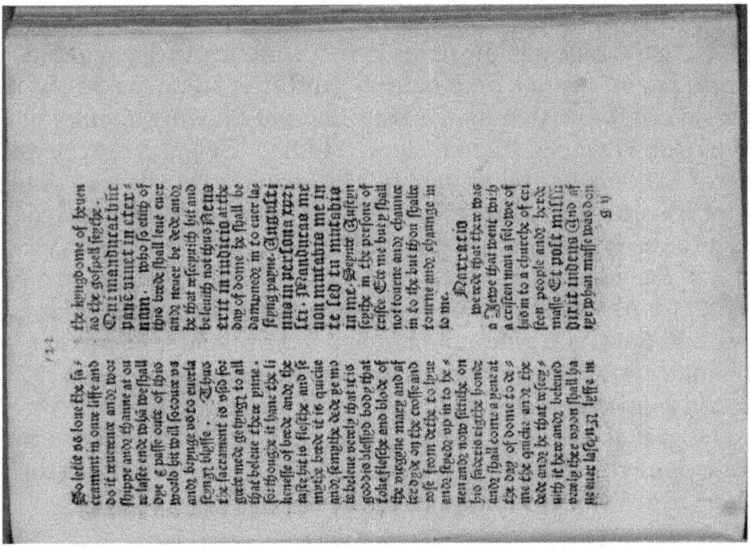

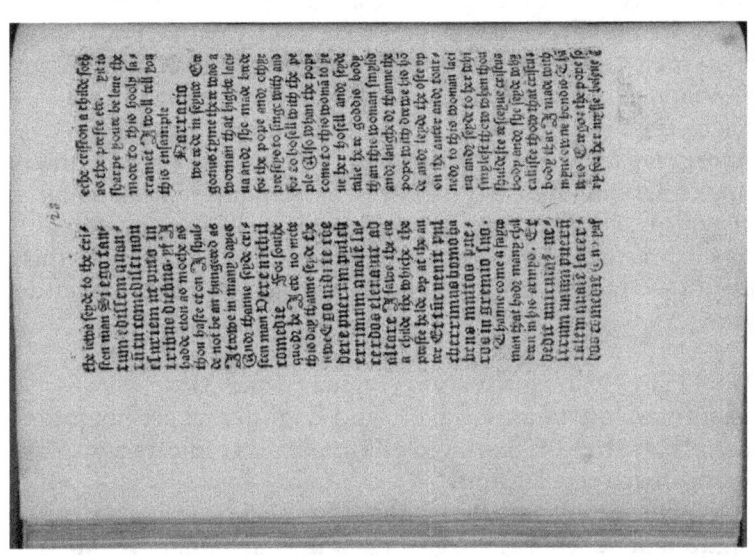

Figure 2. Rood/Printer of Mirk 1486 (STC 17958). Lambeth Palace Library ZZ 1486.9, sig. g2r. With the permission of Lambeth Palace Library.

Figure 3. Rood/Printer of Mirk 1486 (STC 17958). Lambeth Palace Library ZZ 1486.9, sig. g2v. With the permission of Lambeth Palace Library.

don [sig. g2va] the iewe seyde to the cristen man *Si ego tantum edissem quantum tu comedisti non esuriem ut puto in tribus diebus.* yf I hadde eton as moche as thou haste eton I shulde not be an hungered as I trowe in many dayes And thanne seyde cristen man *Uere nichil comedie* For southe quod he I ete no mete this day thanne seyde the iewe *Ego uidi te comedere puerum pulcherrimum qualem sacerdos eleuauit ad altare* I sawe the ete a childe the whiche the preste helde vp at the auter *Et tunc uenit pulcherrimus homo habens multos pueros in gremio suo.* Thanne come a fayre man that hade many children in his armys. *Et dedit unicuiuque uestrum unum puerum talem qualem sacerdos commedit &* he yaf [col. b] eche criston a childe soch as the preste ete.] yit to sharpe youre be leue the more to this hooly sacrament I woll tell you this ensample *Narracio* we rede in seynte Gregorius tyme [...]

Caxton 1491 (STC 17959, sig. f5ra–va) (Figures 4 and 5)
(Square brackets mark quotations in Latin and English that are not found in the manuscripts and the 1483 printed edition; italics indicate a display type, with expansions in regular font.)
he that receyue it here & bileueth verely therupon shal haue euer lastynge life in the kyngdom of heuen. [as the gospel sayth. *Qui manducat hunc panem uiuet ineternum* / Who soo eteth of [col. b] this brede. shall liue euer and neuer be dede] / and he that resceyueth it. and byleueth not thus / [*Reus erit in iudicio* / At the day of dome] he shal be dampned in to euer lastyng peyne / [*Augustinus in persona cristi* / *Manducas me non mutabis me in te sed tu mutaberis in me* / Saynt austen seith in the persone of criste / Ete me but I shall not torne and change in to the. but thou shall torne and change in to me. *Narracio* We rede that there was aiewe that went with a cristen man a felow of his in to a chirche of cristen peple. and herde masse. *Et post missam dixit iudeus* / And after whan masse was done / the iew said to the cristen man / *Si ego tantum edissem quantum tu comedisti non esuriem vt puto in tribus diebus* / Yf I hadde eten as moche as thou haste eten / I sholde not be a hungred / as I trow in thre dayes / And thenne sayd the cristen man to the iew / *Uere nichil comedi.* Forsoth sayd the cristen man to the iewe. I ete noo maner mete this day / thenne sayd the iew [sig. f5va] *Ego vidi te comedere puerum pulcherimum qualem sacerdos eleuauit ad altare* / I sawe the ete a childe þe whiche the preste helde vp at the aulter / *Et tunc venit pulcherimus homo habens multos pueros in gremio suo.* Thenne come there a fayre man that had many childern in his lappe. *Et dedit vnicuique vestrum vnum puerum talem qualem sacerdos comedit* / And he gaaf eche cristen man a childe such as the preste ete.] yet to sharpe your byleue the more to this holy sacrament / I wyll tell you this ensample / *Narracio* We rede in saynt Gregoryes tyme [...]

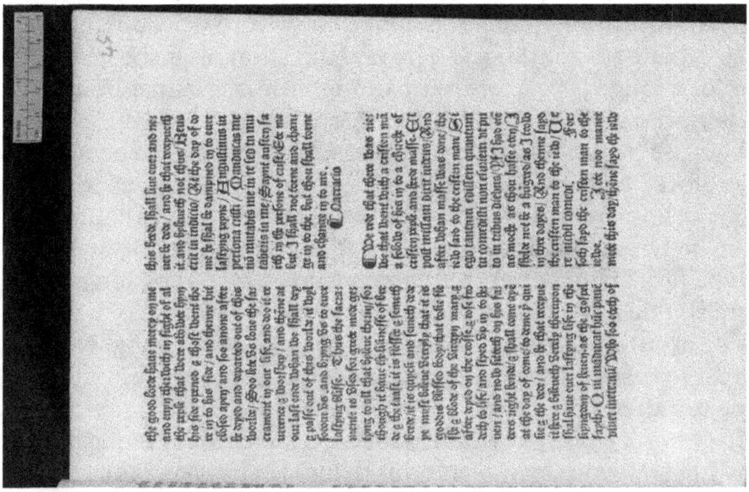

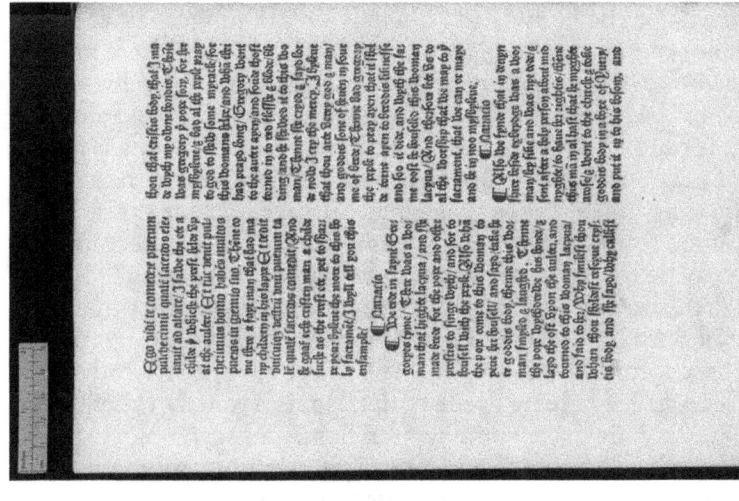

Figure 5. Caxton 1491 (STC 17959). CUL, sig. f5v. With the permission of Cambridge University Library.

Figure 4. Caxton 1491 (STC 17959). CUL, sig. f5r. With the permission of Cambridge University Library.

B. Pentecost Sermon
Powell, ed., *John Mirk's Festial* **39/69–89** (London, BL, MS Cotton Claudius A.II., fol. 76r)
Now to wytyn why þat þe Holy Gost com in lyknes of tonges rather þan any oþer membur of mannus body, and why to ham syttyng infere rather þan standyng. Þan to þe forme, why he com in lyknes of tongys, þis was þe cause: for a tong is þe best membur of a man whyl it is wel rewlyd ande þe werste whan it is oute of rewle. For as Seynt Iamys sayth: "A tong is fyred wyth þe fyre of helle', and may neure be schastysed wyl þat fyre brenneth hur. And for þe tong moste nedys speke þe wordys of þe feyth, þerfore þe Holy Goste com in tongys of fyre. For ryght os blessed fyre ourecomyth and dryueth away þe fyre of leyte, righte so þe fyre of tonges of þe Holy Gost schulde dryuen away and ourecomyn þe fyre of helle þat reyneth þat tyme and ȝet doth in mannus tong, and for encheson þat þe apastolus and alle oþer prechorus aftur hem schuldyn spekyn brennyng wordys, þat is, neyþer for loue ne for hate ne drede of deth sparon to tellyn þe pepul here vyse and here synne þat reyneth wythin hem, and seyn boldely þat whosoeure wil not leue hys synne and amendyn hym bot contyneth to hys deth-day he schal wythoute remedy go to þe fyre of helle, and he þat wil leuyn hys synne and amende hym, þagh he hadde syngyd neuer so greuoslyche beforen, he schal go to þe blessed fyre of hevn, þat is, þe precious loue of God þat brennyth among angelus and alle holy seyntus.

Powell, ed., "A Critical Edition of the *Temporale* **Sermons of MSS Harley 2247 and Royal 18 B XXV"** 3 vols. (unpublished Ph.D. thesis, University of London), II, 23/77–101 (222–223)
Now it is to witte why the Holy Goste come in þe symylitude of brennyng tonges raþer þan in eny oþer parte of mannes body. And whi appered he to þem sittyng raþer þan stonding? To þe first question þis is the reson and answere: for a tonge is þe beste parte or membre of mannes body while it is wele rewlid and wele gyded, and it is þe worst whatn it is evil gyded. And because þe tunge must pronownce, vttir and shewe þe wordis of þe feith, þerefore þe Holi Goste come in þe symylitude of a tunge brennyng. For right as holy men putte away and ouercom þe fyre of lightenyng with prayer, so þe fyre of þe tonge of þe Holy Goste shulde putte away and ouercom þe fyre of lightenyng with prayer, so þe fyre of þe tonge of þe Holy Goste shulde putte away and ouerecom þe fervent fire of hell. And because þe apostelis and all oþer after shuld speke brennyng wordis, þat is to sey, not to cese to preche þe worde of God nor spare for loue, fauoure, mede nor drede of deþe to rebuke syn and vices þat rennyth in þe peple and sey boldely: he þat wolde not leve his syn nor amende his life but contynew in his visyous lyving vnto his dying day he shall goo with-

oute remedy to þe fyre of hell and be dampned withoute ende. And he
þat woll sake his syn and mende his life, also be it he hath synned neuer so
grevously he shall goo to blisse of hevyn.

Caxton 1483 (STC 17957, sigs. e1v–2r)
now to wete why the holy ghoost came in liknesse of tonges rather than
in ony other parte of ma*n*nes body & to hem sittyng rather than stondyng
/ than the first is this cause / for a tonge is best membre of mannes body
while it is wel reuled & the werst whan it is out of reule / for as saynt
Iames sayth a tunge is fyred with fyre of helle that may not be chastysed
whyle the fyre brenneth here & for tunges must speke the wordes of the
feyth therfore the holy ghoost came in liknesse of tunges of fyre / for right
as blessed men ouercome & dryue aweye the fyre of lyghtenyng / right so
the tunge of the fyre of the holy ghoost shold dryue aweye & ouercome
the fyre of helle that reyned that tyme & yet doeth in mannes tunge / &
for encheson that the appostles and al other prechours after hem shold
speke brennyng wordes that is neyther for loue ne for awe / ne for drede
of deth shold spare to telle the peple her synnes that reynyth with hem
& saith who that wyl not leue his synne & amende hym but contynuelly
continueth vnto his lyues ende & to his deth day he shal without remedye
goo to þe fyre of hell / & who [sig. e2r] that leuyth his synne & amende
hym though he haue synned so greuously he shal goo to the blessyd fyre
of heuen that is the precyous loue of god that brenneth amonge aungels &
al other sayntes

"Rood" 1486 (STC 17958, sigs. e6va–f1rb)
(Square brackets mark quotations in Latin and English that are not found
in the manuscripts and the 1483 printed edition; italics indicate a display
type, with expansions in regular font.)
Now hit is to wete why the holy goste more apperyd in to lykenesse of
tonges rathir than in any othir party of mannes body & why he come
to hem sittyng rathir than standyng. As to the furste this is the cause. a
tonge is the beste membre of a mannes body whan hyt [col. b] is in good
rewle and well disposed but whan hyt is oute of rewle hit is the worste.
[*Venenum aspidum sub labiis eorum*[159] Bitter veneme is vnder the tonges
that spekithe euyll seythe Dauid in the sawter.] And as seint Ieme seythe
A cursed tonge is fired with fyre of hell and may not be chastisid while
the fyre brennyth hit And also for tonges muste speke wordis of fyre that
ys sharpe and sperkelyng to sey trouthe and notte spare in prechyng and
techyng to repreue mys dedis for as holy men in olde tyme ouercome and
droue a wey the fyre of lyghtenyng with holy wordes and good preyoures
with the brennyng loue to god ryghte for the fyre of the holy gost shulde

dryue a weye and ouercome the fyre of helle that enuy hath and euyll leuyng that regnyth now in the tonges of moche [sig. f1ra] people and in her herte And for the apostlis & othir prechoris that comythe aftyr hem shulde speke brennyng wordis that is neythir to sharpe nothir for drede nor for loue to sey the trouthe & to tell the people her defautes and to repreue the synne that regneth in hem in many diuerse wyse and so to do and sey the worde of god and to repreue synne. and but they woll leue synne they shall with oute remedy be damned in to the fyre of hell for thoughe thou shuldiste dye spare not to preche the worde of god and telle the trouthe [*Item deus* est *misericors penitentibus peccata sua*.¹⁶⁰ Also god is mercyfull to theym that be sory for her synnes & woll leue hem *Cum uero confessus fuerit et reliquerit ea misericordia consequatur*¹⁶¹ For thoughe a man haue do neuer so moche [col. b] synne and he woll shreyue hym and for sake his synne mercy shall folowe hym and he shall haue for yeuenesse] and so come to the bryghte fyre euer lastyng blysse that is the precious loue of god that brennythe amonge angelis and seyntis in heuen

Caxton 1491 (STC 17959, sig. e6va–b)
(Square brackets mark quotations in Latin and English that are not found in the manuscripts and the 1483 printed edition; italics indicate a display type, with expansions in regular font.)
Now it is to wyte why the holy ghost more appered in to liknesse of tongis rather than in ony other party of mannys body why he come to hem sitting rather thenne stondyng / As to the first / this is the cause / a tonge is the beste membre of a mannys body / whan it is in good rule / and well dysposed. But whan it is out of rule. it is the worst / [*Uenenum aspidum sub labiis eorum* Bitter venym is vnder the tonge / that speketh euyll / sayth dauyd in the psaulter] / And as saynte James sayth / A cursed tonge is fired wyth the fyre of helle / and maye not be chastised while the fire brenneth it And also for tonges muste speke wordis of fyre / that is sharpe and sperkeling to saye trouth / and not spare in prechynge and techyng to repreue mysdedes for as holy men in olde tyme ouer come and droue away the fyre of lyghtnyng with holy wordes and good prayers. wyth the brennynge loue to god / Right for the fyre of the holy ghost shold dryue awaye and ouercome the fire of helle / that enuy hath and euyll liuyng [col. b] that reygneth now in the tongis of moche peple / and in hertes / and for the appostles and other prechers. that cometh after hem shold speke brennyng wordis / that is neyther to sharpe / nother for drede ne for loue to say the trouth / and to tell the peple her defawtes. and to repreue the sinne that regneth in hem. in many dyuerse wyse. & soo to doo. and saye the worde of god. & to repreue sinne / and but they wyll leue sinne they shall wythout remedye be dampned in to the fyre of helle.

For though þu sholdest dey. spare not to preche the worde of god / and telle the trouthe / [*Item deus est misericors penitentibus peccata sua* / Also god is merciful to hem that be sory for her sinnes. and wyll leue hem / *Cum uero confessus fuerit* et *reliquerit ea misericordia consequatur*/ For though a man haue done neuer soo moche sinne and he wyll shryue hym / and for sake his sinne / merci shal folow hym / and he shal haue foryeuenesse] / and soo come to the brighte fyre euerlastyng blisse / That is the precious loue of god that brenneth emonge the angellis & sayntis in the kingdome of heuen

C. Trinity Sunday Sermon
Powell, ed., *John Mirk's Festial* 40/27–39 (London, BL, MS Cotton Claudius A.II.). fol. 77r–v
(Square brackets mark text that is not found in the 1486 and 1491 printed editions.)
For rythe os heretykys in þe begynnyng of þe fayth weryn abowten wyth here smethe wordys and plesyng and falce opynyons to ha distroyed þe feythe of þe Trinite, ryght so now þis Lollardes wyth her smethe wordys and plesyng to þe pepul bene abowtyn to drawen þe pepul fro þe fayth of Holy [fol. 77v] Chyrche [þat holy popys, byschoppes and dotteres taghton and hath ben holdyn and vsyd eure into þis tyme. Wherefore ryght os heretykys in þe begynnyng of Holy Chyrch pursued holy] popes, martyres and confessoures to þe deth, ryght so now þeys Lolleres pursueth men of Holy Chyrche and ben abowtyn in alle þat þei may to vndon hem, if þei myght haue here purpose forth.

Caxton 1483 (STC 17957, sig. e3r)
(Square brackets mark text that is not found in the 1486 and 1491 printed editions)
For right as heretikes in the begynnyng of the feyth were about with her smothe wordes and false opynynons to haue destroyed the feyth of the trynyte / Ryght so now these lollardes with their smothe wordes and plesyng to the peple be about to drawe the peple fro the feyth of holy chirche [that holy popes and doctours haue taughte & haue ben holden and vsed euer in to thys tyme Wherfore right as heretikes in the begynnynge pursueden holy] popes marters and confessours to the deth / Right so now these lollardes pursuen men of holy chirche and ben about in alle that they may to vndoo hem yf they mygth haue theyr purpoos forth

"Rood" 1486 (STC 17958, sig. f3rb)
fore ryghte as heretikes in the be gynnyng of the feythe with her swete wordes and false opynynes where aboute to distroye the feythe of the

hooly Trinite in the same wyse lolleris nowe a dayes with her false spece of gyle be a boute also to with drawe the people from the trewe beleue and feythe of the holy trinite and the beleue and feythe of hooly chirche Popes marteres and confessoures to the dethe Ryghte so now this lolleris purse-withe men of hooly churche and be a boute in all maner weyes that they can and may fynde to distroye and vn do hem so that they myghte haue her purpose.

Caxton 1491 (STC 17959, sig. e8rb)
For right as heretykis in the begynynge of the feyth wyth her swete wordes & false opynyons were aboute to distroye the feyth of the holy trinite / In the same wyse lollers now a dayes wyth her false spice of gile be aboute also to withdraw the peple from the true byleue & feyth of the holy trinyte and the byleue & feyth of holy chirche / Popes martirs and confessours to the deth Right soo now thise lollers pursuen men of holy chirche / and ben aboute in all maner wayes þat they can and may fynde to distroye and vndo hem so that they myghte haue their purpose

NOTES

1. Lotte Hellinga, ed., *Catalogue of Books Printed in the XVth Century Now in the British Library. Part XI: England* ('t Goy-Houten, The Netherlands: Hes & De Graaf, 2007). Hereafter BMC XI. Although no authors are credited on the title page, the three principal contributors were Lotte Hellinga, Paul Needham, and Margaret Lane Ford. The present essay is in particular indebted to Hellinga's work on types and Needham's on paper stocks.
2. I use the spelling "Theodoric," although Hellinga, in her contributions to BMC XI and in Lotte Hellinga, *William Caxton and Early Printing in England* (London: British Library, 2010), uses "Theoderic(us)" in line with the spelling of his name in the two Oxford colophons in which he is named (see below). But for "Theodoric," see Johannes Versor, *Quaestiones super libros Aristotelis De generatione et corruptione*, Datenbank Gesamtkatalog der Wiegendrucke [Union Catalogue of Incunabula Database], GW M50238 (Berlin: Staatsbibliothek zu Berlin, Preussischer Kulturbesitz), http://www.gesamtkatalogderwiegendrucke.de/GWEN.xhtml, and note 140 below.
3. The author is qualified to do this because of her long-term research into Mirk and the *Festial*, including the following editions: Susan Powell, ed., *John Mirk's Festial Edited from British Library MS Cotton Claudius A.II.*, 2 vols., EETS OS 334, 335 (Oxford: Oxford University Press for the Early English Text Society, 2009, 2011); Susan Powell, ed., *The Advent and Nativity Sermons from a Fifteenth-Century Revision of John Mirk's Festial ed. from B.L.*

MSS Harley 2247, Royal 18 B XXV and Gloucester Cathedral Library 22, Middle English Texts 13 (Heidelberg, Germany: Carl Winter, 1981); Susan Powell, ed., *Three Sermons for Nova Festa, together with the Hamus Caritatis*, Middle English Texts 37 (Heidelberg, Germany: Universitätsverlag Winter, 2007). See too note 118 below.

4. No title pages exist for the earliest editions. The print is usually referred to as "Liber Festivalis," but the earliest references to a title are in the colophon to the 1486 edition ("festiuall") and the incipit to the 1491 edition: "Incipit liber qui vocatur festialis." Since Mirk himself asked that the work "be called a Festial" (Powell, *John Mirk's Festial*, Prologue/14–15), *Festial* is used here for both manuscript and print.

5. I am grateful to Professor Nigel Morgan for directing me to this viewpoint from his knowledge of the Sarum calendar. At this date Edward king and martyr would be so called, and his relics at Shaftesbury had little or no cult of public veneration; Nigel Morgan, private communication, June 3, 2013. For a discussion by Needham of the prevalence and types of dating and of signing editions (relevant below), see BMC XI, 317–319.

6. BMC XI, 243.

7. Ibid., 234–244, 385–391. For details of all three printers, see Appendix 1 below.

8. The Germans may have established themselves early in Oxford: "A surprising number of Oxford manuscripts are written by Dutch or German scribes"; Nicolas Barker, *The Oxford University Press and the Spread of Learning: An Illustrated History 1478–1978* (Oxford: Clarendon Press, 1978), 3.

9. Details of date and printer are rare and seemingly random in early German printing. Of around eighty-five editions by the first Cologne printer, Ulrich Zel, only two have colophons with these details; Paul Needham, "Ulrich Zel's Early Quartos Revisited," in *Incunabula on the Move: The Production, Circulation and Collection of Early Printed Books*, ed. Ed Potten and Satoko Tokunaga, Transactions of the Cambridge Bibliographical Society 15:1 (2012) (Cambridge, UK: Cambridge Bibliographical Society, 2014), 9–57, at 9.

10. Appendix 1 below supplements and tabulates details of the editions discussed in this essay; numbers in the text of the essay refer to the numbers of the Rood editions listed in the Appendix *sub* Rood. For full descriptions of the British Library copies of editions identified in BMC XI as by Rood, see BMC XI, 236–243, 385–391 (Plates 22–28). See also the discussion of books in Latin, ibid., 51–53.

11. "Some 21 paper stocks have been recorded in this quarto group [nos. 4–8, 10–12 *sub* Rood in Appendix 1 below], many of them making only a single appearance"; BMC XI, 324.

12. BMC XI, 14. For example, Alan Coates, Kristian Jensen, Cristina Dondi, Bettina Wagner, and Helen Dixon, eds., *A Catalogue of Books Printed in the Fifteenth Century Now in the Bodleian Library*, 6 vols. (Oxford: Oxford

University Press, 2005), item L-126, has a list of books (with their prices) that were to be sold in Oxford in 1483 by Thomas Hunt, "*stacionarius vniuersitatis oxoniensis*"; Falconer Madan, ed., "The Daily Ledger of John Dorne 1520," *Collectanea First Series*, ed. C. R. L. Fletcher, Oxford Historical Society Publications 5 (Oxford: Oxford Historical Society, 1885), 142–143. The list is discussed in Paul Needham, "Continental Printed Books Sold in Oxford, c. 1480–3: Two Trade Records," in *Incunabula: Studies in Fifteenth-Century Printed Books Presented to Lotte Hellinga*, ed. M. Davies (London: British Library, 1999), 243–270.

13. For the full verse with translation, see Daniel Wakelin, "Humanism and Printing," in *A Companion to the Early Printed Book in Britain 1476–1558*, ed. Vincent Gillespie and Susan Powell (Cambridge, UK: Brewer, 2014), 227–247, at 235.

14. As such, Rood is discussed in histories of Oxford University Press. See Harry Carter, *A History of the Oxford University Press: Volume 1: To the Year 1780, with an Appendix Listing the Titles of Books Printed There 1690–1780* (Oxford: Clarendon Press, 1975), 4–12; Barker, *Oxford University Press*, 2–4; Kristian Jensen, "Printing at Oxford in Its European Context 1478–1584," in *The History of Oxford University Press. Volume 1: Beginnings to 1780*, ed. Ian Gadd, Simon Eliot, and W. Roger Louis (Oxford: Oxford University Press, 2013), 31–48, esp. 40–42. All of these provide synopses of the early Oxford press(es), and Carter's is a particularly full account. See also E. Gordon Duff, *The English Provincial Printers, Stationers and Bookbinders to 1557* (Cambridge, UK: Cambridge University Press, 1912), 1–22.

15. Of the five copies in the Bodleian Library in Oxford today, the earliest dates only from a seventeenth-century donation; Coates, et al., *Catalogue . . . Bodleian*, item A-168. For texts studied in schools and at Oxford in the late Middle Ages, see Lotte Hellinga and J. B. Trapp, eds., *The Cambridge History of the Book in Britain. Volume III: 1400–1557* (Cambridge, UK: Cambridge University Press, 1999), esp. J. B. Trapp, "The Humanist Book," 285–315, chap. 14; Kristian Jensen, "Text-Books in the Universities: The Evidence from the Books," 354–379, chap. 14; E. J. Ashworth, "Text-Books: A Case Study—Logic," 380–386, chap. 17; and Nicholas Orme, "Schools and School-Books," 449–469, chap. 22. See also M. B. Parkes, "The Provision of Books," in *The History of the University of Oxford. Volume II: Late Medieval Oxford*, ed. J. I. Catto and Ralph Evans (Oxford: Clarendon Press, 1992), 407–483, and see other chapters in that book. More generally, see Alan Cobban, *English University Life in the Middle Ages* (London: UCL Press, 1999), 149–181.

16. "Et solutum pro v libris vocatis Alexander *De anima*, xxxiii s. iiii d." [and paid for five books called Alexander, *De anima*, 33s. 4d.]. W. D. Macray, *A Register of the Members of St. Mary Magdalen College, Oxford: From the*

Foundation of the College: New Series (London: Henry Frowde, 1894–1915), I:7, entry for 1481, from Magdalen College Archives, LCE/1, fol. 11v.
17. The date January 25, 1433 (Lyndewode, *Constituciones prouinciales*) marks when Lyndewode completed the index to the book.
18. See below for the association of the *Compendium totius grammaticae* with Oxford through its dedicatory verses.
19. James G. Clark, "Lathbury (Lathbery), John (d. 1362), Franciscan Friar and Theologian," in *Oxford Dictionary of National Biography* (Oxford: Oxford University Press, 2004–2014).
20. M17160 (Rood, 1482) is the only entry in the Datenbank Gesamtkatalog der Wiegendrucke [Union Catalogue of Incunabula Database].
21. BMC XI, 68, 239.
22. R. H. Helmholz, "Lyndwood, William (c. 1375–1446), Administrator, Ecclesiastical Lawyer, and Bishop of St. David's," in *Oxford Dictionary of National Biography* (Oxford: Oxford University Press, 2004–2014).
23. STC 17107 (Paris: Andreas Bocard, 1501); STC 17109 (Paris: Wolfgang Hopyl for William Bretton, 1505); STC 17111 (Antwerp: Christoffel van Ruremund, 1525).
24. BMC XI, 32 (within a discussion on tables and indices, 32–33), 239.
25. Madan, "Daily Ledger," nos. 577, 872, 1356, 1600, and index entry on 164.
26. BMC XI, 68. For the Syon copy (probably gifted by Waytt's family or friends for use by the brothers), see Vincent Gillespie, ed., *Syon Abbey*, with A. I. Doyle, ed., *The Libraries of the Carthusians*, Corpus of British Medieval Library Catalogues 9 (London: British Library in association with British Academy, 2001), T.15/SS1.1355.
27. The edition contains two other short works attributed to Jerome. For full descriptions of the British Library copies of two editions (the Rufinus and Aristotle's *Ethica*) identified in BMC XI as by the Printer of Rufinus, see BMC XI, 234–235.
28. Ibid., 13.
29. Ibid., 13, citing Falconer Madan, *The Early Oxford Press: A Bibliography of Printing and Publishing at Oxford "1468"–1640*, Oxford Historical Society 29 (Oxford: Clarendon Press, 1895). All three works ascribed by BMC XI to the Printer of Rufinus are "set in a distinctive gothic type, broad, heavily ligatured, and with some letters with cursive characteristics ... closest to that used by the press which worked for Gerard ten Raem, but it shares some letters with founts used by Ulrich Zel, the first printer at Cologne, and Richard Pafraet, who migrated from Cologne to Deventer"; Barker, *Oxford University Press*, 4. That the Rufinus printer was not ten Raem is argued in A. C. de la Mare and Lotte Hellinga, "The First Book Printed in Oxford: The *Expositio Symboli* of Rufinus," *Transactions of the Cambridge Bibliographical Society* 7 (1978), 184–244.

30. BMC XI, 234; de la Mare and Hellinga, "First Book," 184–244 (de la Mare, "The Printer's Copy and the Tradition of the *Expositio Symboli* of Rufinus," 184–194, Hellinga, "The First Oxford Compositor and His Printer's Copy," 195–209). At this stage the possibility remained (for de la Mare, at least) that the Printer of Rufinus and Rood were the same man, the differences between them the result of "a change from a private backer to institutional support of some kind" (184).
31. The absence of a miter in the Goldwell coat of arms (he became bishop in 1472) raises the question whether the date 1468 might be correct; but see Lotte Hellinga, *William Caxton and Early Printing in England* (London: British Library, 2010), 76–78 and figs. 35, 36.
32. Margaret Lane Ford, "Importation of Printed Books into England and Scotland," in *The Cambridge History of the Book in Britain. Volume III: 1400–1557*, ed. Lotte Hellinga and J. B. Trapp (Cambridge, UK: Cambridge University Press, 1999), 179–201, at 197. On Goldwell, see Rosemary C. E. Hayes, "Goldwell, James (d. 1499), Bishop of Norwich," in *Oxford Dictionary of National Biography* (Oxford: Oxford University Press, 2004–2014).
33. All Souls L.R.4.e.14(2). See Dennis E. Rhodes, *A Catalogue of Incunabula in all the Libraries of Oxford University outside the Bodleian* (Oxford: Clarendon Press, 1982), no. 150. It was not given directly by Goldwell, but since it came from a later bishop of Norwich, John Moore, the assumption is that it was his originally; de la Mare and Hellinga, "First Book," 193–195. For Goldwell's full bequest, see A. B. Emden, *A Biographical Register of the University of Oxford to A.D. 1500*, 3 vols. (Oxford: Clarendon, 1957, 1958, 1959), II:785, sub Goldwell, James; the *Rationale* is printed book xvi.
34. BMC XI, 35, in a discussion of color. Caxton had experimented with color in Bruges. The use of red was a feature of Cologne printers, and Caxton had visited Cologne in 1471–1472 and employed Johann Veldener to supply his type; Barker, *Oxford University Press*, 3. See also Hellinga, *William Caxton*, 44–45, 50–51.
35. Hellinga, *William Caxton*, 76. See also Jensen, "Text-Books," 355.
36. BMC XI, 67. See Coates, et al., *Catalogue . . . Bodleian*, item A-400 (first copy) for details of the *Ethica* and All Souls. This is one of the original bindings, the other being item A-039, the Aegidius. Item R-148 is a Rufinus. No early owners can be identified for the British Library copies of Rufinus and Aristotle; BMC XI, 234–235.
37. Hellinga, *William Caxton*, 78. See further de la Mare and Hellinga, "First Book," 195–209.
38. Perhaps the Printer of Rufinus, having struggled with the Aristotle, returned to Cologne with the information that there was a market for large editions (but that he was not the one to tackle it). BMC XI, 51, calls him "a rather unambitious jobbing printer," but his problem would seem to have been overambition.

39. The success of these Oxford printers in Latin was only preliminary, and Caxton, who relied on publishing in English and so had no overseas competitors, was left the sole printer in England after "Printer of Mirk" ceased business in 1486.
40. BMC XI, 35–36.
41. Ibid., 236–237.
42. J. B. Trapp, "Carmeliano [Carmigliano], Pietro [Petrus Carmelianus, Peter Carmelian] (c. 1451–1527), Poet and Royal Official," in *Oxford Dictionary of National Biography* (Oxford: Oxford University Press, 2004–2014).
43. N. R. Ker, "The Vellum Copies of the Oxford Edition (1482) of Lathbury on Lamentations," *Bodleian Library Record* 2 (1947), 185–188. See also Madan, "Early Oxford Press"; and Hellinga, *William Caxton*, 80–81, figs. 37 and 38.
44. The All Souls fellows were John Hawkyns (1465, also in the All Souls copy of Lathbury—see Coates, et al., *Catalogue . . . Bodleian*, item L-043, third copy), Alison (1469), J. Alysaundyr (1471), John Saunder (1471), and perhaps Richard Cysson (1480) (who is more likely than Thomas, master of Balliol 1512–1518). The University College fellows were Nicholas Mynskyp, collector of university rents 1479/1480 and fellow 1484/1485, and William Hall, fellow 1476–1479. Ker suggests "very tentatively, that the names of subscribers were entered on the leaves as memoranda for the sellers of the vellum"; Ker, "Vellum Copies," 188. Madan earlier suggested that they were parchment sellers or revisers of the print; Madan, *Early Oxford Press*, 256.
45. From the computus roll of John Alisaunder (i.e. J. Alysaundyr of note 44 above) and Nicholas Treble, bursars of All Souls 1480/1481; Ker, "Vellum Copies," 187.
46. A. B. Cobban, "Colleges and Halls 1380–1500," in *The History of the University of Oxford. Volume II: Late Medieval Oxford*, ed. J. I. Catto and Ralph Evans (Oxford: Clarendon Press, 1992), 581–633, at 609–610.
47. The Rufinus manuscript has a monogram and owner identification (fol. 1v) that links it to Robert Thompson, fellow of Magdalen College 1481–1483 and thereafter rector of Marsham, Norfolk, which was in the gift of the bishop of Norwich; de la Mare and Hellinga, "First Book," 187, 194–195, where the only suggestion made is that he perhaps bought it after Goldwell's death when he was rector of St. Peter's Hungate in Norwich (see note 33 above).
48. Trapp, "Humanist Book," 311–312. Other publications attributed by BMC XI to Rood, the *Explanationes in Iob* of Richard Rolle and the *Excitacio fidelis* of St. Augustine (STC 21261 and 922), were also used as schoolbooks.
49. Nicholas Browne, fellow in 1503; BMC XI, 242.
50. The supply of schoolbooks was a constant, if perhaps not a lucrative, trade and it formed the output of the last printer in Oxford, John Scolar (1517–

1528); Elisabeth Leedham-Green, "University Libraries and Book-Sellers," in *The Cambridge History of the Book in Britain. Volume III: 1400–1557*, ed. Lotte Hellinga and J. B. Trapp (Cambridge, UK: Cambridge University Press, 1999), 316–353, at 338.

51. They are now separate; Coates, et al., *Catalogue ... Bodleian*, items A-358 and T-053. For a discussion, see Jensen, "Text-Books," 359, and see further in the same chapter for the *Doctrinale*.
52. The second edition of the *Compendium* (STC 696) ends with the signature m8, the *Vulgaria* (STC 23904) begins n1.
53. For details, see BMC XI, 241.
54. Christopher D. Cook, "Fragments in Westminster Abbey Library," in *Incunabula in the Westminster Abbey and Westminster School Libraries* (London: Bibliographical Society, 2013), 127–142 (fragments 1, 11, and 14). No printed volumes were listed in the inventory made at the dissolution; ibid., 18. Nothing appears to be known of the school's books in the Middle Ages; ibid., 20.
55. Merton College Oxford 27.D.4. See Rhodes, *Catalogue of Incunabula*, xxi and no. 1102(a), for a discussion of vellum copies in All Souls, Balliol, and Westminster Abbey.
56. Ashworth, "Text-Books," 385.
57. Madan, "Daily Ledger," nos. 1024, 1051, 1518, 1720, 1730, 1806, 1813; 482, 505; 1800, and index entry 163–64.
58. See note 16 above. Two of these survive, although rebound; C. Y. Ferdinand, "Library Administration (c. 1475 to 1640)," in *The Cambridge History of Libraries in Britain and Ireland. Volume I: To 1640*, ed. Elisabeth Leedham-Green and Teresa Webber (Cambridge, UK: Cambridge University Press, 2006), 565–591, at 577–578. See Rhodes, *Catalogue of Incunabula*, no. 55(c), (d).
59. Virginia Davis, "Waynflete [Wainflete, Patten], William (c. 1400–1486), Bishop of Winchester and Founder of Magdalen College, Oxford," in *Oxford Dictionary of National Biography* (Oxford: Oxford University Press, 2004–2014); and, for a full account, Virginia Davis, *William Waynflete, Bishop and Educationalist* (Woodbridge, UK: Boydell, 1993), to which I am indebted for details of Waynflete.
60. The discussion below is indebted to Nicholas Orme, *Education in Early Tudor England: Magdalen College Oxford and Its School, 1480–1540*, Magdalen College Occasional Papers 4 (Oxford: Magdalen College, 1998). See also Cobban, "Colleges and Halls," 610–614.
61. On humanist texts printed in England and in English, see Wakelin, "Humanism and Printing," 234–246.
62. Nicholas Orme, "The Magdalen Diaspora," in *Education in Early Tudor England: Magdalen College Oxford and Its School, 1480–1540*, Magdalen

College Occasional Papers 4 (Oxford: Magdalen College, 1998), 51–56. Although destined for a higher plane and not a grammarian, Thomas Wolsey was another fellow of Magdalen and was briefly master of the school (he had left by 1502). See Sybil M. Jack, "Wolsey, Thomas (1470/71–1530), Royal Minister, Archbishop of York, and Cardinal," in *Oxford Dictionary of National Biography* (Oxford: Oxford University Press, 2004–2014).

63. Nicholas Orme, "Anwykyll, John (d. 1487), Schoolmaster and Grammarian," in *Oxford Dictionary of National Biography* (Oxford: Oxford University Press, 2004–2014).
64. BMC XI, 242. Nicholas Orme, "Stanbridge, John (1463–1510), Schoolmaster and Grammarian," in *Oxford Dictionary of National Biography* (Oxford: Oxford University Press, 2004–2014). For books left by Stanbridge and his brother Thomas traceable in Magdalen College Library today, see Rhodes, *Catalogue of Incunabula*, xxiv–xxv.
65. This was not published until after his death; STC 13603.7, 1505?.
66. Nicholas Orme, "Holt, John (d. 1504), Schoolmaster and Grammarian," in *Oxford Dictionary of National Biography* (Oxford: Oxford University Press, 2004–2014); and for a full account, Nicholas Orme, "John Holt (d. 1504), Tudor Schoolmaster and Grammarian," *The Library*, 6th ser., 18 (1996): 283–305.
67. For example, *The Royal Grammar Compiled Formerly by William Lilly*; see *A Short-Title Catalogue of Books Printed in England, Scotland, Ireland, Wales and British America and of English Books Printed in Other Countries, 1641–1700*, compiled by D. Wing, 2nd ed. newly revised and enlarged (New York: Modern Language Association of America, 1994), L2267, 1688. For details of Lily's two "royal" grammars, one in English and one in Latin, see R. D. Smith, "Lily, William (1468?–1522/23, Grammarian and Schoolmaster," in *Oxford Dictionary of National Biography* (Oxford: Oxford University Press, 2004–2014).
68. On both texts and Anwykyll's probable authorship, see Orme, *Education in Early Tudor England*, 15–17.
69. For details, see Davis, *William Waynflete*, 70–72, and for the source see Macray, *Register*, I:8–9 (visit of Founder 1481), 11–12 (visit of Founder 1483).
70. E. Gordon Duff, *Printing in England in the Fifteenth Century: E. Gordon Duff's Bibliography with Supplementary Descriptions, Chronologies and a Census of Copies by Lotte Hellinga* (London: Bibliographical Society and the British Library, 2009), 210. Hereafter Duff/Hellinga. Rood's two editions are Duff/Hellinga nos. 28 and 29, but the source for the verses (both verses, *pace* BMC XI, 54, n. 3) is Duff/Hellinga no. 30 (Deventer, 1489). This is the earliest edition to have the extant verses.
71. For the date Duff/Hellinga, 210; for the quotation BMC XI, 68.

72. British Library IC.55321, described in BMC XI, 240. See also 68 and n. 10, citing James P. Carley, ed., *The Libraries of King Henry VIII*, Corpus of British Medieval Library Catalogues 7 (London: British Library in association with British Academy, 2000), 147, item H2/771. The (perhaps fanciful) suggestion of presentation to Richard III is my own, as is the speculation that the copy of Rood's Lathbury bound in parchment in the year 1483/1484 (Macray, *Register*, 13) might also have been a presentation copy.
73. Emden, *Biographical Register*, III:2003, *sub* "Waynflete, William," lists three manuscripts given by him to Magdalen College and three that he owned.
74. Macray, *Register*, I:8 (from Magdalen College Register A, fols. 7v–8r for September 20, 1481), records that Waynflete brought with him and sent in advance of his 1481 visit "diversos libros quamplurimos pro nova libraria, octingentos aut circiter, praeter libros prius ibidem repertos et legatos ex diversis benefactoribus" [very many different books for the new library, eight hundred or thereabouts, apart from books found there earlier and donated by various benefactors].
75. See note 73 above for the manuscripts; and Ford, "Importation of Printed Books," 181, for the printed books.
76. Rhodes, *Catalogue of Incunabula*, xxiii, noting that the college even today owns 146 incunables, many acquired before 1500.
77. Macray, *Register*, I:7, 10, 13, 15–16.
78. Ibid., I:8.
79. BMC XI, 51 (first two quotations), 68.
80. Ibid., 243.
81. Ibid., 391 and Plate 28. It also has just one initial (G), which is used throughout (as in the introduction to sermons, "Good men and women").
82. Ibid., 387.
83. For example, it had been used for the text in Rood's Lyndewode, with Type 3: 88G for the glossed commentary and Type 5: 92G for headings in the commentary; ibid., 239. Type 5: 92G had been used, with other types, in, for example, Rood's Lyndewode, Rolle, *Logica*, and *Excitatio*; ibid., 239, 241, 242, 243.
84. Ibid., 339.
85. Ibid., 387.
86. Ibid., 28.
87. Ibid., 27. "L" (Liber) is used on verso leaves and Roman numerals on facing rectos.
88. Ibid., 13–14, citing Carter, *History of the Oxford University Press*, 6 and n. 2, which reproduces the relevant entries recording "Dyryke Dowcheman" in Oxford in 1480, "Dydycke" as being paid 23s. 4d. for the mending and gilding of the mace 1481/1482, and "Dedyck Teutonicus" as having left his premises in Oxford 1482/1483. For details of the rented property, see note 137 below.

89. "[H]e is likely to have been one of many men trained as goldsmiths who turned their hands to engraving the punches for making type, in his case with indifferent success"; Carter, *History of the Oxford University Press*, 6. Types 3–5 are of unknown origin (BMC XI, 339), but "all seven of Rood's types have characteristics of the Lower Rhenish school of lettering centred on Cologne"; Carter, *History of the Oxford University Press*, 6, writing before the designation of the Printers of Rufinus and Mirk.
90. The full woodcuts begin the edition (a1r–v); the tiny ones occur in the *Temporale* section, before the sermons for Passion Sunday, the Eve of Pentecost and Pentecost (the same woodcut), and Trinity Sunday, and before the first sermon in the *Sanctorale* (two of St. Andrew); nine half-size ones are found thereafter, before the feasts of SS. Nicholas, Thomas Apostle, Stephen, and John Evangelist, the Holy Innocents, St. Thomas Canterbury, the Circumcision, the Conversion of St. Paul, and the Annunciation. There are no other woodcuts in the following nine quires. See the illustration of the St. Nicholas woodcut in Hellinga, *William Caxton*, 82, fig. 40; also BMC XI, 391.
91. Henry Bradshaw, *Collected Papers of Henry Bradshaw Late University Librarian*, ed. G. W. Prothero (Cambridge, UK: Cambridge University Press, 1889), 84–101, no. VI, "On the Earliest English Engravings of the Indulgence known as the 'Image of Pity.'" Bradshaw points out that of the various Oxford productions at this date, only the *Festial* and the Lyndewode had woodcuts:

> The cut of the author in the Lyndewode, and the eleven large cuts in the *Festial* may perhaps have been the commencement of a series engraved for an edition of the *Golden Legend* which was never executed. They certainly belong to no known books. The five small cuts in the *Festial* apparently belong to a lost Oxford edition of the Primer or *Horae*. (Ibid., 86–87.)

See E. Hodnett, *English Woodcuts*, 1480–1535, Bibliographical Society Illustrated Monographs 22a (London: Bibliographical Society, 1973).
92. Duff/Hellinga, 210.
93. In the colophon Caxton says that he "fynysshed it" November 20, 1483. Since this might refer to the translating rather than the printing, BMC XI, 144, prefers the leeway of "November 20 1483–March 1484." (But for the argument that it is the date of completion of printing, see BMC XI, 319).
94. BMC XI, Appendix, 417–428, "English Paper Stock Tables"; 426–427, "Oxford: Theodericus Rood." Needham does, however, endorse Hellinga's opinion at 323–324.
95. Ibid., 243.

96. Ibid., 15.
97. For the title "Ryal(1)," see the start of the tabula and the colophon (STC 21429).
98. The number of paper stocks is calculated from nos. 47–79; BMC XI, 426–427. For the *Royal Book* and Lathbury stocks, see ibid., 314. Five of the thirty-three *Festial* paper stocks are used by Caxton (ibid., 49, 52, 58, 60, 61; Caxton stocks 132, 231, 204, 228, 93, respectively), in works ranging from 1477 to 1491. Rood no. 52 "Ship" (ibid., 426) does not appear to be correct: it cross-refers to Caxton stock 235, which is "Chalice." No. 52 should probably therefore read "Chalice."
99. Ibid., 426–427.
100. Ibid., 324.
101. Ibid., 243. The argument in this section (Language) is the only one in which I can profess specific expertise through my research on the Festial.
102. N. F. Blake, *William Caxton and English Literary Culture* (London and Rio Grande, OH: Hambledon, 1991), 57–61.
103. Ibid., 60.
104. Ibid., 61.
105. BMC XI, 51.
106. Jensen, *History of Oxford University Press*, 41.
107. This is pointed out in Blake, *William Caxton*, 61.
108. On *vulgaria*, see Wakelin, "Humanism and Printing," 239–241; Orme, *Education in Early Tudor England*, 14; and Orme, "An Early-Tudor Oxford Schoolbook," *Renaissance Quarterly* 34 (1981): 11–39.
109. STC 23904, sigs. n1r, q8v.
110. STC 696, sig. e5r.
111. STC 17958, sig. g2rb–va. The Latin of Rood's display type is italicized here (expansions within the italics are in normal type, while expansions in the English text are italicized). See Appendix 2.A below for the whole insertion, together with the inserted material that directly precedes it, and the equivalent text in British Library MS Cotton Claudius A.II. and in Caxton's 1483 and 1491 editions. Figs. 1–5 provide facsimiles of the 1483, 1486, and 1491 printed texts of this passage.
112. *John Mirk's Festial*, I:xlvii, II:552–53 (K).
113. These are inserted at the equivalent of *John Mirk's Festial*, sermon 39/14, 35, 38, 48, 53. See the full collation, II:646–656. All references to the edited text of *John Mirk's Festial* cite the sermon number followed by a forward slash and then the line references.
114. Inserted in K at the equivalent of *John Mirk's Festial*, sermon 39/38 (and the whole verse quoted), but in Rood at the equivalent of 39/37 and followed at the equivalent of 39/40 by verse 4 ("Et repleti sunt omnes spiritu sancto").
115. "Dominus recitauit nomen pauperis quia ipsum approbauit et nomen

eius in libro scriptum fuit," "Sed nomen diuitis tacuit quia ipsum non approbauit" (asserted as "holy scripture" and perhaps a development of the Vulgate Psalm 71, esp. vv. 71:13–14); "Post ascensionem domini" (a précis of Acts 1:9); "Et apparuerunt illis," "Et repleti" (Acts 2:3, 2:4); "Venenum aspidum sub labiis eorum" (Psalms 13:3, 139:4); "Item deus est misericors penitentibus peccata sua" (Ecclesiasticus 12:3); "Cum uero confessus fuerit et reliquerit ea misericordia consequatur" (Proverbs 28:13). These are inserted at the equivalent of *John Mirk's Festial*, sermon 39/7–13, 22, 37, 40, 73, 86 respectively.

116. *John Mirk's Festial*, sermon 39/11–13. Cf. the paraphrase in Rood, STC 17958, sigs e5rb–va: "For he that can gete good falsely with knackys and mowus he is a wyse man but he that for sakyth the wytte of this worlde is a | fole."
117. STC 17958, sig. e5va.
118. *John Mirk's Festial*, sermon 39/72–73. See Appendix 2.B below for *John Mirk's Festial*, 39/69–89 compared with the revised text of the *Festial* extant in British Library MSS Harley 2247 and Royal 18 B XXV, Caxton's edition of 1483, Rood's edition of 1486, and Caxton's second edition of 1491. For details of the *Festial* revision, see *John Mirk's Festial*, I:lii–lv; Powell, ed., *The Advent and Nativity Sermons*; and for a full edition of the *Temporale* (which includes this sermon), see Susan Powell, "A Critical Edition of the Temporale Sermons of MSS Harley 2247 and Royal 18 B XXV," 3 vols., unpublished Ph.D. thesis, University of London, 1980.
119. STC 17958, sig. e6vb.
120. *John Mirk's Festial*, sermon 39/85–88.
121. STC 17958, sig. f1ra-b.
122. See the collation in *John Mirk's Festial*, II: Appendix III, vii, 646–656.
123. See Appendix 2.B above.
124. Indeed, there may be some reflection of the strangeness of the sometimes macaronic text in Jensen's odd gaffe in referring to Rood's *Festial* as "in an English translation"; Jensen, *History of Oxford University Press*, 41. It may be worth noting too that the English translation of the Latin Vulgate is not that of the Wycliffite bible.
125. BMC XI, 243.
126. Duff/Hellinga, p. 210.
127. BMC XI, 241-3.
128. With the caveat that, since the British Library does not possess copies of the Anwykyll (4, 4a), Cicero (6), or *Doctrinale* (8), BMC XI offers no dates for these.
129. In the *Golden legende* (STC 248760) (BMC XI, 324), which was completed 20 November 20, 1483 (see note 93 above). Needham effectively establishes the principle that shared paper stocks "have a good probability of being

close in time to each other"; Needham, "Ulrich Zel's Early Quartos," 26. In BMC XI he notes that paper stocks are normally used up within three to four years of manufacture but warns against filling in the intervals between dated books with undated books; BMC XI, 320, 332.
130. BMC XI, 324.
131. Ibid.
132. For the printing types, see the individual Rood editions and the overview of types (BMC XI, 236-43, 386-90).
133. Ibid., 323.
134. Ibid., 243 and 15 respectively.
135. Ibid., 320–321, at 320.
136. Caxton seems to have printed nothing between the *Royal Book* (STC 21429), probably early in 1486, and the *Book of Good Maners* (STC 15394, so called from the introduction to the *tabula*), dated May 11, 1487. He commissioned two Sarum service books in Paris on December 4, 1487 and August 14, 1488 and started printing again in the spring of 1489 as the only printer left in England (ibid., 333). The year 1486 is when the London shop of de Machlinia closed, as well as the enterprises of the St. Albans Printer (ibid., 16-19) and perhaps also Rood.
137. BMC XI, 14, n. 4, citing Macray, *Register*, 10, recording a tenement "in quo Dedyck Teutonicus nuper inhabitavit"[in which Dedyck the German recently lived]. The assumption is that the person in question was the same as "Dyryke Dowcheman" responsible for mending and gilding the Oxford mace (see note 88 above) and that both are Theodoric. For "Dyryke Dowcheman" paying rent to Magdalen College for accommodation in 1480 in the part of Oxford "within the gate on the north side" and "Dyryk Rode" paying Magdalen rent in 1482 for a tenement "within the east gate," see H. E. Salter, ed., *A Cartulary of the Hospital of St. John Baptist*, 3 vols., Oxford Historical Society 66, 68, 69 (Oxford: Clarendon Press for the Oxford Historical Society, 1914–1917), I:271–272, 275. See Davis, *William Waynflete*, 86, n. 51. John Cornish and Thomas Uffington (see above) also rented property from Magdalen; Salter, *Cartulary*, 277. For a concise synthesis of the basic facts, with a plan of Oxford locations, see BMC XI, 13–15.
138. For a succinct account of the following details, see BMC XI, 15 (nn. 1–3 for detailed references). My account here is dependent on Ernst Voulliéme, *Der Buchdruck Kölns bis zum Ende des Fünfzehnten Jahrhunderts* (Bonn, Germany: Nachdruck der Ausgabe, 1903, repr. Düsseldorf, Germany: Droste Verlag, 1978), LXII–LXIV, "Theodoricus (Diederich Molner) und Konrad Welker von Boppard, Arnold Therhoernens Nachfolge." Voulliéme notes that nothing more is heard of ther Hoernen after January 2, 1482; ibid., CII, no. 582, within a list of editions CI–CIII. However, he does not positively cite 1482/1483 as his year of death; certainly he was dead

"spätestens Anfang 1484" [at the latest by the beginning of 1484]; ibid., LXII.
139. BMC XI, 52; n. 4 cites S. Corsten, *Die Anfänge des Kölner Buchdrucks* (Cologne, Germany: Greven, 1955), 339; ibid., 338, fig. 6, for ther Hoernen's type.
140. Compare the wording of Rood's first attested Oxford edition, the Alexander, printed "per me Theodericum rood de Colonia." The book in question is Versor, *Quaestiones*; see M50238 in the Datenbank Gesamtkatalog der Wiegendrucke [Union Catalogue of Incunabula Database] at http: www.gesamtkatalogderwiegendrucke.de/docs/VERSJOH.htm#M50238, with a link to a digitized version in the Darmstadt Universitäts- und Landesbibliothek. Here Image 0052 has a colophon (Book 2, fol. xxvr that concludes: "Anno incarnacionis do*min*ice .M.cccc.lxxv. in vigilia sancti Andree apostoli per Theodoricum impressorem Colonie infra sedecim domus"; http://tudigit.ulb.tu-darmstadt.de/show/inc-iii-93/0052?sid 629f41577996e52ede11e8204cd5543a.
141. Voulliéme, *Buchdruck Kölns*, uses the term "Typis Theodorici" but is cautious about ascribing the works so listed to Theodoric or Welker. See ibid., CXXIX ("XXII. Theodoricus," "XXIII. Konrad Welker von Boppard," and "XXII. und XXIII. Typis Theodorici"). BMC XI, 15, is less hesitant: "Theodoricus (Theodericus, Diedrich) Molner continued printing until at least 1488 in association with Konrad Welker von Boppard, who from 1485 was his mother Gertrude's third husband." But see note 143 below. Rood continues to appear in the records until 1495, always in relation to debts incurred; Voulliéme, *Buchdruck Kölns*, LXIV.
142. Rood might mean "rude," "red," or "rood" (cross); Hellinga, *William Caxton*, 79. Of these, the latter seems most likely. William Roberts remarked long ago on "the extraordinary variety of crosses to be found on Printers' Marks used chiefly by the Italian printers"; William Roberts, *Printers' Marks: A Chapter in the History of Typography* (London: George Bell & Sons, 1893), 24, and 25 with a diagram of thirty crosses. Arnold ther Hoernen was the first Cologne printer to adopt a printer's mark; for the mark, which also incorporates crosses, see the colophon dated Cologne May 31, 1477 illustrated in ibid., 157 and the description of the mark, ibid., 159. Duff sits on the fence as to whether Rood and Molner are the same man; Duff, *English Provincial Printers*, 19–20.
143. The editions ascribed to "Theodoricus Molner" in the Datenbank Gesamtkatalog der Wiegendrucke are 08533 (with Johannes Bel and Johann Koelhoff), M16770, M16780, M16779, M3235410, M32355, M32356, M50226, M50238, M50257, and M50264. Apart from the Aristotle volume dated November 29, 1485 (M50238), the Datenbank Gesamtkatalog der Wiegendrucke dates them "c. 1484/5" (08533), or 1485 or 1486. All are commentaries on Aristotle or books on logic. Editions 05307, 05308, 10682, M32354, and M32356 might be Konrad Welker or

Molner and are dated June 5, 1484 (05308) or earlier (05307), "c. 1484/8" (10682), and "c. 1486" (M32354 and M32356). The previous edition of the *Breviarium* (05307, 05308) was printed by Arnold ther Hoernen on May 19, 1481 (05306).

144. See note 93 above.
145. BMC XI, 244.
146. Caxton's first edition of the *Festial* (STC 17957) is largely in quires of 8 ($a-n^8$, $o-p^6$); his second edition (STC 17959) is also largely 8s ($a-p^8$, q^2), followed by a quire of 8 and one of 6 (R^8, s^6) to include three new sermons and a treatise *Hamus caritatis*; Powell, *Three Sermons for Nova Festa*.
147. See, e.g., in Figs. 2 and 3, the poor formation of <u> and <s> (similar to <n> and <a>) in *Reus* and *iudeus* (sig. g2rb) and *habens* (sig. g2va), and of <s> and <t> in *tribus* and *vestrum* (sig. g2va). See also the errors *chaunce* for *chaunge* (sig. g2rb) and *comedie* for *comedi* (sig. g2va).
148. BMC XI, 15.
149. Bradshaw, *Collected Papers*, 86.
150. A possible explanation is that the set of woodcuts for the posited *Legenda aurea* was never completed after it became clear that the project had been shelved. For the disposition of the woodcuts, see note 90 above.
151. As observed in BMC XI, 179. The woodcut is the St. Andrew (STC 17958, sig. h1ra), but it is larger and reversed in Caxton's 1491 edition (STC 17959, sig. f6va).
152. Duff/Hellinga, 210.
153. For the Prologue, see Powell, *John Mirk's Festial*, I:3. Only Rood's edition has the Prologue, not Caxton's earlier edition.
154. See Appendix 2 below for a comparison of the 1483, 1486, and 1491 editions, esp. Appendix 2.C for a lacuna ("that ... holy") in "Rood" 1486 which is replicated in Caxton 1491. STC wrongly records STC 17959 (Caxton 1491) as "Reprints text of 17957" (i.e., Caxton 1486). There is no comment on the text in the Incunabula Short Title Catalogue No. im00621000 at http://istc.bl.uk/search/search.html?operation=recor&rsid=269212&q=2.
155. Davis, *William Waynflete*, 125–126.
156. Susan Powell, "The Secular Clergy," in *A Companion to the Early Printed Book in Britain 1476–1558*, ed. Vincent Gillespie and Susan Powell (Cambridge, UK: Brewer, 2014), 150–175 (155–156, 171–172).
157. John 6:59.
158. Matthew 5:21.
159. Psalms 13:3, 139:4.
160. Cf. Ecclesiasticus 12:3.
161. Proverbs 28:13.

WORKS CITED

Manuscripts, Early Printed Editions, and Archival Sources

Aegidius de Columna. *Tractatus... de peccato originali.* STC 158. Oxford: Printer of Rufinus, March 14, 1479.

Alexander de Alexandria (formerly Alexander of Hales). *Expositio super libros Aristotelis: de anima.* STC 314. Oxford: Rood, October 11, 1481.

Alexander de Villa Dei. *Doctrinale puerorum.* STC 315. Oxford: Rood, 1481–1483.

[Anwykyll], John. *Compendium totius grammaticae.* STC 695, 696. Oxford: Rood, not after 1483.

Aristotle. *Ethica Nichomachea.* STC 752. Oxford: Printer of Rufinus, 1479.

Augustinus. *Sermo de misericordia.* With Richard Rolle, *Explanationes in Iob.* STC 21261. Oxford: Rood, 1481–1483.

———. *Excitacio fidelis ad elemosinam faciendam.* STC 922. Oxford: Rood, 1481–1483.

Book of Good Maners. STC 15394. Westminster: Caxton, May 11, 1487.

Cicero. *Oratio pro T. Milone.* STC 5312. Oxford: Rood, 1481–1483.

Lathbury, John. *Liber moralium super trenis iheremie prophete.* STC 15297. Oxford: Rood, July 31, 1482.

Lyndewode, William. *Constituciones prouinciales.* STC 17102. Oxford: Rood, ca. 1483–1484.

———. British Library IC.55321. STC 17107. Paris: Andreas Bocard, 1501.

———. STC 17109. Paris: Wolfgang Hopyl for William Bretton, 1505.

———. STC 17111. Antwerp: Christoffel van Ruremund, 1525.

Mirk, John. *The Festial.* London, British Library, MS Cotton Claudius A.II.

———. Southwell Minster Library, MS 7.

———. STC 17957. Westminster: Caxton, 1483.

———. STC 17958. Oxford: Printer of Mirk, October 14, 1486.

———. STC 17959. Westminster: Caxton, 1491.

Phalaris. *Epistolae.* STC 19827. Oxford: Rood, 1481(–1485).

Rolle, Richard. *Explanationes in Iob.* With Augustine, *Sermo de misericordia.* STC 21261. Oxford: Rood, 1481–1483.

The Royal Book. STC 21429. Westminster: Caxton, 1485–1486.

The Royal Grammar Compiled Formerly by William Lilly. London: Printed for Awnsham Churchill, 1688.

(?)Stanbridge, John. *Longe Parvula.* STC 23163.13. Oxford: Rood, 1481–1483.

[Swineshede, Richard]. Logica. STC 16693. Oxford: Rood, 1481–1483.

Terence, *Vulgaria Terentii.* STC 23904. Oxford: Rood, not after 1483.

Tyrannius Rufinus. *Expositio sancti Ieronomi in simbolum apostolorum ad papam Laurentium.* STC 21443. Oxford: Printer of Rufinus, December 17, 14[7]8.

Versor, Johannes. *Quaestiones super libros Aristotelis De generatione et corruptione*. GW M50238. Cologne: Theodoricus Molner, November 29, 1485.

Primary Sources

Carley, James P., ed. *The Libraries of King Henry VIII*. Corpus of British Medieval Library Catalogues 7. London: British Library in association with British Academy, 2000.

Catto, Jeremy, and Ralph Evans, eds. *The History of the University of Oxford. Volume II: Late Medieval Oxford*. Oxford: Clarendon Press, 1992.

Clark, James G. "Lathbury (Lathbery), John (d. 1362), Franciscan Friar and Theologian." In *Oxford Dictionary of National Biography*. Oxford: Oxford University Press, 2004–2014.

Coates, Alan, Kristian Jensen, Cristina Dondi, Bettina Wagner, and Helen Dixon, eds. *A Catalogue of Books Printed in the Fifteenth Century Now in the Bodleian Library*. 6 vols. Oxford: Oxford University Press, 2005.

Cook, Christopher D. *Incunabula in the Westminster Abbey and Westminster School Libraries*. London: Bibliographical Society, 2013.

Datenbank Gesamtkatalog der Wiegendrucke [Union Catalogue of Incunabula Database].Berlin: Staatsbibliothek zu Berlin, Stiftung Preussischer Kulturbesitz. English version at http://www.gesamtkatalogderwiegendrucke.de/GWEN.xhtml.

Duff, E. Gordon. *Printing in England in the Fifteenth Century: E. Gordon Duff's Bibliography with Supplementary Descriptions, Chronologies and a Census of Copies by Lotte Hellinga*. London: Bibliographical Society and British Library, 2009.

Emden, A. B. *A Biographical Register of the University of Oxford to A.D. 1500*. 3 vols. Oxford: Clarendon Press, 1957–1959.

Gadd, Ian, Simon Eliot, and W. Roger Louis, eds. *The History of Oxford University Press*. Volume 1: Beginnings to 1780. Oxford: Oxford University Press, 2013.

Gillespie, Vincent, ed. *Syon Abbey*, with A. I. Doyle, ed., *The Libraries of the Carthusians*. Corpus of British Medieval Library Catalogues 9. London: British Library in association with British Academy, 2001.

Hellinga, Lotte, ed. *Catalogue of Books Printed in the XVth Century Now in the British Library. Part XI: England*. 't Goy-Houten, The Netherlands: Hes & De Graaf, 2007.

——— and J. B. Trapp, eds. *The Cambridge History of the Book in Britain. Volume III: 1400–1557*. Cambridge, UK: Cambridge University Press, 1999.

Hodnett, E. *English Woodcuts, 1480–1535*. Bibliographical Society Illustrated Monographs 22a. London: Bibliographical Society, 1973.

Incunabula Short Title Catalogue. British Library. http://www.bl.uk/catalogues/istc/.

Macray, W. D. *A Register of the Members of St. Mary Magdalen College, Oxford: From the Foundation of the College: New Series.* 8 vols. London: Henry Frowde, 1894–1915.

Madan, Falconer. *The Early Oxford Press: A Bibliography of Printing and Publishing at Oxford "1468"–1640.* Oxford Historical Society 29. Oxford: Clarendon Press, 1895.

———, ed. "The Daily Ledger of John Dorne 1520." In *Collectanea First Series*, edited by C. R. L. Fletcher. Oxford Historical Society Publications 5. Oxford: Oxford Historical Society, 1885.

Oxford Dictionary of National Biography. Oxford: Oxford University Press, 2004–2014.

Pollard, A. W., and G. R. Redgrave. *A Short-Title Catalogue of Books Printed in England, Scotland & Ireland and of English Books Printed Abroad 1475–1640.* 2nd ed. edited by W. A. Jackson, F. S. Ferguson, and Katharine F. Pantzer. 3 vols. London: Bibliographical Society, 1976–1991.

Powell, Susan. "A Critical Edition of the Temporale Sermons of MSS Harley 2247 and Royal 18 B XXV." 3 vols. Unpublished Ph.D. thesis, University of London, 1980.

———. "The Secular Clergy." In *A Companion to the Early Printed Book in Britain 1476–1558*, edited by Vincent Gillespie and Susan Powell, 150–175. Cambridge, UK: Brewer, 2014.

———, ed. *The Advent and Nativity Sermons from a Fifteenth-Century Revision of John Mirk's Festial: Edited from B.L. MSS Harley 2247, Royal 18 B XXV and Gloucester Cathedral Library 22.* Middle English Texts 13. Heidelberg, Germany: Carl Winter, 1981.

———, ed. *Three Sermons for Nova Festa, together with the Hamus Caritatis.* Middle English Texts 37. Heidelberg, Germany: Universitätsverlag Winter, 2007.

———, ed. *John Mirk's Festial Edited from British Library MS Cotton Claudius A.II.* 2 vols. EETS OS 334, 335. Oxford: Oxford University Press for the Early English Text Society, 2009, 2011.

Rhodes, D. E. *A Catalogue of Incunabula in All the Libraries of Oxford University outside the Bodleian.* Oxford: Clarendon Press, 1983.

Roberts, William. *Printers' Marks: A Chapter in the History of Typography.* London: George Bell & Sons, 1893.

Salter, H. E., ed. *A Cartulary of the Hospital of St John Baptist.* 3 vols. Oxford Historical Society 66, 68, 69. Oxford: Clarendon Press for the Oxford Historical Society, 1914–1917.

A Short-Title Catalogue of Books Printed in England, Scotland, Ireland, Wales and British America and of English Books Printed in Other Countries, 1641–1700, compiled by D. Wing. 2nd ed. newly revised and enlarged. New York: Modern Language Association of America, 1994.

Secondary Sources

Ashworth, E. J. "Text-Books: A Case Study—Logic." In *The Cambridge History of the Book in Britain. Volume III: 1400–1557*, edited by Lotte Hellinga and J. B. Trapp, 380–386. Cambridge, UK: Cambridge University Press, 1999.

Barker, Nicolas. *The Oxford University Press and the Spread of Learning: An Illustrated History 1478–1978*. Oxford: Clarendon Press, 1978.

Blake, N. F. *William Caxton and English Literary Culture*. London and Rio Grande, OH: Hambledon, 1991.

Bradshaw, Henry. *Collected Papers of Henry Bradshaw, Late University Librarian*, edited by G. W. Prothero. Cambridge, UK: Cambridge University Press, 1889.

Carter, Harry. *A History of the Oxford University Press. Volume 1: To the Year 1780, with an Appendix Listing the Titles of Books Printed There 1690–1780*. Oxford: Clarendon Press, 1975.

Cobban, Alan B. *English University Life in the Middle Ages*. London: UCL Press, 1999.

———. "Colleges and Halls 1380–1500." In *The History of the University of Oxford*, edited by Jeremy Catto and Ralph Evans, 581–633. Oxford: Clarendon Press, 1992.

Corsten, S. *Die Anfänge des Kölner Buchdrucks*. Cologne, Germany: Greven, 1955.

Davis, Virginia. *William Waynflete, Bishop and Educationalist*. Woodbridge, UK: Boydell, 1993.

———. "Waynflete [Wainfleet, Patten], William (c. 1400–1486), Bishop of Winchester and Founder of Magdalen College, Oxford." In *Oxford Dictionary of National Biography*. Oxford: Oxford University Press, 2004–2014.

de la Mare, A. C., and Lotte Hellinga. "The First Book Printed in Oxford: The *Expositio Symboli* of Rufinus." *Transactions of the Cambridge Bibliographical Society* 7 (1978): 184–244.

Duff, E. Gordon. *The English Provincial Printers, Stationers and Bookbinders to 1557*. Cambridge, UK: Cambridge University Press, 1912.

Ferdinand, C. Y. "Library Administration (c. 1475 to 1640)." In *The Cambridge History of Libraries in Britain and Ireland. Volume I: To 1640*, edited by Elisabeth Leedham-Green and Teresa Webber, 565–591. Cambridge, UK: Cambridge University Press, 2006.

Ford, Margaret Lane. "Importation of Printed Books into England and Scotland." In *The Cambridge History of the Book in Britain. Volume III: 1400–1557*, edited by Lotte Hellinga and J. B. Trapp, 179–201. Cambridge, UK: Cambridge University Press, 1999.

Hayes, Rosemary C. E. "Goldwell, James (d. 1499), Bishop of Norwich."

In *Oxford Dictionary of National Biography* (Oxford: Oxford University Press, 2004–2014.
Hellinga, Lotte. *William Caxton and Early Printing in England*. London: British Library, 2010.
Helmholz, R. H. "Lyndwood, William (c. 1375–1446), Administrator, Ecclesiastical Lawyer, and Bishop of St. David's." In *Oxford Dictionary of National Biography*. Oxford: Oxford University Press, 2004–2014.
Jack, Sybil M. "Wolsey, Thomas (1470/71–1530), Royal Minister, Archbishop of York, and Cardinal." In *Oxford Dictionary of National Biography*. Oxford: Oxford University Press, 2004–2014.
Jensen, Kristian. "Text-Books in the Universities: The Evidence from the Books." In *The Cambridge History of the Book in Britain. Volume III: 1400–1557*, edited by Lotte Hellinga and J. B. Trapp, 354–379. Cambridge, UK: Cambridge University Press, 1999.
———. "Printing at Oxford in Its European Context 1478–1584." In *The History of Oxford University Press: Volume 1: Beginnings to 1780*, edited by Ian Gadd, Simon Eliot, and W. Roger Louis, 31–48. Oxford: Oxford University Press, 2013.
Ker, N. R. "The Vellum Copies of the Oxford Edition (1482) of Lathbury on Lamentations." *Bodleian Library Record* 2 (1947): 185–188.
Leedham-Green, Elisabeth. "University Libraries and Book-Sellers." In *The Cambridge History of the Book in Britain. Volume III: 1400–1557*, edited by Lotte Hellinga and J. B. Trapp, 316–353. Cambridge, UK: Cambridge University Press, 1999.
Madan, Falconer. *The Early Oxford Press: A Bibliography of Printing and Publishing at Oxford "1468"–1640*. Oxford Historical Society 29. Oxford: Clarendon Press, 1895.
Needham, Paul. "Continental Printed Books Sold in Oxford, c. 1480–3: Two Trade Records." In *Incunabula: Studies in Fifteenth-Century Printed Books Presented to Lotte Hellinga*, edited by M. Davies, 243–270. London: British Library, 1999.
———. "Ulrich Zel's Early Quartos Revisited." In *Incunabula on the Move: The Production, Circulation and Collection of Early Printed Books*, edited by Ed Potten and Satoko Tokunaga, 9–57. Transactions of the Cambridge Bibliographical Society 15:1 (2012). Cambridge, UK: Cambridge Bibliographical Society, 2014.
Orme, Nicholas. "An Early-Tudor Oxford Schoolbook." *Renaissance Quarterly* 34 (1981): 11–39.
———. "John Holt (d. 1504), Tudor Schoolmaster and Grammarian." *The Library* 6th ser., 18 (1996): 283–305.
———. "Schools and School-Books." In *The Cambridge History of the Book in Britain. Volume III: 1400–1557*, edited by Lotte Hellinga and J. B.

Trapp, 449–469. Cambridge, UK: Cambridge University Press, 1999.
———. *Education in Early Tudor England: Magdalen College Oxford and Its School, 1480–1540.* Magdalen College Occasional Papers 4. Oxford: Magdalen College, 1998.
———. "The Magdalen Diaspora." In *Education in Early Tudor England: Magdalen College Oxford and Its School, 1480–1540.* Magdalen College Occasional Papers 4. Oxford: Magdalen College, 1998.
———. "Anwykyll, John (d. 1487), Schoolmaster and Grammarian." In *Oxford Dictionary of National Biography.* Oxford: Oxford University Press, 2004–2014.
———. "Stanbridge, John (1463–1510), Schoolmaster and Grammarian." In *Oxford Dictionary of National Biography.* Oxford: Oxford University Press, 2004–2014.
———. "Holt, John (d. 1504), Schoolmaster and Grammarian." In *Oxford Dictionary of National Biography.* Oxford: Oxford University Press, 2004–2014.
Parkes, M. B. "The Provision of Books." In *The History of the University of Oxford. Volume II: Late Medieval Oxford,* edited by J. I. Catto and Ralph Evans, 407–483. Oxford: Clarendon Press, 1992.
Smith, R. D. "Lily, William (1468?–1522/23, Grammarian and Schoolmaster." In *Oxford Dictionary of National Biography.* Oxford: Oxford University Press, 2004–2014.
Trapp, J. B. "The Humanist Book." In *The Cambridge History of the Book in Britain.* Volume III: 1400–1557, edited by Lotte Hellinga and J. B. Trapp, 285–316. Cambridge, UK: Cambridge University Press, 1999.
———. "Carmeliano [Carmigliano], Pietro [Petrus Carmelianus, Peter Carmelian] (c. 1451–1527), Poet and Royal Official." In *Oxford Dictionary of National Biography.* Oxford: Oxford University Press, 2004–2014.
Voulliéme, Ernst. *Der Buchdruck Kölns bis zum Ende des Fünfzehnten Jahrhunderts.* Bonn, Germany: Nachdruck der Ausgabe, 1903; repr. Düsseldorf, Germany: Droste Verlag, 1978.
Wakelin, Daniel. "Humanism and Printing." In *A Companion to the Early Printed Book in Britain 1476–1558,* edited by Vincent Gillespie and Susan Powell, 227–247. Cambridge, UK: Brewer, 2014.

The Language of Identity: Henri Estienne's Anti-Italian Polemics

NICHOLAS SHANGLER

France and Italy experienced a mutual cultural and linguistic intertwining beginning in at least the early medieval period. Paul Meyer shows that in the thirteenth century, the French language enjoyed an elevated status in northern Italy.[1] However, by the turn of the sixteenth century, the situation had changed completely, as the rapid cultural evolution of the Italian Renaissance during the fourteenth and fifteenth centuries had outstripped the pace of progress in France. Royal military campaigns in Italy between 1494 and 1525 left three successive French monarchs—Charles VIII, Louis XII, and François I—impressed by the sophistication of their neighbors.[2] These kings and the noblemen who accompanied them returned to France bearing not only the memories and impressions they had forged during their visits but also books, works of art, and other artifacts. Italian artists soon followed, many through the already Italianate city of Lyon. Leonardo da Vinci and Benvenuto Cellini, for instance, were among those who came to live and work in France at the invitation of François I.[3]

The influence of the Italians intensified even further with the marriage of the French prince, the future Henri II, son of François I, to Catherine de Medici in 1533.[4] The ascension of Henri II to the throne in 1547 brought increasing numbers of Italians not only into France but into the fold of the French court.[5] Some of the French began to resent this foreign presence, expressing what we would today identify as nascent nationalistic sentiments. Signs of hostility by the French toward Italians surfaced throughout the Renaissance, increasing in intensity and volume in the later part of the sixteenth century, but are by no means absent even during the medieval period.⁶ Despite the oft-cited desire among the French intellectual class of the Renaissance to travel to Italy, and Rome in particular, as a fundamental part of an erudite education, strong countercurrents lurked close to the surface.⁷ Many courtiers, however, quickly embraced the growing Italianism and affected a language heavily characterized by both Italian words and French words recomposed so as to incorporate fragments of Italian.⁸

A number of prominent voices discouraged their French countrymen from having anything to do with the Italians, urging instead greater respect for French national culture. Among those who began to protest against the intrusion of Italianism in France, particularly with regard to language, a certain Parisian printer, Henri Estienne (1528–1598), distinguished himself by his fervor and for his compelling articulation of the argument in support of the purity of the French language. The son of Robert Estienne (1503–1559), a renowned printer and scholar, Henri Estienne developed from a young age a curiosity and love for languages and books.⁹ However, as a boy, Henri may have acquired other persuasions that would later color his opinion of all things Italian. The Estienne family printing business was originally created by Robert's father, Henri the elder. Robert inherited the business over his two brothers and took it upon himself to complete and to correct, in his eyes, a Latin edition of the New Testament (published in 1523) that his late father had begun. Unfortunately certain passages, written in a style intended to facilitate and render more popular the reading of this text, drew criticism from theologians at the Sorbonne, launching what would become the lifelong persecution of Robert. Each of his several successive editions of the Bible garnered him further censure from the Sorbonne.¹⁰ The constant risk to his life and family took a toll on Robert, which affected his son's perspective on Roman Catholicism and its defenders. As an adult, the Protestant Henri likely held a lasting prejudice that we may see reflected in his anti-Italian views.

Henri Estienne mastered Latin, Greek, and Italian and devoted a significant amount of work to translating, editing, publishing, and collating essential classical texts. Estienne's polemic against the Italianized French employed by French courtiers appears in three separate but related works. Together they form a sort of trilogy, each attacking various aspects of the central problem. The first, *Traicté de la conformité du language françois avec le grec* (1565),¹¹ denies the superiority of Italian by belittling its roots. Estienne claims in his preface that the Italian language owes a far greater debt to French than does French to any Italian heritage. He supports his argument by advancing the idea that French descends directly from Greek and has more in common with Greek than any other language. Since everyone universally recognizes Greek as the greatest language in history, French must therefore be the second greatest. Italian, on the other hand, is but the paltry progeny of Latin. Estienne decries the linguistic inventions of the Italianizing courtiers and instead longingly praises the true French language, "pur et simple, n'ayant rien de fard, ni d'affectation: lequel monsieur le courtisan n'a point encore changé à sa guise, & qui ne tient rien d'emprunt des langues modernes"[12] [pure and simple, showing nothing of varnish, nor affectation: which sir courtier has not yet changed according to his whim, and which borrows nothing from modern languages].

Evidence from two editions of the *Traicté*, the 1565 first printing and a 1569 second edition,[13] demonstrates both Henri Estienne's devotion to his late father and the positive reception of the work. The title page of the 1565 edition, printed by the Estienne workshop in Geneva, bears the notice "En ce Traicté sont descouverts quelques secrets tant de la langue Grecque que de la Françoise: duquel l'auteur & imprimeur est Henri Estiene, fils de feu Robert Estiene" [In this Treatise are revealed several secrets as much of the Greek language as of French: of which the author and printer is Henri Estienne, son of the late Robert Estienne]. The title page of the 1569 edition does not include the mention of Robert Estienne and lists Henri as merely the author. This second edition was published in Paris by Jaques [sic] du Puis with only minor changes to the content, mostly additional examples of French words allegedly derived from Greek.

Henri Estienne continues the attack where he left off with the 1578 publication of his *Deux dialogues du nouveau langage françois italianizé, & autrement desguizé, principalement entre les courtisans de ce temps*[14] [Two dialogues about the new French language italianized, and in other ways disguised, mainly among the courtiers of our time]. The book opens with a series of poems that set the stage for the debate to follow. In the first of the two dialogues, Estienne posits an exchange between a character named Celtophile ("lover of France"), whose role is to prosecute the case against Italianized French, and Philausone ("lover of Italy"), who frequents the court and is charged with defending the practice of mixing French with Italian. Naturally the jury is rigged in favor of Celtophile, with the accused found guilty even before the opening gavel. The two interlocutors find themselves at an impasse at the close of the first dialogue. They agree to reconvene the next morning to continue their discussion and to go together to consult a third party, Philalethe ("lover of Truth"). Over the course of the second dialogue, the topic of their argument gradually progresses to whether French or Italian, considered separately rather than in their blended form, is the greater language. Once Philalethe joins the conversation, he promptly dismantles all of Philausone's reasoning, according an unconditional victory to the French language. Still, Philausone refuses to concede. The book ends with Philalethe promising to demonstrate further the dominance of the French language at a later time.

Keeping Philalethe's promise, the following year, 1579, Henri Estienne published *De la précellence du langage françois*,[15] which he dedicates in the preface to King Henri III "pour m'aquitter de la promesse faicte dernierement à votre Majesté"[16] [to acquit myself of the promise recently made to your Majesty]. Though this work stands as a sequel to the *Deux dialogues*, Philalethe disappears, and Estienne offers the book in his own voice using his real name, opening with a poem entitled "H. Estiene aux François"[17] [H. Estienne to the French people]. Here he broadens the scope of his attacks, no longer limiting himself to rebutting the use of Italianisms at court. Alluding to his own *Traicté*, he reiterates his claims of the self-sufficiency of French with regard to other languages, particularly modern European languages. That said, his main target is still evident:

> Il faut aussi que je responde pourquoy sçachant que nostre langage avoit deux competiteurs, l'Italien et l'Espagnol, je n'ay combatu que l'un, asçavoir l'Italien. Je di donc que je n'ay voulu m'attacher qu'à luy: pource que je m'asseurois que luy ayant faict quitter la place, je pouvois aisément venir à bout de l'Espagnol: veu que je luy estime estre beaucoup inférieur pour les raisons que je deduiray ailleurs.[18]

> [I must also respond to why, knowing that our language had two competitors, Italian and Spanish, I dealt with only one, namely Italian. I say therefore that I wanted to stick to only that one; because I assured myself that having vanquished that one, I could easily dispense with Spanish: seeing that I esteem it to be far inferior for reasons that I will deduce elsewhere.]

He proceeds to define five essential points of comparison—*la gravité, la gentillesse, la bonne grâce, la brièveté*, and *la richesse*—between French and Italian, the relative quantities of which heavily favor the former. Most of Estienne's logic is unsound. He persists in relying upon his fallacious etymologies relating French to Greek, which he first sketched out in the *Traicté*, and then states that any words that seem equivalent between French and Italian are the result of Italian borrowing rather than a common Latin heritage. For example, the Italian *gamba* derives from the French *jambe*, and *caccia* from *chasse*.[19] David Cowling argues that:

> Estienne's vernacular works on borrowing gain considerable internal cohesion, both inter- and intra-textually, through

their deployment of a set of metaphors that are consistently (and, indeed, insistently) used in order to characterize both the process of linguistic borrowing and those who practise it in ways that carefully appeal to the readership's "common ground."[20]

Cowling traces the types of metaphors that Estienne uses and then maps them to the language that scholars today employ when speaking about linguistic purity and loanwords. He finds striking resonances between "much of the persuasive and polemical arsenal marshalled by twentieth-century purists"[21] and that articulated by Estienne.

Estienne clearly harbored grievances against Italy that went beyond the philological. I argue that his attacks on the Italian language and the hybrid Franco-Italian spoken by courtiers were largely motivated by political concerns that raised the critical issue of the connection between language and identity. Estienne loved his native France, declaring in the opening pages of the *Deux dialogues* that "l'honneur et le bien / De mon pays m'est cher comme le mien"[22] [the honor and good / Of my country is [*sic*] as dear to me as my own]. In the *Précellence*, he links his feelings for his country's glory with his projects in support of the French language:

> il luy [Henri III] plaira considerer de quelle importance est ceste entreprise pour l'honneur de son royaume: comme aussi je la puis asseurer qu'elle est procedée d'un cueur qui s'est tousjours monstré zelateur et comme jaloux de l'honneur de sa nation.[23]

> [it will please him [Henri III] to consider the importance of this undertaking for the honor of his kingdom: as I can also assure him that it is carried out by a heart that has always shown itself to be zealous and nearly jealous of the honor of his nation.]

The depth and intensity of his jingoistic sentiments give Estienne a heightened sensitivity to events that in his view negatively affected France.

The anti-Italian sentiment expressed by Estienne and his contemporaries, especially in the second half of the sixteenth century, was in part in reaction to Catherine de Medici and the power exerted by her and her entourage. A large population of Italians accompanied Catherine de Medici into France when she married Henri, the future king, in 1533. Common belief at the time held that the Florentine queen aided her countrymen, once in

France, to profit from favors that allowed them to accumulate substantial political and economic power.[24] Certainly, Estienne laments the physical presence of Italians in France as much as their language's inroads:

> Pourtant soudain vos mots ont mis en jeu,
> Les trouvants ja tous portez sur le lieu,
> N'estant endroit aujourd'huy en la France,
> Où n'ayez faict ou faciez demeurance;
> Mais en la cour, plus qu'en tous autres lieux,
> On a esté de vos mots curieux,
> Car elle est tant de vous Messieurs remplie
> Que c'est desja la petite Italie.[25]

> [However, suddenly, they put your words in play,
> Finding them already all brought to this place,
> There not being anywhere in France today,
> Where you have not made or are not making yourselves at home;
> But at court, more than in any other place,
> One has been curious about your words,
> For it is so full of your kind, sirs,
> That it is already Little Italy.]

He fears that it is too late and that the Italians already wield significant influence everywhere, though their language is still popular primarily at court. According to the testimony of Innocent Gentillet in his 1576 *Anti-Machiavel*, France has suffered a "tyrannie ... pendant quinze ans et plus"[26] [a tyranny ... for more than fifteen years"] under "ceux de la nation de Machiavel (qui tiennent les principaux estats au gouvernement de France)"[27] [those of Machiavelli's nation (who hold the principal roles in the government of France)]. A dangerous alienation, caused by the concentration of influence in the hands of foreigners at the highest levels, has led to the French becoming "étrangers en leur propre pays" [strangers in their own country]. France itself has been "contaminee et souillee de mespris de Dieu, de perfidie, de sodomie, tyrannie, cruauté, pilleries, usures estranges et autres vices detestables, que ces estrangers y sement"[28] [contaminated and sullied by ungodliness, perfidy, sodomy, tyranny, cruelty, pillaging, foreign usury, and other detestable vices, which these foreigners sow there]. Gentillet's mention of "usures" is especially meaningful. Henry Heller details at length how Italian bankers, including Catherine de Medici's own financier, Scipion Sardini, amassed immense wealth.[29] These pecuniary complaints certainly inspired in part the sentiments of anti-Italian partisans.

Yet we cannot place the full burden of blame on the shoulders of the de Medicis. Literary evidence points to French stereotyping of Italians as perverse, sinful, and covetous beginning before the era of Catherine's influence in state affairs, which developed only after the death of her husband, King Henri II, in 1559. Marguerite de Navarre, sister of King François I, includes a scene in her *Heptaméron* (1558) that attests to the negative light in which Italians were popularly cast. Following the recounting of Tale 51, a conversation about Italians ensues:

> "J'avois bien ouy dire," ce dist Longarine, "que les Italiens estoient subjects à trois vices par excellence; mais je n'eusse pas pensé que la vengeance et cruaulté fut allée si avant, que, pour une si petite occasion, elle eut donné si cruelle mort." Saffredent, en riant, luy dist: "Longarine, vous nous avez bien dict l'un des trois vices; mais il faut sçavoir qui sont les deux autres?"—"Si vous ne les sçachiez," ce dist-elle, "je les vous apprendrois, mais je suys seure que vous les sçavez tous."—"Par ces parolles," dist Saffredent, "vous m'estimez bien vitieux?"... "Ne vous esbahissez," dist Simontault, "de ceste cruaulté; car ceulx qui ont passé par Italie en ont vu de si très incroyables, que ceste-cy n'est au pris qu'un petit pecadille."—"Vrayement," dist Geburon, "quant Rivolte fut prins des François, il y avoit ung cappitaine Italien, que l'on estimoit gentil compaignon, lequel, voiant mort ung qui ne luy estoit ennemy que de tenir sa part contraire de Guelfe à Gibelin, luy arracha le cueur du ventre, et, le rotissant sur les charbons à grand haste, le mangea, et, respondant à quelques ungs... que jamais n'avoit mengé si savoureux ne si plaisant morceau que de cestuy-là; et, non content de ce bel acte, tua la femme du mort, et, en arrachant de son ventre le fruict dont elle estoit grosse, le froissa contre les murailles; et emplist d'avoyne les deux corps du mary et de la femme, dedans lesquelz il feit manger ses chevaulx."... "Je croy que vous ne debvez poinct," respondit Simontault, "doubter que la nature de l'Italien est d'aymer plus que nature ce qui est créé seulement pour le service d'icelle."—"C'est bien pis," dist Hircan, "car ilz font leur Dieu des choses qui sont contre nature."[30]

> ["I had heard," said Longarine, "that the Italians are subject to three vices above all others, but I wouldn't have thought that cruelty and the spirit of revenge would have gone so far

as to put someone to death in such a cruel manner for such a trivial reason." Saffredent said to her, laughing: "Longarine, you've mentioned one of the three vices. We must be told about the other two." "If you don't know what they are, then I'll tell you. But I'm sure that you do know what they are, all of them." "Do you mean by that," said Saffredent, "that you think I'm full of vice myself?" "There's no need to be surprised by this act of cruelty we've just heard of," said Simontaut. "People who've travelled through Italy have seen the most incredible things, things which make this a mere peccadillo by comparison." "Yes, indeed," said Geburon. "When Rivolta was taken by the French there was an Italian captain whom everybody regarded as a valiant comrade-at-arms and who came across a man lying dead, a man who was only an enemy in the sense that he had been a Guelph, while the captain was a Ghibelline. He tore the dead man's heart out of his chest, roasted it over a charcoal fire, and ate it. When some people asked what it tasted like, ... he replied that he had never tasted a more delicious or enjoyable morsel. Not content with this fine deed, he killed the dead man's wife, who was pregnant, tore out the fruit of her womb and dashed it against the battlements. He then filled the corpses of both husband and wife with oats and gave them to his horses." ... "One cannot doubt, I think," answered Simontaut, "that it is the nature of Italians to love things created merely for the service of nature more than nature itself." "It's even worse than that," said Hircan, "because they make their God out of things that are against nature."]

Thus, despite what her narrative work owes to Boccaccio's *Decameron*, Marguerite de Navarre's characters describe the Italians as having a treacherous, violent, and unnatural nature.[31] Earlier still, in Bonaventure des Périers' *Nouvelles récréations et joyeux devis*, Tale 88 tells the story, "du temps qu'ilz commencerent à avoir vogue en France"[32] [from the time when [Italians] began to be popular in France], of a crafty Italian charlatan who cheats a simple priest. The priest owns a talented monkey of which he is quite proud, though he bemoans the animal's inability to speak. The Italian "se presente d'une asseurance qui est naturelle à la nation: & va dire à l'Abbé sans oublier les reverances, excellences, & magnificences"[33] [boldly introduced himself, which is typical of that nationality, and said to the abbot, without forgetting the Reverences, Excellencies, and Graces] that he could make the priest's monkey speak. He delivers a long discourse marked by all the artfulness of his brethren:

> L'abbé ouvrit l'oreille à ces raisons Philosophales: & principalement d'autant qu'elles estoyent Italicques. Car les Françoys ont tousjours eu cela de bon, entre autres mauvaises graces de prester plus voulontiers audience & faveur aux estrangers, qu'aux leurs propres.[34]

> [The abbot pricked up his ears at these philosophical reasons and particularly because they were Italic, for the French have always had that fine trait (among other bad qualities) of granting attention and favor more willingly to foreigners than to their own.]

The charlatan's Italian friends rebuke him for the damage he will do to their reputations, until he explains how cleverly he has conceived of his scheme, to pretend to be slowly training the priest's monkey to speak until the priest dies, such that it will never come to light that he is a fraud.

French writers frequently painted Italians as cheats, liars, and masters of artifice, contrasting them with the natural and genuine manner of the Frenchman. Du Bellay, for instance, writes in his "Ode contre les Pétrarquistes," "J'ay oublié l'art de Petrarquizer / Je veulx d'Amour *franchement* deviser / Sans vous flatter, et sans me deguizer"[35] [I have forgotten the art of Petrarchizing / I want to speak frankly of love / Without flattering you, and without disguising myself]. He links "art" to the Italians, and relinquishes it in favor of speaking *franchement*, poetically underscoring the relationship between candor and the French nation. He continues, in the same poem, to distinguish the two countries further on this essential point:

> Noz bons ayeulx, qui cest art demenoient,
> Pour en parler, Pétrarque n'apprenoient,
> Ains franchement leur Dame entretenoient
> Sans fard ou couverture:
> Mais aussi tost qu'Amour s'est faict sçavant,
> Luy, qui estoit François au paravant,
> Est devenu flatteur, et decevant,
> Et de Thusque nature.[36]

> [Our good ancestors, who started this art,
> To speak of it, didn't study Petrarch,

> But rather conversed frankly with their Lady,
> Without artifice or cover;
> But as soon as Love became a savant,
> He, who was previously French,
> Became a flatterer, deceptive,
> And of a Tuscan nature.]

Du Bellay affirms the significant history of the French with his reference to "noz bons ayeulx" [our good ancestors] and urges a return to their principles. We see in this poem a desire to distance the French national traditions from those of Italy. It and other works like it manifest the French struggle for self-definition by opposition to the allegedly superior Italian culture.

Not unrelated to the yearning for cultural recognition, another fear likely motivated the efforts to break the ties with Italy and to dispel any lingering fascination with its culture. The notion of Italian decadence, commonly claimed to be rendered all the more evident by the continued pretensions of the Italian people to a bygone glory, loomed large in the French imagination. Innocent Gentillet cites a Scottish poet, George Buchanan (1505–1582), to highlight the moral past/present disparity that one finds in Italy:

> Jadis Rome par fer et par navalle guerre
> Mit dessous son pouvoir les ondes et la terre.
> Depuis par pieté par science et bonté,
> Les evesques romains ont le ciel surmonté.
> Ne restoit à gaigner aux papes successeurs
> Qu'enfer, qu'ils ont conquis, et en sont possesseurs.[37]
>
> [In times past, Rome, by sword and naval war
> Exerted its power over the seas and the land.
> Since then, through piety, learning, and goodness,
> The Roman bishops attained the heavens,
> Leaving nothing for subsequent popes to capture
> But hell, which they conquered and now possess.]

Gentillet presents a timeline that implicitly evokes another one, that of France present/future. Estienne and his contemporaries may have feared that just as Rome had fallen far to attain the present state of Italy, France would follow an equivalent trajectory if left unchecked.

These issues form the background against which Estienne formulated his anti-Italian invective. The issues of politics, language, and identity remained tightly intertwined. By the time Estienne began composing the *Traicté*, several authors' works manifested an evolving understanding of what language was, how it worked, what it was capable of, and the high stakes involved for whoever could both use language effectively and control "good usage."[38]

On the most fundamental level, my study of Henri Estienne's anti-Italian polemic is a study of language. I discern two distinct uses of language that I address in the coming pages. The most basic of these is the language that Estienne used in composing the work. Second, the object of his invective is again language—specifically French, Italian, and the curious composite of the two spoken in the French court.

A major revolution of twentieth century thought, the basic premise of which was first expressed by Ferdinand de Saussure,[39] is the shift from referential to relational semantics, from regarding the meaning of language as a given object of reference to regarding it as a dynamic function of use. Social practices, specifically, illustrate the ability of words to give voice to a multiplicity of meanings as people use them in unprescribed contexts and for an infinite range of purposes. Rethinking the nature and operation of language forces a reevaluation of the human social world and its dependence upon language as a mediator of reality. We often take language to be a marker of geographical or cultural origin. Timothy Hampton notes:

> If nationalism is produced out of the idea that individual identity is shaped and given purpose by a concept of community of which a common language is the medium . . . the history of nationhood, as a pre-history of nationalism, might be said to involve the struggle to determine language, space, and character, and to define their interaction.[40]

Estienne chose to write his treatises and satires in French. This simple fact is important on several levels. First, and perhaps most pragmatically, his appeals would be understood by a larger portion of the public than if he had written in Latin. Secondly, since language can be a sign of territorialism, by his use of French, Estienne signaled at the outset his intention to stake out his ground. Also, using the vernacular reaffirmed the value of the French language in the face of the Italian challengers, showing that he had no need for their words nor for the Latin of their Roman ancestors.[41]

By the same token, when we use the language of another place, person, or group, we implicate ourselves in the sphere of identity to which that language alludes. The development of a new language, then, necessarily instigates a parallel process of developing a new space. The character Celtophile, we learn, has only recently returned to France from a lengthy stay in Venice. This development lends another layer of complexity to the dialogues. Celtophile speaks as though he is among the last of the true Frenchmen, at least insofar as language goes, yet he frequently refers to being out of touch. He claims in the first dialogue that vis-à-vis listing Italianized words, "C'est à [Philausone] à les cercher, non pas à moy, qui ay esté si long temps absent de France, et ne sçay plus comme on y parle"[42] [It's up to him to find them, not to me, who has been absent from France for so long that I no longer know how they speak there]. Again, in the second dialogue his memory, though sharp enough to cite precise lines from numerous classics of antiquity, falters when asked to recall a certain French word. "Il me semble bien que desja avant mon depart on usoit de ce mot en ceste signification, mais je n'en puis asseurer"[43] [It seems to me that well before my departure this word was used with that meaning, but I can't be positive].

The tension inherent in his persona—at once both insider and stranger—seems fitting, as Estienne's polemical trilogy equally represents a discourse between center and periphery. Celtophile is granted access to a previous time, with a mind and a knowledge of French that remain in a "primitive" or "natural" state, uncontaminated by events following his departure. In Estienne's case, we witness the articulation of a central position—that of the true Frenchman—in the act of being marginalized. The foreign Italian tongue threatens the "pur et nayf françoys," displacing it in a steady reversal of fortunes.

Contemplating the strange and terrible new France, emblematized by the pernicious new language at court, drove Henri Estienne to take up his pen and lash out against the use of Italian. When Estienne heard the Italian and Franco-Italian mixing at court, he reacted to what he perceived as a very tangible invasion, as much so as if Italian soldiers slammed battering rams into the palace doors. Not only borrowing from the Italian vocabulary but allowing the foreign tongue to destroy French words one at a time was unbearable to Estienne. Estienne faults the "ignorante outrecuidance" [ignorant presumptuousness] of the Italianizing courtiers:

> Elle dit que tous mots sont beaux,
> Pourveu que ce soyent mots nouveaux,
> Et puis les accoustre à sa guise,
> Tout ainsi comme elle s'avise.
> Elle coupe la teste aux uns,
> Et rongne la queue à aucuns.
> Quelquefois deux en un assemble,
> Ou un seul estre deux luy semble.
> Bref, ne leur laisse avoir entiers
> Les mots desquels ils sont si fiers,
> Mais fait que chacun s'accommode
> Au plaisir d'elle et à sa mode.[44]

> [She says that all words are beautiful,
> As long as they are new words,
> And then she disguises them as she wishes,
> Just exactly as she takes it into her head to do.
> She cuts the heads off some,
> And trims the tails of others.
> Sometimes two into one she assembles,
> Or one word seems better off being two.
> In short, she doesn't let them [the French] keep whole
> The words of which they are so proud,
> Instead making everyone accommodate
> Her whims and follow her fashion.]

The "ignorant presumptuousness" governing the fabrication of the new *langage courtesan* [courtier language], personified as a woman, appears here as a composite drawn from the whole repertoire of Estienne's nightmares. Manipulative, powerful, and unrelenting, she is personified by Estienne as a cruel, mercurial tyrant who decides what may or may not happen and who forces everyone else to bend to her whim. She takes words and butchers them, lopping off their heads and trimming their tails, but the horror show does not end there: "Quelquefois deux en un assemble, / Ou un seul estre deux luy semble" [Sometimes two into one she assembles, / Or one word seems better off being two]. The decapitated and variously amputated words are then reassembled into ghoulish figures. Yet, contrasting with these monstrous creations, "Elle dit que tous ... sont beaux" [She says that all ... are beautiful] Estienne thus poetically highlights how skewed the courtiers' definition of beauty is to find such practices attractive.

Joachim du Bellay, in *La deffence, et illustration de la langue françoyse* (1549), writes:

> Nul, s'il n'est vrayment du tout ignare, voire privé de Sens commun, ne doute point que les choses n'ayent premierement eté: puis apres les motz avoir eté inventez pour les signifier:[45] & par consequent aux nouvelles choses estre necessaire imposer nouveaux motz.[4]

> [No one, unless he is truly ignorant and deprived of common sense, doubts that things existed first, and then afterward the words got invented to signify them; and thus for new things it is necessary to create new words.]

When debates arose over the validity or intrinsic worth of a given language, the deciding factor was essentially the expanse of the vocabulary. Did a word exist in the young language that could do the same work as words in ancient languages? Could the language accommodate new developments in the arts and sciences with the capability to augment the range of the language? As Ronsard comments in his *Abrégé de l'art poëtique françois*, "plus nous aurons de motz en nostre langue, plus elle sera parfaicte"[47] [the more words we have in our language, the more perfect it will be].

Just such a conception of language found itself solidified by the grammar and spelling manuals that rapidly gained popularity in the sixteenth century. Many of the first grammars aimed to facilitate the translation of existing works into the vernacular as well as the expression of both new and ancient ideas in the young vernacular. Their authors feared that problems with spelling, speech, and punctuation would cause the intended meaning to be lost and to remain fragmented or incompletely formulated:

> Je me suis souvent informé, de plusieurs savans personnages, d'où il aet avenu, que le seul Fransais prononce autremant son langage, qu'il ne l'ecrit. L'Hebrieu, le Grec, & le Latin sont ecris comme on les prononce, avec quelques petites observacions & reigles. Ainsi est-il des langues vulgaires d'aujourdhuy, l'Italiene, l'Espagnole, & l'Alemande, qui sont des plus fameuses de la Chretianté. J'antans qu'il aet ainsi des autres: & que la seule Fransaise, n'observe an son ecriture sa duë prolacion. Qui est un mal & vice bien notable si on y veut aviser de pres. Car outre ce qu'il y ha defaut à ne pouvoir, ou ne savoir represanter par ecrit ce qu'on prononce: il y ha du dommage bien grand, pour ceus qui veulent apprandre ce langage d'autant qu'il leur faut à chaque mot une observacion, de savoir dissimuler quelques lettres an prononcant, lesquelles on ne veut toutesfois permettre aetre omises de l'ecrivain.[48]

> [I have often learned, from several knowledgeable people, that only the Frenchman pronounces his language differently from how he writes it. Hebrew, Greek, and Latin are written as one pronounces them, with several small observations and rules. It is the same with the vernacular languages of today, Italian, Spanish, and German, which are the most famous in Christendom. I hear that it is the same with the others, and that only French does not observe in its writing

its corresponding sounds. Which is a most notable ill and vice if one considers it closely. For other than the fact that it is a problem not to be able, or not to know how, to represent in writing what one is saying, there is a most serious harm for those who want to learn this language, since they must study each word to know how to ignore several letters when speaking, which at the same time one does not always want to allow the writer to omit.]

Laurent Joubert's "Dialogue sur la cacographie fransaize," contained within his *Traité du ris* from which this passage comes, stages a "Fransais" (a Frenchman) and "Wolffgang" (a German) as the interlocutors in a discussion "expliquant les causes de sa [the French language's] corruption"[49] [explaining the causes of its corruption]. The lines cited above belong to the "Fransais," immediately augmenting the force of Joubert's critique. Even a Frenchman can see that his own language is problematic. Nor is this merely a passing concern: Joubert has *often* engaged with this issue with "plusieurs savans personnages" [several knowledgeable people]. Worse yet, the error affects French alone. An unfavorable comparison of French to Hebrew, Greek, or Latin—as Joubert offers here—would not be unexpected and would even have been excusable. The three major classical languages, writes Joubert, operate as they should, with equivalent spelling and pronunciation. However, Joubert follows with the remark that "ainsi est-il des langues vulgaires d'aujourdhuy" [it is the same with the vernacular languages of today], naming Italian as the first example. Joubert's commentary thus contains a much stronger criticism of the French language than may initially be evident.

Many other intellectuals shared the desire for the spelling of the written language to conform to the pronunciation of the spoken language. They reasoned that according the spelling and pronunciation would contribute to a standardization that would heighten understanding and facilitate communication. If the word (the sign) cannot be standardized, then there exists the possibility for the thing (the signified) to be obscured. This clearly shows a referential understanding of language and meaning. However, when the same writers use language—generally in contexts outside of descriptive or prescriptive treatises—in ways that permit or force an examination of its functioning, the works manifest the signs of a manifold creation of meaning. Estienne's fictitious dialogue demonstrates the tension that existed between two ways of conceiving of how words mean. The traditional dualistic system of referential semantics, in which a word points directly and immutably to a preexistent meaning, finds itself uneasily juxtaposed with a notion of relational semantics, where meaning is a dynamic, creative activity.

Estienne devotes a great deal of space to discussing specific words and sounds. His "Remonstrance aux autres courtisans, amateurs du françois italianizé et autrement desguisé" [Remonstrance to the other courtiers, amateurs of the Italianized and otherwise disguised French] prepares the reader of the *Deux dialogues* by sketching out the premise of several specific usages that he attacks throughout the work:

> Pensez à vous, ô courtisans,
> Qui, lourdement barbarisans,[50]
> Tousjours: "J'allion, je venion," dites,
> Contre la promesse que fites
> Au gentil poete Clement,[51]
> Qui s'en courrouçoit asprement.[52]

> [Think of yourselves, oh courtiers,
> Who, greatly barbarizing,
> Always: "I go [plural], I come [plural]," say,
> Contrary to the promise that you made
> To the kind poet Clement,
> Who bitterly complained of that.]

Estienne comments upon two errors in these lines. The first problem is the use of the first-person plural form with the first-person singular pronoun. The courtiers mix up *j'allais* and *nous allions* to produce the incorrect blended form *j'allion*. The second fault, then, is not including the s that should be added to the first-person plural verb ending.[53] These criticisms imply the potential for confusion, though the expressions do not cause confusion when used within the context that gives them the intended meaning. The poet continues:

> Si tant vous aimez le son doux,
> N'estes-vous pas bien de grands fous
> De dire "chouse," au lieu de "chose"?
> De dire "j'ouse," au lieu de "j'ose"?
> Et pour "trois mois," dire "troas moas"?
> Pour "je fay, vay," "je foas, je voas"?
> En la fin, vous direz la "guarre,"
> Place "Maubart," frere "Piarre."[54]

> [If you're so fond of the soft sound,
> Aren't you really quite foolish
> To say "chouse," instead of "chose"? [thing]
> To say "j'ouse," instead of "j'ose"? [I dare]

THE LANGUAGE OF IDENTITY 119

> And for "trois mois," [three months] to say "troas moas"?
> For "je fay, vay," [I do, I go] "je foas, je voas"?
> In the end, you'll say "la guarre," [war]
> Place "Maubart," brother "Piarre."]

The references in the last two lines to what would normally be pronounced "guerre," "Place Maubert," and "frère Pierre" are perhaps the most telling signs of the degree of Estienne's concern. He cannot tolerate the possibility that the words for important things might change in pronunciation, likely fearing that they risk changing in signification as well. War is of clear significance, as well as the common French name Pierre. La Place Maubert is less immediately recognizable but would have been very present in Estienne's mind; the place itself, situated in the neighborhood of the Sorbonne in Paris, in what today is the Fifth Arrondissement, was a preferred location for public executions of printers during the sixteenth century. Etienne Dolet was tortured and burned alive there, on August 3, 1546. Henri Estienne's connection to Dolet's work extends beyond the death of Dolet; for instance, he includes a copy of Dolet's *Annotatiuncula* with his edition of Virgil, self-published in 1575.[55] Dolet was a brother-in-arms in the struggle for the French language and Protestant ideals, and Estienne might have feared that if the names of relevant places and things were altered, the progress of the movement might similarly evaporate. Referential semantics suggests, indeed, that changing the name breaks the connection to the thing.

Estienne ridicules the changing pronunciation of certain words and presents his vision of the resulting confusion of words and objects in ways that show his reader the gravity of the situation:

> **Cel.**: Mais dite-moy, est-ce maintenant la mode de dire "franceses" (comme vous avez dict) et non pas "françoises"? Pareillement de dire "j'estes," "je voudres," "je feres," comme vous avez tantost prononcé?
> **Phil.**: Est-ce tout ce que vous en sçavez? On n'oseroit dire "françois" ni "françoise," sur peine d'estre appelé pedant, mais faut dire "frances" et "franceses," comme "angles" et "angleses"; pareillement "j'estes," "je faises," "je dises," "j'alles," "je venes," non pas "j'estois," "je faisois," "je disois," "j'allois," "je venois"; et ainsi ès autres il faut user du mesme changement.
> **Cel.**: Je croy aussi qu'on ne prononce plus la "roine."
> **Phil.**: Il y a long temps que ceux qui font perfection de prononcer delicatement et à la courtisanesque ont quitté ceste prononciation, et ont mieux aimé dire la "reine."

Cel.: Puisqu'ainsi est, vous me confesserez qu'on ne met point de différence (quant à la prononciation) entre ce que signifie le mot pris du latin *regina*, et entre la signification du mot pris du latin *rana*. Car vous sçavez que une grenouille est aussi appelée *reine* par quelques-uns.[56]

[**Cel.**: But tell me, is it now in fashion to say "franceses" (as you have said) and not "françoises"? Similarly to say "j'estes," "je voudres," "je feres," [*I was, I would like, I would do*] as you pronounced them just now?
Phil.: Is that all that you know about it? One wouldn't dare to say "françois" or "françoise," [*French*] on the pain of being called a pedant, but must say "frances" and "franceses," like "angles" and "angleses" [*English*]; similarly "j'estes," "je faises," "je dises," "j'alles," "je venes," not "j'estois," "je faisois," "je disois," "j'allois," "je venois" [*I was, I was doing, I was saying, I was going, I was coming*]; and so with others it's necessary to make the same changes.
Cel.: I believe, too, that one no longer pronounces "queen" as "la roine."
Phil.: It has been a long time since those who pronounce perfectly and after the courtier style abandoned that pronunciation and preferred to say "la reine."
Cel.: Because it is so, you will admit to me that there is then no difference (as far as the pronunciation) between the signification of the word taken from the Latin *regina*, and that taken from the Latin *rana*. For you know that a frog is also called *reine* by some.]

Here Estienne condemns the changed pronunciation of the sound /*oi*/ into the sound /*e*/. The examples that he chooses—primarily *françois* and *roine*—underscore the danger of allowing the courtiers' language to insinuate itself into formerly pure French. Not only does the new form of the word for "queen" risk signifying a frog instead, through the creation of a homonym that previously did not exist, but the pronunciation of the very word indicating national belonging is changing. The referential semantic model supports exactly the conception of language operation that informs Estienne's polemic.

We see further traces of this referential conception of language in a different way in the moments where Celtophile and Philausone think of an idea or an object and try to map a word onto it. For instance, they begin trying to speak about a man who cares for a tract of forested land. The word *forestier*

THE LANGUAGE OF IDENTITY   121

is suggested, but Celtophile counters that in the current times:

> en escorchant l'italien on dit: *C'est un forestier*, pour dire: *C'est un estranger*, combien est eslongnée ceste signification de celle de "forestier," estant dict en bon et pur langage françois. Car vous sçavez que *forestier* vient de "forest," et pourtant par "forestier" est entendu celuy qui est "garde de forest," qu'on dit aussi "garde de bois."[57]

> [imitating Italian, one says: *He's a forester*, to mean: *He's a foreigner*; how far this meaning is from that of "forester" as it is said in good and pure French. For you know that *forester* comes from "forest," and therefore by "forester" is meant one who is the "keeper of the forest," which one also calls "keeper of the woods."]

Philausone counters, "n'est-il pas ... nommé autrement?" [is it not ... called something else?]. Celtophile admits:

> **Cel.**: Ouy, car quelques-uns l'appellent aussi *gruyer*, voire, aucuns donnent la mesme signification à *verdier*. Mais je ne suis pas de leur opinion, principalement quant à "verdier," car la charge et office du "verdier" semble estre plus honorable, jusques à estre juge de ceux qui mesprennent et delinquent esdictes forests. Et qu'ainsi soit, en quelques lieux on dit *verdier gruyer*.
> **Phil.**: Ce que vous alleguez semble pouvoir aussi tost faire contre vous que pour vous, car quelcun vous respondret que ceux qui adjoustent *gruyer* avec *verdier*, le font afin qu'on ne prenne pas "verdier" pour "forestier," et de là s'ensuivret que "verdier" se prend en deux sortes.[58]

> [**Cel.**: Yes, for some call it also *gruyer* [keeper of the woods], and in fact, some attribute the same meaning to *verdier* [keeper of the woods]. But I am not of their opinion, particularly in regard to *verdier*, because the duty of a "verdier" seems to be much more honorable, to the point of being the judge of those who scorn and violate said forests. And so it is that in several places one says *verdier gruyer*.
> **Phil.**: What you are adducing seems to be able to be just as soon used against you as for you, for someone could re-

spond that those who add *gruyer* to *verdier* do so in order that one will not take "verdier" for "forestier," and from there it would follow that "verdier" has two different meanings.]

This exchange between the two men illustrates the referential semantic system, where a word should point to a predetermined and unchangeable meaning. Philausone's use, in the last line of his reply, of the conditional phrase "s'ensuivret[59] que 'verdier' se prend en deux sortes" [it would follow that "verdier" has two different meanings] highlights the implicit assertion that a word, *verdier* in this case, should not—or cannot—have two meanings. If what certain people might say in response to Celtophile could be equally as true as Celtophile's claim, in other words, then *verdier* would necessarily mean two conflicting things. Putting the verb in the conditional serves to cast doubt upon the validity of such a possibility.

Many passages in the text underscore the relevance of a relational semantic model to the language conception that Estienne uncovers via his dialogues. For instance, we see this shift in the perception of the nature of language during a discussion of the less-cultured and less-educated members of the court. Estienne gives the floor to Celtophile before the start of the dialogues in the quatrain, "Celtophile au lecteur" [Celtophile to the reader]:

> Maint courtisan use de mots nouveaux,
> Qu'il n'entend point, et si les trouve beaux.
> Luy, bigarré, bigarre son langage.
> Mais pardonnons au perroquet en cage.[60]
>
> [Many a courtier uses new words,
> That he does not understand, and thus finds them beautiful.
> He, mixed up, mixes up his language.
> But let's pardon the parrot in his cage.]

Celtophile indicates that the courtiers do not understand the words they use, which he claims is the very basis for their appeal. Almost immediately after this short poem, in the poem "Condoleance au courtisans amateurs du nayf langage françois" [Condolences to the courtiers who are amateurs of the original French language], Estienne echoes the same charge, ridiculing the new courtiers:

> Qui sont tant sots qu'ils font grand cas
> De ces mots qu'ils n'entendent pas,
> Non plus qu'un perroquet en cage

THE LANGUAGE OF IDENTITY

Entend de son parler l'usage.⁶¹

[Who are so stupid that they make a big fuss
About these words that they don't understand,
Any more than a parrot in its cage
Understands the usage of the words it says.]

They Italianize improperly and have no idea what they are saying. Yet, despite the literally nonsensical words, the courtiers still manage to communicate a sense. The sufficiency of the language evidently does not depend upon a fixed preexisting meaning.

This passage includes the second comparison of the courtiers to parrots, first seen in Celtophile's address to the reader cited above.⁶² Parrots, commonly acclaimed for their ability to repeat human language, are not able to generate meaningful speech independently. Many of the courtiers display the same behavior. They borrow blindly from what the more learned members of the court say but have insufficient knowledge to recognize and follow the rules for mixing the languages. For, despite what Philausone claims, even he discloses that there exist both proper and improper ways to formulate new words and conjugations. As a result, quite frequently the courtiers' etymologies are erroneous. Their expressions should be devoid of sense but they are not:

Cel.: Et quant au farcissement de langage pour lequel on se sert de l'Italie, toutes herbes y sont-elles bonnes?
Phil.: Ouy. Et tous les jours on y met de nouvelles.
Cel.: Chacun y en met-il à sa fantaisie?
Phil.: Et quoy donc? Voire tel y en met dont il ne sçait pas dire le nom, mais se contente de luy donner quelque nom à toutes aventures.⁶³

[**Cel.**: And as for the stuffing of the language for which one turns to Italy, are all seasonings good?
Phil.: Yes. And every day one mixes in new ones.
Cel.: Everyone puts some in however he wishes?
Phil.: And what of it? One even puts some in of which he doesn't even know the name, but contents himself with calling it whatever he wishes.]

Philausone says that, "pour parler bon langage courtisan, vostre premiere maxime doit estre de ne cercher ni ryme ni raison en iceluy"⁶⁴ [to speak proper courtier language, your first maxim should be not to seek any rhyme or reason in it.]. Incredulous, Celtophile insists that there must still be respect for the Latin roots of the words that gave birth to the new ones.

> **Cel.**: Vous ne me ferez jamais croire que ceux qui ont le langage latin assez familier pour se pouvoir incontinent souvenir des mots françois pris d'iceluy, ne dient *faire profession*, aussi bien à la cour qu'ailleurs.
> **Phil.**: Il semble que vous imaginiez une cour telle que pourroit estre une cour de parlement, où, à la vérité, on prend un peu garde à telle chose. Mais pensez-vous qu'en la cour du roy, quant au langage, on se regle sur ceux qui gardent quelques regles? Pensez-vous qu'on suive volontiers ceux qui tiennent le droit chemin? Au contraire, on prend plaisir d'aller à travers les chams à l'esgarée, et principalement quand on sçait que quelque grand, ou, pour le moins, quelque mignon, a passé par là, encore qu'il n'y soit passé sans trebuscher plusieurs fois.
> **Cel.**: Et de ceux qui ne parlent point ainsi à l'aventure, mais veulent laisser gouverner leur langage par la raison, qu'en disent-ils?
> **Phil.**: Qu'ils sont des pedans (comme ils usent de ce mot par derision), qu'ils sont des scholarés, qu'ils sont des clericus.[65]

> [**Cel.**: You will never make me believe that those who know Latin well enough to be able to effortlessly recall the French words taken from it don't say *faire profession* [to profess], at court as well as elsewhere.
> **Phil.**: It seems that you imagine a court such as might be a parliamentary court, where, to be sure, one takes a bit of care in such things. But do you think that in the court of the king, as far as language goes, one governs oneself after those who observe the rules? Do you think that one willingly follows those who stick to the righteous path? On the contrary, one delights in traversing the fields willy-nilly, and especially when one knows that some important person or, at least, some minion [possibly: catamite] did the same, and all the more so if he did so without stumbling a few times.
> **Cel.**: And as for those who don't speak so wildly, but want to let reason govern their language, what do they say about them?

Phil.: That they are pedants (as they use that word derisively), that they are learned, that they are clerks.]

Celtophile's discourse relates to decades-old stereotypes of Italians as being dissipated and as morally bankrupt as they were materially wealthy.[66] Philausone's closing remark reveals that the courtiers mock the intelligent and those who value reason. How very Italian of the courtiers to speak "à l'aventure" [wildly], while a Frenchman in true national character would regulate his behavior "par la raison" [by reason]. The reflection on the French court is equally unflattering. Philausone's open flouting of "le droit chemin" [the righteous path] and endorsement of allowing oneself to "aller à travers les chams à l'esgarée" [traverse the fields willy-nilly] clearly betray Estienne's own perspective on a political situation that he sees as corrupt. The dissolute linguistic practices evidently mirror the social practices of the court. The complicit language users—the group of courtiers who have been seduced by the Italo-French—complement each other's ignorant inventions with their own efforts to extract meaning from what the others say. The social contexts and practices in which their expressions appear lend them meaning. The courtiers are using language relationally and inventing new words that can be useful and can signify without logical correlation to established sense or syntax. In relational semantics, "Meanings . . . are not entities or objects corresponding to expressions; they are the uses of expressions; they are the work expressions do."[67]

Such a world is naturally unstable and frightening to Estienne. These worries transcend a mere discussion of language and extend into the realms of politics and identity. Estienne predicts dire material consequences if the use of Italianized French continues unchecked. He pays particular attention, both in the preliminary "Epitre de Monsieur Celtophile aux Ausoniens" and in the course of the dialogues, to the effect that the new language will have on the military. For example, in the "Epitre," he explains:

> Mais, pour parler plus en particulier,
> Ne vous voulant, Messieurs, rien palier,
> Je suis honteux que nos François vont querre
> Entre vos mots ceux qui sont pour la guerre.
> Maladvisez, qui ne prevoyent pas
> Combien ils ont d'infamie en ce cas,
> Et que chacun, leur voyant ceci faire,
> Dira qu'ils ont de vous l'art militaire!
> C'est ce de quoy vous estes plus joyeux,
> C'est ce de quoy estes plus glorieux.
> Et pense bien qu'en quelque terre estrange

Avez acquis une telle louange.
Mais ceux qu'on doit prendre pour bons temoins
Ne pourront pas nier ceci, au moins,
Que quant au faict des armes, au contraire,
François parlans, il ne vous faille taire.
Puis vous sçavez, ès combats et assaux,
Lesquels font plus des exploits martiaux.
Autres, qui n'ont de nos faicts congnoissance,
Ne croiront rien d'une telle vaillance,
Ni ne croiront que la leçon donnons
A vous, Messieurs, non de vous l'apprenons.
Et ne se faut esmerveiller s'on pense
Que d'où les mots, de là vient la science! [69]

[But, to speak more specifically,
Not wanting, sirs, to hide anything from you,
I'm ashamed that our Frenchmen go seeking,
Among your words, those that relate to war.
Ill-informed are they who don't foresee
How grievously mistaken they are in this case,
For one will see them doing so
And will say that they learned the military arts from you!
That's what you are the most joyful about,
That what you feel the most glorious about.
And you think that in some foreign land,
You've acquired such praise.
But those who one should take to be good witnesses
Cannot deny this, at least,
That as far as feats of arms are concerned,
on the contrary,
Frenchmen speaking will make you be quiet.
And then you will know, in combats and attacks,
Those who best do those martial exploits.
Others, who don't know anything about these facts,
Won't believe anything about such valiance,
Nor will they believe that we give the lessons
To you, sirs, rather than us learning from you.
And little wonder if one thinks
That from where the words come, that's where the skill comes.]

Even though the French army will not suddenly become emasculated and impotent, the fact that its language will lead people to believe so will—

THE LANGUAGE OF IDENTITY   127

in Estienne's estimation—bring about in fact the claims that were initially false.

Estienne suggests even from the outset that the new words and those who are using them in new ways are already changing France itself, which comes close to admitting outright the constitutive nature of language. The *Deux dialogues* opens with the poem, "Le livre aux lecteurs" [The Book to the Readers], which offers the following warning to readers:

> Mais en parlant d'un tas de mots nouveaux,
> Il m'a falu parler de ces cerveaux
> Ausquels en tout la nouveauté est belle,
> Tant qu'il [sic] nous font une France nouvelle.[70]

> [But by speaking of a bunch of new words,
> It was necessary for me to speak about these minds
> To whom in everything newness is beautiful,
> So much so that they are making us a whole new France.]

Estienne writes "en parlant," meaning while or by speaking (about these new words), which points to a digression to come in the lines immediately after. This poem and this book discuss some new words, but Estienne also mentions "these minds," metonymically evoking the courtiers. Leaving the words aside for the moment, he expresses a far more troubling thought. These men fancy novelty "en tout," and so much so that they are remaking France itself. In line 4, above, Estienne juxtaposes *ils* and *nous*, "them" and "us," reinforcing the notion of center versus periphery. What distinction does Estienne want the reader to draw between "them" and "us," between the members of the court and the people? Estienne repeats this division of people into opposing sides in the poem, "Condoleance aux courtisans amateurs du nayf langage françois," which also precedes the first dialogue:

> A vous courtisans je n'en veux,
> N'estans de ces audacieux
> Dont l'ignorante outrecuidance
> Veut donner loy à nostre France.[71]

> [To you courtiers I don't want to say anything,
> Not being among the audacious ones
> Whose ignorant presumptuousness
> Wants to impose the law on our France.]

In this instance, he addresses a group of courtiers as *vous*, only these particular courtiers are those who remain stalwart in the defense of pure French despite the Italianizing raging around them. He aligns himself with them while distancing this laudable group from the "audacieux" courtiers whose ignorance threatens to change the law of the land. Line 68 of this poem (the fourth line quoted above) contains the possessive "nostre France." It is "our" France, but who are "we"? It remains unclear at this point whether he extends the rights of co-ownership of France to the "audacieux."

At one moment in the first dialogue, Celtophile, disgusted by all that Philausone has recounted about the language at court, asks in disbelief whether he must adopt the new parlance when he visits the court. Philausone responds, "Ouy, si vous ne voulez avoir un langage à part"[72] [Yes, if you do not want to have a separate language]. Here again the language of exclusion and separation surfaces, challenging Celtophile's sense of belonging. Philausone suggests that he would feel "à part," dissociated from a milieu of which he was formerly a member. Celtophile, like Estienne, seeks to reinstate himself through a return to the language that he considers his own.

Throughout his *Traicté de la conformité du language françois avec le grec*, his *Deux dialogues du nouveau langage françois*, and his *Proiect du livre intitulé de la précellence du langage françois*, Henri Estienne reacts strongly to the mounting Italian influence over the French language. Estienne's anti-Italianism reveals an innovative conception of language, how it works, and the meanings that it may carry. Common belief in the Renaissance period held that reality exists independently of and prior to language, and that language thus describes reality. However, Estienne's works suggest that changes in language will precipitate changes in reality. This view depends upon a different notion of how language operates, namely that language can in fact create reality and establish identity. Estienne's passionate defense of the purity of the French language responds to the corresponding potential corruption of the national character by using his press to attempt to influence the French language as a means of controlling the national identity of the French people. Operating a printing press during the French Renaissance was inherently a public and political act, as the young Estienne learned by watching the troubles experienced by his father. Estienne cleverly plays on this fact to publish linguistic polemics that his allies would recognize as political documents, but that would still shield him from being subjected to the same danger and harassment as printers like his father or the even less fortunate Etienne Dolet.

Xavier University

NOTES

1. Paul Meyer. "De l'expansion de la langue française en Italie pendant le moyen-âge," *Atti del Congresso internazionale di scienze storiche* 4 (Rome: Tip. della R. Accademia dei Lincei, 1904), 61–104.
2. R. J. Knecht, *The Valois: Kings of France, 1328–1589* (London: Hambledon, 2004).
3. Alessandro Vezzosi and Leonardo *Leonardo, Leonardo da Vinci: The Mind of the Renaissance* (New York: Harry N. Abrams, 1997). For more on François I's art patronage, see Janet Cox-Rearick, *The Collection of Francis I: Royal Treasures* (New York: Harry N. Abrams, 1996).
4. R. J. Knecht, *Catherine de' Medici* (London: Longman, 1998).
5. R. J. Knecht, *The French Renaissance Court, 1483–1589* (New Haven, CT: Yale University Press, 2008).
6. Of particular note is the exchange, in the late 1360s and early 1370s, between Petrarch and Jean de Hesdin. In an attempt to lure Pope Urban V to return to Rome from Avignon, Petrarch wrote a treatise in praise of Italy. In response, Jean de Hesdin drafted a lengthy rebuttal of Petrarch's piece. Petrarch replied with the 1373 *Invectiva contra sum qui maledixit Italie*. Later, in 1395, Jean de Montreuil articulated a defense of French national culture in which he demonstrated his awareness of the earlier Petrarchan quarrel. For more, see Ezio Ornato, "La prima fortuna del Petrarca in Francia," *Studi Francesi* 5 (1961): 201–217.
7. For instance, du Bellay, *Regrets*, 95:

> Maudict soit mille fois le Borgne de Libye,
> Qui le coeur des rochers perçant de part en part
> Des Alpes renversa le naturel rampart,
> Pour ouvrir le chemin de France en Italie.
> Mars n'eust empoisonné d'une eternelle envie
> Le coeur de l'Espaignol, et du François soldart,
> Et tant de gens de bien ne seroient en hasart
> De venir perdre icy et l'honneur et la vie.
> Le François corrompu par le vice estranger
> Sa langue et son habit n'eust appris a changer,
> Il n'eust changé ses moeurs en une autre nature.
> Il n'eust point esprouvé le mal qui fait peler,
> Il n'eust fait de son nom la verole appeler,
> Et n'eust fait si souvent d'un bufle sa monture.

Joachim du Bellay, *Regrets*, 95, in *Œuvres poétiques*, ed. Daniel Aris and Françoise Joukovsky, vol. 2 (Paris: Bordas, 1993), 86.

[A thousand times be damned the one-eyed Libyan,
Who, piercing piece by piece the hearts of the rocky
Alps, knocked down the natural ramparts
To pave the way from France into Italy.
Mars would not have poisoned with eternal envy
The heart of the Spaniard, and of the French soldier,
And many good men would not be in jeopardy
Of coming here to lose both their honor and their lives.
The Frenchman corrupted by foreign vice
Would not have learned to change his language and his clothing,
He would not have changed his values to another nature.
He would not have experienced the ill that causes peeling,
He would not have made syphilis called by his name,
And would not so often have made a buffalo his mount.]
(my translation)

8. Peter Rickard, *La langue française au seizième siècle* (Cambridge, UK: Presses Universitaires, 1968).
9. Henri Estienne's paternal grandfather, also named Henri (1470–1520), had himself been a printer.
10. Antoine Auguste Renouard, *Annales de l'imprimerie des Estienne, ou l'histoire de la famille des Estienne et de ses éditions* (Paris: Jules Renouard, 1837). This resource, though dated, contains a thoroughly researched and minutely detailed account of the Estienne family and the known editions that issued from the presses of each generation of these printers.
11. Henri Estienne, *Traicté de la conformité du language françois avec le grec* (Geneva: 1565). Consulted in the Douglas H. Gordon Collection of French Books at the University of Virginia.
12. Ibid., preface, p. V verso. All translations are my own unless otherwise noted.
13. Ibid.
14. Henri Estienne, *Deux dialogues du nouveau langage françois, italianizé et autrement desguizé, principalement entre les courtisans de ce temps* (Geneva: 1578). Consulted in the Douglas H. Gordon Collection of French Books at the University of Virginia; page numbers cited here correspond to the critical edition by Pauline M. Smith: Henri Estienne, *Deux dialogues du nouveau langage françois*, ed. Pauline M Smith (Geneva: Éditions Slatkine, 1980).
15. Henri Estienne, *Proiect du livre intitulé de la precellence du langage françois* (Paris: for Mamert Patisson, 1579). Consulted in the Douglas H. Gordon Collection of French Books at the University of Virginia.
16. Ibid., 1.
17. Ibid., 26.

18. Ibid., 14.
19. Ibid., 273 and 297.
20. David Cowling, "Henri Estienne and French-Italian Code-Switching," in *The French Language and Questions of Identity*, ed. Wandy Ayres-Bennett and Mari C. Jones (London: MHRA and Maney Publishing, 2007), 163. See also David Cowling, "Henri Estienne pourfendeur de l'emprunt linguistique franco-italien," *Moyen Français* 60–61 (2007): 165–173.
21. Cowling, "Henri Estienne and French-Italian Code-Switching," 162.
22. Estienne, *Deux dialogues*, 52, ll. 9–10.
23. Estienne, *Proiect du livre*, 1–2.
24. Much recent scholarship has in many respects rehabilitated the image of Catherine de Medici. See, in particular, Katherine Crawford, *Perilous Performances: Gender and Regency in Early Modern France* (Cambridge, MA: Harvard University Press, 2004); Denis Crouzet, *Le haut coeur de Catherine de Médicis: Une raison politique aux temps de la Saint-Barthélemy* (Paris: Albin Michel, 2005); and Sheila ffolliott, "Casting a Rival into the Shade: Catherine de' Medici and Diane de Poitiers," *Art Journal* (Summer 1989): 138–143.
25. Estienne, *Deux dialogues*, 52, ll. 49–56.
26. Innocent Gentillet, *Anti-Machiavel*, ed. C. Edward Rathé (Geneva: Droz, 1968), 19.
27. Ibid., 36.
28. Ibid., 37.
29. Henry Heller, *Anti-Italianism in Sixteenth-Century France* (Toronto: University of Toronto Press, 2003). For more of Gentillet's complaints against the Italian bankers, see also Gentillet, *Anti-Machiavel*, 42.
30. Marguerite de Navarre, *L'Heptaméron*, ed. Michel François (Paris: Bordas, 1991), 331–332. Translation from: Marguerite de Navarre, *The Heptameron*, trans. P. A. Chilton (New York: Penguin Books, 1984), 429-433.
31. For more on Italian vices, see Gary Ferguson, "Péchés capitaux et 'vices italiens': L'avarice et ses complices dans *L'Heptaméron* de Marguerite de Navarre," *Seizième Siècle* 4.1 (2008): 73–87.
32. Bonaventure des Périers, *Nouvelles récréations et joyeux devis*, ed. Krystyna Kasprzyk (Paris: Librairie Honoré Champion, 1980), 232.
33. Ibid., 230.
34. Ibid., 231. Translation from: Bonaventure Des Périers, *Novel Pastimes and Merry Tales*, trans. Raymond C. La Charité and Virginia A. La Charité (Lexington, KY: U. P. of Kentucky, 1972), 193-195.
35. Joachim du Bellay, *Oeuvres poétiques*, ed. Daniel Aris and Françoise Joukovsky (Paris: Bordas, 1993), 2:190, ll. 1–3 (emphasis added).
36. Ibid., 2:194, ll. 145–152.
37. Gentillet, *Anti-Machiavel*, 358.

38. See, in particular, Geoffroy Tory, *Champ fleury* (1529); du Bellay, *La deffence, et illustration de la langue françoyse* (1549); and Petrus Ramus, *Gramere*, 1st ed. (1562).
39. Ferdinand de Saussure, *Cours de linguistique générale* (Paris: Payot, 1985).
40. Timothy Hampton, *Literature and Nation in the Sixteenth Century: Inventing Renaissance France* (Ithaca, NY: Cornell University Press, 2001), 9.
41. Dante wrote his essay analyzing and supporting the Italian vernacular, *De vulgari eloquentia*, in Latin rather than in the very vernacular he was promoting.
42. Estienne, *Deux dialogues*, 92.
43. Ibid., 269.
44. Ibid., 42–43, ll. 85–96.
45. This idea recalls Genesis 2:19–20, in which God allows Adam to name all of the living creatures.
46. Joachim du Bellay, *Oeuvres complètes*, ed. François Goyet and Olivier Millet (Paris: Champion, 2003), 60.
47. Pierre de Ronsard, *Abrégé de l'art poëtique françois: Art poëtique françoys* (1565 ed.), 12 vols (Geneva: Slatkine Reprints, 1972).
48. Laurent Joubert, *Traité du ris: Contenant son essance, ses causes, et mervelheus effais, curieusemant recerchés [sic] raisonnés & observés* (Paris: Chez Nicolas Chesneau, 1579), 376–377. Consulted in the Douglas H. Gordon Collection of French Books at the University of Virginia.
49. Ibid., 376.
50. It was a commonplace, especially in Italian writing, to refer to the French as barbarians. Here, Estienne reverses the insult, applying the term to the courtiers who borrow the language of the allegedly superior race.
51. Reference to Clément Marot, "Coq en l'asne à L. Jamet," in Clément Marot, *Oeuvres poétiques complètes*, ed. Gérard Defaux (Paris: Bordas, 1993), 86–91.
52. Estienne, *Deux dialogues*, 45, ll. 13–22.
53. Estienne discusses this point further; ibid., 164.
54. Ibid., 46–47, ll. 41–48.
55. Richard Copley Christie, *Étienne Dolet: The Martyr of the Renaissance, 1508–1546* (London: Macmillan and Co., 1899), 505.
56. Estienne, *Deux dialogues*, 82–83.
57. Ibid., 90–91.
58. Ibid., 91.
59. *S'ensuivrait* in modern French; the spelling here reflects Philausone's Italianizing.
60. Ibid., 34, ll. 1–4.
61. Ibid., 42, ll. 72–76.
62. See ibid., 401, for another mention of the *perroquet*, by Philalethe.
63. Ibid., 84–85.

64. Ibid., 240.
65. Ibid., 84.
66. See Heller, *Anti-Italianism*, especially 114–136.
67. W. Haas, "The Theory of Translation," *Philosophy* 37 (1962): 212, 215.
68. This sentiment is echoed in du Bellay, *Regrets*, 9, in *Oeuvres complètes*, 43, ll. 1: "France, mere des arts, des armes & des loix."
69. Estienne, *Deux dialogues*, 56–57, ll. 155–178. Estienne expresses here the same argument as he does in the following excerpt from the *Traicté*:

> le grand mal ... c'est que MM. les courtisans se sont oubliez jusques-là, d'emprunter d'Italie leurs termes de guerre, laissans leurs propres et anciens, sans avoir esgard à la consequence que portoit un tel emprunt; car d'ici à peu d'ans, qui sera celuy qui ne pensera que la France ait appris l'art de la guerre en l'escole d'Italie, quand il verra qu'elle usera de termes italiens? ... Voila comment un jour les disciples auront le bruit d'avoir esté les maistres; et plusieurs casaniers qui se seront tousjours tenus le plus loing des coups qu'ils auront peu, auront bien à leur aise acquis la reputation d'avoir esté les plus vaillans" (p. 24).

> [the great evil ... is that the good sirs, the courtiers, have let themselves get to the point of borrowing from Italy their words used in battle, leaving behind their own ancient ones, without regard to the consequences of such a borrowing; for within a few short years, who will not think that France learned the art of war in the school of the Italians, when he will see that she uses Italian words? ... See how in one day the disciples will be rumored to be the masters; and many cowards who will always have kept themselves as far as possible from the blows of battle will soon at their leisure have gained the reputation of having been the most valiant.]

The end of the Proiect du livre also addresses this same question at length.
70. Estienne, *Deux dialogues*, 34, ll. 5–8.
71. Ibid., 42, ll. 65–68.
72. Ibid., 240.

WORKS CITED

Copley Christie, Richard. *Étienne Dolet: The Martyr of the Renaissance, 1508–1546.* London: Macmillan and Co., 1899.
Cowling, David. "Henri Estienne and French-Italian Code-Switching." In *The French Language and Questions of Identity*, ed. Wandy Ayres-Bennett and Mari C. Jones, 163. London: MHRA and Maney Publishing, 2007.
———. "Henri Estienne pourfendeur de l'emprunt linguistique franco-italien." *Moyen Français* 60–61 (2007): 165–173.
de Navarre, Marguerite. *The Heptameron*, trans. P. A. Chilton. New York: Penguin Books, 1984.
———. *L'Heptaméron*, ed. Michel François. Paris: Bordas, 1991.
de Ronsard, Pierre. *Abrégé de l'art poétique françois: Art poëtique françoys.* 1565 ed. 12 vols. Geneva: Slatkine Reprints, 1972.
des Périers, Bonaventure. *Novel Pastimes and Merry Tales*, trans. Raymond C. and Virginia A. la Charité, 193–195. Lexington: University Press of Kentucky, 1972.
———. *Nouvelles récréations et joyeux devis*, ed. Krystyna Kasprzyk, 232. Paris: Librairie Honoré Champion, 1980.
du Bellay, Joachim. *Oeuvres poétiques*, ed. Daniel Aris and Françoise Joukovsky, 2:190. Paris: Bordas, 1993.
———. *Oeuvres complètes*, ed. François Goyet and Olivier Millet, 60. Paris: Champion, 2003.
Estienne, Henri. *Traicté de la conformité du language françois avec le grec.* Geneva: 1565. Douglas H. Gordon Collection of French Books at the University of Virginia.
———. *Deux dialogues du nouveau langage françois, italianizé et autrement desguizé, principalement entre les courtisans de ce temps.* Geneva: 1578.
———. *Proiect du livre intitulé de la precellence du langage françois.* Paris: Mamert Patisson, 1579.
———. *Deux dialogues du nouveau langage françois*, ed. Pauline M Smith. Geneva: Éditions Slatkine, 1980.
Gentillet, Innocent. *Anti-Machiavel*, ed. C. Edward Rathé, 19. Geneva: Droz, 1968.
Haas, W. "The Theory of Translation." *Philosophy* 37 (1962): 212, 215.
Hampton, Timothy. *Literature and Nation in the Sixteenth Century: Inventing Renaissance France.* Ithaca, New York: Cornell University Press, 2001.
Heller, Henry. *Anti-Italianism in Sixteenth-Century France.* Toronto: University of Toronto Press, 2003.
Joubert, Laurent. *Traité du ris: Contenant son essance, ses causes, et mervelheus effais, curieusemant recerchés raisonnés & observés.* Paris: Chez Nicolas Chesneau, 1579.

Marot, Clément. "Coq en l'asne à L. Jamet." In *Clément Marot, Oeuvres poétiques complètes,* ed. Gérard Defaux, 86–91. Paris: Bordas, 1993.
Meyer, Paul. "De l'expansion de la langue française en Italie pendant le moyen-âge." *Atti del congresso internazionale di scienze storiche,* 4:61–104. Rome: Tip. della R. Accademia dei Lincei, 1904.

Reading Chaucer in the Tower: The Person behind the Pen in an Early-Modern Copy of Chaucer's *Works*

MIMI ENSLEY

In January of 1549, John Harington of Stepney and Kelston was arrested and sent to the Tower of London. There, Harington found himself in a community of eminent prisoners representing some of the most influential names of his day. However, Harington likely had another illustrious companion in Geoffrey Chaucer. Harington possessed a copy of *The workes of Geffray Chaucer newlye printed*, a 1542 William Thynne edition, which he signed and dated to 1550.[1] With Harington, then, we get a rare glimpse of a named reader at work.[2] We find evidence of an early-modern reader encountering the literature of a previous period in a detailed and thoughtful manner, and our understanding of that encounter is informed by Harington's personal circumstances.

Additionally, just as Harington's marginalia interprets Chaucer, any reading of that marginalia is necessarily an interpretation. As Wolfgang Iser argues, the reader "'receives' [the message of the text] by composing it."[3] Thus any act of reading is to some extent an act of creation as well. Harington reads Chaucer and thereby creates an image of Chaucer's poetry for himself. Moreover, Harington creates a record of himself, his interests, and his reading habits through his marginal annotations. When modern readers encounter this marginal self-fashioning years later, we continue this cycle of active reading and interpretation, creating our own image of Harington and of Chaucer through Harington's eyes. We, as later readers, can attempt to piece together Harington's experiences and Harington's Chaucer, but we can never fully recover those entities. We can, however, offer an interpretation grounded in the available evidence, and that interpretation can inform our necessarily limited understanding of how one early-modern reader experienced Chaucer.

Thus the purpose of this paper is twofold. First, I provide an account of the marginalia found in Harington's copy of Chaucer's *Works*. I argue that Harington's marginal annotations intersect with the details we know about his life in ways that reveal how readers in the early-modern period could find relevance in a temporally distant author's work. Second, I offer an interpretation of Harington's marginalia based on the biographical details of his life. In reading Harington's annotations with an eye to his personal history, I seek to give a voice to those oft-lamented anonymous annotators, the hands that appear in our manuscripts and early printed books but are often not connected to the lived experiences of the person attached to the hand. Analysis of a broad corpus of marginal responses can prove fruitful in observing trends and commonalities, as Alison Wiggins shows in her recent study of marginalia from fifty-three early-modern print editions of Chaucer.[4] However, in taking the bird's-eye view, we may risk losing sight of the individual lived experiences that also influenced a reader's annotations and responses. Though I compare Harington with other early-modern annotators of Chaucer, particularly drawing on my own analysis of an annotated Thynne edition held in Chicago's Newberry Library, I emphasize the ways in which knowledge of Harington's biography allows us to talk about his marginalia as something more than merely conventional.

The Person behind the Pen

John Harington—not to be confused with his son, Sir John, who famously translated *Orlando Furioso*—rose in court on the coattails of Sir Thomas Seymour, the brother of Henry VIII's third wife, Jane. Harington began serving Seymour no later and possibly much earlier than 1546.[5] Seymour's power grew after Henry's death, but his circumstances changed drastically when he was arrested and sent to the Tower of London following suspicion about the nature of his relationship with Princess Elizabeth and his alleged plot to gain the Lord Protectorship for himself, usurping it from his brother, Edward.[6] Harington, imprisoned with his master, was questioned about his own role in the scandal and the part he played in setting up a marriage between Lady Jane Grey, the Nine Days Queen, and the young King Edward VI.[7] Though Harington was eventually released from the Tower, Seymour was executed on March 20, 1549, and Harington likely served him up until that date.[8] Harington himself was released in the spring of 1550.

Like many gentlemen of his day, Harington could be described as literary-minded. His manuscript collection of poetry, known as the Arundel

Harington Manuscript, contains examples of Tudor verse from such writers as Thomas Wyatt, Thomas Seymour, and Harington himself. Harington likely collected much of the poetry in the volume during one of his two stints as a prisoner (he was confined a second time from January 1554 to January 1555 on suspicion of involvement in Wyatt's Rebellion).[10] Though Ruth Ahnert notes that the co-occurrence in Arundel Harington of these poems by noted Tower prisoners does not necessarily indicate that Harington and the others sought out or were able to seek out literary communities while imprisoned, she suggests that the poems are united by a sense of place.[11] And regardless of the degree of literary community the Tower afforded its prisoners, we can certainly say that many of those prisoners chose to spend their time engaged in literary activity.

Harington's most notable literary achievement from the Tower is a translation of Cicero's *De amicitia*, which he translated from a French version.[12] In a dedication preceding the book, Harington describes life in the Tower almost idealistically, emphasizing the time for study and contemplation afforded by prison life:

> For thereby founde I great soule profite, a little mind knowlage, some holow hertes, and a few feithfull freendes. Wherby I tried prisonment of the body, to be the libertee of spirite: aduersitee of fortune: the touche stone of freendship, exemption from the world, to be a contempt of vanities: and in the ende quietness of mind, the occasion of study. And thus somewhat altered, to auoide my olde idelnesse, to recompense my lost time, and to take profite of my calamitee, I gaue my selfe among other thynges to study and learne the Frenche tonge.[13]

Judging by the date ascribed in Harington's Chaucer as well as the sheer number of careful annotations—perhaps something Harington would have had time to do only in the confines of a prison cell—it is entirely possible that reading Chaucer constituted a part of Harington's literary activity in the Tower, an "occasion of study" to help him "auoide ... idelnesse" and "recompense ... lost time."

Harington's Marginalia: An Overview

Broadly speaking, we can categorize Harington's marginal annotations into two loosely defined groups. The first group I call "editorial marginalia." With these notes, Harington attempts to correct Thynne's text by adding punctuation or modernizing vocabulary, either to make the text more accessible to himself or potentially to aid readers he believed might follow him.

Relative to his punctuation-focused emendations, which I discuss below, Harington's modernizations of vocabulary are infrequent and cluster near the front of the codex. For instance, at the end of the prologue to the *Canterbury Tales*, the edition reads, "Us thought it was nat worth to make it wyse / And graunted hym without more auyse." Harington strikes through "wyse" and writes "nice" in the margins. He does the same with the words "houe" and "layde" in "The Knight's Tale," replacing them marginally with "haue" and "laid" (fols. 5r, 11r). In "The Book of the Duchess," "whyse" becomes "wise," and in the short poem "Fortune," "hyne" is glossed as "hyena," though in this case Harington does not strike through the original word ("Duchess," l.113, fol. 267v; "Fortune," l.35, fol. 369v).

Harington's added punctuation is much more frequent. Commonly, he will add a comma, colon, or virgule at the end of a line of poetry. He may also envelope a phrase in parentheses if he deems it subordinate or add a double hyphen between a word's component parts if the word is split by a line break. This attention to punctuation occurs in both poetry and prose, but some sections are more heavily punctuated than others. Malcolm Parkes observes that later readers would often add punctuation to both printed books and manuscripts. Though Parkes notes that added layers of punctuation may be difficult to interpret, overall the practice is reader-focused, an attempt to ease an audience's understanding of an older text by updating standards to contemporary practices or individual preferences.[14] Of course, Thynne's 1542 edition is not so distant from Harington's present (1550) to have preserved a system of punctuation that was overly foreign to Harington. Moreover, punctuation in the sixteenth century lacked a standardized system, so Harington would not be updating his text to conform to a set of universal rules. This means that Harington's changes likely reflect a personal desire to add a level of interpretive meaning, to ensure ease of study in the future, and to make the volume accord with his own reading needs.

Harington's most persistent punctuation change is an added bracket that serves as something like a quotation mark. He consistently marks changes in speaker with this flourished bracket, particularly if the new voice is not marked textually until after the speech has begun.[15] So, when Harington reads in *Troilus and Criseyde*, "How hast thou thus unkyndly a longe / Hyd this fro me, thou fole (qd Pandarus)," he returns to the previous line and marks the change of speaker with a bracket, apparently having realized in the second line that there has been a change to Pandarus.[16] He marks this line, presumably, so that on a second reading he or another reader could follow the narrative more efficiently, understanding that there is a new speaker before it is indicated in the text. This heightened attention to speech and changing voices throughout Harington's book also emphasizes the performative elements of Chaucer's text.

With these punctuation changes, then, we also get our first hint of what reading experiences may have been like in the Tower. Prisoners in the early-modern prison system, particularly those with the funds to pay for better conditions, could live relatively comfortably.[17] An oral reading among the "few feithfull freendes" Harington mentions in his dedication to *De amicitia* is certainly a possibility, and the activity would make such added punctuation useful. Whether Harington would have read these texts aloud is ultimately unknowable; however, his changes reflect an interest in the oral nature of Chaucer's poetry and prose, and his emendations certainly would make reading aloud in a group setting easier. Moreover, Harington's added discourse markers suggest a continuation of a medieval scribal practice. As Colette Moore observes, since quotation marks were not yet common practice, medieval scribes used rubrication and other forms of marginalia to indicate speech, particularly when that speech carried a great degree of authority. Moore finds that this practice carried over to the age of print in a similar manner.[18] Harington's flourished brackets, then, seem to be a personalized extension of this common practice.

I classify the second group of marginalia, broadly, as "reader's aids." These are annotations that simultaneously guide Harington's reading of the text and also serve as help for future readers. They summarize key points, mark text out for extraction, highlight the names of characters, or otherwise make sense of the book via an apparatus that externally organizes the text. Underscoring is Harington's preferred method for indicating important and perhaps extractable lines. Less frequently, though still commonly, he draws elaborate manicules. Often, these highlighted segments are the types of sententious phrases we might expect to see decontextualized and written in a commonplace book, and this practice applied in Harington's book reflects a common desire among early-modern audiences to read Chaucer as a moral poet.[19] The drive to extract *sententiae* from Chaucer was so strong that Speght in his 1602 edition marked such phrases with printed manicules similar to Harington's hand-drawn marker. Further, the addition of these "Sentences and prouerbs noted" was important enough for Speght to highlight the feature on his title page, guiding readers toward passages they might copy into a commonplace book.[20] Just as a lack of printed punctuation encouraged Harington to punctuate his own book, in the absence of printed manicules, Harington marked sententious or proverbial passages as he saw fit.[21]

Although the evidence of other early-modern reading practices might lead us to expect cross-references or source citations in Harington's book, these are rare.[22] There are a few notes of this sort, however, and their character can provide details about the resources Harington had at his disposal in the Tower. In the "Reeve's Tale," Harington writes "see in Raynard þ[e] ffoxe" beside "The greatest clerkes ben not the wysest men" (l. 4054, fol. 17r), which is a proverb attested in Caxton's *History of Reynard the Fox* (1481).[23] There is at least one biblical cross-reference—a note indicating "Mathew | xxiii | chap i"—in the first book of the *Testament of Love* (ll. I.497–499, fol. 320r).[24] One might expect that an obviously well-trained and scholastically inclined reader would engage in further source citation; however, the lack of citations may point to an imprisoned reader who did not have recourse to the volumes such a detailed study would require.[25] However, one of Harington's cross-references provides evidence that he had access to at least one more book in the Tower. Harington writes in the dedication to his *Booke of Freendeship* that while he was imprisoned he had the opportunity to "study and learne the Frenche tonge, havyng both skilful prisoners to enstruct me, and therto plenty of bookes to learne the language" (A 2v). It seems one of those "plenty of bookes" in French was the *Roman de la Rose*. In the margins of Chaucer's translation, Harington provides reference to a print edition of the French *Roman* by writing "faux semblant dit cy verite | de tous cas de mendicite" in a break between two sections of Chaucer's translation (between l. 6714 and l. 6715, fol. 161v).

Early print editions of the *Roman* contained what Francis William Bourdillon calls "verse-titles."[26] These brief lines of verse served to divide the long poem into sections, and Harington's note is a copy of one of these French paratextual devices.[27] Harington inscribes the "verse-title" not in the margins but as a heading, indicating that he borrowed the French book's paratext in this single instance. That he did not adapt other "verse-titles" is strange. We might initially think that Harington imported the heading because it was one he remembered from his time outside the Tower. However, the fact that Harington claims he did not learn French until he was imprisoned makes such a scenario unlikely. Thus, if Harington was imprisoned during his reading, he may have had access to a printed *Roman* in addition to his Thynne edition. The selection of this single "verse-title," then, suggests three possibilities. First, Harington could have found this title to be particularly apt and wished to preserve it in Chaucer's version. Second, Harington may have been especially interested in the following section, in which Fals-Semblant suggests that a man who is "so bestyall / That he of no crafte hath science" is justified in begging. Finally, Harington may have only read this single segment of the French version. In that case, his marginalia would also indicate which elements of the French text Harington encountered and which he chose to skip.

Harington also employs marginal notes that signal the topic of a text or section of text.[28] These annotations sometimes occur in Latin, and less often in French, though Harington's preferred marginal language is English. Latin notations occur most frequently in the "Parson's Tale," *The Romaunt of the*

Rose, and the *Treatise on the Astrolabe*—a religious prose treatise, a verse translation, and a scientific tract. The Latin is never extensive and usually consists of a few common words: "quid sit Ira" in the "Parson's Tale" when Ire is formally defined as "the fervent blood of man yquyked in his herte" (l. 535, fol. 108r), and "descriptio Amoris" in *The Romaunt of the Rose* (l. 4703, fol. 151v). The thematic notes in all languages are typically a single word or phrase, and these notes act like a marginal index for the book. In an age before a reader with an electronic edition of a work could search for a word or phrase with a few keystrokes, such marginal indexes must have been useful, particularly because pagination was often erratic.

Most striking of these indexing terms are those Harington applies to the *Canterbury Tales*. In its prefatory material, Thynne's 1542 edition provides readers with two tables of contents, the second of which contains an individual listing of each Canterbury tale and prologue. For most of the tales listed in the table, Harington supplies a brief thematic summary. Reading his notes, we discover that in "The Merchant's Tale" we will find the "benefit of advercitie," that "The Cook's Tale" is about "ill servants," that "The Franklin's Tale" is "of witchecraft," and that the Canon's Yeoman speaks of the "multiplication | and falshod of Chanons." Having these summaries early in the volume would have been a helpful memory tool if Harington wanted to return to a specific tale on later occasions. Other instances of marginal indexing are not applied to whole works; rather they index sections of a text. Thus we see thematic notes like "de penitencia" in a section of "The Parson's Tale" (l. 78, fol. 105r) or "[o]f the love of / [C]hrist / " at the end of *Troilus* (ll. V.1836-7, fol. 212v).[29] Particularly descriptive sections might also receive indexing notes. For instance, when Harington reaches the description of the arena in "The Knight's Tale," he writes "the theatre" and brackets the text column to draw attention to the descriptive section (l. 1889, fol. 6r). Again, these schematizing notes provide Harington with a means of organizing longer works and noting their most striking sections, as if he were selecting passages for a commonplace book. As we see below, he often keys these indexes to moments in the text when Chaucer deals with imprisonment, particularly through a Boethian lens.

More Than a Hand:
A Biographical Reading of Harington's Marginalia

As modern readers, we are doubly removed from Harington's Chaucer. We read Harington reading Chaucer, and we attempt to craft an understanding of Harington's experiences via that reading. We create an image of Harington's imprisoned experiences mediated through his reading of imprisonment, and in this act of interpretation we attempt to refashion Harington and Harington's version of Chaucer. The success of this act of interpretation can never, of course, be empirically tested. And as Wiggins notes, biographical information can often be tantalizing and dangerous for scholars crafting a narrative of reader response from scant marginal evidence.[30] However, the temptation to overgeneralize, to record a marginal response as *merely* conventional or indicative of some broad interest that spanned *all* of Chaucer's sixteenth-century readers, is equally strong. To use a phrase from Robert Darnton, the generalizations may "seem too cosmic for comfort."[31] Thus, if we recognize the limitations of our own roles as readers and interpreters of Harington's marginalia, the biographical information can inform our interpretive efforts and prevent such broad generalities.

Indeed, it is almost impossible not to observe an added layer of personal depth when we read Harington's marginalia in conjunction with the biographical facts of his life, since it is difficult to imagine a case in which the intense personal experiences surrounding Harington's reading did not affect his own response to the text or shape it in ways unique to his personal circumstances.[32] Discerning some of these key interactions between Harington's biography and his marginalia can help remind us that a person with a history always lurks behind the annotations we read and seek to interpret hundreds of years later. We can picture Harington studying Chaucer in his Tower cell, reading aloud to a group of fellow prisoners, and we can imagine how that experience must have shaped his reading practice. Whether or not our image of Harington's imprisonment aligns with his lived experience, his marginal annotations, as I further demonstrate below, do allow for such an image. As Catherine Brown notes, "Medieval readers don't read the way we do; they do things differently. One way to embrace coevalness with them would be to learn to read from them."[33] Though Harington is, of course, not a medieval reader, Brown's sentiment holds true for readers of all historical periods, and to learn to read from Harington, we must know everything we can about the circumstances of his reading, understanding that his personal history is key evidence in decoding his interpretation of Chaucer.

The 1550 date inscribed in Harington's Chaucer is not definitive evidence that he read Chaucer in the Tower, as he was released in the early spring of 1550. However, whether he was recently released or still imprisoned, we would expect the experience to shape his understanding of Chaucer. Harington had seen his fortunes in court climb and plummet. His master, whom by all accounts Harington loved deeply, had recently been executed, and Harington was with him up until his death day. With this in mind, it is no surprise that Harington takes care to mark sections dealing with fortune, sadness, and occasionally imprisonment throughout Chaucer's *Works*. Appropriately, some of his most thoroughly marked texts are those that draw on the Boethian themes expressed in the *Consolation of Philosophy*, which Boethius composed while in prison. In reading and writing, I argue, Harington was able to use Boethius as a bridge from his own present to Chaucer's past, and he appropriated the Boethian material as a means of understanding his own imprisonment.

In "The Knight's Tale," Harington encounters two imprisoned characters in Palamon and Arcite, and the three leaves encompassing the knights' days in prison are of immediate attention for Harington (ll. 1003–1416 fols. 2v–3v). Harington's main form of annotation on these folios is underscoring; however, he also draws three manicules and writes one marginal note. One of Harington's manicules points toward a couplet that must have resonated with a man intimately familiar with the inner workings of court culture— "And therefore, at kynges court my brother / Eche man for hymselfe, there is non other" (ll. 1181–1182, fol. 2v). Harington's deep involvement in the "kynges court" had earned him his imprisonment. At this moment, we can imagine Harington recalling the power struggle between his master Thomas Seymour and Thomas's brother, Edward, the Lord Protector and Duke of Somerset, certainly a case in which "Eche man" was "for hymselfe" in the politics of court.[34]

Though the word "prison" occurs fourteen times across these lines, Harington marks sections containing the word only twice. Instead, it is the particularly emotional sections containing the word "prison" that catch Harington's attention. For example, when Palamon laments the fact that Arcite will be allowed to leave their cell, he states, "For I may wepe and wayle, whyles þat I lyue / wyth all the wo that prison maye me yeue," and Harington underlines the couplet (ll. 1295–1296, fol. 3r). We might envision Harington himself weeping when his own friend and master was led out of the prison, never to return. Many of the other highlighted lines on these folios have a similar emotional quality. Harington also marks, for instance, lines describing Arcite's distress in exile, his "eyen holowe, and grysly to beholde" and his solitary "waylynge all the nyght, makynge mone" (ll. 1363 and 1366, fol. 3v). Though Harington typically underlines couplets or even small sections of a single line, in the case of Arcite's painful exile, he highlights eight lines, a substantially longer passage (ll. 1361–1369). Is Harington here recalling his own days of solitude, exiled from the court culture he knew and perhaps lamenting his own fate? If Harington's reading occurred immediately after his release from the Tower, as is possible, is he identifying with Arcite's newfound freedom, a freedom that he has discovered is just another form of imprisonment?

Of course, a decision to underline a passage is not evidence of what Harington was thinking at the moment of his reading. However, it is clear that something drew him to this section of "The Knight's Tale," and at some level he found that the characters' imprisonments struck an emotional chord as he reflected on his own time in his own Tower. Moreover, later readers encountering this prison-related marginalia likely connect Chaucer's narrative with Harington's lived experiences. We craft an understanding of Harington through this interpretation just as Harington shaped Chaucer's text with his annotating pen.

The most persistent interests reflected in this section, as well as throughout the book, are the Boethian questions of fortune and divine providence. Seven of the nineteen passages Harington underlines throughout the three pages presenting the imprisoned Palamon and Arcite concern this theme (fols. 2v–3v). The section that receives the most attention on these folios is Arcite's Boethian lament:

> Alas, why playnen men so in comune
> That yueth hem full ofte in many a gyse
> well better then hem selfe can devyse
> <u>Some man desyreth to haue rychesse</u>
> <u>That cause is of her murdre or sycknesse</u>
> <u>And some man wolde out of hys prisson fayne</u>
> <u>That in hys house, is of hys meyne slayne</u>
> Infinite harmes bene in thys matere
> <u>We wote nat what thynge we prayen here</u>
> We faren as he, that dronke is as a mouse
> Al dronken man wote well, he hath an house
> But he wote nat, whych the ryght waye thyder
> And to a dronken man the waye is slyder
> And certes in thys worlde so faren we
> <u>We seken fast aftre felicite</u>
> <u>But we go wronge ful ofte truly.</u>
> (ll. 1251–1267, fol. 3r, with Harington's underscoring)

Harington highlights this section in three ways. First, he brackets the entire passage. Second, he underlines several of the lines, selecting the passages concerning prison, prayer, and going wrong despite seeking happiness. And finally, Harington pens a marginal response to the passage, writing, "The provicoun | [of] god is a | [bo]ve | the device | [of] man." In Chaucer, Harington seems to have found a guide for understanding and responding to his own prison situation. In these annotations, he signals his own reliance on God's will in the face of uncontrollable circumstances.

The idea of "the provicoun of god" also sparks Harington's interest in Troilus's Boethian soliloquy in Book 4. Here Harington brackets two and a half columns of text, more than a hundred total lines (ll. 961–1078, fols. 198r–v). He marginally writes "de predestinacione" beside "That forsyght of diuyne purueyaunce" (l. 961, fol. 198r) and "de libero arbitoro /" next to

"And some sayne that nedely there is none / But that free choyce is yeuen us euerychone"(ll. 970–971, fol. 198r). I have observed a similar pattern of marginalia from an annotator writing in a 1532 Thynne edition held at the Newberry Library in Chicago.[35] One of several annotators in this book, the Newberry reader focuses almost exclusively on the concept of free will, an interest we also see reflected in Harington's notes. In this Boethian passage of *Troilus and Criseyde*, the Newberry reader highlights a sententious phrase in three different ways. When responding to the lines, "For al that cometh cometh by necessyte / Thus to ben lorne it is my destyne," the reader underlines the passage, draws a manicule in the margin, and writes "ffre wyl" beside the section (ll. 958–959, fol. 203r). On the following page, the reader, like Harington, brackets the entire first column and marginally writes "[prede] stinacion | fre will" at the top of the bracketed section.[36]

Certainly questions of free will, predestination, providence, and fortune had resonance for many readers in the midst of Reformation-era England. However, Harington's specific situation suggests that his response to these ideas was not merely characteristic of early-modern interests. Instead, we can imagine a reader specifically concerned with his *own* fortune and his *own* predestined circumstances, especially when those circumstances involved a tumultuous life in court that resulted in imprisonment.

The Newberry reader's interest is similarly apparent in Chaucer's *Boece*. This reader focuses most of his attention on Books 4 and 5, and the sections the annotator chooses to underline or distinguish with a manicule frequently contain the words "will" or "fortune." Harington also meticulously reads *Boece*, but again, this interest is informed by his own experiences with imprisonment. *Boece* is one of three items in Thynne's 1542 *Works* that gets a title page, indicating the high status of this text for its early-modern readers. Harington uses the blank verso page afforded by the title page to provide a detailed table of contents for *Boece* (fol. 231v).[37] The blank page is nearly full of Harington's careful, section-by-section summaries written in a cramped but legible hand, as if to maximize the use of the page for these notes. The logical structure of the work invites careful outlining, but the Boethian themes highlighted elsewhere in the volume indicate that Harington was drawn to study this text for more than its scholastic structure.

In his table, Harington has space to outline and summarize only Boethius's first and second books, and he uses most of the page to schematize Book 1. We learn, for example, in Harington's first summary that "Boecius thinketh that poets write fantasies, albeyt their meaning soundeth to | philosophie, if they be depelye studied and well understand ·/." Harington's last note remarks "That theare is nothing certen under heaven ·/," and the previous note tells us "That a man ought not to sorow for the sorowfull chaunce which be past, nomore | than he ought to be glad at the dep*art*ure of joyfull thinge: for death the last day | maketh an end of all·/." These notes respond to Book 2 Metrum 3 and Book 2 Prosa 3, respectively.[38] Having run out of space on his table, Harington continues to summarize passages by squeezing brief comments into the text breaks between sections. His in-text summaries are particularly frequent and detailed in Book 5, which concerns free will. Some are short: "fortune is governed by | divine providence" (5.m1, fol. 261r). Others contain a bit more detail: "god seeth at once all things that | bene are or here after shall come" (5.m2, fol. 261v).

It is clear from other examples of prison writing that Boethius was an attractive figure for describing the circumstances of imprisonment, since the text was incredibly popular among prison-poets of the medieval period. James I of Scotland, for instance, found inspiration in *The Consolation of Philosophy* when he produced his long poem, "The Kingis Quair." James may have written the poem shortly after his release from English imprisonment in 1423, and the text is intimately connected to James's experience in prison.[39] A recent TEAMS edition of "The Kingis Quair" gathers it with several other prison poems from the fifteenth century, and all of them have some connection to Boethian themes.[40] Another such Boethian-inspired prison writer was Thomas Usk, who wrote his *Testament of Love* in response to his shifting political fortunes and imprisonment.[41] As no manuscript of Usk's *Testament* exists, we know about it today because of Thynne's 1532 edition, and Harington read and responded to it in his 1542 book, believing it was Chaucer's.[42]

The annotations in Usk's *Testament* again follow Harington's typical patterns. He underlines proper names, brackets longer passages, and draws manicules by sententious phrases. Some of the more extensive written commentary is overtly moralizing—"want of welth | ofte hindrethe the | worthie" (l. I.401, fol. 319r). Some of the notes are focused on themes—"peace" (fol. 321r). And some of them have a more schematizing purpose—"sondrie example" written beside a list of "ensamples" in the text (ll. I.502–505, fol. 320r). However, as we have seen before, Harington consistently responds to Boethian ideas, particularly passages concerning fortune. He also continues his interest in free will and divine foreknowledge, underlining references to "the auenture of fortune" in the text (l. I.521, fol. 320r) and paying careful attention to Usk's discussion of free will and providence in Book 3.[43] His most specific response to fortune is in an early note. He writes "[t]he true picture | [o]f fortune" and underlines "fortune sheweth her fayrest, whan she thynketh to begyle," highlighting his sense that the truest form of fortune is one that is fickle (ll. I.742–743, fol. 321v). We see fickle fortune again in a passage Harington marks with a flourished bracket:

> Every of tho joyes is tourned into his contrary: For richesse nowe have I poverté, for dignité, nowe am I enprisoned. Instede of power, wretchednesse I suffre, and for glorye of renome I am nowe dispised and foulych hated. Thus hath farn fortune, that sodaynly am I overthrowen and out of al welth dispoyled. (ll. II.992–995, fol. 336v)

He was likely drawn to this section because he too was "nowe... emprisoned," finding himself suffering "wretchednesse" rather than power. By 1550, Harington had already experienced a lengthy stay in the Tower. He was supposed to be discharged in October 1549, but for reasons unknown, he was not released until later (the early spring of 1550). In such a situation, fortune could only seem, at best, unpredictable.[44]

Prison writing continued into the sixteenth century, but Ahnert, in tracing the genre, observes a shift from the medieval to the early-modern periods, finding "a notable lack of Boethian-influenced prison works" in the sixteenth century, when Protestant prisoners "rejected the medieval model of meditative inwardness in favour of new and reconditioned forms that better suited their evangelical agenda."[45] Still, Harington's focus on fortune and free will provides evidence that at least one prisoner read and meditated on Boethian themes. Chaucer's Boethian perspectives on prison may have been Harington's only prison-related reading material, particularly if his library was diminished by his confined conditions. Thus, regardless of broader trends rejecting the Boethian model for prison literature, Harington's personal circumstances made a Boethian connection available, and Harington used that Boethian model as a means of exploring his own imprisoned state.

Before I conclude, I would like to make brief reference to Harington's own prison poetry, as six of the poems in the Arundel Harington manuscript are thought to have been written by Harington in the Tower.[46] Though Harington's prison poetry does not quote Chaucer directly, there are occasional and faint echoes of his reading material. In "At least withdraw your creweltie" (No. 20), written during Harington's second confinement, the speaker claims he has been left in prison for far too long "without all right agaynst all lawse" (l. 6).[47] However, he consoles himself by remembering that the "chaunce" (the fortune) of those holding him now will one day turn:

> But as the Stone that strykes the wall
> Somtyme bownds back on th'urlers hedd
> so your fowle fetche to your fowle fall
> may tourne and noye the brest it bredd. (ll. 37–40)

Here, we might be reminded of Lady Philosophy assuring Boece that "vertues ne be not wythout mede. And that blysffulnesse cometh alway to good folk and infortune cometh alway to wicked folke" (4.pr1, 53–56, fol. 257r). Indeed, Harington, in his reading of Chaucer, has underlined a line to that effect on the next folio: "good folke ben alway stronge and myghtye, and the shrewes ben feble and deserte, and naked of all strengthes" (4.pr2, 8–10, fol. 257v). Remembering that the "shrewes" who imprisoned him will eventually receive "infortune," that the stones they throw will one day return to strike them justly, can be read as a comfort to Harington in his prison cell.

Harington's most doleful poem is "The lyf ys longe that lothsomly doth last" (No. 19). In this elegy, Harington expresses a wish to pass through the "porte" of death into eternal life. He comforts himself with the knowledge that eternal life and freedom will come after a painful life on earth ends:

> Death is a porte wherby we passe to joye
> Lyf ys a lake that drowneth all in payne
> Death is so deare it ceasyth all anoy
> Lyf is so lewd that all it yelds ys vayne
> For as by lyf to bondage man was browght
> Even so by death was freedome lykewyse wrought. (ll. 31–36)

The sentiment is strikingly similar to a couplet we read, and Harington underlines, in "The Knight's Tale:" "Thys world is but a thorowfare full of wo / And we ben pylgrymes, passyng to and fro" (ll. 2847–2848). Though Biblical rather than explicitly Boethian, this sentiment repeated in Harington's poetry suggests that he ruminated on Chaucer as he read.[48] Consciously or unconsciously, his imprisoned reading influenced his own imprisoned writing, and his imprisoned writing influences our interpretation of his imprisonment.

Conclusions

Just as Boethius's imprisonment led him to consider the role of human will, divine providence, chance, and destiny in his writing, a community of imprisoned readers and writers after Boethius, both medieval and early modern, focused on tracing these themes in their own work. Knowledge of Harington's biography shows that his interest in Chaucer's Boethian material may be more influenced by his personal circumstances—his imprisonment—than by any general trend in sixteenth-century Chaucerian reception. Harington had access to Boethian reflections on imprisonment, and he used the books he had in the Tower to reflect upon his own changing fortunes and imprisoned state. Annotations reflecting broad trends in reading techniques and responses to Chaucer are certainly present in Harington's book, but his personal history adds nuance to our generalizations about early-modern reading habits.

Chaucer becomes like Lady Philosophy for Harington, offering him a guide for reflecting on his own imprisonment and the broader questions of free will, fortune, and divine providence. However, Harington's Chaucer acts as more than a Boethian mouthpiece. For Harington, Chaucer is also a means of filling the idle days of imprisonment. He is a companion text to Harington's French lessons, offering another lens to the *Roman* and providing a further perspective on a character Harington finds particularly intriguing, Fals-Semblant. Chaucer was a script for collective reading and perhaps a discussion topic among the prison community in the Tower in 1550. Finally, the book is the means by which Harington can leave his mark for posterity. In the very act of signing and dating his Chaucer, Harington both advertises his ownership of the object and announces to later readers that he once lived and breathed and studied, a declaration that was profoundly meaningful in itself in his tumultuous environment.[49] He crafts an image of himself through this record, and we, as later readers, interpret the image of Harington and interpret Harington's image of Chaucer.

Thus, a biographical reading of Harington's marginalia moves him out of the amorphous group of "sixteenth-century readers of Chaucer." His marginalia gives us unique access to what an early-modern reader in the Tower of London found compelling about a medieval poet's work. Through his notes, we are invited into Harington's reading community; we are encouraged to learn to read as he read and interpret as he interpreted. His notes allow us to envision both an imprisoned reading community and a sophisticated individualized response from a reader invested in tracing the Boethian material throughout Chaucer's corpus. Overall, we are compelled to remember that reading, though it may work within a matrix of conventional expressions, is a highly individualized activity, and the narratives we construct about these readers must take into account the person behind the annotating pen.

University of Notre Dame

Acknowledgments

Thank you to Tim Machan, Kathryn Kerby-Fulton, and Nicole Eddy for their generous feedback on drafts of this essay.

NOTES

1. University of Notre Dame, Hesburgh Library, XLarge PR 1850 1542. There is at least one other annotator in the book, who writes in a later hand and makes cross-references to Milton. However, I focus in this paper only on those annotations by Harington.
2. Of course, Harington is not the only named early-modern reader who

responds to Chaucer's *Works*. For instance, we have access to Pope's copy of the 1598 Speght edition. However, Pope's annotations consist mostly of "c" marks placed beside passages he finds interesting. On Pope's reading of Speght, see David Nokes, "Pope's Chaucer," *Review of English Studies* 27.106 (1976): 180–182. We can also read Ben Jonson's Chaucer. However, Jonson confines his commentary to just three sections of the book: the prefatory "To the Readers" material, "The Remedie of Love," and "Of the Cuckow and the Nightingale." On Jonson's Chaucer, see R. C. Evans, "Ben Jonson's Chaucer," *English Literary Renaissance* 19 (1989): 324–345. For an example of a named reader leaving behind a comparably substantial marginal response in his copy of Speght's edition, see Megan Cook, "How Francis Thynne Read His Chaucer," *Journal of the Early Book Society* 15 (2012): 215–243. Cook connects antiquarian Francis Thynne's annotations in Speght's 1598 Chaucer to his critique of Speght's edition in his published *Animadversions*. Cook notes that Thynne focuses his annotating pen on Speght's paratext and responds to Chaucer with a historical rather than an affective eye. The most famous example of a named early-modern annotator is Gabriel Harvey. On his reading techniques and substantial corpus of marginal annotations, see Lisa Jardine and Anthony Grafton, "'Studied for Action': How Gabriel Harvey Read His Livy," *Past & Present* 129 (1990): 30–78.
3. Wolfgang Iser, "Interaction between Text and Reader," in *The Reader in the Text: Essays on Audience and Interpretation*, ed. Susan Rubin Suleiman and Inge Crosman (Princeton, NY: Princeton University Press, 1980), 107.
4. Alison Wiggins, "What Did Renaissance Readers Write in Their Printed Copies of Chaucer?," *The Library* 9.1 (2008): 1–36.
5. The most complete account of Harington's life is in Ruth Hughey, *John Harington of Stepney: Tudor Gentleman, His Life and Works* (Columbus: Ohio State University Press, 1971).
6. Ibid., 22–29.
7. Ibid., 24–26.
8. Ibid., 29. Seymour was allowed some servants in the Tower.
9. A full edition and description of this manuscript, now London, British Library, Additional MS 28635, is available in Ruth Hughey, ed., *The Arundel Harington Manuscript of Tudor Poetry*, 2 vols. (Columbus: Ohio State University Press, 1960).
10. For a list of those poems in the manuscript supposed to have been composed in the Tower, see Ruth Ahnert, *The Rise of Prison Literature in the Sixteenth Century* (Cambridge, UK: Cambridge University Press, 2013), 91–92.
11. Ibid., 93.
12. The book was printed by Thomas Berthelette in 1550 and released in a second edition in 1562. See Hughey, *John Harington*, 34.

13. A 2r–v. Here and following, references to the book are from John Harington, *The booke of freendeship* (London, 1550), Early English Books Online. An edition is included in Hughey, *John Harington*, 141–190. For a longer analysis of the text, see Ahnert, *Rise of Prison Literature*, 90–100.
14. M. B. Parkes, *Pause and Effect: An Introduction to the History of Punctuation in the West* (Aldershot, UK: Scolar Press, 1992), 5–6. On readers emending the punctuation in incunabula, see Paul Saenger and Michael Heinlen, "Incunable Description and Its Implication for the Analysis of Fifteenth-Century Reading Habits," in *Printing the Written Word: The Social History of Books, circa 1450–1520*, ed. Sandra L. Hindman, 239–249 (Ithaca, NY: Cornell University Press, 1991).
15. In a similar way, annotators of romance manuscripts often marked dialogue and shifts in speakers. For a study of such dialogue markers in *Roman de la Rose* manuscripts, see Sylvia Huot, "'Ci parle l'aucteur': The Rubrication of Voice and Authorship in *Roman de la Rose* Manuscripts," *SubStance* 17.2 (1988): 42–48. Thank you to Nicole Eddy for bringing this similarity to my attention.
16. ll. I.617–618, fol. 171v. Here and following, the text of the quotation is from Thynne's edition. The line numbers are from the *Riverside Chaucer*.
17. Of course, for those without the means to pay for a better prison experience, conditions could be miserable. On the conditions of the early-modern prison see Ahnert, *Rise of Prison Literature*, 11–22. See also Peter Lake and Michael Questier, "Prisons, Priests and People," in *England's Long Reformation, 1500–1800*, ed. Nicholas Tyacke, 195–234 (London: University College London Press, 1997).
18. Colette Moore, *Quoting Speech in Early English* (Cambridge, UK: Cambridge University Press, 2011).
19. On Chaucer's postmedieval reception, see Caroline F. E. Spurgeon, *Five Hundred Years of Chaucer Criticism and Allusion, 1357–1900*, 3 vols. (Cambridge, UK: Cambridge University Press, 1925); Seth Lerer, *Chaucer and His Readers: Imagining the Author in Late-Medieval England* (Princeton, NJ: Princeton University Press, 1993); Seth Lerer, *Courtly Letters in the Age of Henry VIII* (Cambridge, UK: Cambridge University Press, 1997); Joseph A. Dane, *Who Is Buried in Chaucer's Tomb* (East Lansing: Michigan State University Press, 1998); Stephanie Trigg, *Congenial Souls: Reading Chaucer from Medieval to Postmodern* (Minneapolis: University of Minnesota Press, 2002). Spurgeon notes that the understanding of Chaucer as a moral exemplar is "almost exclusively" a sixteenth-century phenomenon, "although there are isolated examples earlier and later." See Spurgeon, *Five Hundred Years*, 1:xciv.
20. For an analysis of Speght's 1602 sententiae, see Clare R. Kinney, "Thomas Speght's Renaissance Chaucer and the *solaas* of *sentence* in *Troilus and Criseyde*," in *Refiguring Chaucer in the Renaissance*, ed. Theresa M. Krier, 66–84 (Gainesville: University of Florida Press, 1998); William Sherman,

Used Books: Marking Readers in the Renaissance (Philadelphia: University of Pennsylvania Press, 2009), 44–45. On commonplace books in the early-modern period, see also Heidi Brayman Hackel, *Reading Material in Early Modern England* (Cambridge, UK: Cambridge University Press, 2005).

21. Antonina Harbus also provides a detailed description of the more than a thousand anonymous marginal notes in a copy of Thynne's 1532 edition held in the Beinecke Library. Harbus notes that although most of the annotations are of a "conventional type," the annotator took particular interest in proverbial material, again something that reflects an interest in extracting material for commonplace books. Harbus's annotator, like Harington, also corrects spelling and punctuation. See Antonina Harbus, "A Renaissance Reader's English Annotations to Thynne's 1532 Edition of Chaucer's *Works*," *Review of English Studies* 59.240 (2007): 342–355.
22. On famous early-modern reader Gabriel Harvey's cross-referencing techniques, see Jardine and Grafton, "Studied for Action," 51.
23. See the note to the line in the *Riverside Chaucer*.
24. Here and following, line numbers from Usk are taken from Thomas Usk, *The Testament of Love*, ed. R. Allen Shoaf (Kalamazoo, MI: Medieval Institute Publications, 1998).
25. Fifteenth-century manuscripts of Chaucer often contained such source citation, particularly in "The Wife of Bath's Prologue." For a treatment of these scribal glosses, see Theresa Tinkle, "The Wife of Bath's Marginal Authority," *Studies in the Age of Chaucer* 32 (2010): 67–110.
26. Francis William Bourdillon, *The Early Editions of the Roman de la Rose* (London: Bibliographical Society, 1906), 97.
27. Bourdillon records the lines as the 66th verse-title.
28. On this practice applied in incunabula, see Saenger and Heinlen, "Incunable Description," 249–250.
29. The annotation at fol. 212v is cropped, as are many other examples of Harington's marginalia. Here and following, the letters in brackets are my emendations.
30. Wiggins, "What Did Renaissance Readers Write," 12.
31. Robert Darnton, "First Steps toward a History of Reading," in *The Kiss of Lamourette: Reflections in Cultural History* (New York: W.W. Norton, 1990), 162.
32. For other studies that demonstrate the value of reading marginalia biographically, see Carl Grindley's analysis of the Ayscough family's reading of *Piers Plowman* in the sixteenth century: Carl Grindley, "The Life of a Book: British Library Manuscript Additional 35157 in Historical Context" (PhD diss., University of Glasgow, 1996). See also Karrie Fuller's work on Sir Adrian Fortescue's reading of Langland in 1532: Karrie Fuller, "Langland in the Early Modern Household," in *New Directions in Medieval*

Manuscript Studies and Reading Practices, ed. Kathryn Kerby-Fulton, John J. Thompson, and Sarah Baechle, 333–334 (Notre Dame, IN: University of Notre Dame Press, 2014).

33. Catherine Brown, "In the Middle," *Journal of Medieval and Early Modern Studies* 30.3 (2000): 547–574.
34. For a brief summary of Thomas's supposed plots against Edward, see G. W. Bernard, "Thomas Seymour," in *Oxford Dictionary of National Biography*, ed. H. C. G. Matthew and Brian Harrison (Oxford: University Press, 2004).
35. Newberry Library, Case 6A 112. In addition, I have also examined two 1542 Thynne editions in the Newberry collections, one of which contains substantial manuscript marginalia (Vault Case Y 185. C4055). I plan to provide a full analysis of the marginal notes in these and other Thynne examples as part of a longer study. It is worth noting at this stage that the multiple annotators in both Case Y 185 and Case 6A 112 use similar reading techniques to Harington's. Annotators in both examples, for example, marginally index sections, underline sententious phrases, and draw manicules.
36. The annotation is unfortunately cropped on the far left side. The "predestinacion" reading is my best guess based on the context. A third word, below "fre will" is cropped to the extent that it is unreadable.
37. Notably, Harington does not provide a table of contents for the two other texts with title pages—*The Canterbury Tales* and *The Romance of the Rose*.
38. Thanks to Jesse Lander for allowing me to read a paper he presented at the International Congress on Medieval Studies entitled "Reading and (Re)marking: A Tudor Gentleman Encounters Chaucer." He reads Harington's table of contents closely and concludes that some of Harington's summaries offer polemical expansions on Chaucer's text.
39. Linne R. Mooney and Mary-Jo Arn, "*The Kingis Quair*: Introduction," in *The Kingis Quair and Other Prison Poems*, ed. Linne R. Mooney and Mary-Jo Arn (Kalamazoo, MI: Medieval Institute Publications, 2005), available at http://d.lib.rochester.edu/teams/text/mooney-and-arn-kingis-quair-and-other-prison-poems-kingis-quair-introduction.
40. Mooney and Arn, "General Introduction," in *The Kingis Quair and Other Prison Poems*, available at http://d.lib.rochester.edu/teams/text/mooney-and-arn-kingis-quair-and-other-prison-poems-introduction.
41. On Usk's biography, see Paul Strohm, "Politics and Poetics: Usk and Chaucer in the 1380s," in *Literary Practice and Social Change in Britain, 1380–1530*, ed. Lee Patterson, 83–112 (Berkeley: University of California Press, 1990). The date of Usk's *Testament* is unknown, and many scholars try to place it during one of Usk's imprisonments. Strohm notes that we need not interpret Usk's prison literally or autobiographically, and he dates the text to 1385–1386, the period between Usk's two imprisonments. See Strohm, "Politics and Poetics," 97 n. 18.

42. Harington references Chaucer by name in an annotation on fol. cccxxv, equating the textual "I" in l.I.545 ("I was drawe to ben assentaunt") with Chaucer himself.
43. He underlines, for example, passages such as "to good service longeth good dede goodly don thorowe fre choice in hert" and "Every man hath free arbitrement to chose good or yvel to performe" (3.216, 3.222, fol. cccxliiv).
44. Hughey, *John Harington*, 30.
45. Ahnert, *Rise of Prison Literature*, 4–5. The exception is Thomas More's *A Dialogue of Comfort against Tribulation*.
46. Ahnert, *Rise of Prison Literature*, 91.
47. Here and following, all quotations from Harington's poetry are taken from the edition in Hughey, *Arundel Harington Manuscript*. For Hughey's brief discussion, see Hughey, *John Harington*, 48–49.
48. On the biblical source of this sentiment, see the note to the line in the *Riverside Chaucer*.
49. The prison graffiti that several prisoners left behind on the walls of the Tower is a related practice. See Ruth Ahnert, "Writing in the Tower of London during the Reformation, ca. 1530–1558," *Huntington Library Quarterly* 72.2 (2009): 168–192, esp. 172–178.

WORKS CITED

Ahnert, Ruth. *The Rise of Prison Literature in the Sixteenth Century*. Cambridge, UK: Cambridge University Press, 2013.

———. "Writing in the Tower of London during the Reformation, ca. 1530–1558." *Huntington Library Quarterly* 72.2 (2009): 168–92.

Bernard, G. W. "Thomas Seymour." In *Oxford Dictionary of National Biography*, edited by H. C. G. Matthew and Brian Harrison. Oxford: Oxford University Press, 2004. http://www.oxforddnb.com/view/article/25181.

Bourdillon, Francis William. *The Early Editions of the Roman de la Rose*. London: Bibliographical Society, 1906.

Brown, Catherine. "In the Middle." *Journal of Medieval and Early Modern Studies* 30.3 (2000): 547–574.

Chaucer, Geoffrey. *The Riverside Chaucer*. Edited by Larry D. Benson. 3rd ed. Boston: Houghton Mifflin, 1987.

———. *The Works of Geffray Chaucer Newly Printed, with Dyuers Workes Whiche Were Neuer in Print Before*. London: Thomas Godfray, 1532.

———. *The Workes of Geffray Chaucer Newlye printed, Wyth Dyuers Workes Whych were Neuer in Print Before*. London: Richard Grafton, 1542.

Cook, Megan. "How Francis Thynne Read His Chaucer." *Journal of the Early Book Society* 15 (2012): 215–243.

Dane, Joseph A. *Who Is Buried in Chaucer's Tomb*. East Lansing, MI: Michigan State University Press, 1998.

Darnton, Robert. "First Steps toward a History of Reading." In *The Kiss of Lamourette: Reflections in Cultural History*, 154–187. New York: Norton, 1990.
Evans, R. C. "Ben Jonson's Chaucer." *English Literary Renaissance* 19.3 (1989): 324–345.
Fuller, Karrie. "Langland in the Early Modern Household." In *New Directions in Medieval Manuscript Studies and Reading Practices*, edited by Kathryn Kerby-Fulton, John J. Thompson, and Sarah Baechle, 324–342. Notre Dame, IN: University of Notre Dame Press, 2014.
Grindley, Carl. "The Life of a Book: British Library Manuscript Additional 35157 in Historical Context." PhD diss., University of Glasgow, 1996.
Hackel, Heidi Brayman. *Reading Material in Early Modern England*. Cambridge, UK: Cambridge University Press, 2005.
Harbus, Antonina. "A Renaissance Reader's English Annotations to Thynne's 1532 Edition of Chaucer's Works." *Review of English Studies* 59.240 (2007): 342–355.
Harington, John. *The booke of freendeship*. London, 1550.
Hughey, Ruth. *John Harington of Stepney: Tudor Gentleman, His Life and Works*. Columbus: Ohio State University Press, 1971.
———, ed. *The Arundel Harington Manuscript of Tudor Poetry*. 2 vols. Columbus: Ohio State University Press, 1960.
Huot, Sylvia. "'Ci parle l'aucteur': The Rubrication of Voice and Authorship in *Roman de la Rose* Manuscripts." *SubStance: A Review of Theory and Literary Criticism* 17.2 (1988): 42–48.
Iser, Wolfgang. "Interaction between Text and Reader." In *The Reader in the Text: Essays on Audience and Interpretation*, edited by Susan Rubin Suleiman and Inge Crosman, 106–119. Princeton, NJ: Princeton University Press, 1980.
Jardine, Lisa, and Anthony Grafton. "'Studied for Action': How Gabriel Harvey Read His Livy." *Past & Present* 129 (1990): 30–78.
Kinney, Clare R. "Thomas Speght's Renaissance Chaucer and the solaas of sentence in Troilus and Criseyde." In *Refiguring Chaucer in the Renaissance*, edited by Theresa M. Krier, 66–84. Gainesville: University of Florida Press.
Lake, Peter, and Michael Questier. "Prisons, Priests and People." In *England's Long Reformation, 1500–1800*, edited by Nicholas Tyacke, 195–234. London: University College London Press, 1997.
Lerer, Seth. *Chaucer and His Readers: Imagining the Author in Late-Medieval England*. Princeton, NJ: Princeton University Press, 1993.
———. *Courtly Letters in the Age of Henry VIII*. Cambridge, UK: Cambridge University Press, 1997.
Mooney, Linne R., and Mary-Jo Arn. *The Kingis Quair and Other Prison Poems*. Kalamazoo, MI: Medieval Institute Publications, 2005.

Moore, Colette. *Quoting Speech in Early English*. Cambridge, UK: Cambridge University Press, 2011.
Nokes, David. "Pope's Chaucer." *Review of English Studies* 27.106 (1976): 180–182.
Parkes, M. B. *Pause and Effect: An Introduction to the History of Punctuation in the West*. Aldershot, UK: Scolar Press, 1992.
Saenger, Paul, and Michael Heinlen. "Incunable Description and Its Implication for the Analysis of Fifteenth-Century Reading Habits." In *Printing the Written Word: The Social History of Books, circa 1450–1520*, edited by Sandra L. Hindman, 225–258. Ithaca, NY: Cornell University Press, 1991.
Sherman, William. *Used Books: Marking Readers in the Renaissance*. Philadelphia: University of Pennsylvania Press, 2009.
Spurgeon, Caroline F. E. *Five Hundred Years of Chaucer Criticism and Allusion, 1357–1900*. 3 vols. Cambridge, UK: Cambridge University Press, 1925.
Strohm, Paul. "Politics and Poetics: Usk and Chaucer in the 1380s." In *Literary Practice and Social Change in Britain, 1380–1530*, edited by Lee Patterson, 83–112. Berkeley: University of California Press, 1990.
Tinkle, Theresa. "The Wife of Bath's Marginal Authority." *Studies in the Age of Chaucer* 32 (2010): 67–110.
Trigg, Stephanie. *Congenial Souls: Reading Chaucer from Medieval to Postmodern*. Minneapolis: University of Minnesota Press, 2002.
Usk, Thomas. *The Testament of Love*. Edited by R. Allen Shoaf. Kalamazoo, MI: Medieval Institute Publications, 1998.
Wiggins, Alison. "What Did Renaissance Readers Write in their Printed Copies of Chaucer?" *The Library* 9.1 (2008): 3–36.

Annotated Books

Annotations to Chaucer's *Works* (1532). Chicago, Newberry Library Case 6A 112.
Annotations to Chaucer's *Works* (1542). Chicago, Newberry Library Vault Case Y 185. C4055.
Harington, John. Annotations to Chaucer's *Works* (1542). South Bend, IN, University of Notre Dame, Hesburgh Library XLarge PR 1850 1542.

Les Vies des Femmes Célèbres: Antoine Dufour, Jean Pichore, and a Manuscript's Debt to an Italian Printed Book

ANNELIESE POLLOCK RENCK

The ornate manuscript presented to Anne of Brittany by Antoine Dufour, *Les Vies des femmes célèbres* (Nantes, Musée Dobrée, ms. XVII), has been the object of extended study.[1] Written in 1504,[2] the manuscript was then illuminated by Jean Pichore, Parisian artist, by 1506.[3] We unfortunately do not know of any documents describing the production of this work: Dufour states in his prologue that Anne commissioned it,[4] but beyond this detail, the role that the queen played in the production of the manuscript remains unknown. We are unable to ascertain, for example, if Anne specified how Dufour was to represent the women in his text or which women he was to include. We do not know if the writer then communicated with the Parisian illuminator in order to convey his wishes concerning the iconography contained in the manuscript. However, a careful examination of both the text and the images of *Les Vies des femmes célèbres* shows that author and artist coordinated their work in some manner and that the individuals involved in the codex's production translated and adapted multiple sources, including an Italian incunabulum, in constructing their manuscript for the queen.

Dufour's Text:
A Translation via Compilation of Two Latin Sources from Italy

Antoine Dufour relied on at least two Latin texts in composing his *Vies des femmes célèbres*: Boccaccio's *De mulieribus claris* (ca. 1362) and Jacopo

Filippo Foresti da Bergamo's *De plurimis claris selectisque mulieribus*, a Latin adaptation of Boccaccio's work, published in Ferrara in 1497, and again in 1521.[5] Writing in France in the first decade of the sixteenth century, Dufour wove these two sources together, creating his own unique tapestry distinct from and yet reliant on the threads of both Italian authors.[6]

Around 1362, Giovanni Boccaccio dedicated his *De mulieribus claris* to Andrea Aciaiuoli, Countess of Altavilla.[7] Consisting of 104 biographies of famous women from antiquity and the Old Testament, this was the first collection of biographies in Western literature to present only women.[8] *De mulieribus claris* enjoyed enormous success both in its original Latin and in translation in numerous languages throughout the fifteenth and sixteenth centuries.[9] Jacopo Filippo Foresti da Bergamo's *De plurimis claris selectisque mulieris* was compiled primarily from *De mulieribus claris*, the Bible, and Sabadino degli Arienti's *Gynevera de le clare donne* (ca. 1489–1490 and 1492).[10] According to Steven Kolsky, *De plurimis* emerged in a sociopolitical context in late-fifteenth-century Italy, in which noblewomen saw *De mulieribus*'s presentation of powerful women as an opportunity to follow the example of female political action set forth in Boccaccio's work.[11]

While Boccaccio created an opposition between good and bad women in his Preface, specifying that he would not treat Christian women, Foresti borrowed Boccaccio's rhetoric but delineated two camps of women: on the one hand, pagans such as Semiramis, Medea, Athalia, Olympia, and Cleopatra, and on the other, Christian women such as Sarah, Judith, and Esther. As Kolsky writes, "the compiler methodically juxtaposes the Boccaccian women with his own additions in order to define the *De Plurimis* as a Christian work." [12]

Antoine Dufour's text carefully compiles and adapts Boccaccio's and Foresti's works, creating a "translation" that responds to rather than reproduces its sources.[13] *Les Vies des femmes célèbres* is comprised of ninety-one biographies, sixty-four of which also appear in *De mulieribus claris*, and all of which appear in Foresti's *De plurimis*. Many of these ninety-one biographies follow Boccaccio's text so closely that there is little doubt as to the French translator's utilization of the Latin source. The remaining twenty-seven biographies draw certain details from a variety of texts, but all of the women described in Dufour's work appear in Foresti's compendium, and the French author's biographies mirror almost exactly the order of those in the *De plurimis*.[14]

An examination of Semiramis's biography in each work helps us understand how Dufour compiled his version from both Foresti's and Boccaccio's texts. Foresti placed his biography of Sarah, a heroine absent from Boccaccio's compendium, directly before that of Semiramis in his text, pointing out in the second woman's case how dissimilar she was from her biblical contemporary—a parallel that Dufour takes up in his text as well.[15] Although Foresti's biography of Semiramis is very similar to that of Boccaccio's, as he employs the same Latin word for word in the majority of the text, Foresti's inclusion of Sarah in his compendium departs from his Latin source, as does the parallel between the two heroines established by the Italian author cited above. The comparison between Sarah and Semiramis is then taken up by Dufour, strongly suggesting the French author's familiarity with the *De plurimis*.[16]

At the end of Semiramis's biography, Foresti includes a description of the inscription on her tomb and King Darius's opening of the tomb,[17] an anecdote retained by Dufour[18] but not found in Boccaccio's text.[19] However, Dufour adds an additional sentence to the end of her biography, reminding the reader that Semiramis was killed by her son—a detail also recounted by Boccaccio at the end of his biography but omitted by Foresti.[20] The narrative of Semiramis's story thus demonstrates how Dufour combines or compiles translated passages from both Latin sources.

Although Dufour specifically included the anecdote recounting Semiramis's death, we also see textual instances where the French translator has, by contrast, omitted descriptions related to violent acts, as in the case of Joanna of Naples's biography. Joanna of Naples (1326–1382) ascended to the Neapolitan throne at the age of seventeen. As Elizabeth Casteen notes, Joanna was a subject of some controversy as a female ruler, and "her queenship thus became the background for discussions about royal succession, hereditary principle, and the nature and definition of sovereignty."[21]

Seen in this light, the fact that Dufour chose (via Foresti) to include Joanna in his compendium of famous women is in itself significant: dedicating his collection of famous women's biographies to the current French queen, the translator inserts himself into contemporary debates surrounding conceptions of sovereignty and in particular female rule. Jeanneau notes that Joanna of Naples is idealized in the sixteenth-century French text, since Dufour significantly does not mention the fact that she was rumored to have murdered her first husband.[22] By idealizing Joanna, Dufour is able to draw parallels between her and Anne of Brittany as both virtuous and politically active women.[23]

Yet the choice of Joanna of Naples also underlines Dufour's adaptation of two Latin texts from Italy into a biography that is more relevant to readers in sixteenth-century France. Both Boccaccio's and Foresti's texts glorify not only Joanna but also Italy, its people, and its land, whereas Dufour shifts focus back onto Joanna and her accomplishments. Additionally, where the Latin texts devote much time discussing Joanna's strength (the trials she withstood, the people she disciplined), the French version discusses at greater length Joanna's charity, her "consolation, comfort, and aid for widows, the poor, the sick, and orphans" ("consolation, confort et ayde des vefves, povres, malades et orphelins")[24] and the fact that she "nourished strangers and indigent people as much as others, built and financed monasteries and hospitals, and received in magnificence and liberally treated clerics and lettered men" ("estrangiers et indigens autant que aultres substantoit; monastères, hospitaulx édiffioit et nourrissoit, clercz, lectrez et vertueux magnificquement recevoit et libéralement tractoit").[25]

While Dufour may indeed have emphasized these traits in Joanna in order to draw parallels between herself and his patroness, Anne of Brittany, he also surely did so in order to make this famous woman more understandable for his female readers (the queen and her female entourage). They would have been able to see in Joanna a figure to admire as similar not only to themselves but also more generally to their own cultural and historical framework. Rather than a shining example of the strength of Italy, as Joanna was heralded to be in Boccaccio's and Foresti's texts, Joanna emerges in Anne of Brittany's manuscript as an example of female piety, charity, and power.

Images as Translated Presentations of Women

While it is certainly clear that Dufour adapted at least two Latin textual sources, we may also observe that ms. XVII's illuminator, Jean Pichore, also utilized both visual and verbal models, perhaps even those found in the first edition of *De plurimis*, in constructing the miniatures contained within *Les Vies des femmes célèbres*. Jean Pichore ran a very large workshop in Paris, where he worked as an illuminator and bookmaker from 1502 to 1521.[26] He and his workshop artists illuminated a number of codices for Louise of Savoy[27] and two other manuscripts treating famous women.[28] Caroline Zöhl attests to Pichore's Italian source materials,[29] which were effected in part by his collaboration with artists for Cardinal Georges of Amboîse.[30]

Pichore also worked extensively for Louis XII and/or Anne of Brittany. He illuminated an ornate copy of the *Remèdes de l'une et l'autre fortune* (BnF fr. 225; ca. 1503)[31] and a French translation of Petrarch's *Triomphes* (BnF fr. 594) for Louis XII.[32] Additionally, Zöhl attributes a copy of Plutarch's *Discours sur le mariage de Pollion et d'Eurydice*, commemorating the marriage of Anne and Louis around 1499 (Saint Petersburg, Russian National Library, Fr.Q.v.III,3), to the Parisian artist.[33] Finally, Pichore and his workshop contributed five miniatures to a volume made upon the queen's death, *Relation des obsèques d'Anne de Bretagne* (Paris, Petit Palais, Dutuit 665).[34]

As Zöhl's work shows extensively, Jean Pichore's contacts and oeuvre can underline for us the varying iconographical traditions that he drew upon (Italian and French, classical and Gothic), his patrons (Georges of Amboîse, Louise of Savoy, Louis XII, and Anne of Brittany), and his collaboration with other artists from a wide geographical area and media (manuscript and print). It is this range of artistic development that emerges in Pichore's illuminations of *Les Vies des femmes célèbres*, underlining further the manuscript's existence as a compilation of multiple sources, both visual and textual.

It is clear that Pichore took great care in aligning his depiction of at least some of the famous women with those described in Dufour's text. As an example of the intertwined roles of text and image in the manuscript, we may cite Zenobia, a woman warrior whom Dufour describes as carrying a "standard whose motto was the honor of ladies" ("estandart, qui estoit l'honneur des dames pour sa devise").[35] Although the inscription painted by Pichore in his representation of her banner is difficult to decipher—because the first word, "Lonneur" (= l'honneur [the honor]) is not properly abbreviated—it reads "Lone des dames." Sophie Cassagnes-Brouquet is thus correct in describing the motto as "une inscription en l'honneur des dames."[36] Pichore's miniature, integrating the detail of the inscription on Zenobia's flag from Dufour's text, indicates the illuminator's engagement with the manuscript's verbal narrative.

In Pichore's portrait of Medea in *Les Vies des femmes célèbres*, the female protagonist sits at a table covered by a cloth, pen in hand (Fig. 1). Instead of writing on the letter before her, however, she plunges her pen into the heart of her dead infant. To my knowledge, only Dufour's text describes this detail in the heroine's biography: "to reach the summit of her cruelty, Medea wrote villainous letters to Jason with blood from the heart of her dead infant" ("pour achever le comble de sa cruaulté, du sang du cueur de son filz, fist à Jason villaines lettres").[37] Including an important feature from Dufour's biography of Medea, Pichore thus utilizes this verbal source in his miniature. It is impossible to know, without some sort of documentation, exactly why Pichore decided to paint Medea writing a letter in her infant's blood. Nonetheless, the inclusion of this very dramatic characteristic in the manuscript's iconographical program suggests that the artist had access in some manner to Dufour's text.

Yet Pichore also, I posit, combines Dufour's text with contemporary iconographical sources in sculpting his portrait of Medea. In particular, the Parisian illuminator's familiarity with the many portrayals of women in the process of writing found in numerous manuscripts at the end of the fifteenth century[38] highlights the importance of Medea's pose as writer here. While the image of a woman writing is found only three times in *Les Vies des femmes célèbres*, this representation of the learned female appears to have become a prevalent tradition in the late fifteenth century—a tradition into which Pichore also inserted himself in his miniatures of Nicostrata (fol. 21) and Blesillia (fol. 61).

The case of Medea in *Les Vies des femmes célèbres*, however, distinguishes itself through Pichore's and Dufour's depiction of the heroine's bloody letter-

Figure 1. Medea, Nantes, Musée Dobrée, ms. 17, fol. 18v. © Musée Dobrée – Grand patrimoine de Loire-Atlantique.

writing. I have found one other textual and iconographical depiction of a woman writing a letter in blood, and a roughly contemporary one at that. In BnF fr. 874 (ca. 1502),[39] a manuscript version of the *XXI Epistres d'Ovide* to whose iconographical program Pichore contributed,[40] the scribe includes rubrics introducing each of Ovid's translated letters. The preface to Hypermnestra's epistle explains that as punishment for disobeying her father, she is to be put in jail and each day will have a part cut off from her body until the day she dies. The rubric, unique to this manuscript exemplar, indicates that Hypermnestra composes an epistle to her husband using the blood of her severed leg.[41] This textual detail, present only in BnF fr. 874, is taken up by the manuscript's illuminator, whether Pichore himself or another artist with whom he collaborated in its production. The elaborate illumination of Hypermnestra found in BnF fr. 874 (Fig. 2) is the only visual reference to a heroine writing a letter in blood, other than Pichore's depiction of Medea in the *Vies des femmes célèbres* manuscript, that I have found so far. Whether or not Pichore—and/or his collaborators—consciously refers to the BnF fr. 874 rubric in this depiction of Hypermnestra, the miniature in Anne's manuscript certainly appears to combine the traditional depiction of women writing letters found in the *XXI Epistres* with an important feature from Dufour's biography of Medea—that of her writing in her child's blood—translating both verbal and visual sources in creating something of his own innovation.

One final source for Pichore's iconographical program, or at least that of the manuscript's rubricator, may be proposed, as the placement and format of the illuminations in Anne of Brittany's copy of *Les Vies des femmes célèbres* mirrors closely that of Foresti's original incunabulum. The 1497 edition of *De plurimis* begins with a title page (fol. 1r), and then a full-page illustration of Foresti presenting his work to its female dedicatee, Beatrice of Aragon (fol. 1v), the author's prologue (fol. 2r–3v), a table of contents (fol. 4r–5r), and finally a full-page illustration containing eight square religious scenes related to Mary and Christ (fol. 5v). After multiple folios recounting Mary's biography, each biography begins with a square historiated initial and a rubric announcing the heroine to follow. Many but not all biographies include a small illustration inserted into the text at the beginning of the scenario just below the rubric.

Queen Anne's commissioned book presents significant similarities in its formatting, especially with regard to the placement and size of its miniatures. Pichore's iconography, like the Italian printed edition, contains two full-page miniatures that visually mirror those included by Foresti, one showing Dufour's presentation to Anne of Brittany (fol. 1r), and the other containing six square scenes depicting Mary and Christ (fol. 2r). As in the printed edition, these two miniatures visually bracket the transla

Figure 2. Hypermnestra, Paris, Bibliothèque Nationale de France, ms.français 874, fol. 175v.

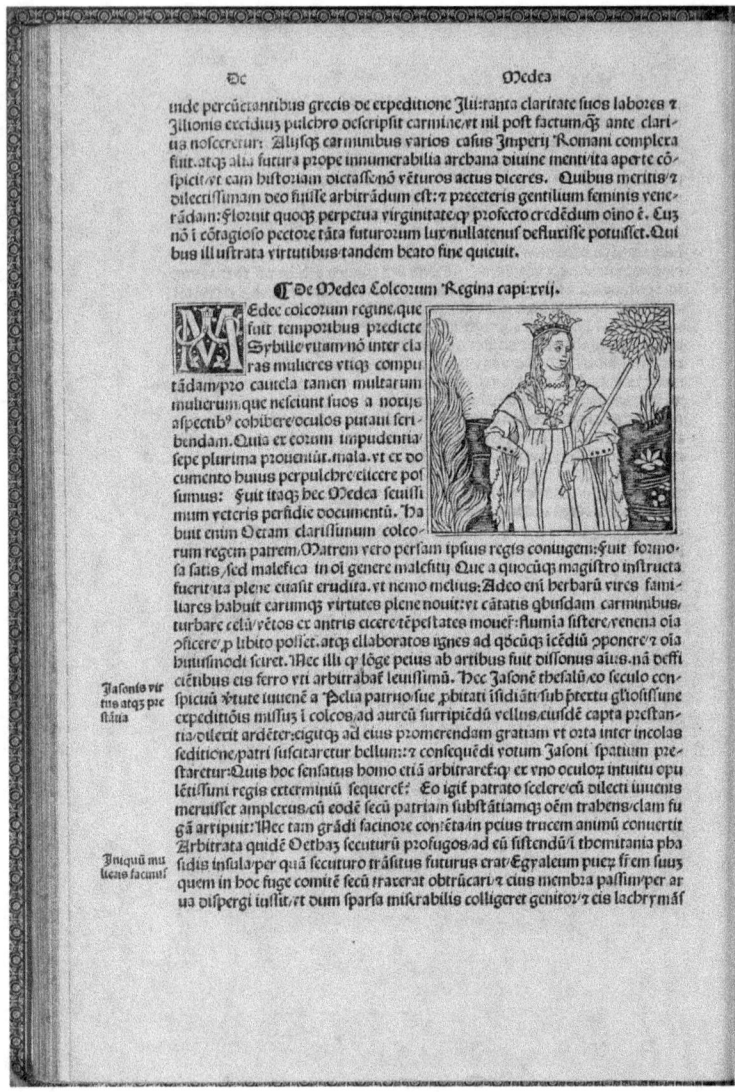

Figure 3. Medea, Los Angeles, Getty Research Institute (81693), fol. 22v.

tor's Prologue (fol. 1v). Thereafter, each biography begins with a square historiated initial, and where accompanied by a miniature, a square-shaped image of the woman in question that lines up with the first line of her biography. The example of Medea (Figs. 1 and 3) reveals the similarities between the mise-en-page found in Foresti's printed edition and that of the later manuscript: both include square historiated initials, miniatures surrounded by a simple square border, and a single column of text into which the miniatures are inserted flush with the first line. While Foresti's printed edition does preface each biography with a rubric, these rubrics are not printed in a separate color and indeed are sometimes set apart from the body of the biography by a blank space between them and first line of text, thus serving much the same function as the simple space between biographies that the manuscript makers incorporated into the page layout.

Whether Jean Pichore himself drew from Foresti's printed edition remains unclear. There do seem to be certain compositional similarities between the two presentation scenes (Figs. 4 and 5)—namely, the presence of two religious figures, one at the back with his arms folded, and the inclusion of the Annunciation scene prefacing Mary's biography (Figs. 6 and 7). In addition, certain details found in Pichore's miniatures could have been drawn from the printed illustrations. For example, the small figures painted by Pichore to decorate Medea's writing desk (Fig. 1), in particular the one holding a sticklike object over his shoulder, display the same sort of childish violence found in the lower margins of the 1497 edition's presentation scene (Fig. 5); Joan of Arc (Dufour, fol. 76v) wears the same armor in both versions, and her horse has the same bridle and saddle as a soldier in those same margins of Foresti's printed book (Fig. 5). However, these details are not conclusive enough to say with any surety whether the Parisian illuminator, although known for his usage of Italian source materials and his ability to draw upon multiple sources, employed this particular Italian printed edition as a model or inspiration for his work in Queen Anne's manuscript.

What is clear, however, is that this 1497 printed edition from Italy was used by Antoine Dufour as model for both the content and the ordering of his ninety-one biographies of famous women, and that whoever formatted the manuscript itself chose to follow the Italian source's layout for the two full-page miniatures and the smaller ones accompanying the women's biographies. Although further inquiry is required as to Jean Pichore's potential reliance upon the printed materials used by the manuscript's author, the likely presence of a copy of Foresti's printed edition in the hands of Antoine Dufour and the individual responsible for the manuscript's formatting point to interesting implications for scholarship surrounding the transition from manuscript to print, namely, that especially in Paris around 1500, the two

Figure 4. Anne of Brittany and Antoine Dufour, Nantes, Musée Dobrée, ms. 17, fol. 1r. © C. Hémon, Musée Dobrée – Grand patrimoine de Loire Atlantique.

LES VIES DES FEMMES CÉLÈBRES   169

Figure 5. Isabeau of Bavaria and Jacopo Filippo Foresti da Bergamo, Los Angeles, Getty Research Institute (81693), fol. 1v.

Figure 6. Annunciation and Scenes relating to the life of Mary, Nantes, Musée Dobrée, ms. 17, fol. 2r. © C. Hémon, Musée Dobrée – Grand patrimoine de Loire-Atlantique.

LES VIES DES FEMMES CÉLÈBRES 171

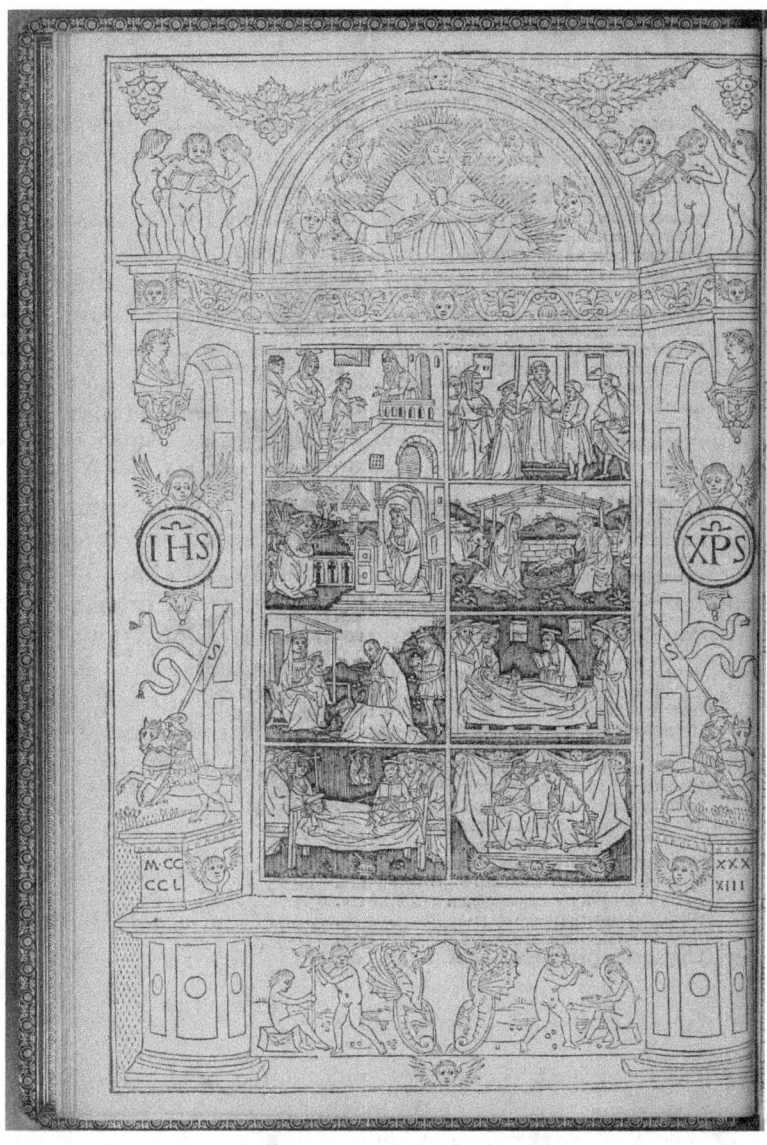

Figure 7. Scenes relating to the life of Mary, Los Angeles, Getty Research Institute (81693) fol. 5v.

forms of reproduction existed in tandem and even in cooperation with each other, each tradition drawing from, adapting, and mirroring the other. Although much work has been carried out on the usage of manuscript sources in constructing printed editions, *Les Vies des femmes célèbres* provides an example of the reverse also being true: that manuscript makers drew upon printed sources as well.[42]

This study of one particular manuscript can be added to a growing list of scholarship within the last few decades that has revealed the movement of printed editions from Italy to Paris in the last years of the fifteenth century. Kathrin Giogoli and John Block Friedman show that Robinet Testard adapted elements from the so-called Mantegna tarot cards in a number of his works, and in particular a French translation of Boccaccio's *De mulieribus claris*, BnF fr. 599;[43] most recently, Sonja Drimmer reveals the trajectory of a humanist from Italy, to Paris, and then to England in 1507[44] and the very portability of the print resources that he brought with him on his journey and whose graphics are imitated in his manuscripts.[45] The study of these iconographical and human trajectories is revealing not only for literary and art-historical scholars but also for researchers interested in constructing a broader history of cultural exchange between Italy and France at the end of the Middle Ages and in examining questions of manuscript and printed book production at the end of the fifteenth century and the beginning of the sixteenth. Ultimately, this brief article sheds light on the fluid nature of exchange between manuscript and print in Parisian workshops around 1500 and the role that Italian books played in bringing the Renaissance to France.

Bucknell University

Acknowledgments

I would like to thank Cynthia Brown, James Conrad, and Edward English for their review and suggestions.

NOTES

1. See Cynthia J. Brown, *The Queen's Library: Image-Making at the Court of Anne of Brittany, 1477–1514* (Philadelphia: University of Pennsylvania Press, 2011), 144–166; and Cynthia J. Brown, "The 'Famous-Women' *Topos* in Early Sixteenth-Century France: Echoes of Christine de Pizan," in *"Riens ne m'est seur que la chose incertaine": Etudes sur l'art d'écrire au Moyen Âge offertes à Eric Hicks par ses élèves, collègues, amies et amis*, ed. J.-Cl. Mühlethaler and D. Billotte (Geneva: Editions Slatkine, 2001), 149–160; Sophie Cassagnes-Brouquet, *Un manuscrit d'Anne de Bretagne. Les Vies des femmes célèbres d'Antoine Dufour* (Rennes, France: Éditions Ouest-

France, 2007); and Michelle Szkilnik, "Antoine Dufour's *Vies des femmes célèbres*," in *The Cultural and Political Legacy of Anne de Bretagne: Negotiating Convention in Books and Documents*, ed. Cynthia J. Brown (Cambridge, UK: D.S. Brewer, 2010), 65–80.

2. Dufour dates his text in the Prologue. See Antoine Dufour, *Les Vies des femmes célèbres*, ed. G. Jeanneau (Geneva: Librairie Droz S.A., 1970), 1. All citations of Dufour's text are taken from this edition; all translations from the Middle French are my own.

3. See Claire Aptel, Nathalie Biotteau, Marie Richard, and Jacques Santrot, eds., *Thomas Dobrée 1800–1895: Un homme, un musée* (Nantes and Paris: Musée Thomas Dobrée and Somogy Éditions d'Art, 1997), 167–168. For the attribution of the miniatures to Jean Pichore, see François Avril and Nicole Reynaud, *Les Manuscrits à peintures en France, 1440–1520* (Paris: Flammarion, 1993), 415.

4. Dufour writes, "knowing the depth and the height of the virtues of the elevated, powerful and excellent princess my lady Anne of Brittany, queen of France and duchess of Brittany, I . . . , by the commandment of this lady, . . . wanted to translate the present book into mother tongue" ("congnoissant l'abisme et le comble de vertus estre en treshaulte, trespuissante et tres excellente dame et princesse ma dame Anne de Bretaigne, royne de France et duchesse de Bretaigne, je . . . , par le commandement d'icelle, . . . ay bien voulu translater ce présent livre en maternel langage,"); Dufour, *Vies des femmes*, 1.

5. The 1497 edition of *De plurimis* was published by Lorenzo de'Rossi in Ferrara; in 1521, Johannes Ravisius Textor inserted it into his anthology, the *De memorabilibus et claris mulieribus aliquot diversorum scriptorum opera*, printed in Paris. For further information on how and why this adaptation was written, see Stephen D. Kolsky, *The Ghost of Boccaccio: Writings on Famous Women in Renaissance Italy* (Turnhout, Belgium: Brepols, 2005), 117–147. All references to Foresti's text are from Los Angeles, Getty Research Institute (81693). In referencing the work, I use two separate foliations. For the paratextual material, I refer to the actual foliation of the incunabulum, counting from 1 to 5; for the remainder of the printed book, I refer to the printed foliation as appears in roman numerals in the top right corner of each recto folio. As Dufour wrote his text ca. 1504, it was this edition rather than the 1521 version of Foresti's work that the author of the *Vies des femmes célèbres* must have consulted.

6. Other scholars have debated Dufour's utilization of these two Latin texts in composing his *Vies des femmes célèbres*. Peter F. Sands, "Antoine Dufour, Jacques Philippe and 'le racheter des hommes,'" *Bibliothèque d'Humanisme et Renaissance* 39 (1977): 81–87, asserts that Dufour indeed relied heavily on Foresti's work. G. Jeanneau responds to Sands's claim in G. Jeanneau,

"Dufour et son modèle," *Bibliothèque d'Humanisme et Renaissance* 39 (1977): 89–90, with an analysis of the French author's divergence from Foresti's 1497 adaptation of Boccaccio.

7. Giovanni Boccaccio, *Famous Women*, ed. Virginia Brown (Cambridge, MA: Harvard University Press, 2001), xx. All citations from Boccaccio's text are taken from this edition.
8. Ibid., xi.
9. For a brief summary of these translations and editions, see ibid., xx–xxii. See also "Chronologies of *Querelle des femmes* Texts," and "Lists of Manuscripts, Incunables, and Early Printed Editions," in Helen J. Swift, *Gender, Writing, and Performance: Men Defending Women in Late Medieval France (1440–1535)* (New York: Oxford University Press, 2008), 247–250 and 251–254.
10. Kolsky, *Ghost of Boccaccio*, 5.
11. Ibid., 7–8 and 111–116.
12. Ibid., 123.
13. Dufour writes that he wished to "translate the present book into mother tongue" ("translater ce présent livre en maternal langage") (1), but also states that he does so in order to "restrain the tongues of those who have only seen or heard inventions and lies" ("brider la langue de ceulx qui ne ont veu ny leu que fables et mensonges"); Dufour, *Vies des femmes*, 1–2. In other words, although he claims to have translated an unidentified source, he also complains that he has been unable to find a source that speaks well of women and thus has decided to provide one himself.
14. Dufour combines certain biographies—e.g., Foresti's "Mamea Egyptiorum regina" and "Mamea Alexandri Augusti parente" (Foresti, *De plurimis*, fol. 103v) are both discussed by Dufour in one biography, "Mammée" (Dufour, *Vies des femmes*, 128–130)—but otherwise remains faithful to the order of Foresti's biographies with one exception: Foresti's work lists Proba (Foresti, *De plurimis*, fol. 115v–116r) before Galla Placidia (Foresti, *De plurimis*, fol. 118r–120r), whereas Dufour includes both these women in his text but places Galla Placidia (Dufour, *Vies des femmes*, 139) before Proba (Dufour, *Vies des femmes*, 142).
15. Foresti writes, "Semiramis, the eminent queen of Assyria in the times of the aforementioned Sara, with military discipline disguised her sex, committed many great and egregious sins, which indeed (although they were regarded so differently from the deeds of Sara) nevertheless recall to our memory that very famous woman." The Latin reads, "Semiramis insignis Assyriorum Regina temporibus Sare predicte militari disciplina sexum mentita suum grandia plurima et egregia facinora gessit que quidem (etsi dissimila Sare facinoribus sint habita) illam tamen clarissimam plurimum reddunt." (Foresti, *De plurimis*, fol. 14v); Dufour writes that Semiramis was a "woman as lascivious and vicious as Sara was prudent and virtuous" ("femme aussi lubrique et

vicieuse que Sarra fut prudente et vertueuse"); Dufour, *Vies des femmes*, 23.
16. Swift, *Gender, Writing*, 203, notes the "temporal contextualization" surrounding Semiramis and Sarah employed by Foresti and Dufour. I point out that Foresti compares not only the temporal era of the two female protagonists but also the worth of their deeds.
17. Foresti writes of Semiramis's tomb, "As Plutarch reports, she constructed a tomb for herself, in which she wrote these things down in writings: 'whatever king might need money, after this monument is opened, take what you want!' And so Darius King of the Persias, when the stone had been raised, discovered no money, but he did find other writings that said 'if you weren't such a bad man and insatiable for coin, you would not have disturbed the grave of these corpses.'" The Latin reads, "Ut plutarchus refert sibi sepulchrum extruxit inquo hec litteris scripsit: 'Quicumque rex pecuniis indiguerit, patefacto hoc monumento que volveris accipito.' Itaque darius persarum rex lapide sublato pecuniarum nihil invenuit, sed alias litteras reperit que hec dicerent ni malus vir esses, ac numis insaciabilis cadaverum loculus non moveres"; Foresti, *De plurimis*, fol. 17r.
18. "Before her death, [Semiramis] had a tomb built and had written on it, 'Whoever opens this tomb will find countless treasures.' A long time afterwards, Darius, king of Persia, had the tomb opened, and, expecting to find this treasure, found an inscription of this sort: 'If it were not for your avarice, you would not have smelled the stench of the dead.'" ("Devant sa mort, [Semiramis] fist construire ung sépulchre et fist mettre dessus: 'Quiconques ouvrira ce sépulchre trouvera innumérables trésors.' Darius, roy de Perse, long temps après, le fist ouvrir et, cuidant trouver ce trésor, trouva ung escripteau de ceste sorte: 'Si n'eust esté ton avarice, tu n'eusses pas sentu la puanteur des mors'"); Dufour, *Vies des femmes*, 24.
19. Boccaccio, *Famous Women*, 24.
20. Dufour writes, "And thus as she lived wickedly, she died wickedly, for she was killed by her own son" ("Et, ainsi qu'elle avoit meschamment vescu, meschamment elle mourut, car de son filz elle fut tuée"); Dufour, *Vies des femmes*, 24; Boccaccio, *Famous Women*, 24.
21. Elizabeth Casteen, "Sex and Politics in Naples: The Regnant Queenship of Johanna I," *Journal of the Historical Society* 11 (2011): 183–210.
22. Dufour, *Vies des Femmes*, 160.
23. Ibid., LII. Corroborating Jeanneau's argument are the similarities between the presentation miniature depicting Anne receiving the book (fol. 1r) and that of Joanna (fol. 75v): both women, seated on a throne, wear a red dress and a black headscarf. Brown, *Queen's Library*, 150–159, discusses in more detail a number of female figures, including Joanna, who are verbally and visually associated with Anne de Bretagne. Casteen, "Sex and Politics," 185, notes that "Johanna and her supporters sought to identify her with

commonly accepted positive attributes of aristocratic femininity, such as piety and compassion." In taking up Joanna's image a century later, then, Dufour associates his patroness with these virtues as well.

24. Dufour, *Vies des femmes*, 160.
25. Ibid., 161.
26. Caroline Zöhl, "Ovide, *Les Héroïdes*," in *France 1500: entre Moyen Age et Renaissance*, ed. Geneviève Bresc-Bautier, Thierry Crépin-Leblond, Elisabeth Taburet-Delahaye, and Martha Wolff (Paris: Éditions de la Réunion des musées nationaux, 2010), 126.
27. Pichore illuminated several manuscripts for Louise of Savoy, such as the *Chants royaux du Puy de Notre-Dame d'Amiens* (BnF fr. 145), a copy of the *Remèdes de l'une et l'autre fortune* (BnF fr. 224), and BnF fr. 421, *Trespassement de Saint Jerôme* (Zöhl, "Ovide," 126–127). Additionally, a manuscript version of the *XXI Epistres d'Ovide* painted by Pichore contains Louise's emblems: BnF fr. 873 (ibid., 126). See also Caroline Zöhl, *Jean Pichore: Buchmaler, Graphiker und Verleger in Paris um 1500* (Turnhout, Belgium: Brepols, 2005), 189.
28. Zöhl, "Ovide," 125–126, attributes to Pichore four manuscript versions of the *XXI Epistres d'Ovide*: BnF fr. 873, BnF fr. 874, Bibliothèque de l'Assemblée nationale, ms. 1466, and Vienna, ÖNB, cod. 2624. Zöhl attributes the decoration of BnF fr. 874 to Pichore in collaboration with other Parisian painters.
29. Concerning ms. 1466 (*XXI Epistres d'Ovide*), which she dates between 1505 and 1510, now housed at the Bibliothèque de l'Assemblée nationale, Zöhl argues that "the monumental figures, the antique costumes decorated with motifs in vogue at the time, the architecture, and the frames clearly show the imprint of Italian models" ("les figures monumentales, les costumes antiques ornés de motifs alors en vogue, l'architecture et les cadres portent résolument l'empreinte des modèles italiens"); ibid., 125. Zöhl explains that Pichore had access to these models from printed works and manuscripts from Italy as well as those that Georges of Amboîse acquired in 1501 from Frederick III of Aragon.
30. Georges of Amboîse bought 108 volumes from Frederick III of Aragon sometime between 1502 and 1503; see Gennaro Toscano, "Le cardinal Georges d'Amboise (1460–1510) collectionneur et bibliophile," in *Les Cardinaux de la Renaissance et la modernité artistique*, ed. Frédérique Lemerle, Yves Pauwels, and Gennaro Toscano (Villeneuve d'Ascq, France: IRHiS— Institut de Recherches Historiques du Septentrion, 2009), paragraph 44, available at http://hleno.revues.org/217. These volumes are listed in Léopold Delisle, *Cabinet des manuscrits de la bibliothèque impériale* (Paris: Imprimerie Impériale, 1868), 233–238. Pichore illustrated a number of manuscripts for the cardinal between 1502 and 1503. As Toscano notes, "the collection of Italian manuscripts, acquired by the Cardinal of Amboîse

and present in Normandy since the beginning of the sixteenth century, held great importance in the diffusion and knowledge of the decorative repertoires of the Italian Renaissance" ("la collection de manuscrits italiens, acquise par le cardinal d'Amboîse et présente en Normandie dès le début du XVIe siècle, eut une grande importance pour la diffusion et la connaissance des répertoires décoratifs de la Renaissance italienne"); Toscano, "Cardinal," paragraph 74.
31. Zöhl, *Jean Pichore*, 19.
32. Toscano, "Cardinal," paragraph 68, asserts that these manuscripts were "more than likely" ("sans doute") commissioned by Georges of Amboîse. See also Zöhl, *Jean Pichore*, 189–190.
33. Zöhl, *Jean Pichore*, 22 and 193.
34. Ibid., 191. This manuscript is also referred to as *Le trépas de l'Hermine regrettée*. For an edition of its text, see Cynthia J. Brown and Elizabeth A. R. Brown, "Le trespas de l'hermine regrettee: A Critical Edition," in *"Qu'il mecte ma povre ame en céleste lumière." Les funérailles d'une reine: Anne de Bretagne (1514), textes, images et manuscrits*, ed. Jean Luc Deuffic (Turnhout, Belgium: Brepols, 2014). For more on the manuscript's illuminations, see Pierre-Gilles Girault, "Le trépas de l'hermine regrettée. Un récit des funérailles d'Anne de Bretagne enluminé par Jean Pichore," *Art de l'Enluminure* 48 (2014): 46–61.
35. Dufour, *Vies des femmes*, 119.
36. Cassagnes-Brouquet, *Manuscrit d'Anne de Bretagne*, 79.
37. Dufour, *Vies des femmes*, 40.
38. In particular, Pichore's own illuminations in manuscript exemplars of the *XXI Epistres d'Ovide* (BnF fr. 873 and 874, Paris, Chambre des Députés, ms. 1466, and Vienna, Österreichische Nationalbibliothek, codex 2624) can point to the artist's familiarity with this visual *topos*.
39. On fol. 1r of this manuscript, a prologue unique to this exemplar reads, "Here begin the *Letters of Ovid* that were translated by the late gentleman the bishop of Angoulême named Octovien of Saint Gelais" ("Cy commence les epistres d'Ovide lesquelles ont esté translatees par feu monsieur l'evesque d'Angoulesme nommé Octovien de Saint Gelais"; my transcription and translation. I have added all punctuation, the accent aigu to masculine past participles, the accent grave to distinguish "à" from "a," and capitalization in the case of proper nouns and the first letter of sentences). This rubric thus indicates that the manuscript, or at least this folio, whose hand is the same as one found throughout the codex, was confected after 1502, the year of its translator's death.
40. See note 28.
41. The French rubric reads: "The father, wanting to know if his daughters had carried out his order, came to count the number of dead and found that

the youngest daughter, named Hypermnestra, had not killed her husband. For this reason, he had her taken and imprisoned, and condemned her to have one body part cut off each day until she died. And the first day, he had her leg cut off. Using the blood that flowed from this wound, she wrote to Lynus her husband the letter that follows." ("Le pere, voulant scavoir se ses filles avoyent fait son commandement, vint compter le nombre des mors et trouva que la plus jeune nommee Ypermestra n'avoit pas tué son mary. Par quoy la fist prendre et emprisonner et la condempna à avoir chascun jour ung membre coupé jusques à tant qu'elle fust morte. Et le premier jour luy fist couper une jambe dont du sang qui en sailloit elle escripvit à Lynus son mary l'espitre qui s'ensuit"); fol. 169r; my transcription and translation.

42. Sandra Hindman, "The Illustrations," in *The Danse Macabre of Women: Ms. fr. 995 of the Bibliothèque Nationale*, ed. Anne Tukey Harrison (Kent, OH: Kent State University Press, 1994), argues that a manuscript's illuminations originate in and modify, or upgrade, earlier woodcuts. Hindman further shows how this modified program of illustration envisages a royal female audience, perhaps Anne of Brittany or Margaret of Austria, in its transformation of a pictorial cycle mocking the female sex into one of praise. For a more general study, see Sandra Hindman and James Douglas Farquhar, *Pen to Press: Illustrated Manuscripts and Printed Books in the First Century of Printing* (Baltimore, MD: Art Department, University of Maryland, 1977).

43. Kathrin Giogoli and John Block Friedman, "Robinet Testard, Court Illuminator: His Manuscripts and His Debt to the Graphic Arts," *Journal of the Early Book Society* 8 (2005): 143–88.

44. Drimmer writes, "in 1507 the Mantuan friar Filippo Alberici journeyed to England, via Paris, in search of a literary patron"; Sonja Drimmer, "111: Filippo Alberici (?), *Hieroglyphica* and Emblematic Inscriptions, British Library, Royal 12 C. iii," in *Royal Manuscripts: The Genius of Illumination*, ed. Scot McKendrick, John Lowden, and Kathleen Doyle (London: British Library, 2011), 330.

45. Sonja Drimmer, "From Egypt to England, via Manuscript and Print: An Illustrated Hieroglyphica," paper presented to the Thirteenth Biennial Conference of the Early Book Society, St. Andrews, Scotland, Jan. 1, 2013. See also Drimmer, "111: Filippo Alberici (?)."

WORKS CITED

Primary Sources

Foresti da Bergamo, Jacopo Filippo. *De plurimis claris selectisque mulieribus*. Ferrara, 1497. Los Angeles, Getty Research Institute (81693).

Ovid, *Heroides*, translated by Octovien de Saint-Gelais:
  Paris, Bibiliothèque nationale de France, manuscript français 873.
  Paris, Bibiliothèque nationale de France, manuscript français 874.
  Paris, Chambre des Députés, manuscript 1466.
  Vienna, Österreichische Nationalbibliothek, codex 2624.

Secondary Sources

Aptel, Claire, Nathalie Biotteau, Marie Richard, and Jacques Santrot, eds. *Thomas Dobrée 1800-1895: Un homme, un musée*. Nantes and Paris: Musée Thomas Dobrée and Somogy Éditions d'Art, 1997.

Avril, François, and Nicole Raynaud. *Les Manuscrits à peintures en France, 1440–1520*. Paris: Flammarion, 1993.

Boccaccio, Giovanni. *Famous Women*, edited and translated by Virginia Brown. Cambridge, MA: Harvard University Press, 2001.

Brown, Cynthia Jane. "The 'Famous-Women' Topos in Early Sixteenth-Century France: Echoes of Christine De Pizan." In *"Riens ne m'est seur que la chose incertaine": Études sur l'art d'écrire au Moyen Âge offertes à Eric Hicks par ses élèves, collègues, amies et amis*, edited by J.-Cl. Mühlethaler and D. Billotte, 149–160. Geneva: Editions Slatkine, 2001.

———. *The Queen's Library: Image-Making at the Court of Anne of Brittany, 1477–1514*. Philadelphia: University of Pennsylvania Press, 2011.

———, and Elizabeth A. R. Brown. "Le trespas de l'hermine regrettee: A Critical Edition." In *"Qu'il mecte ma povre ame en céleste lumière." Les funérailles d'une reine: Anne de Bretagne (1514), textes, images et manuscrits*, edited by Jean Luc Deuffic, 46–61. Turnhout, Belgium: Brepols, 2014.

Cassagnes-Brouquet, Sophie. *Un manuscrit d'Anne de Bretagne: Les vies des femmes célèbres d'Antoine Dufour*. Rennes, France: Éditions Ouest-France, 2007.

Casteen, Elizabeth. "Sex and Politics in Naples: The Regnant Queenship of Johanna I." *Journal of the Historical Society* 11 (2011): 183–210.

Delisle, Léopold. *Cabinet des manuscrits de la bibliothèque impériale*. Paris: Imprimerie Impériale, 1868.

Drimmer, Sonja. "111: Filippo Alberici (?), *Hieroglyphica* and Emblematic Inscriptions, British Library, Royal 12 C. iii." In *Royal Manuscripts: The Genius of Illumination*, edited by Scot McKendrick, John Lowden, and Kathleen Doyle, 330. London: British Library, 2011.

———. "From Egypt to England, via Manuscript and Print: An Illustrated *Hieroglyphica*." Paper presented to the Thirteenth Biennial Conference of the Early Book Society, St. Andrews, Scotland, Jan. 1, 2013.

Dufour, Antoine. *Les Vies des femmes célèbres*, edited by G. Jeanneau. Geneva: Librairie Droz S.A., 1970.

Farquhar, James Douglas, and Sandra Hindman. *Pen to Press: Illustrated Manuscripts and Printed Books in the First Century of Printing*. Baltimore, MD: Art Department, University of Maryland, 1977.

Friedman, John Block, and Kathrin Giogoli. "Robinet Testard, Court Illuminator: His Manuscripts and His Debt to the Graphic Arts." *Journal of the Early Book Society* 8 (2005): 143–188.

Girault, Pierre-Gilles. "Le trépas de l'hermine regrettée. Un récit des funérailles d'Anne de Bretagne enluminé par Jean Pichore." *Art de l'Enluminure* 48 (2014): 46–61.

Hindman, Sandra. "The Illustrations." In *The Danse Macabre of Women: Ms. fr. 995 of the Bibliothèque Nationale*, edited by Anne Tukey Harrison, 15–25. Kent, OH: Kent State University Press, 1994.

Jeanneau, G. "Dufour et son modèle." *Bibliothèque d'Humanisme et Renaissance* 39 (1977): 89–90.

Kolsky, Stephen D. *The Ghost of Boccaccio: Writings on Famous Women in Renaissance Italy*. Turnhout, Belgium: Brepols, 2005.

Sands, Peter F. "Antoine Dufour, Jacques Philippe and 'le racheter des hommes.'" *Bibliothèque d'Humanisme et Renaissance* 39 (1977): 81–87.

Swift, Helen J. *Gender, Writing, and Performance: Men Defending Women in Late Medieval France (1440–1535)*. New York: Oxford University Press, 2008.

Szkilnik, Michelle. "Antoine Dufour's Vies des femmes célèbres." In *The Cultural and Political Legacy of Anne de Bretagne: Negotiating Convention in Books and Documents*, edited by Cynthia J. Brown, 65–80. Cambridge, UK: D.S. Brewer, 2010.

Toscano, Gennaro. "Le cardinal Georges d'Amboise (1460–1510) collectionneur et bibliophile." In *Les Cardinaux de la Renaissance et la modernité artistique*, edited by Frédérique Lemerle, Yves Pauwels, and Gennaro Toscano. Villeneuve d'Ascq, France: IRHiS—Institut de Recherches Historiques du Septentrion, 2009.

Zöhl, Caroline. *Jean Pichore: Buchmaler, Graphiker und Verleger in Paris um 1500*. Turnhout, Belgium: Brepols, 2005.

———. "Ovide, Les Héroïdes." In *France 1500: entre Moyen Age et Renaissance*, edited by Geneviève Bresc-Bautier, Thierry Crépin-Leblond, Elisabeth Taburet-Delahaye, and Martha Wolff, 125–126. Paris: Éditions de la Réunion des Musées Nationaux, 2010.

Nota Bene: Brief Notes on Manuscripts and Early Printed Books

Highlighting Little-Known or Recently Uncovered Items or Related Issues

The Sizes of Middle English Books, ca. 1390–1430

RALPH HANNA

Before M. R. James's innovative "descriptive catalogues," manuscript cataloguers had seen their primary responsibility as advertising the contents of the collections they described. As a result, they were rather vague about reporting the sizes of the books they included. In such accounts, which include many still in use presenting Oxford collections, indications of book sizes have been assimilated to those customary in describing printed books, with designations like "large folio," "quarto," and so on. Similarly, E. W. B. Nicholson's shelfmarks for continuing Bodleian collections in language classifications such as "Eng.th." relied exclusively upon book size, based on the height of the spine, in this case the narrower six categories designated, from largest to smallest, "a-f."[1]

James's innovation—the precise measurement in inches of a book's height and width—is exact and helpful. But in insisting upon the individual instance, it also renders detail chaotic and thus fails to register what was abundantly obvious to earlier researchers. They saw, broadly speaking, that medieval books were produced in common and repeated sizes. However, in assimilating these features to common print-book formats, the cataloguers were peering through the wrong end of the telescope. Print books display the forms they do *because* they continue common medieval forms of production; paper mills turned out sheets that could be accommodated to forms already familiar from the world of parchment. However, a major point I stress in the following analysis is that machine production imposes certain constraints not present in manuscript, and although descriptive, the designations assigned to manuscripts by Victorian cataloguers are ultimately misleading in bibliographical terms.

I owe my interest in this problem entirely to Elizabeth Solopova and Anne Hudson. As part of their ongoing Leverhulme-funded investigation of the manuscripts of the Wycliffite Bible, they invited me to survey the sixty-nine relevant books now preserved in Oxford.[2] These books have traditionally been seen as somewhat problematic qua manuscripts of the Bible. The normal Bible model, surviving in many thousands of copies, had been established in Paris from 1230 and later, and consisted of small, portable volumes in relatively fixed formats. In contrast, the English examples prove to be remarkably diverse, ranging from full Bibles too heavy to move with any degree of ease (e.g., the two-volume London, British Library, MSS Egerton 618+617) to tiny selective bits, usually New Testament selections, that would fit with ease into the pocket of a modern pair of trousers (e.g., Bodleian MS Rawlinson C.237+238 and MS Lyell 26).[3]

But while these may not generally resemble Paris Bibles, they do seem to me recognizable as English books. That is, the forms in which they were produced (here specifically their sizes) remind me of a broad range of Middle English literary manuscripts. The shapes in which the Wycliffite Bible is received were cloned off those usual elsewhere (and which became fairly ubiquitous in English book culture). From a Middle English codicological perspective, there is very little original or distinctive about Lollard books. This essay examines some evidence for normal Middle English production standards, as these are reflected across the Lollard volumes, while also offering a specific indication of the logic underlying these book sizes.

Very few of these biblical manuscripts are datable in any precise way. Their scripts tend to be rather informal versions of set hands that show minimal variation over time. But, on the whole, one assumes that the majority of them will have emerged in the early fifteenth century (for example, they include negligible evidence of even passing influence of secretary scripts). Thus the relevant comparison class is with Middle English books produced between the construction of Lollard scripture (late 1370s?) and the 1430s, that is, books one would date s. xiv ex., xiv/xv, and xv in. Strikingly, my survey will reveal that with perhaps half a dozen marginal exceptions (something like 10 percent of the sample), the sizes of Wycliffite Bibles gather into groups, four in all. Moreover, these groupings are of a sort that would have been recognizable to Victorian manuscript cataloguers, although the individual confirmations of each group imply a different interpretation from that which the cataloguers implicitly offered.[4]

From the broader Middle English perspective of book production, the striking thing about the full run of these Bibles is their avoidance of what I think of, at least in a general way, as "the standard literary format" of contemporary books. I consider as models of this procedure a wide range of books communicating *Piers Plowman* B and C, most usually as their single text. I identify about seventeen relevant manuscripts of this poem, produced more or less contemporaneously with Lollard scripture, in such a format. In these volumes, the mean gross dimensions are a leaf 275 to 290 millimeters high and 185 millimeters wide.[5]

These copies of *Piers* are important because they reflect a production history that began in London within the poet's lifetime. On any count, *Piers Plowman* appears to have been the most popular literary text of the period to around 1410, and the standards of production here will have had a formative influence on the conception "book" shared by later producers. This is not simply a unique feature—as is most everything else about *Piers Plowman*; such production can be paralleled in other popular texts far from so limited in locale of production.

To begin with nonmetropolitan examples, one might cite an extensive swathe of early copies of *The Prick of Conscience*. There are about twenty relevant volumes of this text that show no visible London presence until a single odd copy from the 1450s. Their mean dimensions closely resemble those of the *Piers Plowman* copies: 265 to 270 millimeters high, 180 millimeters wide. The format is similarly well attested with another nonmetropolitan text, Richard Rolle's English Psalter in fourteen relevant copies with mean dimensions 280 to 285 millimeters high, 200 millimeters wide. And the format also occurs frequently with another text whose circulation appears generally London-centered, in nine to eleven early copies of Nicholas Love's *Mirror of the Blessed Life of Jesus Christ* with mean dimensions 280 millimeters high, 195 millimeters wide. Strikingly, only the Ur- (and rather problematic) copy of Chaucer's *Canterbury Tales*, Hengwrt, is at all comparable with these books; it measures 290 millimeters by 210 millimeters, and the only early and similarly sized copy of this text is Egerton 2726 at 305 millimeters by 205 millimeters (its close cogener Cambridge Dd. 4.24, of the same textual species but on paper with parchment outer and inner bifolia, measures 290 mm x 205 mm).[6]

These figures should be sufficient to indicate that there is widespread standard size of literary manuscript of about 280 to 290 millimeters in height.[7] The width of the page varies, although probably predictably, given the differing types of work on offer: *Prick of Conscience* manuscripts are narrower than the remainder because they are devoted to double-column short-line poetry; the psalters are a bit wider to accommodate prose double columns; the Hengwrt *Canterbury Tales* is (insufficiently) wide because it was intended to receive at least some glosses. Indeed, as J. P. Gumbert demonstrates in a study that underwrites and inspires this one, the width of a volume can probably be discounted as an independent function; he shows that traditionally the ratio of a book's height to its width has tended toward a constant, the so-called "golden section." His arguments imply that the Victorian cataloguers of Oxford collections were probably correct in emphasizing book height.[8]

The books I describe here belong to a normative form of literary production—but not one at all normative among manuscripts of the Wycliffite Bible. In my group of just about seventy volumes, one can find this book size in only ten examples, 14 percent of the sample. The mean dimensions of this small group are 280-285 millimeters by 195 millimeters.[9]

Indeed, rather than the norm of Bible production, these "standard format" copies are marginally less widely attested in Oxford collections than are larger examples of Wycliffite Bibles. These are books a Victorian cataloguer would have identified as "large folio," well over 300 millimeters in height, a dozen in total. These, all examples of full Bibles, in some cases only one volume from a set, can only have sat on a lectern and can only have been intended for some variety of group reading. They rebuff the notion that Lollardy was prosecuted or necessarily clandestine, since not only are they not capable of being easily hidden, they usually exhibit high production values, frequently including painting, and thus required extended professional involvement. These volumes display mean dimensions of 395 millimeters by 265 millimeters.[10]

These volumes may also be paralleled in contemporary book culture. For example, there is a good run of oversized, often highly decorated copies of Rolle's Psalter, eleven in all. The mean dimensions of these are nearly identical with those of the large bibles, 385 millimeters high by 260 millimeters wide. Although *The Prick of Conscience* is much more apt to appear in a small devotional volume than in a large anthology, even discounting the poem's appearance in the enormous Vernon and Simeon manuscripts, there are least seven relevant books. These display wide variations in size, as do the Bibles, but a somewhat smaller mean size, 335 millimeters by 220 millimeters; eliminating the three smallest (MV 44 and 45, SR 13), which may be especially large examples of "standard literary" format, their *average* dimensions are 360 millimeters by 250 millimeters. The Ellesmere *Canterbury Tales* (El) always stands apart (it measures 400 mm x 280 mm), but the early seminal copies of the *Tales* generally display the smaller end of this format, with mean dimensions comparable to large manuscripts anthologizing *The Prick of Conscience*, 335 millimeters by 225 millimeters.[11]

Both "standard literary" format and "large folios" represent minority productions among Wycliffite Bibles. But comparing these two forms of book points to one not necessarily expected coalescence of data. That is, if one considers the relation of the two sizes of book, one can see that if one takes a leaf from the larger book (385 mm x 270 mm) and folds it horizontally across the center of the leaf, one will construct a bifolium in which each leaf roughly corresponds in size to the leaves of the smaller books (270 mm x

190+ mm). It is thus very likely that the two different book sizes represent only different ways of handling the same material support.

Since all these volumes are parchment, the size of this support must be determined by the usable skin derived from what one may call "the standard English sheep." Long ago, Graham Pollard estimated that such a skin would provide a surface roughly 1200 millimeters by 900 millimeters.[12] Pollard's guess is confirmed by the dimensions of the largest surviving medieval English volumes; books like these include the well-known Simeon and Vernon manuscripts (585 mm x 395 mm and 545 mm x 395 mm, respectively). Their dimensions imply that these immense lectern books offer leaves formed from a single skin folded twice (first across the spine, then along it).[13] In them, each eight-leaf quire consists of two such skins, with each skin in what a print bibliographer would describe as folding "in quarto" (thus "4° quired in 8s").

While it is slightly digressive, one feature thrown up by Simeon and Vernon deserves some recognition. Both books retain very nearly the full vertical extent of Pollard's hypothesized average skin, in quarto fold. But this is not true of their horizontal dimensions, which are significantly narrower than the 450 millimeters one might expect Pollard's skin to yield. However, this is an entirely predictable discrepancy; the "waste" areas of a parchment skin, those usually considered not fit for formal use, always fall along the outer edges of what will become leaves in a finished book—the point where the skin originally lay along the sheep's thigh and belly. In contrast, virtually the entire vertical dimension of the original skin is potentially usable.[14]

On the basis of this analysis, one can explain the construction of those book sizes I am calling "large folio" and "standard literary format." A leaf of Vernon manuscript dimensions represents an original skin area of roughly 600 millimeters by 400 millimeters. Folding such a leaf horizontally across its center will produce a bifolium in which each leaf measures roughly 400 millimeters by 300 millimeters, comparable to the leaves of books in the format I am calling "large folio." Quires in these books, then, must represent bibliographical octavos, with each quire comprised of a single skin folded three times.

Further, "standard literary format," as my earlier argument shows, must represent half the original skin area of these "large folios"/octavos. However, such books, because they are routinely quired in eights, cannot have been produced simply by an additional folding of a full skin, for this would result in quires of sixteen leaves ("16mo" in the parlance of printed-book formats). Instead, these books must have been produced from half-skins by cutting a single skin in the middle across the spine to produce two equal parts. One of these pieces, roughly 600 millimeters by 400 millimeters, must be folded twice ("in quarto") to achieve the observed confirmations of "standard literary format," approximately 300 millimeters by 200 millimeters. The resulting quires are thus bibliographically comparable to those of Vernon and other supersized books, for they are also "quartos quired in 8s"—but with the qualification, "from half-skins."

However, as I have indicated, neither of these "standard formats" is widely reproduced among manuscripts of the Wycliffite Bible. Nearly 70 percent of the sample represents books in considerably smaller formats. Here I would draw attention to one range of comparable books that appear like mushrooms after the rain all over England, just contemporary with Lollard Bibles. These are small-format books of devotional materials, the sort of texts introduced to readers by Carl Horstmann's *Yorkshire Writers*.[15] At least a couple of examples are or are derived from metropolitan work (e.g., Oxford, Bodleian Library, MS Bodley 923 or Oxford, University College, MS 97), but books in this sizing show as well a wide provincial dispersion. They differ from Wycliffite Bibles in important ways; for example, they are customarily not in double columns but long lines, and usually in cursive-based scripts, not textura. But their size shows significant similarities to many Wycliffite examples. The fourteen contemporary volumes I have chosen for comparison display mean dimensions of 210 millimeters by 145 millimeters.[16]

Comparably sized books form a very heavily populated area of Wycliffite Bible production. Around 42 percent of my sample, twenty-nine books in all, are roughly of the same size as the widely dispersed devotional miscellanies I have just described. Surveying this extensive sample as a whole, overall the mean dimensions of these volumes are 195 millimeters by 130 millimeters, that is generally within the production range of larger Parisian pocket Bibles, which they often mimic fairly intelligently. Indeed, the larger books in this portion of the sample, of sizes just at the customary upper limit usually associated with Parisian pocket Bibles (200 mm), clearly resemble Middle English devotional books in size, with a mean dimensions of 205 millimeters by 145 millimeters.[17]

Once again, these dimensions may be readily correlated with examples already discussed. The larger part of this sample shows dimensions that replicate the relations already uncovered in comparing "standard literary format"/bibliographical half-skin quarto with "large folio"/ bibliographical octavo. That is, if one takes a leaf from a book in "standard literary format," about 270 millimeters by 190 millimeters, and folds it across its horizontal center, one will produce a bifolium in which each leaf has the approximate dimensions 190 millimeters by 135 millimeters, just about the mean size of the Bibles. In a wide range of instances, page dimensions are again half those of the next-larger-sized customary book format. "Devotional format" religious miscellanies and the comparable Lollard Bibles have been produced by folding the same parchment half-sheet one further time, and they represent legitimate bibliographical "octavos" from *half-skins* (not the "quartos" of Bodley's nineteenth-century cataloguers).

As I have suggested, Paris pocket Bibles are typically very small books; a large example is roughly the size of the octavos just discussed.[18] Thus one should not be surprised to find that a substantial portion of my Wycliffite Bible sample is comprised of unusually small books, not a format particularly common in Middle English book culture (although certainly well paralleled among Latin liturgical and paraliturgical materials, e.g., "pocket" Breviaries and Books of Hours). About 20 percent of the sample, thirteen books, are of these dimensions—and thus close to 60 percent of the Oxford Bibles are in distinctly portable formats. The mean dimensions of these smaller volumes are 135 to 140 millimeters by 90 millimeters. While, as I have indicated, this is not a particularly common size for a Middle English book, I find four readily comparable small devotional volumes, with slightly larger mean dimensions of 145 to 150 millimeters by 95 to 105 millimeters.[19]

Once again, these mini-volumes are, as one might have predicted, just half the size of the next larger frequently occurring book size. Folding a leaf from a devotional miscellany, about 200 millimeters by 135 to 145 millimeters, in half should produce a bifolium in which each leaf has dimensions 135 to 145 millimeters by 90 to 100 millimeters, just about what one observes here. A Victorian cataloguer would have referred to a book of this size as "16mo." However, the quiring of these volumes, typically in eights, like the vast run of Middle English books, would imply that such a designation is probably inaccurate. Although the size of a "16mo" print book, these are bibliographically "quartos" ("4° quired in 8s") but produced from full skins cut into quarters. Like those individuals responsible for books in "standard literary format," these book producers achieved this size reduction not by additional folding but by beginning their work with a half-skin halved yet again; this they simply folded twice to produce "quartos quired in 8s" *from quarter-skins.*

Thus it seems to me possible to exaggerate unduly the disparate shapes of Middle English Bibles. Quite simply, when the producers of Wycliffite Bibles came to form their volumes, they did so with an eye to contemporary perceptions of the proper way to disseminate literary materials written in English. This book surround provided ready models for their production procedures, and only at the very smallest (and relatively unusual) end of the production range did these individuals look directly toward the model that had initially stimulated their efforts, the Parisian pocket book of the preceding century. Further, I hope to have demonstrated that these customary book sizes are neither capricious nor accidental; rather, they represent specific responses to conditions imposed by the very material from which books are customarily created, the sheepskin.

Keble College, Oxford

NOTES

1. James's first catalogue was M.R. James, *A Descriptive Catalogue of the Manuscripts in the Library of Eton College* (Cambridge, UK: Cambridge University Press, 1895). Relevant Oxford predecessors include the sequence of 'Bodleian Quarto Catalogues," beginning with the Ashmole collection in 1845, and Henry O. Coxe's survey of college collections (1852); for Nicholson, who may have adopted this format to facilitate efficient storage, see further Ralph Hanna, *The Index of Middle English Prose Handlist XII: Smaller Bodleian Collections* (Cambridge, UK: D. S. Brewer, 1997), xi, with references.
2. These I identify throughout by the (inherited) numbers assigned in the most recent listing of copies, Mary Dove, *The First English Bible: The Text and Context of the Wycliffite Versions* (Cambridge, UK: Cambridge University Press, 2007), 298–303, with, in parentheses, the shortened shelfmarks that will be used in Anne Hudson and Elizabeth Solopova's forthcoming publications on the Wycliffite Bible. Dove misses a very few examples, and I also consider copies of two texts outside her numerical scheme but relying upon Wycliffite scripture: the Glossed Gospels and the translation of Clement of Llanthony, *Oon of Foure*. I am particularly grateful to Elizabeth Solopova, who is cataloguing these books, for sharing with me her measurements of all the copies.
3. Laura Light provides the most basic discussion of Parisian production; see most recently, Laura Light, "The Thirteenth-Century Pandect and the Liturgy: Bibles with Missals," in *Form and Function in the Late Medieval Bible*, ed. Eyal Poleg and Laura Light (Leiden, The Netherlands: Brill, 2013), 185–215 (and the references there to her earlier discussions, 186 n. 7, 198 n. 33). On the Wycliffite examples, cf. Christopher de Hamel, *The Book: A History of the Bible* (London: Phaidon, 2001), 180: "Looked at from [a Parisian] perspective, Wycliffite manuscripts of the Scriptures are hardly Bibles at all." However, this English deviance is far from unique; cf. Sabina Magrini, "Production and Use of Latin Bible Manuscripts in Italy during the Thirteenth and Fourteenth Centuries," *Manuscripta* 51 (2007): 209–251. My comments here are scarcely predicated upon the whole archive, but my sample covers roughly 25 percent of the survival of this, the most popular Middle English book.
4. In the discussion below, I restrict my sample to books on parchment. I have rounded all measurements to the nearest 5 mm (narrower specifications run afoul of both one's accuracy in measuring as well as modest internal variations in the individual books). Because with one exception, all the volumes are on handmade parchment, not some modern machined product, one should probably assume variations in the initial product of up to at least 10 percent. (In the context I am discussing, this is actually a very small

dimension, at most 25–30 mm, or just about an inch.) Moreover, one must always remember that the books have been through binders' planing—and perhaps multiple times—and all the dimensions we see are likely to be 5–10 mm smaller than the originals.

5. The relevant examples are those assigned sigla C^2 F L M R W Y in George Kane and E. Talbot Donaldson, eds, *Piers Plowman: The B Version* (London: Athlone, 1975), 1–14; and G MP P^2 Q S V X Z W in George Russell and George Kane, eds, *Piers Plowman: The C Version* (London: Athlone, 1997), 1–18.

6. For the first, see Robert E. Lewis and Angus McIntosh, *A Descriptive Guide to the Manuscripts of the* Prick of Conscience, Medium Ævum Monographs n.s. 12 (Oxford: Society for the Study of Medieval Languages and Literature, 1982); these are the copies there designated MV 8, 16, 48, 54, 59, 61, 68, 69, 73, 78, 82–83, 90, 91; and SR 1, 4–6, 15. For Rolle's prose Psalter, see Ralph Hanna, *The English Manuscripts of Richard Rolle: A Descriptive Catalogue* (Exeter, UK: Exeter University Press, 2010), where these are items 1, 23, 38, 43, 44, 50, 62, 77, 95, 99, 100, 107, 109, 113 (nos. 23 and 99 are slightly larger than the remainder). For Love, see Michael G. Sargent, ed., *The Mirror of the Blessed Life of Jesus Christ: A Full Critical Edition* (Exeter, UK: Exeter University Press, 2005), 104–142, where the relevant books are A^1 A^2 Ad^1 Bc Hm^2 Ld Mm Tk^2, with Cc^2 and Ro slightly larger than the remainder.

7. The centrality and persistence of this as a standard format may be indicated by the fact that I composed this essay on the standard British paper size that is called "A4," 297 mm high x 210 mm wide. One can easily convert the book sizes I describe here into early modern and later paper stocks by referring to Philip Gaskell, *A New Introduction to Bibliography* (Oxford: Clarendon, 1972, 1974), 73–75.

8. See J. P. Gumbert, "The Sizes of Manuscripts: Some Statistics and Notes," in *Hellinga Festschrift/Feestbundel/Mélanges* (Amsterdam: Israel, 1980), 277–288, esp. 283–285, where Gumbert takes up the later fourteenth- and fifteenth-century *paper* books in his Continental sample.

9. The relevant books are Dove's 64 (Bodl. 771), 70 (e Mus. 110), 72 (Fairfax 11), 75 (Junius 29), 89 (Ashmole 1517), 90 (Bodl. 183: one of two MSS that Dove numbers as "90": see n. 17 below), 97 (New 66), as well as Oxford, Bodleian Library, MS Holkham misc. 40 and two copies of the Glossed Gospels, Oxford, Bodleian Library, MS Bodley 143 and MS Laud misc. 235. Dove 99 (New 320) also displays this format but is on paper and securely datable s. $xv^{3/4}$; Dove 190 (Worc. Col. E. 10.7) consists of fragmentary leaves that appear to have originally been of comparable dimensions (as also, one might note, the equally fragmentary Me of *The Canterbury Tales*).

10. These books, nearly all described in some detail at Dove, *First English Bible*, 253–264, include her numbers 60 (Bodl. 277), 61 (Bodl. 296), 65 (Bodl. 959), 71 (Fairfax 2), 87 (Douce 369/1), 91 (ChCh 145), 94,

(CCCO 4), 95 (CCCO 20), 96 (Linc. Col. lat. 119), 101 (Queen's 388), 103 (Oxf. St. John's 7), and Oxford, Bodleian Library, MS Bodley 243 of the Glossed Gospels. One of these volumes, MS Bodley 277 (Dove's no. 60), is specifically marked for refectory reading, presumably at the London Charterhouse, to which Henry VI gave it; for images, see de Hamel, *Book*, 183–184, figs. 130–131.

11. For oversized copies of the prose Psalter, see catalogue items 5, 6, 24, 55, 57, 72, 79, 86, 96, 102, and 116. Also comparable are the massive anthologies at the head of the manuscript tradition of *The Prick*, Lewis-McIntosh's MV 27, 34, 44, as well as MV 45, 56, 92, and (unusually because the text is sole) SR 13. Among early copies of *The Canterbury Tales*, one can point to Ha^4 Cp Gg Pw La (and the format is nigh ubiquitous in copies of Gower's bulky *Confessio Amantis*).

12. Graham Pollard, "Notes on the Size of the Sheet," *The Library* 4th ser. 22 (1941): 105–137, at 110: "The average size of a sheepskin, I am told, is 3 by 4 feet."

13. See Léon Gilissen, "La composition des cahiers: Le pliage du parchemin et l'imposition," *Scriptorium* 26 (1972): 3–33.

14. See further Erik Kwakkel, "Discarded Parchment as Writing Support in English Manuscript Culture," *English Manuscript Studies* 17 (2012): 238–261. However, there are certainly hints that the edges of skins originally at the sheep's head and tail might also present problems of quality. For example, in a further very large book, The Wollaton Antiphonal (University of Nottingham Library, MS 250), dimensions 600 mm x 400 mm, a number of sheets required "sizing up" to match those used elsewhere in the book; this involved pasting strips about 30–35 mm high to the upper edges of some leaves. While this may simply indicate that the very large sheets necessary for this production were sometimes not available, it may point to quality problems associable with the sheep's head and tail.

15. Carl Horstmann, *Yorkshire Writers*, 2 vols. (London: Swan Sonnenschein, 1895–1896).

16. Most of these are those described in Hanna, *The English Manuscripts of Richard Rolle*, as nos. 12, 13, 21, 35, 48, 59, 68, 87, 91, 94, 103, but the list is capable of significant expansion, here limited to Oxford, Bodleian Library, MS Laud misc. 656, MS Bodley 923 (a London book), and MS Bodley 647 (Lollard tracts). A majority of the copies of *The Prick of Conscience*, more than 50 examples in all, also exhibit this format, although their usual dimensions are slightly larger.

17. The relevant volumes (larger examples starred) are Dove's numbers 54 (Laud misc. 33), 55 (Laud misc. 36), 56 (Laud misc. 182), *57 (Laud misc. 207), *62 (Bodl. 531), 63 (Bodl. 665), *69 (Selden supra 51), 73 (Fairfax 21), *76 (Dugdale 46), *78 (Rawl. C.257), 80, (Rawl. C.259), 81 (Rawl.

C.752), 82 (Rawl. C.888), 83 (Gough Eccl. Top. 5), 85 (Douce 240), 86 (Douce 265), *88 (Douce 370), 90 (Brasenose 10: the other of two MSS which Dove numbers as "90": see n. 9 above), 92 (ChCh 146), 93 (ChCh 147), 98 (New 67), 102 (Queen's 369), 104 (Oxf. St. John's 79), 105 (Univ. 96), as well as Oxford, Bodleian Library, MS Douce 258, *MS Douce 265 flyleaves (from a different MS from the rest), * MS Laud misc. 388, Oxford, Christ Church, MS Allestree L.4.1 (*Oon of Foure*), and *Oxford, Trinity College, MS 93. Four additional books (which, if included here, would take the total to 33) appear to me most likely large examples of this production size; these are Dove's nos. 58 (Laud misc. 361), 66, with extensive margins to accommodate glosses (Bodl. 554), 79 (Rawl. C.258), and MS Bodley 481 (*Oon of Foure*). These display mean dimensions of 230 mm x 160 mm; they may be comparable to smaller-format "devotional" versions of Love's *Mirror*, Sargent's Ad^3 Fo Ar^2 Tr^2 with mean 235–240 mm x 170 mm, as well as to many copies of *The Prick*.

18. See the actual-size reproduction of two fairly typical examples in Scot McKendrick and Kathleen Doyle, *Bible Manuscripts: 1400 Years of Scribes and Scripture* (London: British Library, 2007), 110–111, plates 97–98. Both books accord with the typical English dimensions adduced later in this paragraph, 140 and 145 mm high x 90 mm wide, respectively.

19. These are Dove's nos. 52 (Laud misc. 24), 53 (Laud misc. 25), 67 (Bodl. 979), 68 (Selden supra 49), 74 (Hatton 111), 77 (Rawl. C.237/238, two vols.), 81 (Rawl. C.752), 84 (Douce 36), 100 (Oriel 80), 166/218 (Lyell 27), 189 (Lyell 26), and MS Bodley 978 (*Oon of Foure*). For analogies, see Hanna, *English Manuscripts of Richard Rolle*, nos. 20, 92, 104, and BL, MS Royal 17 A.xxvi; in addition, note (as Thorlac Turville-Petre points out to me) London, British Library, MS Harley 913 (Fr. Michael of Kildare's poems from the 1330s) with dimensions 140 mm x 95 mm.

Oxford, Bodleian Library, MS Laud Misc. 740 and New York, Public Library, MS Spencer 19: A Common History?

KATHRYN WALLS

Oxford, Bodleian Library, MS Laud Misc. 740 (henceforth "O"), is a copy of *The Pilgrimage of the Lyfe of the Manhode* (henceforth, the *Life*), a literal translation into Middle English prose of the first recension of Guillaume de Deguileville's *Pèlerinage de la vie humaine* (the *Vie*). New York, Public Library, MS Spencer 19 ("S"), is a copy of *The Pilgrimage of the Soul*, a translation of de Deguileville's sequel to the *Vie*, the *Pèlerinage de l'âme*. As others before me have recognized, these two manuscripts appear to be have been produced in the same workshop by what Rosemary Potz McGerr (editor of S) describes as "an organised group of artists supplying books to members of the aristocracy with ties in the Northeast Midlands in the second quarter of the fifteenth century."[1] That the manuscripts began life as a pair is consistent with the fact that the first known owner (and probably the commissioner) of S appears to have owned O as well. To quote McGerr:

> Evidence about S's earliest known owner appears on flyleaf Av, where a fifteenth-century hand has written, "Liber domini Thome Comorworth militis." Sir Thomas Cumberworth of Somerby Lincolnshire, was Sheriff and Member of Parliament for Lincolnshire and died in 1451. Cumberworth's will records his gift of a copy of the *Soul*, which he calls "my boke of grasdew of the sow[l]e," to the priest at the chantry of the Virgin Mary founded by Cumberworth in the parish church

at Somerby in 1437. Cumberworth's gift of "my boke of grasdaw" to the priest of the other chantry he founded [that of the Trinity] indicates that he owned a copy of the prose *Life* as well. Though Cumberworth's name does not appear in [O], this may well be his copy, given its similarities to S.[2]

Since Cumberworth bequeathed S to one priest and O to another, one might conclude that the MSS were separated on Cumberworth's death and that, as a consequence, they remained so. Indeed, these interconnected conclusions are those drawn, albeit tacitly, by the modern editors both of the *Life* and of the *Soul*. My purpose in what follows is to point out that it is possible, even likely, that S and O remained together until the early seventeenth century. While my hypothesis was prompted by the discovery of a previously unremarked annotation in S that is similar to the many annotations entered into O by William Baspoole (probably in the 1620s), I represent it chronologically.

I begin, then, with Cumberworth's will. From what is known about the accommodations of chantry priests in the period, it seems likely that the intended recipients of the manuscripts would have lived in a single priests' house.[3] Cumberworth might have envisaged their storing the two manuscripts there. Alternatively, he might have envisaged the storage of both manuscripts in the church. This latter possibility is suggested by his stipulation concerning two undifferentiated cupboards for the storage of vestments: one cupboard was to go to one priest and one to the other.[4] That Sir Thomas bequeathed a collection of relics and also a single mill horse to "[his] Chauntre prests" further indicates that he viewed these priests much as a unit.[5] In bequeathing his copies of Deguileville's *Life* and *Soul* to his chantry priests, then, Sir Thomas may well have been attempting to ensure that they remained together.

But if Sir Thomas wanted the books to be maintained as a pair, it is an open question as to whether the chantry priests nominated as their recipients by Sir Thomas ever took possession of them. Sir Thomas Cumberworth's will stipulated that they were to remain in the possession of his chantry priests "& ther successurs."[6] At some point, as shown below, this proviso was ignored. Perhaps, right from the start, Sir Thomas's executors were obstructed in the fulfillment of their duty by the principal heir, Sir Thomas's grandnephew Sir Robert Constable of Flamborough in Yorkshire.[7] Their "suppowellorse" (or supervisors) included Sir Robert,[8] and Sir Thomas also stipulated that Sir Robert was to make the final decision as to the disposal of any possession that might "fal in trawers [disputes] or in contrare consayetes of this last will betwen [his] sectures [executors]."[9] Furthermore, Sir Thomas bequeathed his "boke of the talys of cantyrbury" to Sir Robert's wife "Annes" (Agnes).[10] Sir Robert may have taken advantage of his position in order to supplement his wife's valuable manuscript with two more and taken all three back to Yorkshire. If so, this would go some way to explain how S (and perhaps O) came into the hands of its (or their) next known owner, Dame Agnes (née Scrope), whose first husband, Sir Christopher Boynton, lived in East Heslerton, twenty miles northwest of Sir Robert's village of Flamborough.[11]

Dame Agnes's ownership is indicated by a note entered on a flyleaf of S by one "Isabell Lumley" ("Here beginnith the boke cald Grace Dieu giffen unto the / Monasterye of Marrick by Dame Agnes Radcliff onn / whose sowl Ihesu haue mercye. Amen. / Per me Isabell Lumley").[12] Agnes had become a nun soon after the death in 1485 at the Battle of Bosworth Field of her second husband, the Lancastrian knight Sir Richard Ratcliffe (or Radcliffe) of the North Yorkshire village of Sedbury.[13] Since (i) S also bears (again, on a flyleaf) a sixteenth-century inscription of ownership of one "John Cowper" ("By me John Cowper anrs thes buke"),[14] and (ii) the prioress at the time of Marrick's dissolution in 1539 was one Christabella Cowper, who had granted a lease to a John Cowper in the previous year, it may well be that, as others before me have concluded, the John Cowper who entered his name into S was a relative of Christabella who had acquired S from her.[15] Indeed (although this point has gone unnoticed to date) such a presumption carries conviction in view of the fact that Christabella had a nephew by the name of John Cowper, that nephew being the bastard son of one of her two brothers.[16] A "John Jackeson otherwise called John Cowper of Comberworthe in the County of Lincolne," whose will was proved in 1558, is likely to have been this nephew, perhaps especially given his alternative surname, which could be that of his mother or stepfather, a name taken in the absence of his natural father.[17] The trail then goes cold, although we know that as McGerr notes, "[b]y the seventeenth century, S was in the possession of Henry Percy, ninth Earl of Northumberland, who died in 1632."[18]

If, as I want to suggest, the history of S until its acquisition by Percy was shared by O, the question arises as to why S contains the evidence of its history while O does not. A probable answer lies in the fact that while S remains with its flyleaves in its original binding, O, which lacks flyleaves, was rebound in the early seventeenth century (at which point, we may presume, it lost its flyleaves).[19] It was, as already noted, upon the flyleaves of S that Cumberworth, Lumley, and Cowper entered their indications of ownership.

Hard information relating to the possession of O until the seventeenth century is—in the absence of flyleaves—confined, as noted by Avril Henry (the editor of the *Life*) to a sixteenth-century autograph in the upper margin of folio 129v, the last page of the text: "This is Amb[r]ose Sutton's Book," an autograph that narrowly escaped cropping when the manuscript was rebound.[20] No suggestions have thus far been offered as to the identity of this owner. A likely candidate is the Ambrose Sutton who served as a member of Parliament for the Lincolnshire seat of Great Grimsby in 1554.[21] Significantly for my hypothesis, Sutton was a Lincolnshire public figure of whom Cowper ("of Comberworthe in the County of Lincolne") might well have been aware. It may be, then, that Sutton, the known owner of O, acquired both O and S from Cowper. The life spans of Cowper (d. 1558) and Sutton (1530–1592) certainly overlap in a way consistent with a scenario according to which Cowper passed the manuscripts to Sutton.

The early-seventeenth-century evidence relating to the ownership of O comes not from the manuscript itself but indirectly, via the colophon in a 1655 manuscript copy of *The Pilgrime* (Cambridge, University Library, MS Ff. 6. 30)–*The Pilgrime* being a revised version of the *Life* authored by William Baspoole in c.1630.[22] This colophon records that Baspoole "did copy ... out" *The Pilgrime* from an "originall" that he subsequently gave to Archbishop Laud.[23] As Marguerite Stobo and I demonstrate elsewhere, one of the two medieval manuscripts used by Baspoole was in fact O. The evidence is in part textual, there being many echoes in *The Pilgrime* of O's textual idiosyncrasies. A large number of the illustrations in the first fair copy of that text (Cambridge, Magdalene College, MS Pepys 2258) likewise betray the influence of the illuminations in O.[24] Most significant for the present investigation, however, is the frequent appearance among the marginal annotations in O of a seventeenth-century Italic hand that, as Rosemond Tuve was the first to observe, reappears in the headings and annotations in the Pepys manuscript.[25] This is almost certainly the hand of Baspoole himself, as may be inferred from the fact that most of the annotations in MS Laud Misc. 740 appear to have been entered in order to promote the incipiently Laudian dimensions of the text, dimensions that Baspoole exaggerates in his own revised version of it.[26] (As noted below, Baspoole entered a further set of annotations in a hand characterized by Tuve as "pseudo-Gothic.")

Unlike O, S is generally free of annotations entered subsequent to its date of composition. On folio 92v, however, it bears a previously undiscussed marginal note in a seventeenth-century Italic hand (see Fig. 1).[27] This appears in the left margin alongside a sentence in the thirtieth chapter, headed "The tra*n*stator [sic] declareth more opynly the nature of the soule to commou*n* vnderstondynge."[28] The context is a lecture on the subject of the capacities of the soul delivered for the benefit of the narrator-protagonist by a lady called Doctrine.[29] The sentence at stake, spoken by Doctrine, reads:

> The flesh, that is the flesshly part of the soule, coueyteth ayen the spirit and the spirit agenst the flessh, so that thise two alwey ben ad*uer*saries to gydres and not with stondynge

this contrariousite thise two ben ve*rr*ely one in substau*n*ce so that I mene not that a man hath two soules, but that he hath a soule of two nature[s], fleschly and goostly.³⁰

As shown in Figure 1, the marginal annotation in an Italic hand summarizes this material: "The soule of two natures, sensual & ghostly."

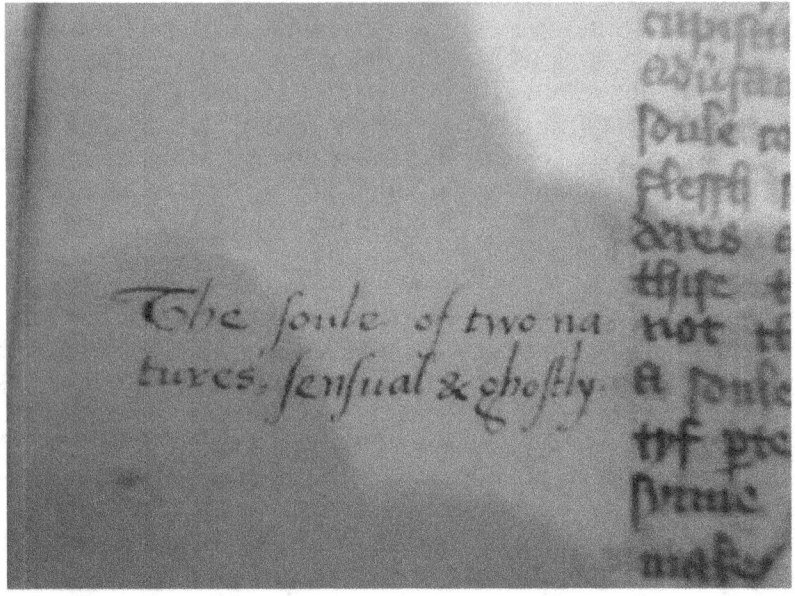

Figure 1. New York Public Library, MS Spencer 19, folio 92v. Courtesy of the New York Public Library.

William Baspoole had a particular interest in the constitution of the soul.³¹ In O on folio 54r, a passage that is part of an extensive disquisition by Reason on the antagonism that characterizes the relationship between the soul and the body (*Life*, ll. 3097–3448) is prefaced with a marginal annotation in Baspoole's pseudo-Gothic handwriting that reads: "The 7 leaues following doe declare the manifould miserys of *the* sowle, through *the* contynuall tentation of *the* flesh. Reade wi*th* patience, then Judg."³² In the Pepys manuscript of *The Pilgrime*, too, Reason's evocation of the nobility of the soul and the enmity toward it of the body is marked for special attention by marginal bracketing and the word "note."³³

It is impossible, on the basis of the single annotation in S, to prove that

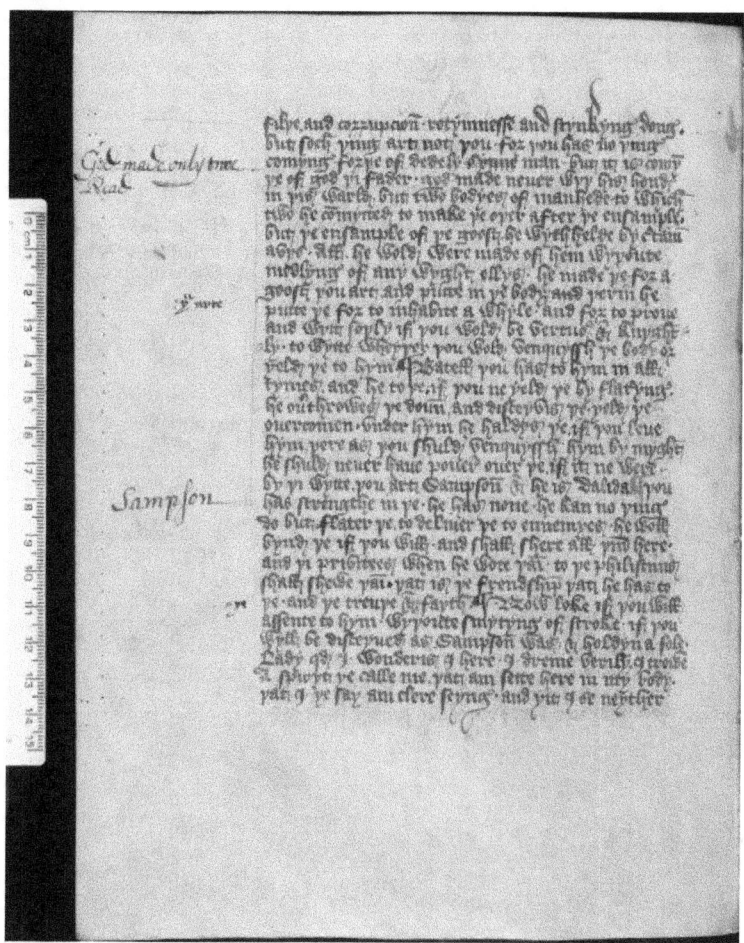

Figure 2. Oxford, Bodleian Library, MS Laud Misc. 740, folio 56v. Courtesy of the Bodleian Library, University of Oxford.

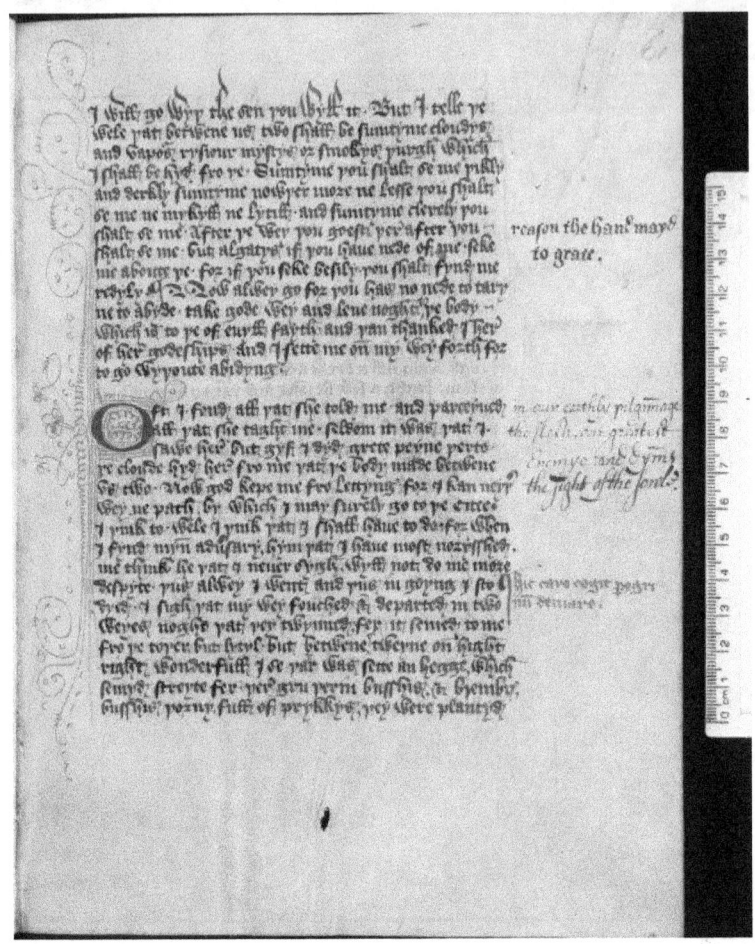

Figure 3. Oxford, Bodleian Library, MS Laud Misc. 740, folio 61r. Courtesy of the Bodleian Library, University of Oxford. For the Italic hand annotation see the center right margin.

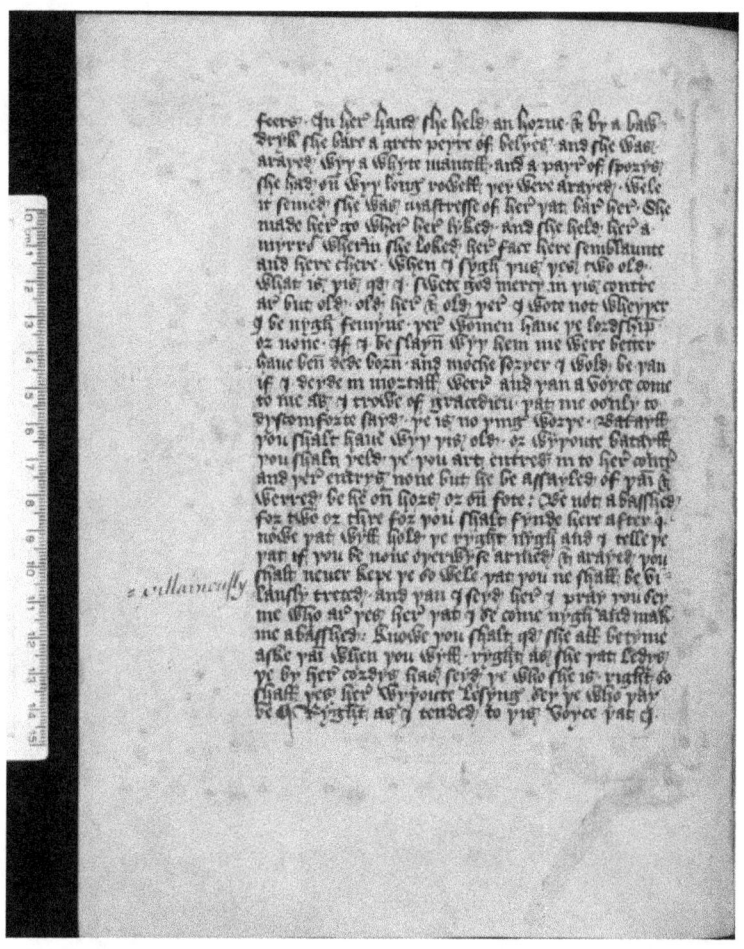

Figure 4. Oxford, Bodleian Library, MS Laud Misc. 740, folio 69v. Courtesy of the Bodleian Library, University of Oxford.

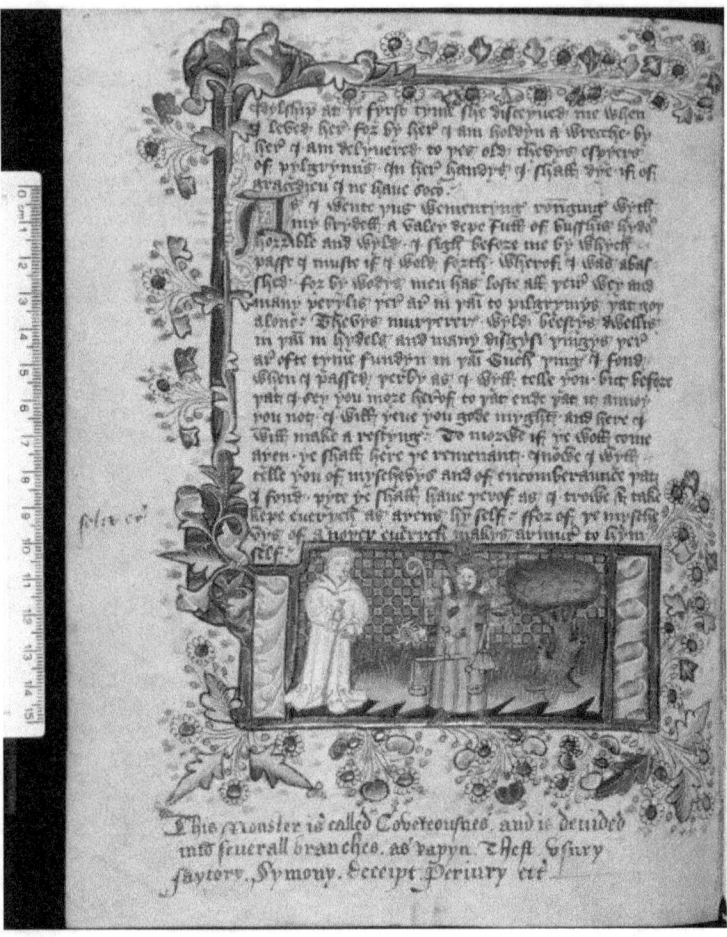

Figure 5. Oxford, Bodleian Library, MS Laud Misc. 740, folio 85v. Courtesy of the Bodleian Library, University of Oxford.

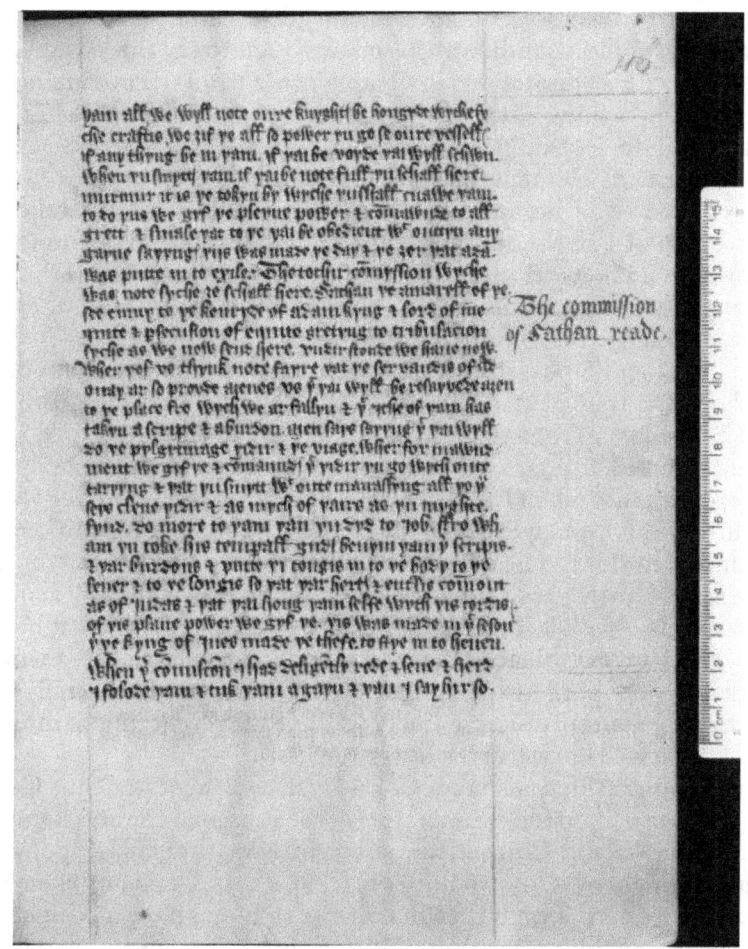

Figure 6. Oxford, Bodleian Library, MS Laud Misc. 740, folio 116r. Courtesy of the Bodleian Library, University of Oxford.

it was entered by Baspoole. On the other hand, it is impossible to prove that it was not. Baspoole's handwriting is inconsistent to say the least. As noted above, some of his annotations in O are written in an unconvincing imitation of the handwriting of the medieval scribes (the hand characterized by Tuve as "pseudo-Gothic"), some are written in a chiefly pseudo-Gothic style that contains elements of Italic, some are written in Italic contaminated by pseudo-Gothic, and some might be described as pure Italic. Thus, while the capital T in the annotation of S (Fig. 1) is not to be found in any of Baspoole's Italic-hand annotations in O, it is on the model of the capital T that appears in some of his pseudo-Gothic annotations—in, for example, the words "Theft" (Fig. 5) and "The" (Fig. 6). [34]

If both O and S passed through the hands of William Baspoole, it is most likely that they were acquired by him together and thus at the same time. The evidence from O points to a period in or before 1633, since O has Laud's names, titles, and the date 1633 inscribed on its first page. I say "or before" because when Laud became archbishop in September 1633 and began inscribing his acquisitions in this way, he included manuscripts he had acquired earlier.[35] The evidence relating to S indicates that it must have been before Henry Percy's death in 1632. Percy may well have acquired S from Baspoole. As we know, Baspoole gave a manuscript of what he saw as a proto-Laudian text to Laud. He may have thought the *Soul*—a work that in its treatment of purgatory might be described as quintessentially Catholic—fitting for Percy. Although Percy was not a Catholic, his Catholic connections were well known, even notorious.[36]

A final point: the transference of S (and, as I suggest, O) to Cumberworth, a village named for the ancestors of their original commissioner, is remarkable. Christabella Cowper, the person who was probably responsible for the transfer, might have known the Constables, the descendants of Sir Thomas's nephew Robert. John Jackeson Cowper (whom I have identified as the owner who names himself as "John Cowper" in S) certainly did—as revealed in his will, he had leased grounds from a "Sir Marmaduke Constable knight." This Sir Marmaduke must have been the son of Sir Marmaduke [knight of the body of Richard III], and grandson of the Sir Robert Constable who (according to my hypothesis) carried the manuscripts out of Lincolnshire into Yorkshire in the first place. If Christabella had been in touch with the Constables, she could have learned from them of the history of the manuscript (or of both manuscripts), and chosen to dispose of it (or them) accordingly. But it is perhaps more likely that she simply concluded, thanks to the identification of Sir Thomas Cumberworth as the owner of S on flyleaf Av, that the manuscript (or manuscripts) came from Cumberworth. Either way, it would seem that the prior history of the manuscript (or manuscripts) was important to Christabella and that it played a part in its (or their) subsequent history.

In summary, my hypothesis as to the ownership of S and O until they fell into the hands of Baspoole is as follows: (i) Sir Thomas Cumberworth, (ii) Sir Thomas's heir Sir Robert Constable of Yorkshire, (iii) Dame Agnes, also of Yorkshire, (iv) Marrick Priory, where Dame Agnes, by then a widow and a nun, had died, (v) Christabella Cowper, the prioress of Marrick at the time of its dissolution, (vi) Christabella's nephew John Cowper of Cumberworth in Lincolnshire, (vii) Sir Ambrose Sutton, Member of Parliament for Great Grimsby in Lincolnshire, and (viii) after the death of Sutton in 1592, a person or persons unknown who acquired the manuscripts from him and retailed them to Baspoole. Paradoxically enough, while it is Baspoole's hand in both manuscripts that is the clue to their common history, it was probably Baspoole who brought that common history to an end.

Victoria University of Wellington

NOTES

1. Rosemary Potz McGerr, ed., *The Pilgrimage of the Soul: A Critical Edition of the Middle English Dream Vision*, vol. 1 (New York: Garland, 1990), lxxxiii. For the relevant measurements, see (for O) Avril Henry, ed., *The Pilgrimage of the Lyfe of the Manhode*, vol. 1, EETS 288 (Oxford: Oxford University Press, 1985), xliii; and (for S) McGerr, *Pilgrimage of the Soul*, 1:lxxx. On the scribes, see Henry, *Pilgrimage of the Lyfe*, 1:xlv–xlviii; and McGerr, *Pilgrimage of the Soul*, 1:lxxx–lxxi. On the decorations and illustrations, see Henry, *Pilgrimage of the Lyfe*, 1:xlii–xliii; McGerr, *Pilgrimage of the Soul*, 1:lxxxi–lxxxii; and Kathleen L. Scott, *Later Gothic Manuscripts 1390–1490*, 2 vols. (London: Harvey Miller, 1996), 2:218.
2. McGerr, *Pilgrimage of the Soul*, 1:lxxxiii. There are several Lincolnshire villages named Somerby and Somersby. Cumberworth's Somerby (he refers to it in his will as "Someretby") is in Lindsey near Glanford-Brigg. It lies about forty miles north of the village of Cumberworth. For the identification of the second chantry (or, as it is described in Sir Thomas Cumberworth's will, "auter" [altar]), see the complete transcription in Andrew Clark, ed., *Lincoln Diocese Documents 1450–1544*, EETS, OS 149 (London: Kegan Paul, Trench, Trübner & Co., Humphrey Milford, Oxford University Press, 1914), 44–57, 48.
3. On the sharing of accommodations by chantry priests, see K. L. Wood-Legh, *Perpetual Chantries in Britain* (Cambridge, UK: Cambridge University Press, 1965), esp. 234–239.
4. Clark, *Lincoln Diocese*, 48.
5. For the relics, see ibid., 47. For the horse, see ibid., 48.
6. Ibid., 48.

7. In the will he is referred to throughout as Sir Thomas's "neveu" (and his wife as Sir Thomas's niece).
8. Clark, *Lincoln Diocese*, 56.
9. Ibid., 57.
10. Ibid., 49.
11. For the biography of Dame Agnes, see Mary C. Erler, "Exchange of Books between Nuns and Laywomen: Three Surviving Examples," in *New Science out of Old Books: Studies in Manuscripts and Early Printed Books in Honour of A. I. Doyle*, ed. Richard Beadle and A. J. Piper (London: Scolar Press, 1995), 360–370. East Heslerton is even closer to Burton Agnes, home of Sir Robert's daughter (another Agnes), wife of Sir Walter Griffith. For the Constable family history, see Rosemary Horrox, "Constable Family (Per. C. 1300–1488), Gentry," in *Oxford Dictionary of National Biography* (Oxford: Oxford University Press, 2004–2014).
12. Flyleaf Cv. Cf. McGerr, *Pilgrimage of the Soul*, 1:lxxxiv.
13. Erler, "Exchange of Books," 363, notes that Dame Agnes's commission to veil was issued on September 20, 1485. Isabel herself has been variously identified as the daughter, daughter-in-law, and stepdaughter of Dame Agnes in T. Whitaker, *History of Richmondshire* (London: Printed for Longman, Hurst, Rees, Orme, and Browne, Hurst, Robinson, and Co., and Robinson and Hernaman, 1823), 77; Thomas Edward Watson, *History and Pedigree of the Family of Lewen* (London: Mitchell, Hughes and Clark, 1919), 175; Victor Hugo Paltsits, *The Petworth Manuscript of "Grace Diuw"* or *"The Pilgrimage of the Soul"* (New York: New York Public Library, 1928), 6; McGerr, *Pilgrimage of the Soul*, 1:lxxxiv.
14. Flyleaf Cr. Cf. McGerr, *Pilgrimage of the Soul*, 1:lxxxiv.
15. On the dissolution of Marrick Priory, see John W. Clay, ed., *Yorkshire Monasteries: Suppression Papers*, Yorkshire Archeological Society Record Series 48 (London: Mitchell Hughes and Clark, 1912), 134–135; cited in McGerr, *Pilgrimage of the Soul*, 1:lxxxiv, cxxiii. On Christabella's leases, Erler, "Exchange of Books," 363–334, cites John H. Tillotson, *Marrick Priory: A Nunnery in Late Medieval Yorkshire*, Borthwick Paper 75 (York, UK: Borthwick Institute, 1989), 39, n. 40.
16. Christabella was one of the sisters of Edward Cowper (also known as Kirkby), abbot of Rievaulx. Claire Cross mentions John, "his brother's bastard son" (son, that is, of Edward's brother, who was also named John) in her entry on Edward; see Claire Cross, "Cowper, Edward (d. 1557)," in *Oxford Dictionary of National Biography* (Oxford: Oxford University Press, 2004–2014).
17. The will is held at the Public Record Office, Catalogue Reference: PROB/11/40, Image Reference: 252.
18. McGerr, *Pilgrimage of the Soul*, 1:lxxiv, cites G. R. Batho, "The Library of the

'Wizard' Earl: Henry Percy, Ninth Earl of Northumberland (1564–1632)," *The Library* 15 (1960): 246–261. S. Paltsits, *Petworth Manuscript*, 7, cites "a report of 'The Manuscripts of the Right Honourable Lord Leconfield, at Petworth House, co. Sussex,' . . . contributed by Alfred J. Horwood to the *Sixth Report* of the Royal Commission on Historical Manuscripts, part 1 (London, 1877) . . . where [S] is described on 288, no. 2."

19. On the rebinding of O in the seventeenth century, see Nicole Gilroy, "The Repair and Rebinding of *The Pilgrimage of Human Life* at the Bodleian Library," *The New Bookbinder* 29 (1999): 17–26. Gilroy's article is accompanied by photographs, one of which (on p. 18) shows the spine of the volume with the seventeenth-century sewing in place, along with marks and threads indicative of the medieval sewing positions.

20. Henry identifies what she describes as "a tantalisingly cropped line (or passage) in the same hand" above the autograph. She also records "by f. 128^v William Buk [...] ... and by f. 63^r *Wb, Arc'bish.y.Th.* (?)." See Henry, *Pilgrimage of the Lyfe*, 1:xlv. It may be worth noting that William Booth was Archbishop of York from 1452 to 1464.

21. For the details of Ambrose Sutton's career, see the entry under his name in S. T. Bindoff, ed., *The History of Parliament: The House of Commons 1509–1982* (n.p.: Boydell and Brewer, 1982).

22. The Cambridge copy exists, according to its colophon, at three or possibly four removes from the first fair copy of Baspoole's text, which—as Magdalene College Cambridge MS Pepys 2258—is extant. It will be evident that *The Pilgrime* circulated in manuscript. Three manuscripts are extant. See William Baspoole, *The Pilgrime*, ed. Kathryn Walls with Marguerite Stobo, Renaissance English Text Society (Tempe: Arizona Center for Medieval and Renaissance Studies, 2008). For the colophon discussed here, see ibid., 5.

23. *The Pilgrime* is strictly speaking not a copy, although it is designed to seem like one. It is, rather, a heavily revised version of the *Life*. But the point is incidental here.

24. See Walls and Stobo, *Pilgrime*, 11–12 (for the textual echoes), and 51–82 (on the illustrations). See also Rosemond Tuve, *Allegorical Imagery: Some Mediaeval Texts and Their Posterity* (Princeton, NJ: Princeton University Press, 1966), 152–218.

25. Tuve, *Allegorical Imagery*, 202–204 (fig. 64), 212–213 (figs. 89, 90).

26. On Baspoole as the common annotator, see Walls and Stobo, *Pilgrime*, 15–28. For the Laudian character of the bulk of the annotations in O (annotations that correspond with the Laudian ideology that informs Baspoole's revision of the *Life* in/as *The Pilgrime*), see Kathryn Walls, "'A Prophetique Dreame of the Churche': William Baspoole's Laudian Reception of the Medieval *Pilgrimage of the Lyfe of the Manhode*," in *Centered on the Word: Literature,*

Scripture, and the Tudor-Stuart Middle Way, ed. Daniel W. Doerksen and Christopher Hodgkins (Newark, NJ: University of Delaware Press, 2004), 245–276. On the Laudian character of Baspoole's adaptations of the *Life* in *The Pilgrime*, see Walls and Stobo, Pilgrime, 91–122.

27. This note is recorded (but without any indication of hand or date) by M. Dorothea Barry in her edition of the MS (then known as the "Petworth MS"); M. Dorothea Barry, "The Pilgrimage of the Soul: A Fifteenth Century English Prose Version of 'Le Pèlerinage de l'Ame' by Guillaume de Guileville. Transcribed and edited from the Petworth MS," PhD diss., University of Toronto, 1931, 183, n. 1.
28. Barry, "Pilgrimage," 180.
29. Doctrine's responses to the questions of the narrator-protagonist extend from line 6841 to line 7204 in the original *Ame*. This material is rendered in the twenty-seventh to thirtieth chapters of Book IV in the English translation—according, that is, to the Spencer MS. But chapter 30 has indeed, as announced in the chapter heading, been added by the translator. For the French original, see J. J. Stürzinger, ed. *Le Pèlerinage de l'âme* (London: Roxburghe Club, 1895).
30. Barry, "Pilgrimage," 182–183.
31. This is not to say that the relevant thematic material in the *Life* and the *Soul* are identical. The passage on the subject in the *Life* (true to Deguileville) dwells on the antagonism between soul and body. The passage in the *Soul* (added by the English translator) focuses on a division that, although similarly oppositional, is represented as lying not between soul and body but between different elements of the soul.
32. Baspoole's note, reproduced here in Fig. 2 (upper left margin), is in fact linked with the same long disquisition. It appears at a subsequent point at which Reason explains that the corrupt state of our bodies is to be attributed not to God as Creator but to their descent from the bodies of our originally perfect but ultimately fallen first parents; see Henry, *Pilgrimage of the Lyfe*, ll. 3235 ff. See Walls and Stobo, *Pilgrime*, 413.
33. See Walls and Stobo, *Pilgrime*, 412–413.
34. There is, however, no precedent in Baspoole's annotations in O for the form of the "g" in "ghostly."
35. See R. W. Hunt, ed., *A Summary Catalogue of Western Manuscripts in the Bodleian Library at Oxford*, vol. 1 (Oxford: Clarendon Press, 1953), 129; and Walls and Stobo, *Pilgrime*, 6–7.
36. On Percy's Catholic connections, see Mark Nicholls, "Percy, Henry, Ninth Earl of Northumberland (1564–1632)," in *Oxford Dictionary of National Biography* (Oxford: Oxford University Press, 2004–2014).

A Previously Unrecognized French *Alexander* Romance

J. R. MATTISON

Sefer Alexandros Mokdon, a Hebrew version of the King Alexander legend, stands out in the larger corpus of Alexander romances because "the source of the greater part of the episodes in this deviant versions [*sic*] remains unknown."[1] It is attested in two extant manuscripts, Oxford, Bodleian Library, MS Heb. d. 11, folios 265r–277v, and Modena, Estense Library, MS 53, Italian, and a third manuscript, last seen in Damascus, which is now lost. *Sefer Alexandros* has posed a scholarly problem since the first editions of the Bodleian and Modena manuscripts were published at the end of the nineteenth century, with almost all subsequent studies confirming its "deviant" nature.[2] In contrast to the majority of Western Alexander romances, the tale did not derive from the tenth-century *Historia de Preliis* and its various Greek recensions.[3] Many of its episodes—"much more marvelous and fabulous" than occidental ones[4]—have had no known comparable versions until now.[5]

Yale University, Beinecke Rare Book and Manuscript Library, MS 918 is a third extant witness to the contents of *Sefer Alexandros*, albeit to a version of the text in another language. The fragment, consisting of two consecutive bifolia drawn from the middle of a quire, survives because it was reused as binding material for a tall book—a format similar to books used as ledgers—although the intervening years have damaged certain areas of text.[6] A later hand has twice written "roid*arum* person*arum* bouiarum" [of carts, of people, of cows], hinting at the folios' later use.[7] The version in this fragment does not simply echo *Sefer Alexandros* but closely imitates the details of it as attested in Bodleian Library, MS Heb. d. 11.[8] It does this despite the fact that the fragment is in French whereas the previously attested text is in Hebrew.

The following passage from each manuscript clearly demonstrates the closeness of the two texts. Beinecke Library, MS 918 reads:

> Li Roys ala parler aus Juis. Si les toua quil demoroient dedens les pauillons. ki estoient taint de toutes manieres de colours. Si vint au pauillon ou ilh troua .j. viel homme. ki se seioit deuant son pauillon et tenoit son liure en sa main. Li Roys le salua. Et ilh ne li respondi point. Li Roys li dist. Je sui chirconcis aussi com tu ies. si sui Roys et fius de Roy. Quant li viels hons loy. si se leua contre lui. et parla a lui. et le fist seior en son pauellon. et lounor a moult durement.⁹

> [The king went to talk to the Jews. He found them where they lived within tents, which were painted in a variety of colors. He went to the tent where he found an old man who sat in front of the tent and held his book in his hand. The king greeted him and he did not respond to him at all. The king said to him, "I am circumcised, just as you are. I am a king and the son of a king." When the old man heard him, he rose before him and spoke to him and brought him into his tent and honored him greatly.]

The same passage in Bodleian Library, MS Heb. d. 11 is as follows, in a modern English translation of the Hebrew:

> The king went to the Jews and found them dwelling in tents dyed in many colors. Entering one tent, he found an old man sitting with his book in his hand. The king greeted him with "Peace," but he did not reply. The king said: "I am circumcised just as you are and I am king, son of a king." Hearing this, the old man arose, spoke with him and showed him great honor by seating him in his tent.¹⁰

Each detail in the Hebrew text is also found in the French version in the same order. Such exactness is present not only in this passage; the entire fragment of French prose in Beinecke Library, MS 918 parallels the analogous passages of Hebrew prose in Bodleian Library, MS Heb. d. 11 from the moment when the king and his army search the bodies of the women they have killed until Alexander tastes manna in the land of Sydonie, where the fragment ends. Both the French and Hebrew texts recount Alexander's conversation with an old Jewish man, a leader of the Ten Tribes, in which the king declares that he is circumcised and the old man expounds upon Jewish laws and customs, drawing on the Old Testament and the Babylonian Talmud in his responses. For example, the old man declares, "nous trouons en notre loy que .v. de nous en chaceront bien cent des vos. Ce cent des nos en chaceront bien .xm. des vos: que notre anemi doient cheoir deuant nous a glaiue" [We find in our laws that five of us would defeat 100 of you and 100 of us would defeat 1,000 of you: our enemies should fall before us by sword], in a passage that reprises Leviticus 26:8.[11]

Little is known about the origins of the manuscript Beinecke Library, MS 918; its paleographical features suggest that the manuscript most likely dates to the fourth quarter of the thirteenth century or the first quarter of the fourteenth century.[12] The single scribe writes in a dialect of Old French that uses *ilh* for the third-person singular and plural *cas sujet* instead of the more common *il*; such a spelling is associated with the Walloon dialect of north-western France.[13] Writing in a two-column layout with twenty-one lines of text, the scribe uses red to highlight capital letters throughout the text; he uses a single paraph to mark Alexander's entrance into the "terre de Mares." Its small size, lack of decoration, and sometimes clumsy letter formation indicate that this was unlikely to be a luxury book.[14]

It is, in spite of its appearance, an important manuscript as a witness to a version of the Alexander legend in French that was previously attested only in Hebrew. That this Alexander legend should be discovered in French raises many questions: what is the relationship between Beinecke Library, MS 918 and Bodleian Library, MS Heb. d. 11? According to a colophon in the latter, Eleazer, son of Asher ha-Levi, completed the manuscript in 1325, although the legend may have originated some time between the seventh and twelfth centuries.[15] The two fourteenth-century codices are therefore contemporary. With so few witnesses to this particular version of the Alexander romance, it is tempting to see a direct link between the two books. However, the French and Hebrew texts each employ proper names in their own language, so neither appears derived directly from the other. For example, in Beinecke Library, MS 918, Alexander's scribe is "Manessier," but in Bodleian Library, MS Heb. d. 11, he is "Menachem." Similarly, the names of the geographic regions—such as "Mares" in the French and "Amrisa" in the Hebrew—conform to the language of the text. The use of Hebrew proper names in the French text might have helped elucidate which manuscript came first, but such is not the case.

Why would a Hebrew tale emphasizing Jewish sources and asserting Jewish power and independence appear in French? Given the presentation of Alexander in the Hebrew version, the reappearance is striking, for this tale would seem to appeal most to a Jewish, Hebrew-reading audience rather than a French-reading one. In contrast to the better-known Alexander legends that tell of the king's defeat or enclosure of the Ten Tribes, this version presents a circumcised Alexander and a powerful Jewish people who defy him.[16] The ideal Jewish life of scriptural study that the old man describes to Alexander "strikes a strong resonating chord with... Messianic material."[17] Such episodes are hardly in line with widespread medieval anti-Judaism and might have been difficult for a medieval Christian audience to accept unquestioningly. Perhaps significantly, the episodes of *Sefer Alexandros* preserved in Beinecke Library, MS 918 are those that Saskia Dönitz specifically points to as being "derived from Jewish motifs... these deviations from the source material show the intention of the anonymous author: he wanted to recast Alexander's life into a Jewish framework."[18] That is, the contents of this version of the story suggest that the French text attested in the fragment would most likely be a translation of a work originally composed in Hebrew for a Jewish readership.

The translation of such a Jewish text out of the language of the Jews provokes further consideration of the original readership of the French text. Who would have been the intended audience for Beinecke Library, MS 918? French Jews sometimes composed their texts in French but seemed to prefer to read and write in Hebrew characters.[19] Kristen Fudeman notes that there is only one known Jewish manuscript from the period written in French in the Roman alphabet: a 1273 French translation of the *Commencement de sapience* by Hagin le Juif.[20] Beinecke Library, MS 918, if translated from Hebrew into French for a Jewish audience, might be a second such example. The content, with its particular emphasis on Jewish power, would seem to appeal most to a Jewish audience, yet it could also be the case that the text was translated out of Hebrew into French for a gentile readership that was able to disregard the Jewish implications of the romance.

These questions and accompanying complications are only the beginning of the study of Beinecke Library, MS 918: this seemingly modest fragment could provide new insight not only into the history of the transmission of Alexander romances—particularly the understudied Hebrew version—but also into medieval Jewish literature and the relationships between Jewish and French communities in the late thirteenth and early fourteenth centuries.

Jesus College, University of Oxford

Acknowledgments
I would like to thank Jessica Brantley, Jonathan Cayer, Hindy Najman, Anne Schindel, Aaron Vanides, Anders Winroth, and Shlomo Zuckier for their kind help and support.

NOTES

1. W. Jac. van Bekkum, "Medieval Hebrew Versions of the Alexander Romance," in *Medieval Antiquity*, ed. Andries Welkenhuysen, Herman Braet, and Werner Verbeke (Leuven, Belgium: Leuven University Press, 1995), 293–303, at 299. For similar views, see Rosalie Reich, *The Tales of Alexander of Macedonia* (New York: Ktav, 1972), 6; Moses Gaster, "An Old Hebrew Romance of Alexander," *Journal of the Royal Asiatic Society of Great Britain and Ireland*, 1897, 485–549, at 498; and Israel J. Kazis, *The Book of Gests of Alexander of Macedon* (Cambridge, MA: Medieval Academy of America, 1962), 33. See Saskia Dönitz, "Alexander the Great in Medieval Hebrew Tradition," in *A Companion to Alexander Literature in the Middle Ages*, ed. Z. David Zuwiyya (Boston: Brill, 2011), 21–41, for a survey of this version's place within the Hebrew tradition as well as a detailed plot summary.
2. Gaster, "Old Hebrew Romance," 485–549, printing a translation; and I. Lévi, "Sefer Alexandros Mokdon," in *Festschrift zum achtzigsten Geburtstage Moritz Steinschneiders* (Leipzig, Germany: Harrassowitz: 1896), 142–163, printing the original.
3. Reich, *Tales of Alexander*, xii; Kazis, *Book of Gests*, 33–35.
4. W. Jac. van Bekkum, "Alexander the Great in Medieval Hebrew Literature," *Journal of the Warburg and Courtauld Institutes* 49 (1986): 218–226, at 224.
5. Gaster, "Old Hebrew Romance," 489–490.
6. Elizabeth Hebbard, "Beinecke 918," lecture given at the Beinecke Rare Book and Manuscript Library, Yale University, April 11, 2013, makes similar observations.
7. New Haven, Yale University, Beinecke Rare Book and Manuscript Library, MS 918, fol. 3v. I thank Anders Winroth and Aaron Vanides for help with this translation. The same hand has also written *fictus* across the page; this could perhaps be a later user's comment ("false, fictitious") on the Alexander story.
8. Because only Oxford, Bodleian Library, MS Heb. d. 11, has been edited and translated into English, it serves as the basis of comparison. A. Y. Harkavy described the Damascus manuscript in Russian in 1892 before it was lost. Gaster, "Old Hebrew Romance," 490, dismisses the Damascus manuscript, believing it to be a "comparatively modern copy." The Modena manuscript has not been studied in the twentieth or twenty-first centuries.
9. Beinecke MS 918, fols. 2v, col. b–3r, col. a. I have silently expanded the abbreviations in this extract but have not otherwise altered the spelling from the manuscript. All French translations are my own.
10. Reich, *Tales of Alexander*, 113.
11. Beinecke MS 918, fols. 3r, col. b–3v, col. a. The holes and stains on the parchment obscure many places in the text that cite the Old Testament

which are legible in Bodleian Library, MS Heb. d. 11. See Reich, *Tales of Alexander*, 112, 114.
12. The style of northern gothic textualis used in the manuscript is consistent with those dating from the later part of the thirteenth century and into the fourteenth century. The letter *i* is topped with diacritical markings, situating the script around 1300, yet the second compartment of *g* remains below the baseline, placing the manuscript before 1400. The high number of biting letter combinations and the horizontal approach strokes on the ascenders of *b*, *h*, and *l* also date the manuscript to the late thirteenth to early fourteenth century. On these features, see Albert Derolez, *The Paleography of Gothic Manuscript Books* (Cambridge, UK: Cambridge University Press, 2003), 73–101.
13. Geneviève Hansenohr and Guy Raynaud de Lage, *Introduction à l'ancien français* (Paris: Sedes, 1989), 72.
14. Each folio measures approximately 224 mm by 140 mm.
15. See Arthur Ernest Cowley and Adolf Neubauer, *Catalogue of the Hebrew Manuscripts in the Bodleian Library*, 2 vols. (Oxford: Clarendon Press, 1886–1906), ii, 208–216, for a description of the colophon. See Kazis, *Book of Gests*, 32, for dating of the tale.
16. See George Cary, *The Medieval Alexander* (Cambridge, UK: Cambridge University Press, 1956), 18, for a description of the enclosure of the Ten Tribes. See Andrew Runni Anderson, *Alexander's Gate, Gog and Magog, and the Inclosed Nations* (Cambridge, MA: Medieval Academy of America, 1937), 60; and Shamma Aharonm Boyarin, "Diasporic Culture and the Makings of Alexander Romances," Ph.D. diss., University of California, Berkeley, 2008, 47, for discussions of Jewish power in this version of Alexander legend.
17. Boyarin, "Diasporic Culture," 84.
18. Dönitz, "Alexander the Great," 37.
19. Kristen Fudeman, *Vernacular Voices: Language and Identity in Medieval French Jewish Communities* (Philadelphia: University of Pennsylvania Press, 2010), 1, 5, 17. Fudeman calls this practice of writing in French with Hebrew characters "Hebraico-French"; ibid., 5.
20. Ibid., 5.

A Previously Unidentified *Somniale Danielis* Text in Takamiya MS 33 with an Updated Handlist of Latin *Somniale* Texts from England

ALEXANDRA REIDER

Takamiya MS 33, now on deposit at the Beinecke Rare Book and Manuscript Library at Yale University, is an illuminated manuscript of medical, scientific, and astrological texts written on parchment in Latin and Middle English. The manuscript has been disbound and in its present form consists of nine quires partially sewn together. The first folio is fairly worn. The distinctive borders might suggest a date for the manuscript in the 1480s.[1] The script, which can be described as a bastard anglicana with elements of secretary, might suggest a date more generally within the period from the 1480s to just after 1500.[2] The last text in Takamiya MS 33, which occupies folios 57r to 63v, has gone formally unidentified in the most complete available catalogue of the collection, that compiled by the owner, Professor Toshiyuki Takamiya; he describes it as "a dream book."[3]

This Latin *oneirokritkon* is a previously unidentified text within the tradition of the *Somniale Danielis*. The "Daniel dreambook" is a "Christianised dream key manual" held to be written in Greek sometime between the fourth and seventh centuries, though the surviving material record begins with Latin versions in manuscripts that date only from the ninth century.[4] In Takamiya MS 33, the dreambook's rubric does not introduce it as such (which is key, and more on which below), but comparison of the text with those presented in Steven R. Fischer's *The Complete Medieval Dreambook* and Lawrence T. Martin's *Somniale Danielis: An Edition* shows that the majority of the dreams and associated significations in Takamiya MS 33 derive from known texts in the tradition, even if not in the specific pairing found in Takamiya MS 33 itself.[5] Variation within the roster is the norm among *Somniale* texts: "some dreams and their interpretations appear frequently, while others are preserved in only a few manuscripts."[6] The *Somniale* text in Takamiya MS 33 likely the 40th Latin witness to the tradition that is of English origin.[7] (For an updated working handlist of the Latin *Somniale Danielis* texts thought to be from England, see the Appendix below.)

Somniale Danielis in Takamiya MS 33 comprises 458 dreams, which makes it quite long for this tradition.[8] Even so, the work appears to be atelous, as Linda Ehrsam Voigts notes.[9] The text is in two columns: dreams on the left and significations on the right, with a red line connecting them. The alphabetical list begins on folio 57r with the dream-and-signification set *arma portare se videre—honorem significat*, and it ends on the bottom of folio 63v with *vestimenta linea habere—pecuniam habere*. These are also the concluding words of the manuscript; there are no further complete folios and no *explicit*. The lack of *explicit* is notable: in London, British Library, MS Additional 15236, a *Somniale* text also ends shortly into the letter *V*, but the presence of an *explicit* indicates that the text was judged to be complete.[10] With no such *explicit* in Takamiya MS 33, there is reason to suggest that the already-long dreambook went on, or was originally intended to go on even longer.

While most of the significations are a terse one or two words, such as *honorem* or *periculum*, a few end in *significat* or *significant*, the latter practice being standard within the *Somniale* tradition.[11] The text is in alphabetical order by the headword of the dream, though the order of headwords within each letter is less predictable, and there are some other oddities: notably, the Latin preposition *in*, rather than the nominal object of the preposition, serves as the headword for most of the *I* section. Each new initial letter, progressing through the alphabet, is introduced with a two-line decorated initial in gold leaf, except for *A*, which is a four-line initial. Decorative borders ornament the top and left margin of the first folio, folio 57r.

One of the reasons such a popular work—the most popular dream interpretation text in the Middle Ages,[12] even "one of the most popular books in medieval Europe"[13]—has been hitherto unidentified must be its misleading rubric. Though the rubric mentions prophets, it makes no specific mention of Daniel, as is standard but not required in this tradition.[14] Instead, it foregrounds Aristotle. The Latin rubric reads: "Sompnus est legamentum [*sic*] omnium sensum [*sic*] ab arestotile de sompno et vigilia et nota quod sompnus est triplex scilicet primo modo ab angelis et secundo ab hominibus tercio modo a demonis spiritus prophetarum non semper est subditus prophetis." This translates as: "'Sleep is the binding of all the senses,' from

Aristotle's *On Sleep and Waking*, and note that sleep is three-fold: namely, the first kind is from the angels; the second is from men; the third is from demons. The spirit of the prophets is not always subject to the prophets."[15]

Typically, when the *Somniale* is not attributed to Daniel by name, either the text is still identified as the work of a prophet or there is no introductory material at all.[16] Neither circumstance is the case here. And although the rubric does not introduce the text as Aristotle's *De somno et vigilia*, it does cite that work, and not *Somniale Danielis*, at the outset. This Aristotelian red herring is all the more significant because, as Lorenzo DiTommaso notes, "while it was possible—albeit within a limited range—for substantively identical texts to be associated with more than one biblical, mythological, or historical figure, the *Somniale* resolutely remained the sole province of Daniel."[17] Though the rubric falls one step short of attributing the work to Aristotle, it still calls into question Daniel's seemingly exclusive right to the material: "spiritus prophetarum non semper est subditus prophetis," indeed.

As misleading as the *Somniale* rubric is, it also suggests a reason for the text's inclusion in the manuscript. The focus on Aristotle in the rubric of this text recalls the rubric of the manuscript's first text, John Lydgate and Benedict Burgh's poem, *Secrees of Old Philosoffres*. *Secrees* is an English verse translation of *Secretum secretorum*, the popular pseudo-Aristotelian Latin prose treatise. The rubric of *Secrees* in Takamiya MS 33 puts Aristotle on the first folio of the manuscript: "Of the crafte of phisonomye whiche doth trete of the qualitees and condicions of the membre of man and of the Image of Ypocras whiche Arestotele wrote to kynge Alisaunder." The presence of this particular *Somniale* and its rubric in Takamiya MS 33 thus creates a "bookend" effect.

Lydgate and Burgh's poem also appears with the same rubric in Cambridge, Gonville and Caius College, MS 336/725.[18] The second half of this other manuscript is a "twin" of Takamiya MS 33 in most of its textual contents and visual details. The same decidedly distinctive line filler, made up of alternating red and blue running *x*'s," fills out the rubric's last line in both manuscripts. The four-line decorated "I" at the beginning of the poem, as well as the one-line alternating red and blue initials at the beginning of each stanza, are markedly similar in style in both manuscripts. More broadly, the design of the paraph marks and, perhaps most strikingly, of the ornate borders that mark new texts is consistent across the "Takamiya portion" of the manuscript at Gonville and Caius College and Takamiya MS 33 itself.[19]

The motif of Aristotle writing to Alexander makes another appearance in both manuscripts, though Aristotelian elements ultimately feature more prominently in Takamiya MS 33. The main text of the *Tractatus nobilis de regimine sanitatis* begins, "Aristoles [*sic*] autem scribens Alexandro" (Takamiya MS 33, fol. 38r; Gonville and Caius MS 336/725, fol.140r). This work occurs roughly halfway through Takamiya MS 33 and the corresponding material in Gonville and Caius College, MS 336/725, punctuating the volumes with an Aristotle-and-Alexander mid-point that recalls the rubric of Lydgate and Burgh's *Secrees*. Takamiya MS 33 cites the classical authority, but not Alexander, a third time with its Aristotelian *Somniale* text. There is no *Somniale*, with or without an Aristotelian rubric, in the Cambridge "twin," and none of the works therein after the *Tractatus* mention Aristotle. The dreambook's rubric thus reveals that the thematic interest in Aristotle — which may also be an interest in structural symmetry — is stronger in Takamiya MS 33.

The structurally and thematically unifying arc that *Somniale* anchors may have been extrinsic to the design of Takamiya MS 33: *Somniale* shows signs of existing as a unit separate from the rest of the manuscript, to which it then may have been appended as a booklet.[20] The structure of the folios supports this: the first leaf of this work, folio 57, is a singleton, which is followed by a quire of six further folios. These seven folios comprise the "booklet" I consider, though if it were an independent unit at one time, it may have been longer. A stub of very worn parchment after the final leaf, folio 63, wraps around the entire booklet and is pasted along the gutter of folio 57, though it is now partly peeling off.[21] This stub has stains on both the recto and verso that are not on the *Somniale* booklet. Last, the configuration of the bifolia in this last portion of the manuscript is especially problematic. The single folio at folio 57 is curious; even more curiously, the hair and flesh sides of the parchment do not match across openings except across folios 60v to 61r, although the text is continuous throughout, from folios 57r to 63v.[22]

In addition to the codicological singularities of this *Somniale*, there are other reasons, beyond the booklet, to suggest that the dreambook may once have been separate. In further support of the possibility that these leaves were a later appendage, folio 56, the final extant folio in the quire immediately preceding *Somniale Danielis*, was originally left blank, though it had been ruled in what appears to be brown crayon: medicinal recipes are added in a later hand on both sides of the leaf.[23] Had the dream text been part of the manuscript's original design, it would presumably have followed the preceding text directly, given that there was suitably formatted space available: the *Sominale* folios are ruled in a similar brown waxy crayon. Further evidence that the dream text might not have been part of the manuscript's original design is the fact that this is the only text in Takamiya MS 33 not to appear in its twin manuscript, Cambridge, Gonville and Caius College, MS 336/725.[24]

Yet however codicologically distinct the *Somniale* text is, the visual and structural continuities bespeak a concerted cohesion across the manuscript. Crucially, the booklet with *Somniale* has the same decorator and style of decoration in its border, initials and line fillers as the rest of the manuscript. There is also no discernible difference in the booklet's script. There was a clear effort expended to integrate this material visually with that preceding.

And, as discussed above, the somewhat misdirecting rubrication of *Somniale* nevertheless creates a structural "bookend" effect with its nod to Aristotle.

The integration is an important complicating factor that raises the question of how long *Somniale Danielis* was separate from the rest of the volume. The possibility that the material originated independently is perfectly in line with Ralph Hanna's description of booklets as providing booksellers with "ready stock, especially of popular texts," which *Somniale* certainly was.[25] Independent circulation would also explain the degree to which the outer stub is worn. Yet the decorative and structural cohesion across the whole manuscript is undeniable.[26] The booklet may have been produced and appended directly after production of the rest of the volume. Further codicological study of contemporaneous copies of *Somniale Danielis* might reveal whether there is precedence for booklets containing it to circulate independently in England in the period and might thereby shed some light on reasons for the assembly and present structure of Takamiya MS 33.

Future comparative work on Takamiya MS 33 and Gonville and Caius College, MS 336/725 must take into account the presence and the idiosyncrasies of the Takamiya copy of *Somniale Danielis* as well as the ramifications of its codicology. One may already distinguish between the twins by noting the great length of Gonville and Caius Library MS 336/725 (172 folios) compared to Takamiya MS 33 (63 folios) and registering all that is absent from the latter. But it is worth emphasizing that one may also, although it is less obvious to do so, reverse the process and tell the twins apart by noting the larger presence of overarching thematic and structural interests in Takamiya MS 33. At precisely what point in its making or use was Takamiya MS 33 thus "framed" by the addition of a *Somniale Danielis* that acknowledges the authority of Aristotle is now one of the questions for future research.[27]

Yale University

Acknowledgments

My thanks are due to Anya Adair, Daniel Cowling, Lorenzo DiTommaso, Roland Folter, Ralph Hanna, Traugott Lawler, David McKitterick, Henry Parkes, Kathleen L. Scott, Barbara A. Shailor, Toshiyuki Takamiya, M. Teresa Tavormina, and Daniel Wakelin. I am also grateful to the librarians of the Gonville and Caius College for the permission to examine MS 336/725.

APPENDIX: AN UPDATED HANDLIST OF LATIN TEXTS OF
SOMNIALE DANIELIS FROM ENGLAND

In *Zur Bedeutung von Schlaf und Traum im Mittelalter*, Maria Elisabeth Wittmer-Butsch provides two tables that sort eighty-two Latin manuscripts of *Somniale Danielis* by origin and date.[28] Lorenzo DiTommaso augments Wittmer-Butsch's inventory and rearranges it, furnishing references to 126 Latin *Somniale Danielis* manuscripts as part of his heroic catalogue and bibliography of apocryphal Daniel literature, which is sorted by language and indicates date but not origin.[29] Below, I provide an updated working handlist of Latin texts of *Somniale Danielis* from England. I have corrected Wittmer-Butsch's tabulation against my own research into the 126 Latin manuscripts in DiTommaso's inventory.[30]

All but two of Wittmer-Butsch's assumptions of English origin for Latin manuscripts in English libraries stand. London, Wellcome Medical Library, MS 508 is, N. R. Ker notes, from Germany.[31] Further, the manuscript from B. S. Cron's private library and from which he published a limited-run edition and translation is, the prefatory material to his book suggests, from France.[32] In addition to Takamiya MS 33, now in New Haven, Connecticut, three other English *Somniale* texts are found in non-English libraries. Wittmer-Butsch was perhaps hasty in assuming Germanic origin for two manuscripts in Berlin's Staatsbibliothek that are in fact English; and a Vossiani manuscript in Leiden is also English, though it dates to the seventeenth century and thus falls outside Wittmer-Butsch's medieval purview.[33]

The following handlist should not be taken as an exhaustive account of copies of *Somniale Danielis* from England but rather as a further step in that direction. I have checked the catalogue information and available scholarship on DiTommaso's 126 Latin manuscripts to see where English origin is noted. The dates and folio/page numbers listed below are taken from his inventory unless otherwise stated. Witnesses not hitherto proposed as English in origin are in bold.

1. **Berlin, Staatsbibliothek zu Berlin Preußischer Kulturbesitz, MS theo. 4° 10 (s.xv), fols. 63r–64r.**[34]
2. **Berlin, Staatsbibliothek zu Berlin Preußischer Kulturbesitz, MS lat. 4° 70 (s.xiv), fols. 226r, col. a–229r, col. b.**[35]
3. Cambridge, Corpus Christi College, MS 301 (s.xiv), pp. 198–202.
4. Cambridge, Corpus Christi College, MS 466 (s.xiv), pp. 131, 228–231.
5. Cambridge, Corpus Christi College, MS 481 (s.xiii/xiv), pp. 404–418.
6. Cambridge, Pembroke College, MS 103 (s.x), fols. 75r–77v.
7. **Cambridge, Peterhouse, MS 222 (s.xiv), fols. 1r–8v.**[36]
8. Cambridge, Trinity College, MS O.1.57 (s.xv), fols. 119r–124r.

9. Cambridge, Trinity College, MS O.8.21 (s.xv–xvi), fols. 134r–149v.[37]
10. Cambridge, University Library, MS Gg.i.1 (s.xiv), fols. 394v–397r.
11. Cambridge, University Library, MS Ii.vi.17 (s.xv), fols. 112r–117v.
12. **Leicester, Old Town Hall Library, MS 4 (s.xiii–xiv), pp. 33–34.**[38]
13. **Leiden, Universiteitsbibliotheek, MS Vossiani lat. O. 52 (s.xvii), fols. 101r–109v.**[39]
14. London, British Library, MS Additional 15236 (s.xiii/xiv), fols. 161v–168v.
15. London, British Library, MS Cotton Tiberius A.iii (s.xi), fols. 27r–31v.
16. London, British Library, MS Cotton Tiberius A.iii (s.xi), fols. 31v–32r.
17. **London, British Library, MS Cotton Tiberius A.iii (s.xi), fols. 32r–v.**[40]
18. London, British Library, MS Cotton Titus D.xxvi (c. 1040), fols. 11v–16r.
19. **London, British Library, MS Egerton 821 (s.xii/xiii), fols. 12r–14v.**[41]
20. London, British Library, MS Egerton 847 (s.xv), fols. 21v–26v.
21. London, British Library, MS Harley 2558 (s.xiv), fols. 191r, col.a–191v, col.b.
22. London, British Library, MS Royal 8.E.x. (c. 1315), fols. 114v–117r.
23. London, British Library, MS Royal 12.C.xii (s.xiii/xiv), fols. 81v–86v.
24. London, British Library, MS Royal 13.D.i (c. 1385), fols. 247v–248r.
25. London, British Library, MS Sloane 475 (s.xi/xii), fols. 217v–218r.[42]
26. **London, British Library, MS Sloane 1009 (s.xv), fols. 58r–61v.**[43]
27. **London, British Library, MS Sloane 2561 (s.xvii), fol. 55.**[44]
28. London, British Library, MS Sloane 3281 (s.xiii/xiv), fols. 39r–47r.[45]
29. London, British Library, MS Sloane 3542 (s.xiii–xvi), fols. 41v–44v.[46]
30. **London, Royal Society of Antiquaries, 306 (s.xv), fols. 64r–71v.**[47]
31. **New Haven, Beinecke Rare Book and Manuscript Library at Yale University, Takamiya MS 33 (s.xv), fols. 57r–63v.**
32. Oxford, All Souls College, MS 81 (s.xv), fols. 166r–172r.
33. Oxford, All Souls College, MS 81 (s.xvi), fols. 205r–211v.
34. **Oxford, All Souls College, MS 81 (s.xv), fols. 232r–238v.**[48]
35. Oxford, Bodleian Library, MS Bodley 177 (s.xiv), fol. 64r.
36. Oxford, Bodleian Library, MS Bodley 581 (s.xiv), fols. 6r–8v.
37. Oxford, Bodleian Library, MS Digby 81 (s.xiii), fols. 99v–101v.
38. Oxford, Bodleian Library, MS Digby 86 (s.xiii), fols. 34v–40r.
39. Oxford, Bodleian Library, MS Lyell 35 (s.xv), fols. 5r, 19r–23v, 25v.
40. Oxford, Bodleian Library, MS Selden Supra 74 (s.xiii), fol. 14ra.

NOTES

1. K. L. Scott proposes this date to me in email correspondence from Nov. 18–19, 2014. The rose pen frame of the borders indicates a date in the last quarter of the fifteenth century; see Kathleen L. Scott, *Dated and Datable English Manuscript Borders: c. 1395–1499* (London: Bibliographical Society and British Library, 2002), 9. Further, in correspondence she notes that

both the relatively free curling of the larger borders and the consistent use of green lobes point to a date of the 1480s and that the leaf motifs are not oversized enough in relation to the other motifs in the sprays (as they are in ibid., pl. 37a) to suggest a date as late as the 1490s. In correspondence of November 26, 2014, she observes that a very similar lower border decorates a page of *Boke of the xii patriarkys* in Cambridge, University Library, MS Ff.6.33, though that manuscript also differentiates itself with a "bar down the left margin" and "a less rigorous upper border," as well as a different scribe. Laura Saetveit Miles, "Scribes at Syon: The Communal Usage and Production of Legislative Manuscripts at the English Birgittine House," in *Saint Birgitta, Syon and Vadstena: Papers from A Symposium in Stockholm, 4–6 October 2007*, ed. Claes Gejrot, Sara Risberg, and Mia Åkestam, Konferenser 73 (Stockholm: Kungl. Vitterhets Historie och Antikvitets Akadamien, 2010): 71–88, at 71, notes that the hand in Cambridge, University Library, MS Ff.6.33 is that of William Darker, who died in 1512, but Anya Adair has suggested to me that the script of Takamiya MS 33 is not William Darker. Contrast examples of his hand: see A. I. Doyle, "William Darker: the Work of an English Carthusian Scribe," in *Medieval Manuscripts, Their Makers and Users: A Special Issue of Viator in Honor of Richard and Mary Rouse* (Turnhout, Belgium: Brepols, 2011), 199–211; and an example of Darker's fere-textura in M. B. Parkes, *English Cursive Book Hands: 1250–1500* (Oxford: Clarendon Press, 1969), pl. 8(ii).

2. Ralph Hanna notes, in email correspondence of February 20, 2015:

> The hand itself I would date s. xv^{ex} (i.e. after 1470) or s. x v$^{4/4}$ (more specifically 1480s–1490s). There are some things in it that are more reminiscent of 16th-century secretary than of 15th, although they are not consistent features, rather forms in variation with others. Here I am thinking of things like [on fol. 1r] near the foot, the two examples of **g** that have a "horn" above the upper cup on the right side only and a dangly lower lobe.

He also points out "the **w** with pronouncedly prominent v on the front end and the final stroke (the second **v**) reduced to a relatively small **o**-sized loop." Based on this evidence, he concludes that these features:

> may only suggest that this is someone "upgrading" a script they are more used to writing, a document hand (but which trickles in here and there as they go), than anything about dating. But simultaneously, it does suggest that I wouldn't automatically exclude dating this "s. xv/xvi," that is leaving open the possibil-

ity that it might be just after 1500 (rather than, say, specifically c. 1485–1500).

A useful English comparator is Oxford, Bodleian Library, MS Bodley 831 from 1493; see Andrew G. Watson, *Catalogue of Dated and Datable Manuscripts c. 435–1600 in Oxford Libraries*, 2 vols. (Oxford: Clarendon Press, 1984), no. 115, pl. 788.

3. Toshiyuki Takamiya, "A Handlist of Western Medieval Manuscripts in the Takamiya Collection," in *The Medieval Book: Glosses from Friends & Colleagues of Christopher de Hamel*, ed. James H. Marrow, Richard A. Linenthal, and William Noel ('t Goy-Houten, The Netherlands: Hes & De Graaf, 2010): 421–440, at 428. There is no mention of the manuscript in Takami Matsuda, Richard A. Linenthal, and John Scahill, eds., *The Medieval Book and a Modern Collector: Essays in Honour of Toshiyuki Takamiya* (Cambridge, UK, and Tokyo: D. S. Brewer & Yushodo Press, 2004); nor in Simon Horobin and Linne R. Mooney, eds., *Middle English Texts in Transition: A Festschrift Dedicated to Toshiyuki Takamiya on his 70th birthday*, Manuscript Culture in the British Isles 6 (York, UK: York Medieval Press in association with Boydell & Brewer, 2014).
4. Steven M. Oberhelman, *Dreambooks in Byzantium: Six Oneirocritica in Translation, with Commentary and Introduction* (Hampshire, UK: Ashgate, 2008), 2–4.
5. Steven R. Fischer, *The Complete Medieval Dreambook: A Multilingual, Alphabetical Somnia Danielis Collation* (Bern: Peter Lang Publishers, 1982); and Lawrence T. Martin, *Somniale Danielis: An Edition of a Medieval Latin Dream Interpretation Handbook*, Lateinische Sprache und Literatur des Mittelalters 10 (Frankfurt am Main, Germany: Peter D. Lang, 1981).
6. Lorenzo DiTommaso, *The Book of Daniel and the Apocryphal Daniel Literature*, Studia in Veteris Testamenti Pseudepigrapha 20 (Leiden, The Netherlands: Brill, 2005), 237. For a summary of the (inconclusive state of the) *oneirokritikon*'s textual criticism, see ibid., 239.
7. There are also witnesses to the tradition in Old English, Middle English, Middle Welsh, Middle Irish, Old Icelandic, German, French, Italian, Hebrew, Armenian, and Coptic; ibid., 389–394.
8. Ibid., 237.
9. Linda Ehrsam Voigts, "The 'Sloane Group': Related Scientific and Medical Manuscripts from the Fifteenth Century in the Sloane Collection," *British Library Journal* 16 (1990): 26–57, at 33.
10. Martin, *Somniale Danielis*, 15.
11. DiTommaso, *Book of Daniel*, 237.
12. Ibid., 236.
13. Gabriel Turville-Petre, "Dream Symbols in Old Icelandic Literature," in

Festschrift Walter Baetke, dargebracht zu seinem 80. Geburtstag am 28 März 1964, ed. Kurt Rudolf, Rolf Heller, and Ernst Walter (Weimar, Germany: Hermann Böhlaus Nachfolger, 1966), 343–354, at 349.

14. For a sample of the variety of titles of and prologues to the *Somniale*, see the narrative descriptions of thirty-two of the Latin witnesses in Martin, *Somniale Danielis*, 14–60.
15. The rubric's most explicit allusion is to Aristotle, but it also incorporates Alan of Lille, who explains in *De arte praedicatoria* that sleep is threefold (*Patrologia Latina* 210.195D–196A), and St. Paul, who says in 1 Corinthians 14:32 that the spirits of prophets are subject to the prophets. I am grateful to Traugott Lawler for his help in puzzling out the rubric.
16. Martin, *Somniale Danielis*, 14–60.
17. DiTommaso, *Book of Daniel*, 243.
18. Cambridge, Gonville and Caius College, MS 336/725, fol. 104r. (This manuscript has two sets of foliation: I use the first, recorded in ink.) Voigts, "Sloane Group," 27, gives the most complete consideration so far of the two manuscripts in tandem.
19. In correspondence of November 19, 2014, Kathleen L. Scott proposes that the two manuscripts had the same decorator.
20. For the most recent survey on the "booklet" and the questions it raises, see Alexandra Gillespie, "Medieval Books, Their Booklets, and Booklet Theory," in *Manuscript Miscellanies, c. 1450–1700*, ed. Richard Beadle and Colin Burrow, *English Manuscript Studies 1100–1700* 16 (London: British Library, 2011), 1–29.
21. Cf. Pamela R. Robinson's sixth feature of a "booklet": "Its outer leaves may be soiled or rubbed, suggesting that the 'booklet' circulated independently for some time before being bound up with others." See P. R. Robinson, "The 'Booklet': A Self-Contained Unit in Composite Manuscripts," *Codicologica* 3 (1980): 46–69, at 48.
22. Such disjointedness is not visible in other parts of the manuscript. Cf. Ralph Hanna's additional feature of a "booklet": "Variation in the material from which different parts of a manuscript are made: shifts between paper and vellum, shifts (insofar as these are recognizable) among kinds or qualities of vellum, shifts among different paper stocks"; Ralph Hanna, "Booklets in Medieval Manuscripts: Further Considerations," *Studies in Bibliography* 39 (1986): 100–111, at 108.
23. This portion of the manuscript (fols. 51r–56v) preceding the *Somniale* booklet shows signs of being a booklet as well. Fol. 51r has a stub pasted down the gutter, now partly peeling off, like that on fol. 57r. Instead of being attached to a larger outer stub, however, this fol. 51r stub simply folds behind to the other side of the quire, where it is one of three stubs in total. Cf. P. R. Robinson's ninth feature of a "booklet":

> The last page (or pages) of a "booklet" may have been left blank because the text did not fill the "booklet." A "booklet" in which the concluding text is complete may lack its last leaf (or leaves), suggesting that a blank endleaf (or leaves) has been cut away when the "booklet" was bound up with others.

Robinson, "Booklet," 48. It is also worth mentioning that the preceding quire, fols. 47r–50v, has four stubs at the end.

24. I follow Tess Tavormina in noting that though the "Takamiya portion" of the Gonville and Caius manuscript mainly starts on fol. 104, shared material also exists on fols. 60r–63r (Takamiya MS 33 fols. 51r–53v) and on fols. 96r–97v (Takamiya MS 33 fols. 54r–55v). Her comments to this effect are recorded in email correspondence with the Gonville and Caius College Library from April 15, 2014, which is preserved in the manuscript's annotated catalogue there. I add to this observation that it is these five folios, as well as the ruled folio originally left blank, that in the Takamiya manuscript together form the quire preceding *Somniale* (see note 23). There is no similar indication that these folios (fols. 60r–63r, fols. 96r–97v) are codicologically distinct in the Gonville and Caius volume. Fols. 60r–63r are in a quire that consists of fols. 57–64. Fols. 96r–97v are in a quire that consists of fols. 93–99. The material that starts halfway down the second column on fol. 60r in Gonville and Caius MS 336/725 stands at the head of the first column on the corresponding folio in Takamiya MS 33, fol. 51r. The material is less well fitted to its new setting in the second instance: the top half of fol. 96r in the Gonville and Caius manuscript is occupied by text continuous from fol. 95v; on the corresponding folio in Takamiya MS 33, 54r: fol., there is a blank space. The impetus to place these two different texts alongside one another in the Takamiya manuscript may have been visual and/or thematic. They are similarly laid out, with lists of items visually linked by red brackets. They are also similar in content: both lists detail medicines. It is nevertheless clear that these texts are different: the first is a mix of English headings situated above the lists and primarily Latin list-entries; the second is entirely in Latin with Latin headings in the margin. The decoration is also somewhat different between the two texts: decorated gold-leaf initials mark off the English headings of the first text; blue paraph marks divide the entries in the second. It is interesting to note that in the Takamiya manuscript, the second text in the booklet (fols. 54r–55v) reproduces the full text of its Gonville and Caius counterpart (fols. 96r–97v). The first text in the booklet (fols. 51r–53v) reproduces only the end of the text that in Gonville and Caius MS 336/725 runs from fols. 57v–63r. The reproduction of the end and its *explicit* in this case cleverly gives the impression that a full text has been reproduced.

25. Hanna, "Booklets in Medieval Manuscripts," 101.
26. Hanna writes, "The producer of a codex, in a single-quire booklet, possesses a bibliographical unit which can potentially be fitted into nearly any context." Ibid., 105. What is striking about the Takamiya MS 33 *Somniale* booklet is how perfectly it fits into its current context. It was also certainly not cheap to produce, another feature Hanna cites to explain the typical booklet's appeal; Ibid., 102.
27. Gillespie lays out a variety of motivations for booklet production, one of which may ultimately best explain the codicology of Takamiya MS 33:

> In the absence of some contemporary narrative about it, or a great deal of circumstantial evidence, how is a codicologist meant to distinguish a composite manuscript made up from booklets put into circulation by authors as booklets, from one made by scribes imitating this authorial format, from one made up from booklets copied for the purposes of stocking a shop? The conditions in which a scribe (or an author) might find it useful to make books from booklets are also various: when he was collaborating with others; when his patron's needs seemed likely to shift unexpectedly; when he was not sure where his next exemplar was coming from; when his own work was routinely interrupted by other tasks; when his exemplar seemed "easily divisible" and he judged that the copy he was making might also be best in some flexible form.

See Gillespie, "Medieval Books," 21. Given the complicated "twin" relationship that Takamiya MS 33 has with Gonville and Caius MS 336/725, it may prove particularly useful to think through the options involving an exemplar.
28. Maria Elisabeth Wittmer-Butsch, *Zur Bedeutung von Schlaf und Traum im Mittelalter*, Medium Aevum Quotidianum, 1 (Krems, Austria: Medium Aevum Quotidianum, 1990), 178–179. Wittmer-Butsch's tables promise the "Verbreitung der lateinischen Handschriften und Fragmente des 'Somniale Danielis'" across different spans of time; ibid., 178–179. Whether *Verbreitung* [distribution] entails origin or provenance is not immediately clear: she covers both. She also delineates her categories variously. She alternates between sorting manuscripts into bounded countries (as in *Italien*) and into language zones (as in *Deutsches Sprachgebiet*). DiTommaso asserts that "in her tables M.E. Wittmer-Butsch merely lists the manuscripts by their shelf marks" (DiTommaso, *Book of Daniel*, 240); that is, that she takes note only of their present location. This methodology would certainly explain how two English manuscripts ended up in the realm of *Deutsches*

Sprachgebiet [see items 1 and 2 in the Handlist] and how she assumes an English origin for the Wellcome Library manuscript from Germany [see further in the Appendix], but it is not the only rationale she uses. She does note the Italian origin of Uppsala, Universitetsbibliotek (Carolina), MS C.664 and the French origin of London, British Library, Harley MS 3017, so I can only assume that she is most concerned with presenting origin.

29. DiTommaso, *Book of Daniel*, 379–389. DiTommaso's research considerably increases the number of known manuscripts containing *Somniale Danielis*, adding upwards of forty Latin texts to Wittmer-Butsch's tally. One reason, though a minor one, for this increase is an expanded set of criteria. DiTommaso, who is most concerned with classifying the witnesses by language, includes three Latin texts from the seventeenth and eighteenth centuries; Wittmer-Butsch limits her inquiries to witnesses from the ninth through sixteenth centuries.

30. I have made every effort to track down information about the last Latin manuscript in DiTommaso's inventory, which was purportedly in the private collection of Professor August Conrady, a sinologist at the University of Leipzig. See "August Conrady," *Universität Leipzig: Geschichte*, last modified August 10, 2011, http://www.uni-leipzig.de/~ostasien/institut/geschichte/august-conrady. I have been unable to find any information about this *Somniale* text specifically, but DiTommaso has generously provided me with a reference to a Latin lunation in a manuscript in the Conrady collection. In an email of January 15, 2015, he writes, "Interesting but not probative is the fact that this text was a lunation, and lunations frequently precede or follow copies of the *Somniale* in MS." See Hardin Craig, *The Works of John Metham, including The Romance of Amoryus and Cleopes* (London: Kegan Paul, Trench, Trübner & Co., for the Early English Text Society, 1906), xxxix.

31. N. R. Ker, *Medieval Manuscripts in British Libraries*, vol. 1, London (Oxford: Clarendon Press, 1969), 398.

32. Cron writes:

> This list of dreams and their interpretations is written in a hand of probably the fourteenth century on some blank leaves in the middle of a thirteenth century manuscript of the *Treatise on the Virtues and Vices* of Guillaume Pérault, Bishops of Lyons (died before 1260), that formerly belonged to the monastery, now Cathedral, of St. Benignus at Dijon.

B. S. Cron, "Note on Text & Translation," in *A Mediaeval Dream Book: Printed from the original Latin with an English translation* (London: Gogmagog Press, 1963), n.p.

33. See items 1, 2, and 13 and the accompanying notes in Appendix: An Updated Handlist.
34. Assigned by Wittmer-Butsch, *Zur Bedeutung von Schlaf und Traum*, to *Deutsches Sprachgebiet*. For a record of English origin, see Valentin Rose, *Verzeichniss der lateinischen Handschriften der Königlichen Bibliothek zu Berlin, zweiter Band: Die Handschriften der kurfürstlichen Bibliothek und der kurfürstlichen Lande, dritte Abteilung* (Berlin: A. Asher & Co., 1905), 1161–1164. The portion of the manuscript with the *Somniale* also contains the work of the Oxford-affiliated scholastics Walter Burley, John of Wales, and Robert Holcot.
35. Assigned by Wittmer-Butsch, *Zur Bedeutung von Schlaf und Traum*, to *Deutsches Sprachgebiet*. For a record of English origin, see Rose, *Verzeichniss*, 1216–1221.
36. M. R. James, *A Descriptive Catalogue of the Manuscripts in the Library of Peterhouse* (Cambridge, UK: Cambridge University Press, 1899), 271–275.
37. I am grateful to David McKitterick for providing me with the folio numbers, which were added after James compiled his catalogue and are thus not in M. R. James, *The Western Manuscripts in the Library of Trinity College, Cambridge: A Descriptive Catalogue*, vol. 3, *Containing an Account of the Manuscripts Standing in Class O* (Cambridge, UK: Cambridge University Press, 1902), 409–410. They are also not included in DiTommaso's inventory.
38. N. R. Ker, *Medieval Manuscripts in British Libraries*, vol. 3, *Lampeter–Oxford* (Oxford: Clarendon Press, 1983), 77–79.
39. S. xvii is too late for Wittmer-Butsch's purview. For a record of English origin, see K. A. de Meyier, *Codices Vossiani Latini, Pars III: Codices in Octavo* (Leiden, The Netherlands: Bibliotheca Universitatis Leidensis, 1977), 97–98.
40. Wittmer-Butsch does not acknowledge the presence of multiple copies of the Latin *Somniale* in Cotton Tiberius A.iii; by DiTommaso's count, there are five, the last two of which he notes are in Latin and Old English. (I have omitted these two from my handlist on account of their being primarily in Old English. See R. M. Liuzza, *Anglo-Saxon Prognostics: An Edition and Translation of Texts from London, British Library, MS Cotton Tiberius A.iii*, Anglo-Saxon Texts 8 (Cambridge, UK: D. S. Brewer, 2011), 178-189 and 208-211.) She does, however, cite two separate versions in Oxford, All Souls College, MS 81 (in which, by DiTommaso's count, there are three). To err on the side of caution, and because, per DiTommaso, three versions of the text abut in Cotton Tiberius A.iii, I assume that she has omitted one, not two, texts.
41. László Sándor Chardonnens and R. M. Liuzza both refer to it as English. See L. S. Chardonnens, *Anglo-Saxon Prognostics, 900–1100: Study and Texts*, Brill's Texts and Sources in Intellectual History 3 (Leiden, The Netherlands: Brill, 2007), 113, 395, 479; and Liuzza, *Anglo-Saxon Prognostics*, 30 n. 105 and esp. 42 for mention of *Somniale*.

42. According to Liuzza, this manuscript is "possibly English." See R. M. Liuzza, "Anglo-Saxon prognostics in context: a survey and handlist of manuscripts," *Anglo-Saxon England* 30 (2001): 181–230, at 225–227. Chardonnens, *Anglo-Saxon Prognostics*, 42-43, is cautious about the posited English origin for the relevant part of the manuscript. The manuscript is listed in Helmut Gneuss and Michael Lapidge, *Anglo-Saxon Manuscripts: A Bibliographical Handlist of Manuscripts and Manuscript Fragments Written or Owned in England up to 1100* (Toronto: University of Toronto, 2014), 400, where it is attributed to an "English or Anglo-Norman scribe."
43. I acquire the date and folio numbers from the detailed manuscript description available online. See Rebecca Farnham, "London, British Library, Sloane 1009 (vol. 1)," in *Manuscripts of the West Midlands: A Catalogue of Vernacular Manuscript Books of the English West Midlands, c. 1300–c. 1475* (Birmingham, UK: University of Birmingham, 2009), http://www.hrionline.ac.uk/mwm.
44. S. xvii is too late for Wittmer-Butsch's purview. Further work is needed to place the *Somniale*, specifically, in England with certainty, but at least some parts of the manuscript, which is a collection of fragments that span six centuries, are from England; see the *British Library Online Catalogue*, http://searcharchives.bl.uk; as well as "Detailed Record of Sloane 2561," *British Library Catalogue of Illuminated Manuscripts*, last revised November 30, 2005, http://www.bl.uk/catalogues/illuminatedmanuscripts/.
45. Martin, *Somniale Danielis*, 27, posits an origin of either England or France for the manuscript. The *British Library Online Catalogue* specifies that the dream text is English.
46. Further work must be done on placing and dating the component parts of this manuscript, which is, per the *British Library Online Catalogue* entry, a composite volume of texts from different centuries and in several different languages: English, Latin, Dutch, German, and French. Wittmer-Butsch places the manuscript in England, but as seen, her rationale in determining *Verbreitung* is somewhat inconsistent. Chardonnens also places the manuscript in England; see L. S. Chardonnens, "Mantic Alphabets in Medieval Western Manuscripts and Early Printed Books," *Modern Philology* 110.3 (2013): 340–366, at 360.
47. Ker, *Medieval Manuscripts*, 1:310.
48. See note 42.

New Findings in a Late-Medieval Catechetic Prose Sequence

MICHAEL MADRINKIAN

Oxford, Bodleian Library, Laud Misc. 656 contains a sequence of three unpublished prose texts: an "Exposition on the Creed," a Decalogue tract entitled *Decem mandata*, and a catalogue of sentences from the books of wisdom entitled *Proverbia Salomonis*. The manuscript tradition of these three works is very small; only three other manuscripts share any of the same texts. While it has previously been thought that *Decem mandata*, the longest of the three, was the only item to appear in other manuscripts, this article draws attention to two other witnesses to the "Exposition on the Creed," both of which appear in conjunction with *Decem mandata*. It also discusses the implications of this discovery for the relationship between the texts, suggesting that they originally formed a textual sequence and were transmitted as such. The various manifestations of the prose sequence, moreover, show the ways in which the texts were adapted for different material and social contexts and thus show their role in the unstable environment of religious writing in the early fifteenth century.

According to S. J. Ogilvie-Thomson's volume of *The Index of Middle English Prose (IMEP)* on the Bodleian Library's Laudian collection, the text of *Decem mandata* appears in two other manuscripts in addition to MS Laud Misc. 656: London, Westminster School, MS 3 and Cambridge, Trinity College, B.14.54.[1] Although the other two texts in Laud's sequence, the "Exposition on the Creed" and *Proverbia Salomonis*, are listed in the *IMEP*, both are treated as unique to MS Laud Misc. 656. While this appears to be correct for *Proverbia Salomonis*, the *IMEP* overlooks the fact that a version of the "Exposition on the Creed" also appears alongside the copy of *Decem mandata* in Trinity College MS B.14.54.[2] In Trinity, the "Exposition on the

Creed" follows the same sequence as it does in MS Laud Misc. 656, directly preceding *Decem mandata*. One of the reasons the editors of the *IMEP* overlooked this seemingly obvious connection may be that the text of the "Exposition" in Trinity College MS B.14.54 has a number of textual variations from that in MS Laud Misc. 656. Also omitted from all catalogue references to these works is the fact that both the "Exposition on the Creed" and *Decem mandata* appear in sequence in London, British Library, Harley MS 2343.[3] The texts in MS Harley 2343 are closely related to those in Trinity College MS B.14.54, though its copy of *Decem mandata* has several significant additions, which are discussed further below.

I

Before the texts themselves can be discussed, some information about their respective manuscripts and textual transmission is necessary. MS Laud Misc. 656, which contains the full sequence, is a vernacular English manuscript dated roughly to end of the fourteenth century. The manuscript, which is copied throughout by one scribe, appears to be a fairly low-grade production, being written on rough parchment in a cursive anglicana hand with very little consideration for aesthetic value or presentation of the texts. MS Laud Misc. 656 also lacks any of the decorative features common to the commercial book trade in this period, which could potentially indicate a monastic origin.

The manuscript consists of two booklets, which appear to have been together since the early stages of production. Both booklets are in the same handwriting and appear to be consistently formatted throughout; therefore there is nothing to suggest that the scribe did not originally intend to put them together. The first booklet contains two major alliterative works, *The Siege of Jerusalem* and the C version of *Piers Plowman*, while the second is comprised solely of the prose sequence under present consideration. The second booklet is significantly shorter than the first, the prose items occupying only eighteen folios (fols. 117r–125v).[4] The dialectal forms used by the scribe throughout the manuscript's various texts are generally characteristic of the Southwest Midlands.[5] Throughout the prose texts, however, are relict forms more characteristic of the East Midlands.[6] It seems either that this scribe acquired the exemplar of the prose texts from a more easterly region or that the texts were originally composed in this dialect.

The second manuscript in which *Decem mandata* appears, Westminster School MS 3 (s.xv^{in}), is an extensive miscellany of religious and devotional texts containing eighteen items and 232 folios. Ralph Hanna has treated this manuscript comprehensively, situating its copying in London, on the evidence of later provenance.[7] In Westminster School MS 3, *Decem mandata* (here titled "þe ten comaundementis of god") is copied by the main scribe of the manuscript (Scribe 1) and appears in a separate booklet, of which it is the sole occupant (fols. 163r–180r). As Hanna argues, the manuscript was most likely a planned work, and *Decem mandata* seems to be conceived of as part of the whole. According to Hanna, the multiple scribes of Westminster School MS 3 employ an East Midlands dialect, leading him to conclude that they were part of "that well-documented migration from the central East Midlands to London."[8] This dialect concords roughly with the relict forms found in the prose texts in MS Laud Misc. 656.[9]

Composed about the same time as Westminster School MS 3, around the turn of the fifteenth century, is London, British Library, Harley MS 2343, a collection of catechetic texts in the vernacular that contains both the "Exposition on the Creed" and *Decem mandata* in sequence (fols. 1v–78v). These two texts occupy the majority of the space in Harley 2343; the seventeen other items are all quite brief, most simply listing various elements of the catechesis. The manuscript itself is very small (90 mm x 60 mm), perhaps designed as a portable guide to devotion, and is copied throughout by one scribe. The features of layout and script are very similar to those in the Westminster School manuscript, and it is possible they were produced in similar contexts. The dialect in the sequence also corresponds almost invariably to the central East Midlands, particularly the area around Bedfordshire, Huntingdonshire, and Cambridgeshire, similar to the forms present in the other manuscripts.[10] This dialect carries throughout all of the texts in Harley 2343, suggesting either that it was the scribe's own orthography or that all the texts were sourced from that region.

The final manuscript in which the "Exposition on the Creed" is paired with *Decem mandata*, Cambridge, Trinity College MS B.14.54 (fols. 1r–93v), is another small devotional manuscript (130 mm x 85 mm), datable to the third quarter of the fifteenth century.[11] Intriguingly, the three other texts in the manuscript, *The Sixteen Conditions of Christ's Charity, The Five Bodily Wits, and The Five Ghostly Wits*, are also found (albeit in different versions) in MS Harley 2343. The hand of MS B.14.54 is identifiable as that of Stephen Dodesham, one of the most prolific of recorded copyists in the later Middle Ages. Dodesham was first active in the mid-fifteenth century, apparently as a professional copyist of the London book trade. In the 1460s, he joined the Carthusian order, residing in Witham and later in Sheen.[12] This manuscript appears to be characteristic of Dodesham's later work, in which he tends to use short *r* and kidney-shaped *s*,[13] which would mean that it was likely copied during his time as a Carthusian. Trinity College B.14.54 may also have connections to Syon Abbey, for which Dodesham is known to have previously copied manuscripts,[14] as the text on folios 89r–99v is palimpsest over copies of indulgences for visiting Syon.[15] Given the monastic appearance of MS Laud Misc. 656 (as noted above), these two manuscripts together suggest that the prose texts they share might have been transmitted in networks of religious houses.

How such networks might have been structured is difficult to say. The dearth of manuscript witnesses to these texts makes any judgment about their relationships somewhat tenuous. The texts in MS Laud Misc. 656, however, are significantly different from those in the other three manuscripts. In all three texts, MS Laud Misc. 656 differs in its scriptural citations, which list only the book and chapter number; for example, "exodi 20 *capitulo*,"[16] which in the other manuscripts reads, "Þe first comaundement of god of þe first table is writen in þe book of Exodi þe xx chapitre."[17] The "Exposition on the Creed" in MS Laud Misc. 656 also contains some more significant variations from the other texts, such as shifting the order of verses in a passage and adding or subtracting biblical references. Given that none of these variations would require further knowledge, it is impossible to determine whether they are attributable to authorial revision or scribal intervention. The sequence in MS Laud Misc. 656 is thus most difficult to place; it is possible that it descends from a stage of revision antecedent to the archetype of the other three manuscripts; yet it could equally be a postarchetypal scribal abridgement, perhaps to save space.

The copy of *Decem mandata* in MS Laud Misc. 656 shares in common with the copy in Westminster School MS 3 the omission of a substantial passage under the first commandment that discusses the cherubim on the Arc of the Covenant (Exod. 25) and the brass serpent of Moses (Num. 21). This passage, which is attested in MS Harley 2343 and Trinity College MS B.14.54, seems generally in keeping with the text's style, and there is no reason to believe it is not authorial. Yet there are also further layers of revision that appear in MS Harley 2343, including two unique passages in the prologue and a lengthy conclusion unattested in any of the other extant manuscripts. These added passages are stylistically quite different from the rest of the text. In contrast to the sequence's expository style (which is discussed below), these passages adopt a traditionally didactic tone. The added conclusion, moreover, which elaborates on the benefits of keeping the commandments, is somewhat rambling and lacks the sequence's rhetorical potency. The unique passages thus seem most likely to be the work of a later interpolator. The substantial nature of these revisions, however, including the addition of scriptural material, would suggest a reviser or revisers with substantial biblical knowledge.

As noted above, *Proverbia Salomonis*, the third text in the sequence, is extant only in MS Laud Misc. 656. While it is possible that *Proverbia Salomonis* was and remained unique to this manuscript, several factors make this unlikely. First, it has been noted that the relict dialectal forms in the prose texts in MS Laud Misc. 656 seem to be different from that of the scribe, and thus *Proverbia Salomonis* cannot have been originally composed by this scribe. Second, considering that *Proverbia Salomonis* reflects the same style and rhetorical structure as the other texts, it seems likely to have been intended as part of the original sequence.

Based on these manuscript witnesses, a possible solution to the sequence's textual transmission is provided by the following stemma:

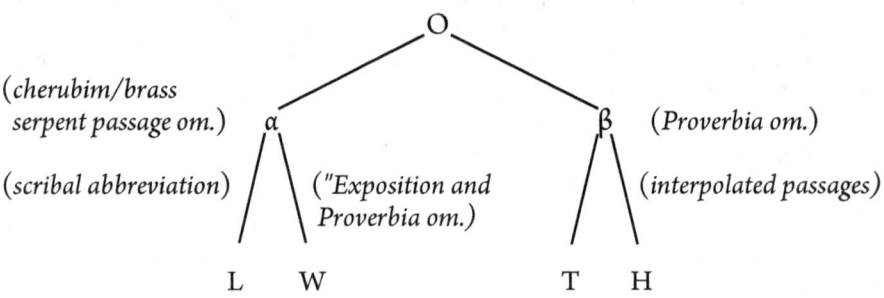

Here the archetype, which contained all three texts of the sequence, is split into two hypearchetypes, *alpha* and *beta*, distinguished by *alpha*'s omission of the cherubim/brass serpent passage in *Decem mandata* and the omission of *Proverbia Salomonis* from the sequence in *beta*. In the *alpha* strand, MS Laud Misc. 656's text would subsequently have edited the sequence to a "bare bones" version, while Westminster School MS 3 extracted *Decem mandata* for independent use. The texts in the *beta* tradition seem to have remained somewhat stable, save for the interpolated passages in MS Harley 2343. While there are other possible interpretations of the evidence, this process of transmission seems most plausible.

II

Having discussed the circumstances of the manuscripts, let us turn to the texts of the sequence under consideration. The "Exposition on the Creed," *Decem mandata*, and *Proverbia Salomonis* are works of moral and doctrinal didacticism. Catechetic texts such as these were extremely common in devotional manuscripts of the fourteenth and fifteenth centuries and became increasingly popular in the vernacular.[18] Where the present sequence differs from other devotional literature is in its employment of scripture alone, using no authorial voice or moralization. The three texts are composed solely of translated scriptural quotations and paraphrase, borrowing predominantly from the Old Testament, especially the books of history, the prophetic books, the wisdom books, and the Pentateuch. The authorial silence in the texts fosters a deliberate unoriginality; they speak *through* scripture rather than about it, thereby adopting its incontrovertible authority.

The uniformity of this unique style in the three texts suggests that they might have been composed together by the same author, a possibility reinforced by the positioning of the "Exposition on the Creed" and *Decem mandata* together in three different manuscripts. At the same time, however, the appearance of *Decem mandata* alone in Westminster School MS 3 shows that the sequence was also malleable enough that individual units could be used separately from the others.[19] The sequence's clever use of scriptural paraphrase indicates that the composer of the texts was a learned and erudite reader of scripture, most likely a cleric, who was able to summon an impressive number of biblical passages. The fact that the scriptural citations are all given in the vernacular indicates that the catechetic sequence was most likely composed, in the first instance at least, for lay practice, though they might also have reached readerships of enclosed religious. Based on the late-fourteenth-century script of MS Laud Misc. 656, we may assume a *terminus ad quem* for the composition of the texts of sometime in the 1390s.

The "Exposition on the Creed" is a prose treatise that paraphrases and elaborates on the Apostles' Creed. It begins by attributing each line of the Creed to various New Testament apostles; for example, "Peter þe apostle seiþ I bileue in god fadere almy3ty makere of heuen *and* of erþe."[20] This formula, in which the apostles each speak a part of the Creed, is attested in a wide range of Middle English prose and poetry and is found in the Pseudo-Augustinian sermon, *De symbolo*.[21] Each article of the Creed is illustrated with examples from scripture illustrating the respective beliefs, which have been translated and paraphrased.[22] After it has fully expounded the Creed, the tract extends into a commentary on belief (again, conveyed only through verses of scripture), which includes biblical examples of some Old Testament exemplars of faith, Abel, Enoch, Noah, Abraham, Lot, and Isaac, demonstrating the benefits that each received for the fortitude of his belief. The text thus situates the Creed within a historical and typological perspective. It displays the connections between the figures and events of the Old Testament and the apostles of the New and demonstrates the relationship of these examples to the beliefs of the contemporary Church.

The second text in the sequence, *Decem mandata*, which Ralph Hanna has called "a rather strange decalogue tract,"[23] is by far the longest of the three prose texts. It begins with a brief prologue establishing the importance of knowing the Ten Commandments.[24] The text is divided into ten sections, each of which corresponds to one of the commandments,[25] and as with the other items, it is almost entirely comprised of scriptural quotations, using Old Testament translations and paraphrase. In its exposition, *Decem mandata* appears to be more interested in providing examples of the commandments being broken and the punishment that follows than in showing them being upheld. It employs long passages from scripture, unbroken by commentary, that provide examples of the sins implicit in the Decalogue, such as the Israelites' stoning of the Sabbath-breaker (Num. 15), Joab's murders of Abner and Amasa and his subsequent killing by Benaiah (1 Kings 2), Shechem's rape of Dinah (Gen. 34), David's coveting of Uriah's wife (2 Sam. 11), and numerous others. This perspective provides a useful context for understanding the commandments. Rather than explaining to the readers why they should follow the injunctions, it lets scripture speak for itself, demonstrating the consequences of neglecting the Decalogue through poignant biblical illustrations.

The final text of the sequence in MS Laud Misc. 656, *Proverbia Salomonis*, is a very brief tract, the shortest of the three. While it employs the same use of scriptural paraphrase, it differs from the other texts in being more didactic than example-based. As its Latin title (taken from the colophon) suggests, the text consists primarily of biblical injunctions from the Book of Proverbs, elucidating the book's practical wisdom to outline the basic principles of Christian virtue.[26] While the text is somewhat concerned with personal piety, overall it is more focused on one's responsibility to the larger community, for instance, in a consistent emphasis on the virtue of charity.[27]

III

In understanding the intentions behind the texts, it is important to consider the surrounding social milieu, especially the theological tensions of the period. Copied in the late fourteenth century, the earliest manuscript, MS Laud Misc. 656, was produced during the rise of the Wycliffite reformist movement. On the whole, the content of the texts seems relatively orthodox, though there are some subtle inferences that might suggest a certain reformist proclivity.[28] It is significant to note, for instance, that there are no references to any of the sacraments, saints, or clerical orders; rather, there is a focus solely on scripture and the common people. There are also, incidentally, certain passages of scripture in the texts that appear to have been sourced from the Wycliffite Bible,[29] though in the 1390s, when the prose sequence was most likely composed, this cannot be taken as conclusive evidence of sympathy with Lollard thought.[30]

Of the three texts, *Decem mandata* contains the most potential evidence for reformist leanings. The Decalogue was extremely important for the Lollards and was a common vehicle for polemical commentary, as Fiona Somerset notes.[31] As Anne Hudson similarly observes, Decalogue tracts in this period were quite frequently condemned as heretical, as the first injunction, proscribing idolatry, "gave opportunity for disquisitions on the evils of images."[32] Such a tendency can, perhaps, be seen in *Decem mandata*, especially as the first injunction is one of the most heavily expounded divisions of the text. It is also significant that the biblical passages chosen to illustrate the idolatrous use of graven images are all highly condemnatory of false priests, reflecting the common Wycliffite criticisms of the clergy. The first paraphrased passage, from 1 Kings 18, asserts that:

> þer were amonge þe children of israel foure hundred *and* fifty of fals prestis *and* of fals prophetis þat worschipeden an ymage þat hiȝt bale *and* also þey tauȝten þe peple for to worschipe hit.[33]

This is followed by one of the longest segments of biblical paraphrase in the entire text, from the apocryphal Chapter 14 of Daniel, which says, similarly:

> In babyloyne weren seuenty prestes *and* þey worscipeden an ymage þat hiȝte bele *and* also þey tauȝten þe kyng *and* þe peple forto worschipe hit.[34]

In the biblical accounts, both of these passages end with all of the false priests being killed. The scriptural excerpts are thus ideal for Wycliffite appropriation, as they can at once be used as both a warning against idolatry and a scathing critique of the false clerics who support it.

The possibility of Lollard rhetoric is even stronger in the passage about the cherubim and the brass serpent, expounding another instance of idolatry amongst the Israelites and further condemning the "folie of the prestes." The passage also includes a rare authorial digression on the worship of the crucifix:

> þus herby me semeþ wel þat cristen men may make *and* haue crucifixes in þe chirche for to bringe men in mynde of þe passioun of oure lorde ihesu crist ... but the crosse shulde not be made forto be worshiped neiþer praied to neiþer offrid to .. . not forto worshipe no manere of ymagerie ne pray þerto for helpe ne offre þerto but in mynde of þe passioun of crist.[35]

This sentiment seems to further reflect the Lollard anxiety over images, in which the crucifix was a crucial question.[36] While the passage does not condemn the crucifix itself, it makes a deliberate point to reprove the idolatrous worship thereof. Amanda Moss notes, however, that it does not contain any of the more radically iconoclastic language of some Lollard texts and suggests that this may instead be a reformist critique of Lollard arguments.[37] It is possible that the more controversial nature of this passage could explain its omission in the alpha hypearchetype.

Yet the most obvious Lollard rhetoric appears in the interpolated text in MS Harley 2343, which shows a particular distaste for the worship of images, calling it an "abhomynacioun to god."[38] One of the two added passages in *Decem mandata*'s introduction is a long didactic excursus on idolatry. Integral to this passage is a philosophical argument about the relationship between intellection and belief, suggesting that material images distract one from the abstract knowing necessary to love God: "siþ noman loueþ his god but aftir þat he knowiþ him . siþ knowinge mesuriþ loue . hou inwardli schulde we traueile forto knowe we oure god . and fle alle errouris þat fallen in þis knowinge."[39] This emphasis on an inner cognition of God is fundamental to Wycliffite ideology. In particular, its assertion that "þingis þat ben vnsensible . passen in goodnesse þingis þat ben sensible" reflects a common Wycliffite exhortation to reject "sensible" or material signs for an "unsensible" or immaterial knowing.[40]

The sequence in Trinity College MS B.14.54 and MS Harley 2343 also shows an awareness of the threat of censorship.[41] While the "Exposition on the Creed" in MS Laud Misc. 656 ends with the brief statement: "þis þat ȝe han now herde is þe riȝtful bileue withoute þe whiche no man may be ysaued" (fol. 118r), in MS Harley 2343 and MS B.14.54 this ending reads:

> in þis wise thus it endiþ withouten eny more Natheles if eny man can finde in this Crede eny errour or heresie and grounde him in holy writte I wol mekely reuoke it and lerne to bileue better.[42]

This evidences a recognition of the precarious nature of religious writing in the period.[43] Yet the tone is also quietly assertive, noting that any critic must first "grounde him in holy writte." It seems to suggest that whoever believes the speaker to be a heretic will most likely be proven wrong by the Bible. Here, as with the sequence's reliance on expository scriptural translation, the text again presents scripture as the insurmountable last word, superseding any human discourse.

From the evidence that has been presented, then, we may conclude that although the texts in this sequence cannot be called Wycliffite in any definitive sense, they appear to be conscious of and informed by reformist ideology and to have made some efforts to guard themselves from censure. The sequence, moreover, was obviously recognized as bearing this potential, a fact made particularly evident by the Lollard interpolations of MS Harley 2343. The unique and somewhat ingenious style of the texts, moreover, is the ultimate safeguard against condemnation. In presenting a simple concatenation of biblical passages, the texts are almost unimpeachable; if one questions their assertions, one questions scripture itself. As demonstrated above, the consistency of the sequence's unique stylistic structure suggests that it was probably composed as a sequential unit. Yet the disparate nature of the sequence's textual history and the multiple stages of revision in which it exists show its malleability throughout the course of its transmission. The texts in the sequence were adapted to suit various contexts, with some manuscripts curbing and others furthering its subversive potential. The sequence thus offers a valuable insight into the lives of catechetic texts in the fifteenth century and the unstable theological territory that they navigated.

Christ Church, Oxford

NOTES

1. S. J. Ogilvie-Thomson, *The Index of Middle English Prose: Manuscripts in the Laudian Collection, Bodleian Library, Oxford* (Cambridge, UK: D. S. Brewer, 2000), 77–78.
2. The description of Cambridge, Trinity College, MS B.14.54 in Linne Mooney, *The Index of Middle English Prose, Handlist XI: Manuscripts in the Library of Trinity College, Cambridge* (Cambridge, UK: D. S. Brewer, 1995), 16–17, lists no other witnesses for either of the two texts. None of these texts is listed in P. S. Jolliffe, *A Checklist of Middle English Prose Writings of Spiritual Guidance* (Toronto, Canada: Pontifical Institute of Mediaeval Studies, 1974).
3. In the footnotes to his doctoral thesis, Philip Durkin observes that these two texts are shared between London, British Library, MS Harley 2343 and Trinity College MS B.14.54, but he does not note their appearance in any other manuscripts; Philip Durkin, "A Study of Oxford, Trinity College, MS 86, with Editions of Selected Texts, and with Special Reference to Late Middle English Prose Forms of Confession" (Ph.D. dissertation, University of Oxford, 1994), 68–114, 138, nn. 21 and 22.
4. For a full description of Oxford, Bodleian Library, MS Laud Misc. 656, see Ralph Hanna and David Lawton, eds., *The Siege of Jerusalem* (Oxford: Oxford University Press, 2003), xiii–xiv.
5. These Southwest Midland features include *hure* [hear], *3o* [she], *pro3* [through], *to-gedres* [together], and *seueþ* [seventh]. Data for these spelling forms are gathered from Angus McIntosh, M. L. Samuels, and Michael Benskin, eds., *A Linguistic Atlas of Late Mediaeval English* (Aberdeen, Scotland: Aberdeen University Press, 1986).
6. These eastern spellings include *dou3teres* [daughters], *3yue* [give], *praien* [pray], *seiden* [said], *seyn* [saying], *seien* [see], and *þo* [those].

7. See Ralph Hanna, "The Origins and Production of Westminster School Ms. 3," *Studies in Bibliography* 41 (1988), 197–218, 206; reprinted in Ralph Hanna, *Pursuing History: Middle English Manuscripts and Their Texts* (Stanford, CA: Stanford University Press, 1996), 35–47.
8. Ibid., 206.
9. Ibid., 206, also notes that despite the eastern dialect features in the manuscript, a number of the texts in London, Westminster School MS 3 have distinctly western connections, which could be attributable to "a western customer, who had access to and provided the copyists with exemplars from home, or from some geographically equivalent route." Such lines of east-west exchange could explain the occurrence of the texts in Laud Misc. 656, a seemingly southwestern provincial manuscript.
10. The significant dialect features in the manuscript include *douȝtris* [daughters], *iȝen* [eyes], *ȝouen* [given], *lijf* [life], *preie* [pray], *siȝ* [saw], *schulen* shall (pl.)], *seiden* [said (pl.)], *weren* [were (pl.)], and *wolen* [will (pl.)].
11. See M. R. James, *The Western Manuscripts in the Library of Trinity College, Cambridge: A Descriptive Catalogue*, vol. I (Cambridge, UK: Cambridge University Press, 1900), 463.
12. For more on Stephen Dodesham, see A. I. Doyle, "Stephen Dodesham of Witham and Sheen," in *Of the Making of Books: Medieval Manuscripts, Their Scribes and Readers: Essays Presented to M. B. Parkes*, ed. Pamela Robinson and Rivkah Zim (Aldershot, UK: Scolar Press, 1997), 94–115; Simon Horobin, "The Scribe of Bodleian Library MS Bodley 619 and the Circulation of Chaucer's *Treatise on the Astrolabe*," *Studies in the Age of Chaucer* 31 (2009), 109–124; and Linne Mooney, "Vernacular Literary Manuscripts and Their Scribes," in *The Production of Books in England 1350-1500*, ed. Alexandra Gillespie and Daniel Wakelin (Cambridge, UK: Cambridge University Press, 2011), 192–211, 206–207.
13. See Horobin, "Scribe of Bodley 619," 121.
14. Dodesham's earliest datable work is the *Sanctilogium salvatoris* in Karlsruhe, Badische Landesbibliothek, MS Sankt Georgen 12, which he apparently copied for Syon Abbey, most likely during his time as a professional scribe; Doyle, "Stephen Dodesham," 98–101.
15. Doyle, "Stephen Dodesham," 106; and Mooney, *IMEP*, 17.
16. Laud Misc. 656, fol. 118r.
17. Westminster School MS 3, fol. 163r. Another feature common to all manuscripts apart from Laud Misc. 656 is the use of introductions to each commandment, e.g., "Here bigynneþ þe fourþe comaundement *and* þe first of þe secounde table"; Trinity College MS B.14.54, fol. 169r.
18. On the proliferation of vernacular manuals of religion in the fourteenth century, see Vincent Gillespie, "Vernacular Books of Religion," in *Book Production and Publishing in Britain 1375-1475*, ed. Jeremy Griffiths and

Derek Pearsall (Cambridge, UK: Cambridge University Press, 1989), 318.
19. This tendency to extract portions from longer catechetic sequences can be seen in Oxford, Bodleian Library, MS Ashmole 61, where the *Speculum christiani*'s section on the Decalogue is used as a stand-alone text. It also seems to be common for treatises on the Ten Commandments to be reused in multiple manuscripts. One such Decalogue text appears in London, British Library, Harley MS 2398 (fols. 1r–4r); BL MS Cotton Titus D.xix, fols. 120r–146v; BL Harley MS 211, fols. 47r–65r; and St. Albans Cathedral Library Catechetica (see Ogilvie-Thompson, *IMEP*, 3). Another version appears in BL MS Add. 17013, fols. 2r–85v; BL MS Add. 2283, fols. 92r–115v; and San Marino, CA, Huntington Library, MS HM 147, fols. 1r–113v.
20. Laud Misc. 656, fol. 117r.
21. See J. Burke Severs and Albert E. Hartung, eds., *A Manual of the Writings in Middle English 1050–1500*, vol. 7 (New Haven, CT: Connecticut Academy of Arts and Sciences, 1986), 2283, 2511–2512.
22. The text's longest biblical reference paraphrases the "Field of Dry Bones" episode of Ezekiel 37:1–14 to illustrate the eleventh article of the Creed, the resurrection of the body.
23. Hanna, "Origins and Production," 202. For a more detailed discussion of this text see Amanda Moss, "'Þat þine opun dedis be a trewe book': Reading around Arundel's Constitutions," *After Arundel: Religious Writing in Fifteenth-Century England*, ed. Vincent Gillespie and Kantik Ghosh (Turnhout: Brepols, 2011), 395–412.
24. The prologue to *Decem mandata* is fairly conventional for Decalogue treatises. Its citation of Matthew 19:16–22, in which Jesus establishes the importance of the Ten Commandments, is used in numerous introductions to such texts. Similarly, the phrase "euery man *and* woman," which is used throughout the prologue, also appears to be a common trope.
25. The enumeration of the commandments in *Decem mandata* follows the standard Augustinian division. The longer headings in the Harley, Westminster, and Trinity manuscripts introduce the division of the two tables, which again follows the Augustinian model. For the Decalogue's division see Lesley Smith, *The Ten Commandments: Interpreting the Bible in the Medieval World* (Leiden, The Netherlands: Brill, 2014), 65–75.
26. Although the Book of Proverbs is the text's primary focus, it also quotes from Ecclesiastes, Isaiah, Jeremiah, Micah, Ecclesiasticus (Sirach), Wisdom, and II Maccabees.
27. E.g., the injunction to aid the poor from Proverbs 21 in Laud Misc. 656, fol. 125r.
28. A. I. Doyle, "Stephen Dodesham," 106, notes of the Trinity College texts that "some passages suggest a Lollard antecedent or interpolation."
29. The passages that share the Wycliffite Bible's translations exactly or nearly

exactly include: Isa. 7:14, Dan. 9:26, Prov. 19:26, Zech. 5:2, Prov. 6:27–34, Mic. 6:8, Jer. 48:10, Isa. 24:2, Prov. 10:19, and Isa. 10:1–2.

30. The use of the Wycliffite Bible was not prohibited until 1407, when Thomas Arundel, archbishop of Canterbury, "inhibited any public or private use or dissemination of the translation of the Bible made in Wyclif's time, or of any translation made later than that, unless licensed by the diocesan bishop or by a provincial council." Mary Dove, *The Earliest Advocates of the English Bible: The Texts of the Medieval Debate* (Exeter, UK: University of Exeter Press, 2010), xix.

31. Fiona Somerset, *Feeling Like Saints: Lollard Writings after Wyclif* (Ithaca, NY: Cornell University Press, 2014), 64. See, e.g., the Wycliffite exposition of the Ten Commandments in Sidney Sussex College MS 74, a collection of Lollard sermons.

32. Anne Hudson, *The Premature Reformation* (Oxford: Oxford University Press, 1988), 484. See also Margaret Aston, *Lollards and Reformers: Images and Literacy in Late Medieval Religion* (London: Hambledon Press, 1984), 135–192.

33. Laud Misc. 656, fol. 118v.

34. Ibid., fol. 118v.

35. Trinity College MS B.14.54, fol. 24r.

36. Margaret Aston, "Lollards and the Cross," in *Lollards and Their Influence in Late Medieval England*, ed. Fiona Somerset, Jill C. Havens, Derrick G. Pitard (Woodbridge, Suffolk: Boydell Press, 2003), 99–113. Also see Hudson, Premature Reformation, 301–307.

37. Moss, "Þat þine opun dedis," 404–405. Moss compares the passage to Wyclif's view in his De mandatis divinis that "the use of images was legitimate, as long as they were used to stimulate religious affections and were not worshipped" (405).

38. MS Harley 2343, fols. 32v–33r.

39. Ibid., fol. 17v.

40. Ibid., fol. 18r. See Shannon Gayk, *Image, Text, and Religious Reform in Fifteenth-Century England* (Cambridge, UK: Cambridge University Press, 2010), 53–54, quoting this line from Harley 2343.

41. For more on the effects of censorship on the religious literature of the period, see Nicholas Watson, "Censorship and Cultural Change in Late-Medieval England: Vernacular Theology, the Oxford Translation Debate, and Arundel's Constitutions of 1409," *Speculum* 70 (1995), 822–865.

42. Trinity College MS B.14.54, fol. 17v.

43. Given that this disclaimer appears in both the Trinity manuscript and the earlier Harley manuscript, Amanda Moss's speculation that it may have been added by Dodesham himself cannot be correct (Moss, "Þat þine opun dedis," 407).

Tracing Neurological Disorders in the Handwriting of Medieval Scribes: Using the Past to Inform the Future

DEBORAH THORPE

A new interdisciplinary project has begun at the Centre for Chronic Diseases and Disorders (C2D2) at the University of York entitled "Tracing Neurodegenerative Disorders in the Handwriting of Medieval Scribes: Using the Past to Inform the Future." This note describes the project, which was introduced at the Early Book Society Conference, Oxford, in June 2015. This research extends beyond a one-year "discipline-hopping internship" at C2D2 (2014–2015) called "Tracing Executive Function Impairment in the Handwriting of Medieval Scribes."[1] The further two-year interdisciplinary program pushes beyond its pilot study into a focus on how historical analysis can enhance our modern understanding of diseases and disorders. In the new study, funded through a C2D2 fellowship,[2] we have the following aims and objectives.

In the era before the invention of the printing presses, handwriting was a profession through which scribes could earn a living, and in a monastic context, the production of handwritten texts was an extended and deliberative act of worship. The initial aim of the project is to establish the practical impact of movement disorders caused by neurological conditions on the lives and work of medieval writers. In order to achieve this, I have set the objectives of establishing the changes in scribes' handwriting as they aged normally; determining what changes may be attributable to neurological conditions such as Parkinson's disease, essential tremor, Alzheimer's disease, and stroke; analyzing the practical impact of these distortions on scribes' productivity and the nature of their work; and exploring intersections with non-motor symptoms (for instance, problems with sentence structuring and spelling), and concurrent conditions such as eyesight deterioration and the effects of alcohol consumption. Thus, we hope to enhance our understanding of the lives of the individuals who produced medieval texts, shedding more light on conditions that may, or may not, have terminated or prematurely ended their writing activities.

We shall next explore whether scrutinizing historical handwriting affected by disorder can contribute to modern techniques for medical handwriting analysis. The analysis of distorted handwriting in current clinical medicine and research is well documented. Studies of patients drawing an Archimedean spiral have demonstrated the impact of neurological disorders on the movement of the wrist joints used to produce the shape. Research into the writing of letters and words can shed light not only on motor disorders but also on problems in planning sequential strokes, letters, and words.

The first objective is to compare the nature of medieval and modern handwriting in the context of chronic diseases and disorders, examining distortions visually to establish and compare the impact of movement disorders on the formation of letter strokes. Once these malformations have been identified, the second objective is to train evolutionary algorithms to recognize and classify them. The final objective is to explore the potential for transferable outcomes in the development of medical diagnostic and monitoring equipment. The digital study of medieval disordered handwriting forms an unusual synthesis of disciplinary approaches, which has potential to demonstrate the value of collaboration between the humanities and sciences. The project will make connections between scholars from a range of backgrounds, thus ensuring that its outcomes are communicable within each of its constituent disciplines.

This project forms part of the Intelligent Systems group of the University of York's Electronics Department, which includes several Ph.D. students working on projects relating to computer-aided medical diagnosis and applied evolutionary algorithms. The primary mentor is Stephen Smith, who has experience of digitally assessing pen movements in drawings from patients with a range of neurological conditions. This project provides us an opportunity to apply this expertise to static scans of handwriting, forming an experimental contrast to his work on live participants. Smith has collaborations with specialists at the University of California San Francisco Medical Center, Leeds General Infirmary, and the Royal Liverpool and Broadgreen Hospitals. I have formed collaborations of my own at these institutions over the course of the internship.

As second mentor, Linne Mooney will advise on the historical and cultural context of Middle English literature. This project is an interdisciplinary application of paleographic expertise that has not been attempted before. Research into the health of scribes complements research on the production and reception of medieval books.

In addition to its core team, the project benefits from an advisory board built up over the course of the year-long internship. A key collaborator is Jane Alty of the Neurology Department of the Leeds Teaching Hospitals National Health Service Trust and the Hull York Medical School. Working with Alty, a consultant neurologist with a specialist interest in movement disorders, has resulted in a study of the tremor of the thirteenth-century Tremulous Hand of Worcester (explained in more detail below). Numerous other scholars have provided guidance and inspiration in the course of planning and beginning the project from the fields of history, literature, neurology, psychiatry, linguistics, electronics, and computer science.

The research design comprises both exploratory and explanatory components. The exploratory element investigates medieval handwriting using a combination of traditional paleographic analysis and digital processing in order to uncover previously undetected signs of movement disorders. The explanatory phase uses the data generated by the evolutionary algorithms to inform our contemporary understanding of the human experience of disease and disorder and possibly contribute to the development of diagnostic and monitoring equipment. Although the project has implications for our understanding of the medieval period, we also envision outcomes that will enhance our modern understanding of diseases and disorders.

Aging has a demonstrable impact on the planning and movement abilities needed to produce handwritten words. With age there is deterioration in the main brain areas related to executive functions, the cognitive functions required for the performance of complex everyday activities (see note 1). This is exemplified in a writing experiment by Sara Rosenblum and colleagues, where elderly people were found to spend considerably longer with their pen in air (as opposed to on the paper), produced a larger script, and took longer to perform a written task.[3]

Medieval writers displayed considerable interest in the effects of aging on perception, movement, and coordination. For example, the Reeve of Chaucer's "Reeve's Prologue" has "unweelde" or weak limbs.[4] The old man, "Elde," of the fourteenth-century text *The Parlement of the Thre Ages*, complains that age has "sotted" or blurred his sight and "encrampeschet" or deformed his hands.[5] Medieval and early-modern medical treatises and the classical tracts that influenced them depict a general weakening of the body with age. Gabriele Zerbi's *Gerontocomia* (1489) describes how "the strength of old people likewise ebbs away and their bodies grow heavy with cold."[6] These texts account also for difficulties with visual perception, as described in Maximianus's *Elegies* specifically in relation to reading and writing: "If I read books, the letters split in two | the page I knew seems larger than it was."[7]

There has been a wealth of studies of aging and associated medical conditions in the medieval period, many focusing on what can be gleaned from literary texts, documentary sources, and archaeological records.[8] The fourteenth-century poem "God Send Us Paciens in Oure Oolde Age" describes the onset of a range of age-related afflictions. Certain of these ailments, such as tremors, may imply the onset of neurological disorders: "Oure heed, oure hondis, þo wolen schake | And oure leggis wole tremble where we go."[9] But in the absence of additional evidence, the perils of retrospective diagnosis may outweigh the benefits. Differences in terminology and the fact that medieval texts often describe symptoms that may suggest a number of conditions might lead us to the wrong conclusions. In contrast, the material evidence preserved in surviving handwriting might prove more reliable; the impact of movement disorders on the hands and handwriting should be universal, or at the very least similar. Medieval manuscripts capture a material record of aging: traces of human brains, eyes, arms, and hands becoming older. Thus this project analyzes the changes that develop over time in medieval handwriting as a scribe aged normally: the "ordered quills."

We are collecting case studies of medieval scribes with particularly well-documented writing careers. Combining paleographic research and medical handwriting analysis, we aim in this project to use chronological evidence to shed more light on the impact of aging on the life of a writer. Proposed case studies include Thomas Hoccleve, whose career is well documented, though he seems to have lived only to his late fifties; other scribes are recorded as living longer, and John Shirley may have reached his nineties.

In addition to traditional paleographic study, digitized samples of handwriting by these scribes will be analyzed using a combination of image-processing and evolutionary computation techniques. Evolutionary algorithms will analyze and define the distortions caused by aging, which will be progressed into detecting signs of developing neurological conditions.

Evidence for age-related visual impairment and eye problems will likely present itself in the writing of certain aging scribes.[10] Cataracts and macular degeneration are common causes of age-related eyesight deterioration today. Paleographic evidence of deterioration in the planning abilities of medieval scribes, possibly caused by eyesight deterioration, has already been detected; Theresa O'Byrne has uncovered evidence for aging and potential eyesight problems in the work of the Irish scribe Nicholas Bellewe.[11] She observes that by the time the scribe was an old man, his distinctive script had begun to show signs of deterioration, possibly due to visual impairment. As other scribes often had long and prolific careers, it is likely that further cases of age-related handwriting distortion will present themselves for analysis.

The first test case has been studied in collaboration with Jane Alty in an article to be published by *Brain* entitled, "What Type of Tremor Did the Medieval 'Tremulous Hand of Worcester' Have?"[12] This is, to the best of our knowledge, the first detailed analysis of the handwriting in the context of disease and disorder by a paleographer and neurologist in collaboration. The study finds evidence that suggests essential tremor (ET) as the most likely diagnosis. As part of the differential and as a correlate for the medieval writing, a modern sample was taken from a seventy-five-year-old man with ET, using a calligraphy pen. The modern man's movement disorder had a comparable impact upon the writing, supporting the diagnosis of ET for the Tremulous Hand of Worcester.

Once evidence for a movement disorder has been identified, the project proceeds to analyze its effect on the life of a scribe. In *Gout: The Patrician Malady*, medical historians Roy Porter and G. S. Rousseau justify their research on what might be considered "a rather trifling condition": "historical pathology mainly consists of chronic conditions, attacking the musculoskeletal system, the respiratory system, the nervous system, and of course the brain—not in themselves fatal, but incurable, typically debilitating, sometimes crippling and inordinately painful."[13] Though neurological disease could never be considered trifling, certain conditions might have escaped both record and study, being noninfectious, often nonfatal, and of varying or progressing degrees of severity. Even the most debilitating disorders might present mild symptoms at first, sometimes for many years. Thus the project will trace the ongoing impact of movement disorders in scribes' handwriting, asking whether neurological conditions would alter or prematurely terminate a career.

Evidence in the writing of the Tremulous Hand of Worcester suggests that certain scribes were prolific despite the onset and progression of a disorder. This scribe's apparent lack of cognitive problems supported the diagnosis of essential tremor as opposed to Parkinson's disease.[14] His continued ability to spell words well, his unusual ability to translate from Old English in this period, and the neatness of his writing despite the intrusion of his tremor likely all contributed to his continued work as a writer. The next stage will be to scrutinize the output of other scribes with degenerative disorders to widen the scope of this study into the practical impact of neurological conditions.

The project's second and third aims focus on historical material as a way of enhancing our modern understanding of chronic diseases and disorders. Porter and Rousseau call attention to a need for enhanced understanding of degenerative diseases in an era of greater longevity.[15] In this spirit, our study examines historical neurological disorders in order to contribute to and broaden our contemporary knowledge. Since the impact of medieval and contemporary movement disorders on handwriting is comparable, we anticipate that investigations in static handwriting analysis will lead to insights into monitoring living patients, possibly by developing diagnostic equipment.[16]

The project seeks to affect clinical practice by inviting neurologists and other medical practitioners to reevaluate the paradigms of their work and debate existing understanding of neurological conditions in the light of historical research. This work has already begun through the co-authored article in *Brain*, which not only invites neurologists to consider tremor conditions in historical context but also creates connections between past and present through its comparative analysis of medieval and modern handwriting.

This project forms unconventional synergies between disciplinary approaches and intends to make contributions in each of its constituent fields. A key element of the research is its collaborative approach. (For this reason, I invite correspondence, comments, and offers of collaboration through my institutional contact details or through response in the *Journal of the Early Book Society*.). Within electronics, the study offers the opportunity to apply digital image processing and evolutionary computation to historical sources in a way that provides an experimental contrast to work on live participants. Within the biological sciences, the study will enrich our understanding of the relationship between brain functioning and activity performance in handwriting. It will add historical context to biomedical studies of Parkinson's, Alzheimer's, and stroke. Within the humanities, we will discover more about effects of disease and age-related impairments that may have affected or prematurely ended the careers of professional medieval scribes. It creates an application of paleography that stimulates discussions with scholars in disability studies and thus widens the scope of existing research into the lives and work of historical writers.

University of York

Acknowledgments

Several collaborators have contributed ideas and inspiration in the development and ongoing research of this project. In particular, I would like to thank project mentors Stephen Smith and Linne Mooney; collaborators Jane Alty and Markus Schiegg; and Theresa O'Byrne and Derek Pearsall for information that contributed to this review.

NOTES

1. "Executive function" is "an umbrella term that encompasses high-level cognitive functions required for the performance of complex everyday activities, such as planning and organization, reasoning and problem solving, conceptual thought, self-correction and judgment, and decision making."

Sara Rosenblum, Batya Engel-Yeger, and Yael Fogel, "Age-Related Changes in Executive Control and Their Relationships with Activity Performance in Handwriting," *Human Movement Science* 32.2 (2013): 364, available at http://www.ncbi.nlm.nih.gov/pubmed/23558056.
2. The project is part-funded by the Wellcome Trust (ref. 105624) through the Centre for Chronic Diseases and Disorders (C2D2) at the University of York.
3. Rosenblum, Engel-Yeger, and Fogel, "Age-Related Changes," 363–376.
4. Geoffrey Chaucer, *The Canterbury Tales*, in *The Riverside Chaucer*, ed. L. D. Benson (Oxford: Oxford University Press, 2008), 1:3886.
5. Warren Ginsberg, ed., *Wynnere and Wastoure: and, The Parlement of the Thre Ages* (Kalamazoo, MI: Western Michigan University Press, 1992), ll. 286–287.
6. L. R. Lind, ed., *Gabriele Zerbi: On the Care of the Aged; and Maximianus, Elegies on Old Age and Love* (Philadelphia, PA: American Philosophical Society, 1988), 18.
7. Lind, *Gabriele Zerbi*, 56, ll. 145–146.
8. For aging in the medieval period, see, e.g., Joel T. Rosenthal, *Old Age in Late Medieval England* (Philadelphia: University of Pennsylvania Press, 1996); Shulamith Shahar and Yael Lotan, *Growing Old in the Middle Ages: 'Winter Clothes Us in Shadow and Pain'* (London: Routledge, 1997); and Albrecht Classen, ed., *Old Age in the Middle Ages and the Renaissance: Interdisciplinary Approaches to a Neglected Topic* (Berlin: de Gruyter, 2007).
9. Frederick James Furnivall, ed., *Hymns to the Virgin & Christ, the Parliament of Devils, and Other Religious Poems*, EETS os 24 (London: Trench, Trübner, 1867), 114.
10. For a general introduction to visual impairment in the medieval period, see Edward Wheatley, *Stumbling Blocks before the Blind: Medieval Constructions of a Disability* (Ann Arbor: University of Michigan Press, 2010).
11. Theresa O'Byrne, "Manuscript Creation in Dublin: The Scribe of Bodleian e. Museo MS 232 and Longleat MS 29," in *New Directions in Medieval Manuscript Studies and Reading Practices: Essays in Honor of Derek Pearsall*, ed. Kathryn Kerby-Fulton, John J. Thompson, and Sarah Baechle (Notre Dame, IN: University of Notre Dame Press, 2014), 271–291. I am grateful to Theresa O'Byrne for sharing her copy of this chapter with me and to Derek Pearsall for putting us in touch.
12. Deborah Thorpe and Jane Alty, "What Type of Tremor Did the Medieval 'Tremulous Hand of Worcester' Have?," *Brain* 138 (October 2015): available at http://dx.doi.org/10.1093/brain/awv232.
13. Roy Porter and G. S. Rousseau, *Gout: The Patrician Malady* (New Haven, CT: Yale University Press, 1998), 2.
14. For a comprehensive study of the work of the Tremulous Hand, see Christine Franzen, *The Tremulous Hand of Worcester: A Study of Old English in the Thirteenth Century* (Oxford: Clarendon Press, 1991).

15. Porter and Rousseau, *Gout*, 3.
16. ClearSky Medical Diagnostics, which "specialises in medical devices for the diagnosis and monitoring of Parkinson's disease, Alzheimer's disease and a range of other neurodegenerative conditions." http://www.clearskymd.com.

Descriptive Reviews

FRANCISCO ALONSO ALMEIDA
A Middle English Medical Remedy Book: Edited from Glasgow University Library MS Hunter 185. Middle English Texts 50. Heidelberg, Germany: Universitätsverlag Winter, 2014. 143 pp.

Earlier this year a team of scientists working with Dr. Christina Lee (Nottingham University) discovered that a remedy preserved in the Anglo-Saxon work known as *Bald's Leechbook* is extremely effective against the superbug methicillin-resistant staphylococcus aureus (MRSA). The ninth-century recipe—an apparently simple eye salve made from onion, garlic, and cow bile—killed up to 90 percent of MRSA bacteria. The scientists believe that the recipe itself, rather than any one single ingredient, is effective against the bug. If we needed a good reason to take seriously medieval materia medica, this certainly would be it; those of us accustomed to grappling with manuscripts, handwriting, and binding on a daily basis, rather than MRSA, however, already know that such texts are fascinating for manuscript studies in general as well as for thinking through concepts such as textual form, structure and production, audience and readership, as well as social and economic issues.

Francisco Alonso Almeida's edition for the Middle English Texts series concerns a work that is broadly similar to *Bald's Leechbook*. It is a collection of what might be termed "popular medicine" (9) preserved in a single witness: Glasgow University Library MS Hunter 185 (H), which manuscript is described as a "compendium of texts dealing with plants for medical purposes followed by medical notes and remedies" (20). Essentially, the volume divides into five identifiable parts and contains some notes in Latin on ingredients with curative properties and on qualities of medicinal products, a herbal, a collection of medical recipes in Middle English, as well as some items in French. Almeida edits the entirety of the manuscript (which consists of only 67 fols.), including the Latin and French items and marginal notations. According to Almeida the manuscript was copied in two stages, around 1400, and is localizable to Gloucester and to Kent.

The most significant part of H is the final section, which includes medical recipes (over 200), prognostic texts, and charms in Middle English and which is in the hands of both of the scribes responsible for the copying of the manuscript. A cursory look through the recipes that relate to ailments of the eye did not reveal a treatment similar to the supercure found in *Bald's Leechbook*, but there are several others: for cataracts, for sore and watery eyes, and for bleary eyes, recipes that vary between those that are very simple indeed and those requiring several ingredients and often several days' work.

In his introduction, the editor notes that remedy books from this period contain either recipes that can be easily excerpted and adapted for inclusion or use elsewhere, or recipes that are dependent on other parts of the collection for efficacy or for sense. This collection of recipes seems to correspond in the main to the second of these categories; the way in which the scribes attempted to organize the recipes—a cap-à-pie system—is not consistent throughout, but there is at least some sense that the recipes are operational as a collection rather than as stand-alone pieces. For instance, recipe number 78, "for euel herying of man or of woman," is followed by another that is simply entitled "[a]lso for þe same." Moreover there is some slippage between recipes and prognostications, as one might expect to find in *receptaria*, which draw their material from the folk tradition and which preserve the blend of therapy, prediction, and folk belief inherent to that tradition. Indeed the sources for *receptaria* such as this one are difficult to trace since many of their elements are indebted to the oral tradition. Nonetheless, Almeida finds synergies and points of comparison between the medical recipes in MS Hunter 185 and, for instance, the more learned *Compendium medicinae* attributed to Gilbertus Anglicae, which had a wide circulation in Middle English (the editor also finds similarities between his texts and the *Liber de diversis medicinis*).

The edition includes a lengthy and informative discussion of the form and structure of the recipe texts found here within the context of wider work, including an analysis of the social features of H but privileging the linguistic features. The section on social features notes that there are three languages present, indicating that the "intended audience would have included physicians with a knowledge of Latin as well as lay folk, who were instructed in English" (43). Despite the well-acknowledged difficulties in establishing intended audience(s) for works like *receptaria* that are so varied and wide-ranging (and, from the 1400s, so ubiquitous), it seems to me that Almeida's close linguistic reading of the recipes (including the quantities, utensils required, etc.) and of other features of both the manuscript and the recipes might have prompted a more detailed discussion of this matter. The editor observes that the intended audience for such works is generally determined by language, but perhaps the detail—linguistic and otherwise—found in the recipes could provide a rich vein of information that might reveal something of the intended readership.

Nonetheless, this is a careful and informative edition that includes a fairly extensive apparatus (including a very useful summary of the contents, annotated and numbered to correspond to the recipes in the main part of the edition), a detailed commentary, and an excellent glossary. And although the texts edited by Almeida are of the sort with which most readers of this review will be familiar, many works of popular medicine and science from the Middle Ages remain unedited and underappreciated; indeed, the editor himself notes that "[e]ditions of collections similar to that in H are few" (9). This situation is steadily being corrected, chiefly because of Almeida and other scholars as well as series such as Middle English Texts that actively encourage editions of such material. Almeida is to be commended for his thoughtful, careful, and thorough work on a collection of rich (and perhaps still useful) remedies.

Carrie Griffin, University of Limerick

JOANNA BELLIS, ED.
John Page's The Siege of Rouen:
Edited from London, British Library MS Egerton 1995.
Heidelberg, Germany: Universitätsverlag Winter, 2015.
lxxvii + 185 pp. 6 B&W plates, incl. 1 map.

The siege of Rouen lasted from August 1418 to January 1419 and was part of the inevitable hard slog needed to realize Henry V's ambitions in France. The unexpected victory at Agincourt in October 1415 had brought him little in the way of territorial gain, though the battle established his reputation for all time and killed so many members of the nobility of France that it took years for the country to recover. By the summer of 1418, Caen and Cherbourg had fallen, and most of the "English" duchy of Normandy had been occupied. Rouen on the Seine, almost as large and wealthy as Paris, had to be next.

Historical sources on the siege seem many and varied: on the French/Burgundian side are the chronicles by Jean de Wavrin, Enguerrand de Monstrelet, Jean Lefèvre de Saint-Rémy, Pierre de Fénin, and Michel Pintoin (*Religieux de Saint-Denis*). Wavrin, Monstrelet, and Lefèvre, however, all used the same pro-Burgundian account, and the differences between them are merely scribal; Fénin and Pintoin are very brief, and the latter in particularly is very vague. On the English side there are, apparently, Thomas of Walsingham, Thomas Otterbourne, Adam of Usk, and various *vitae* and *gesta* of Henry V by anonymous or doubtful authors. Otterbourne, however, copied Walsingham, who was very brief anyway, just as was Adam of Usk, who merely makes reference to the siege. Some of the *vitae* do not even cover the relevant years; others give very little information, and their texts turn out to be intricately and confusingly related, that is, copied from each other. The only "English" sources that offer more detail are the Latin chronicle by

John Strecche and the English *Brut*—and they both turn out to have relied heavily on the text under review here, the *Brut* to the point of changing into literal quotation, in verse, about half-way down the story.

John Page's poem is clearly of great importance not only to scholars of English but certainly to historians as well. According to his own words he was an eyewitness, and nothing in his lively and very readable text makes one doubt his claim. Understandably biased in Henry's favor and emphasizing the king's benevolence where possible, the poet is at the same time full of understanding for the suffering of the besieged, detailing, for example, the prices the starving Rouennais had to pay for horsemeat, dogs, and rats, describing the incredible misery of the *bouches inutiles* that the town had expelled and the English would not allow to leave the ditch they were sheltering in, and comparing the sartorial splendor of the English lords to the rags of the citizens when they met. As a historical source the poem is exceptional; as a literary text it also holds its own.

The present edition offers everything manuscript scholars and students of English literature could wish for. Historians might perhaps wish for a little more, but they are being handed the tools for their own undertakings. An introduction elucidates the history of the text before this edition, emphasizes its value and its use by the *Brut*, lists previous editions, and explains the historical context; the editor is very brief and vague about the other sources for the siege, but there is a good map (made for the French translation of 1867). There follows a full discussion of the many John Pages who could possibly have written the text, circa thirty in all, many of them soldiers—who are in fact unlikely authors, as previous editors of the poem have also argued. I would like to add that a soldier would not have been as upset by the clearing of the land around Rouen by its inhabitants, which included the destruction of many churches. This was essential from a military point of view, preventing the English from using any buildings, but a cleric serving the English king might well have been appalled at this "cyrsyde deede" (line 62). Second, there is a detail not mentioned by any of the editors, present or previous: the phrase used in line 665, "Withyn hys owne an emperoure," in the context of Henry's position as rightful king, is a translation of a legal concept used particularly for the kings of France and usually expressed in Latin: "*Rex est imperator in regno suo.*" It does not seem the kind of quotation that would spring to a soldier's mind.

The introduction continues with the date, audience, language, meter, and afterlife of the *Siege*. The description of the fourteen surviving manuscripts (not all known to previous editors), of which only two offer a complete text whereas most of them are versions of the *Brut*, is extensive and illustrated with various tables. The text itself is presented cleanly, without undue attempts to indicate the scribal idiosyncrasies even of the base manuscript, BL Egerton 1995. Twenty-six separate pages of "Textual Variants" and eight of "Textual Notes" should satisfy any critic. The "Commentary" provides explanation of editorial decisions and some discussion of historical points and literary and cultural allusions, and is followed by a glossary and a list of people and places. Finally an appendix prints the text as it was summarized in prose in the *Brut* chronicle, excluding the section in verse that was copied verbatim into that chronicle. The bibliography is subdivided into several sections, and there is unfortunately no index of any kind.

In many ways, of course, this edition supersedes the 1927 one by Heribert Huscher, but I found that his thorough study is also still worth consulting, and indeed, the present editor freely acknowledges her great debt to Huscher. Also I cannot help feeling that we have come a long way in the wrong direction if German quotations need to be translated for academic readers of today.

Livia Visser-Fuchs, Independent Scholar

PETER W. M. BLAYNEY
The Stationers' Company and the Printers of London, 1501–1557. 2 vols. Cambridge: Cambridge University Press, 2013. 1,300 pp.

"Monumental": the word that springs most immediately to the tips of a reviewer's fingers upon contemplating the 1,300 pages of Peter Blayney's *The Stationers' Company and the Printers of London, 1501–1557*. It is certainly an impressively heavy piece of scholarship; the reviewer and the reviews editor had quite a time working out how to get it from Britain to Canada (or, for that matter, across the room). But the word "monumental" is perhaps the wrong one. A monumental structure has a metonymic relationship to its object: a monument is something grand that commemorates something even grander. This is not quite what Blayney offers here. As he explains in his preface, his intention on starting the project was corrective rather than comprehensive. Finding that Cyprian Blagden's *The Stationers' Company: A History, 1403–1959* "dismisses nearly two centuries (1357–1553) in just over twelve pages (21–33) in which there is scarcely a paragraph free of factual errors, unfounded assumptions, or both" (xxi), he set out to provide scholars of the early-modern book trade with a better history by rereading and reinterpreting every early source he could find. No other scholar could have done this with Blayney's meticulous care or formidable expertise. If the attention to detail and correction of "unfounded assumptions" comes at the expense of grand narratives, which it sometimes does, this seems a small price to pay for work of reference that will serve so many so well.

Blayney's study is, in short, an extraordinary feat of scholarship. He successfully marshals "virtually every mention of any printer, Stationer, or other person active in the book trade" (xix) whom he has found for the period 1501 to 1557 and builds a host of compelling new arguments about the history of that trade. The first chapter will be particularly edifying for members of the Early Book Society, whose interests lie at the intersection of manuscript and print cultures. In this chapter, he gives the first authoritative account of the rise of the occupation of "stationer" in medieval England, the founding of the Stationers' Company in 1403, and the impact of the advent of printing on the established book trade. It may seem strange that this story needs to be told, but it does. Blayney publishes critical, missing facts—about the moment when and the reasons why Richard Pynson and Wynkyn de Worde joined the Stationers' Company, for example.

He also corrects some major misapprehensions. William Caxton was a mercer, as many who study him are quick to note. But as a member of that liveried and distinguished guild, he had nothing to fear from the stationers, as some have claimed he did in order to account for his decision to set up shop in Westminster, outside the walls of the City of London. To take another example, scholarship on an 1484 act of Parliament that exempted bookmen from new trade regulation is the source of a "widespread fantasy that the proviso resembled a general Bill of Rights, emancipating alien book merchants" (44). Blayney shows that in fact the proviso protected them from new rules but left them subject to every other ordinary regulation and tax.

There are riches in subsequent chapters for the student of sixteenth-century English printing. Each of these chapters covers somewhere between a half and a whole decade. Each follows the same structure: a discussion of printers who began work in the greater London area in that period, an account of provincial printing at the same moment, developments in the trade at large and in the careers of major players, additional archival discoveries, and analysis of the import trade. Taken together, the chapters provide new biographies of every known printer and/or Stationer and many who were entirely unknown until Blayney turned up a document describing them. In some cases, a previously minor figure is shown to have had a major role in the history of the English book trade. For example, Elizabeth Pickering, the widow of Robert Redman and printer in her own right (and under her maiden name), emerges as a force behind the Stationers' Marian Charter, in the quest for which two of her husbands after Redman—William and Ranulph Cholmeley—acted as principals.

There will be readers who find Blayney's take-no-prisoners style dispiriting as he dismantles whatever he finds slipshod, speculative, or plain wrong in others' scholarship. But anyone with an interest in early Tudor history—bookish, literary, economic, or social—owes him an incalculable debt for the thousands of hours he has labored to set the record straight and recover what had been lost. It may seem that Blayney never met an argument he liked as much as he liked correcting it. But the next time any of us makes an argument about early English printing, we will be much better for his extraordinary generosity and his example.

Alexandra Gillespie, University of Toronto

THOMAS A. BREDEHOFT
The Visible Text: Textual Production and Reproduction from Beowulf *to* Maus.
Oxford Textual Perspectives.
Oxford: Oxford University Press, 2014. x + 182 pp.

Thomas Bredehoft's little book of textual theory is deliberately provocative. *Beowulf*, existing only in its single, unadorned, unattributed manuscript, is, he declares, not a text (19). The same presumably applies to *Pearl* and the other poems of MS Cotton Nero A.x, whose manuscript circumstances he explicitly compares to those of "the bulk of classical Old English poetry" (74), but by then he is no longer making this point.

Beowulf is instead a "textual artefact," whereas texts, for Bredehoft, must be either "subject to the logic of the copy" or accompanied by defining paratext. He means by the former phrase that texts, in his view, are "implicated in an economy of reproduction," that is, exist for the purposes of being copied, with an underlying implication of failure, as a copy can never exactly reproduce an original. More broadly, he argues that we should distinguish between ideologies (rather than simply technologies) of production and reproduction. There is no evidence, he maintains, that *Beowulf*, in its surviving manuscript form, was a copy of another manuscript in the normally understood sense of "copy." Moreover, he suggests, the making of the extant *Beowulf* manuscript was probably seen at the time as making earlier versions redundant, and any such might have been deliberately destroyed. That is to say, *Beowulf* and many other Anglo-Saxon manuscripts were created as single, one-off productions, as unique artifacts—the economy of reproduction was not operating. In the Gothic period, however, the ideology changed and reproduction became the norm, hence the survival of many texts in multiple copies (with the need for accompanying paratext), with the difference from the subsequent print era being that scribes had a "moving target" attitude to the originals of what they were copying, aware that two manuscript copies of a text will necessarily differ from one another (the concept of manuscript variance).

This perceived difference between the two periods is the most interesting theoretical aspect of Bredehoft's book for the medievalist, particularly the early medievalist. For example, he allots the versions of *The Dream of the Rood* on the Ruthwell and Brussels crosses the same status as that in the Vercelli manuscript. All three, he argues, are "unique, non-medial, non-text artefacts or productions" (45). None of them is a "copy." But Bredehoft presents his theories without regard to developments, as the centuries passed, in literacy, education, or scribal methodology, let alone in social, economic, and institutional life more generally, and he himself acknowledges that the paradigms he advances represent no more than dominant tendencies. His book, indeed, proceeds by way of multiple repetitions and qualifications of the main points, as he tries to make everything fit the argument (translations cause particular difficulty), and there is inevitable special pleading. For instance, he is well aware that Bede wanted his *Historia ecclesiastica* "to be embedded within the ideology of textual reproduction" (30), but his attempt to argue that the multiple scribal copies of this work were unique productions in a way different from multiple copies of works written in the Gothic period is not convincing. Later, Chaucer's concern for "trewe" copying in his words to Adam and the lack of paratext surrounding copies of *Piers Plowman* do not mean, we find, that the Gothic ideology, as he defines it, is not still operating in these cases. (Fortunately, perhaps, there is no mention of the obsessive corrector John Capgrave.)

Another weakness is that Bredehoft believes himself to be newly overturning scholarly positions that have in fact long since been abandoned. Thus he asserts that scholars still build their "entire theoretical perspective ... upon an understanding of scribal activity as inherently reproductive, in the sense that it separates authors from scribes as separate (and hierarchical) loci of authority" (54). Similarly, his strictures that we must "take much more seriously the testimony of manuscripts that have been conventionally devalued because they show the highest degree of variance" (166) are scarcely as revolutionary as he seems to think, and his consideration of these matters does not extend to editorial theory.

Following the chapters on the Anglo-Saxon and Gothic periods, the book moves forward to consider the ideology of typographic print reproduction, which Bredehoft argues is characterized by a particular failure ever to represent successfully the author's original ("the printed text necessarily fails to be a manuscript," 98). Book-makers, he says, have tried to counteract this failure principally by producing "editions," which deploy a variety of paratexts as bulwarks of authority, with the difference from the Gothic model being that the ideal of a "correct" text (which need never have existed in reality) is always in the background. He also considers the ideology of facsimiles, seen as another response to the perceived failures of print.

Bredehoft's book ends with a chapter on modern comics, which he argues are a new and different kind of text, defined as a deliberate sequence of juxtaposed combinations of image and text, or simply of juxtaposed images without linguistic component. Controversially he insists that it is a mistake to think of comics as a hybrid of textual and visual forms, and that even wordless comics are texts (unlike, therefore, *Beowulf*), on the basis that an act of interpretation is an act of reading. This chapter, entitled "Comics Textual Production," takes the author into some of his most ingenious arguing, as he attempts (as it were) to justify the summary on the back cover of the book which pairs Anglo-Saxon manuscripts and modern comics as "productions" against the contrary pairing of late-medieval manuscripts and printed books ("reproductions"). Comics, he now contends, are productions as well as reproductions, because there is no entirely separate stage of original artwork that ends up being reproduced, and therefore comics, ideologically, are not facsimiles: "A comics work ... produces something brand new as it reproduces" (138). There is no mention of artists' books, which might have supplied a better example of modern-day "production" (in his original terms), if that is what he had wanted.

The Visible Text is thought-provoking, and Thomas Bredehoft has assembled an impressively wide-ranging number of case studies. But the book is more likely to be of value to the textual theorist than the medievalist.

Oliver Pickering, University of Leeds

LAURA CLEAVER AND HELEN CONRAD O'BRIAIN
Latin Psalter Manuscripts in Trinity College Dublin and the Chester Beatty Library.
Dublin: Four Courts Press, 2015.
104 pp. + 3 B&W and 35 color figures.

Medieval commentators regarded the Psalms as a *summa* or digest of the entire Bible, a verbally dense and therefore exegetically rewarding account of the wisdom of both the Old and New Testaments. It is in a way fitting, then, for thirteen medieval psalters now in two Dublin collections—one well known and the other less so—to receive a comprehensive catalogue and overview in this short, educative, and handsomely produced volume. In *Latin Psalter Manuscripts in Trinity College Dublin and the Chester Beatty Library,* Laura Cleaver and Helen Conrad O'Briain compress a wide range of ideas about the history, translation, decoration, and collection of medieval psalters, as well as individual catalogue descriptions and pictures of each of the manuscripts at hand, into just over one hundred pages. To borrow one of its author's analogies for the outsized theological importance of the short Latin *tituli* that precede many medieval psalms, this book punches above its weight.

It consists of four main parts: an introduction to the Psalms and medieval psalters by Helen Conrad O'Briain (15–22); an essay on psalter decoration (23–38) and another on the patronage and provenance of the thirteen psalters (39–49) by Laura Cleaver; and finally, a long catalogue entry for each of these manuscripts (51–96), done, I presume, by both authors together, although that is never stated. All of this matter is preceded by a brief preface in which the authors explain that in order to concentrate on "the Psalter as a devotional book" (13), they exclude from consideration complete Bibles that incorporate the entire Book of Psalms and various types of liturgical codices—breviaries, antiphonals, and Books of Hours—that draw on them selectively. The volume concludes with a helpful glossary of terms, from "Anglicana" through "Vulgate" (97–99), and a bibliography (101–104).

Because some of the types of manuscripts excluded are among our most important evidence for the devotional vitality of the Psalter during the Middle Ages, one wonders how Cleaver and O'Briain define "devotion" for the purposes of their book. They do not make their definition explicit. O'Briain's introduction, "The Book of Psalms or Psalter," is nevertheless a deft account of the Psalter's history as "a self-contained collection" of biblical poems (16), its translation and retranslation in late antiquity by St. Jerome, and its centrality to Latin literacy and Christian prayer throughout the Middle Ages. O'Briain surveys the most relevant scholarship on each of her key subjects and looks ahead to some of the most compelling manuscripts catalogued in the book: the octavo Ricemarch Psalter (Trinity MS 50), for example, produced in Wales during the eleventh century in imitation of eighth-century Irish handwriting and decoration, which is distinctive in containing the text of Jerome's final revision of the Psalter against the original Hebrew, the *Hebraicum*, a version that had no liturgical currency throughout the Middle Ages but was of keen interest to scholars; and the folio Winchcombe Psalter (Trinity MS 53), copied in England in the mid-twelfth century, where Jerome's second translation and the text used in the Divine Office, the *Gallicanum*, and the *Hebraicum* appear in parallel columns.

Both of these psalters, I think, were designed with study in mind—an activity that was central to the devout life especially of medieval monks, who were attuned to the Christological readings of the Psalms that O'Briain emphasizes (19). Another important point, which O'Briain touches on but does not have the chance to pursue, is the dual private and public lives of some of the manuscripts in the catalogue, such as a Gallican psalter from mid-thirteenth-century Augsburg (Chester Beatty MS W.40) that contains persistent marginal instructions in German on when and how to recite certain psalms. Many medieval manuscripts were used within both individual and social contexts. But the Psalter was special in its bibliographic duality throughout the Middle Ages because of the intense personal and communal nature of psalm language itself; according to medieval exegetes, the Psalmist always speaks at once for himself and on behalf of our common humanity.

Cleaver, too, is adept at concision, making a number of points that encourage further investigation. The opening of her first essay, on psalter decoration, could serve undergraduates as a crash course in the processes of manuscript production: parchment making, the construction of a quire, and miniature painting. Her more substantial theme here, however, is the impressive range of images of David—and, to a lesser degree, other saints, sinners, and animals (including grotesques)—that appear throughout the thirteen Dublin psalters. Cleaver has an eye for the telling detail, distinguishing, for instance, between the different kinds of musical instruments David plays in specific miniatures and focusing attention on slight variations between portraits of the Psalmist in the Trinity and Chester Beatty manuscripts and their analogues elsewhere.

One example I found intriguing, given the superb high-resolution color photographs provided throughout this book by the publishers, juxtaposes David in Trinity College MS 92 and in National Library of Scotland MS 18 gesturing toward the pages of a psalter held open by choristers (31). Cleaver remarks several distinguishing features between the two images, and I became so infected with her enthusiasm that I noticed one she missed: whereas in the Trinity manuscript David points to the musical notes above the text of the Psalms, in the National Library of Scotland manuscript he points to the words. Given that both miniatures illustrate the opening to Psalm 97, *Cantate Domino canticum novum* [Sing to the Lord a new song] and that a lively debate persisted throughout the Middle Ages over whether this song should be identified with the musical performance of the Psalms or their moral performance by way of good thoughts and deeds, this variant—like those Cleaver notices—may have a witty theological significance.

Cleaver's second essay, on patronage and provenance, is likewise full of interesting and suggestive details. She begins by concentrating on five psalters given to Trinity in 1661 as part of the library of Archbishop Ussher (MSS 53, 69, 91, 93, and 600), describing from some of Ussher's notes in a book now at the Bodleian (MS Rawl. D. 1290, a page of which is reproduced here), "a network of scholars who borrowed each other's books in pursuit of their interests" (40). Later, she provides useful facts about different seventeenth-century owners of other Trinity psalters, and in her pages on Alfred Chester Beatty, brand-new (to me) details about that collector's habits: how they recall but at the same time need to be distinguished from those of an early ideological collector such as Ussher. Cleaver's subtle probing of the pre-seventeenth-century provenance and politics of Trinity MS 92, a large-format Gallican psalter made at the end of the fourteenth century in London, is also engaging. In three closely argued pages she explores how a leaf from a 1508 printed missal added at the end of this manuscript, with its red Lancastrian roses, "resonates with the initials in the Psalter" (42), which also employ a red rose motif, thereby suggesting a possible royal provenance for the codex.

This balance between description and analysis is apparent as well in the book's catalogue entries. These are arranged in chronological order, so that Trinity and Chester Beatty manuscripts are intermingled in their order of presentation, the earliest item being the previously mentioned Ricemarch Psalter (ca. 1079) and the latest an Italian psalter and hymnal (ca. 1450–1500) that depicts on its *Beatus* page a regal and saintly David who wears both a crown and a nimbus. The entries are expansive, some of them running to fifteen hundred words. While each follows the same general format, taking up in turn the manuscript's size and date, followed by information concerning its possible use, a description of its handwriting, evaluation of its decoration, and an account of its other distinguishing features, such as loss of leaves, prefaced and appended texts, and so on, the authors tend to emphasize the visual appeal of the psalters above all their other features.

In a couple of instances, where the manuscripts involve more elaborate and non-Davidic cycles of imagery—for example, a series of saints in the Chester Beatty MS W. 40, and in the calendar section of Trinity College MS 90, a Psalter-Hours from Belgium, a series of the labors of the months—the authors provide meticulous accounts of the decoration. These, like some of Cleaver's observations in her essays, reach beyond the Dublin collections to associate the manuscripts with related codices elsewhere—in the case of Trinity MS 90's labors of the months, for example, with its sister manuscript, British Library Additional MS 21114. On occasion, however, one wishes for more codicological or archival information. We are told, for instance, that Trinity MS 92, discussed above, is missing fifty-eight of its folios, about a third of the book, but not beyond one detail what it lacks or why. Trinity MS 69, a Latin and Middle English psalter with appended vernacular texts once owned by Ussher, is, as the authors note, related to another copy of the same text in Princeton's Scheide Library, MS 143. This manuscript is also worth connecting, however, with another important Ussher psalter at Trinity, MS 70, a Wycliffite primer containing psalms, psalm glosses, and related Middle English prose. MS 70, unfortunately, was one of those codices excluded from consideration by Cleaver and O'Briain.

Latin Psalter Manuscripts in Trinity College Dublin and the Chester Beatty Library has its limitations, but within those it succeeds admirably in calling focused attention to thirteen underappreciated manuscripts that represent, in terms of their date, textual variations, and decorative schemes, the full range of significance of the Psalms for medieval readers, clerical and lay alike. I have no doubt that the useful spadework done by Cleaver and O'Briain on these psalters will, as they hope, encourage "further research on these and other treasures in two of Dublin's collections of manuscripts" (13).

Michael P. Kuczynski, Tulane University

BRENDA DUNN-LARDEAU, ED.
Catalogue des imprimés des XVe et XVIe siècles dans les collections de l'Université de Québec à Montréal.
Montréal: Presses de l'Université du Québec, 2013. viii + 326 pp. 153 color plates.

This erudite, lavishly illustrated catalogue was created by the Groupe de Recherche Multidisciplinaire de Montréal sur les Livres Anciens (XVe–XVIIIe Siècles) [Montreal Multidisciplinary Research Group on Early Books (15th–18th Century)], which is comprised of the Québécois book historians Brenda Dunn-Lardeau (project leader); Janick Auberger, Claire Le Brun-Gouanvic, and Richard Virr (co-researchers); and several additional collaborators, including Manuel Nicolaon and Sandy Ferreira Carreiro, and other scholars named on page 15 of the *Catalogue des imprimés des XVe et XVIe siècles dans les collections de l'Université de Québec à Montréal*. This catalogue is the first to enumerate and describe the manuscripts and early printed books held at the Université de Québec à Montréal (UQÀM). The collection includes seventy-one works, or ninety-four volumes, comprising a total of five manuscripts and eighty-nine printed works. In the introduction, Dunn-Lardeau explains that since the manuscripts have all been analyzed and described previously, the catalogue includes only the printed texts (sixty-six titles in eighty-nine volumes). Unfortunately, and this is but a minor critique of this excellent scholarly work, the studies of the manuscripts are in publications that are not widely available outside Québec, and so it would have been useful to include them in this catalogue in order fully to highlight the quality and extent of the collection at UQÀM.

The collection dates to 1969, the year of the university's foundation, and it is derived primarily from the former Jesuit college, Sainte-Marie (1848–1969); books were also donated by the École Normale de Jacques-Cartier

(1857–1969), the École des Beaux-Arts de Montréal (1922–1969), and other private and institutional benefactors. Given the collection's provenance, it reflects, not surprisingly, the Jesuits' humanist didactic and intellectual preoccupations. The books from Sainte-Marie include classical and Renaissance texts of diverse genres: histories, narratives of travel and exploration, religious texts (including many that are attributed to Protestant authors or printers), counter-Reformation doctrine, philological works, and educational manuals. The Jesuits played an important role in Québec, and the Order is responsible for amassing impressive libraries that now form significant bibliographic repositories in Québécois, such as the Archive of the Jesuits in Canada, the Bibliothèque de la Compagnie de Jesus held at Collège Jean-de-Brébeuf, and, of course, this collection at UQÀM.

The sole incunabulum held at UQÀM—Pomponius Mela's *Cosmographia*, printed in 1482—was donated by the École Normale de Jacques-Cartier. Theodor de Bry's *America pars II, pars VI,* and *pars IX* as well as *Indiæ Orientalis pars I, pars VI,* and *pars XI,* which are noteworthy for their rich, detailed illustrations and maps of America, Congo, and Guinea, also derive from the École Normale de Jacques-Cartier. The 1547 edition of Gilles Corrozet's *Icones historiarum Veteris Testamenti,* the sole volume bequeathed by the École des Beaux-Arts de Montréal, is another highlight of the collection: this visual, emblematic representation of the New Testament contains ninety-four attractive woodcuts designed by Hans Holbein.

The *Catalogue des imprimés des XVe et XVIe siècles dans les collections de l'Université de Québec à Montréal* is thoughtfully presented, enabling scholars to access the entries in multiple ways according to their particular needs. The sixty-six entries are arranged alphabetically by author, and they are followed by indices of illustrations; of authors, editors, translators, and illustrators; of printers and publishers; and of places of publication. These diverse indices will enable scholars easily to locate texts of interest and they also provide useful overviews of the collection's contents; for example, they rapidly illuminate where specific authors or printers are responsible for multiple texts and show the breakdown of the texts' geographical provenance.

Extensive, pertinent information is provided for each of the sixty-six entries, including the author, title, date, and place of publication; the language of composition; a brief outline of the work's content and importance; a detailed description of the title page; diplomatic transcriptions of the title page and colophon; a full collation; a list of contents; an account of illustrations and all other visual elements; a report of fonts used; the dimensions of the paper and descriptions of identifiable watermarks; any copy-specific information; the call number; a bibliography of the reference materials used to compile the entry; and details of the volume's presentation in any exhibits or expositions. This information is complemented by an abundance of high-quality color plates of images likely to be of interest to scholars, such as title pages, printers' devices, woodcuts and engravings, maps, provenance marks, specialized fonts, complex page layouts, decorated fore-edges, manuscript inscriptions, or remarkable bindings. A selection of these images is available on the research group's Web site at http://www.livresanciens.uqam.ca.

The entries are all thorough and clearly presented; they are the product of meticulous, solid bibliographical research. Images have been selected with care to illuminate the beauty, interest, value, and iconographic idiosyncrasies of the texts. Not only is this catalogue an aesthetic joy to peruse, but it also contains a wealth of information about each item in the collection and sheds light on the practices of book collection in Québécois religious and educational institutions.

Joyce Boro, Université de Montréal

OTON DE GRANSON
Poems, ed. and trans. Peter Nicholson and Joan Grenier-Winther.
Oxford Textual Perspectives.
Kalamazoo, MI: TEAMS Medieval Institute Publications, 2015. 406 pp.

Oton de Granson (sometimes spelled "Grandson," ca. 1340s–1397), described in the introduction to this volume as a "knight, diplomat, and poet," is perhaps best known to most English-speaking scholars as playing a minor or supporting role as a contemporary of Geoffrey Chaucer, who cites him by name in his *Complaint of Venus*, a work crafted by Chaucer via a loose translation of a sequence of five balades by Granson. Peter Nicholson and Joan Grenier-Winther's welcome new TEAMS edition of Granson's large and diverse body of work will, however, it is hoped, enable English-speaking readers to extend their engagement with his literary production beyond this oft-cited link to Chaucer.

Granson, who wrote in French, hailed from the noble classes of the County of Savoy (in modern-day Switzerland); however, during his extremely eventful and peripatetic lifetime he also spent extended periods living in England, joining the English armed forces and in 1374 entering the service of John of Gaunt (where he could have encountered Chaucer). As well as Chaucer, he seems to have numbered the French poet Eustache Deschamps among his friends; one of Deschamps' best-known balades records a comically unsettling incident in Calais involving himself, Granson, and some English soldiers. As a result of Granson's English military service, which he continued off and on throughout his lifetime, he also spent time in Spain (in prison), Prussia, and Palestine; one Catalan manuscript containing some of his works survives. He died in Savoy as the result of a duel fought to reclaim his inheritance from apparently unjust confiscation.

As even this short summary of his life attests, Granson is a figure situated within a range of complex and important diplomatic, social, cultural, and linguistic networks at the close of the fourteenth century, networks that have recently come under fresh critical scrutiny. Renewed focus on the impact of multilingualism and a range of intercultural connections upon medieval writing and writers, and the intertwined relationships between "English" and "French" writing in particular, provides a new context in which to read Granson's works: evidently proficient in English as well as his native Savoyard French, Granson was a participant and reader embedded within an extremely fertile cross-channel literary culture that had an impact on his own and others' works in diverse ways.

The standard edition of Granson has remained until recently that of Arthur Piaget, *Oton de Grandson, sa vie et ses poésies* (Lausanne, Switzerland: Payot, 1941). Grenier-Winther brought out a new edition in 2010, *Oton de Granson: Poésies* (Paris: Champion, 2010): both of these editions are, of course, in French. The present English-language edition, which is equipped with a facing-page modern English translation, will serve an important role in allowing non-French-speaking scholars and especially students a much greater access to Granson's work.

The edition is equipped with a compact and clear introduction to Granson's life and works and a useful summary of the (sometimes complicated) manuscript evidence that has given rise to the suggested canon of his works. Perhaps more detailed descriptions of the manuscripts would have been useful; however, it is also understandable that this is not given priority in an edition primarily aimed at classroom use, as the TEAMS editions are. The textual notes, which do not provide a complete list of manuscript variants, do provide a helpful concordance enabling the reader to consult the more extensive notes in Grenier-Winther's 2010 edition and in Piaget. The explanatory notes provided for each poem are useful and clear, flagging important allusions to other well-known texts (e.g., *The Romance of the Rose*) for a student reader.

Given the variation in order and appearance of Granson's works across different manuscripts, the editors have taken the sensible decision to group poems formally, beginning with rondeaux and ballades and then moving to longer forms, culminating in the multiformat "Livre Messire Ode." The English translations provided by the editors are fluent and idiomatic: in places, perhaps, a little too much so. Of course, the "difficulty" of the translation provided has to be tempered by the fact that this edition is aimed at a wide-ranging student audience, some of whom are unlikely to have come across medieval French before; but some students might (paradoxically) find the French a little easier to disentangle if the English syntax followed it more closely and therefore read slightly *less* idiomatically. However, this is a very minor quibble with a very useful and clear edition that will, it is hoped, enable Granson's varied and interesting literary work to be much more widely known and studied than is currently the case.

Olivia Robinson, Brasenose College, Oxford

SUSANNA FEIN AND MICHAEL JOHNSTON, EDS.
Robert Thornton and His Books,
Essays on the Lincoln and London Thornton Manuscripts.
York, UK: York Medieval Press, 2014. xii + 310 pp. + 27 figures.

The essays in this volume offer an excellent opportunity to take stock of where we are now in terms of the small industry of scholarship that has taken as its focus the life and career of the fifteenth-century North Yorkshire gentleman scribe and book producer, Robert Thornton of East Newton in the parish of Stonegrave and the wapentake of Ryedale. This is no bad thing, since, in terms of the history of books before printing, the figure of Robert Thornton and the achievement memorialized by his two surviving codices are often taken as representative in several important ways of what it meant to be a single late-medieval English regional copyist and book producer. The editors show they are fully cognizant of this detail in their complementary overviews of the scribe-compiler and his books. Thus, in the introduction to this volume, Michael Johnston offers an object lesson in the relative value of microhistory in preference to the *grand récit* as applied method for this kind of largely codicological study, while in chapter 1, Susanna Fein surveys the extant corpus of material copied by Thornton and gives an updated list of contents for his two surviving manuscripts, usefully now keyed to both *The Digital Index of Middle English Verse* and *A New Index of Middle English Verse*.

There follow three essays by "Thornton" scholarly veterans. George Keiser offers a new reflection on the life and milieu of the scribe in the light of his graphemic analysis of different forms the scribe used at what one must assume were different career stages. Joel Fredell then takes as his starting point the evidence he has gathered regarding unique decorative features in the production of books in late-medieval York and applies these to the Thornton books and a study of the booklet production method. It is remarkable that all the contributors to the volume now agree that a system of booklets and "proto-booklets" (but not necessarily always the same textual units in the manuscripts that Johnston, Fein, Keiser, and Fredell have identified and characterized) must have played a critical role in the writing and compiling processes of the items in the two Thornton books under such sustained close scrutiny in this volume.

Perhaps more controversially, the next essay, by Ralph Hanna and Thorlac Turville-Petre, questions the kind of profile that can be built up around the Thornton scribe by analysis of the codicological assumptions and editorial method underlying the standard modern edition of the alliterative *Morte Arthure*, published in 1984. Hanna and Turville-Petre describe how, in the thirty years since its publication, work on Middle English dialects and on the constraints governing the metrics of alliterative verse has led them to challenge some of the readings offered by this edition, where Thornton's accuracy as a scribe and his "good ear" for alliterative poetry are largely taken for granted. They offer instead what is tactfully described in their essay title as a prolegomenon for a future edition. The justification for this is based on their conclusion that "the text as transmitted by Thornton is often inaccurate" (146) and that "Thornton's *Morte* is at least a third-generation copy with numerous erroneous accretions" (155).

The next essays focus more specifically on "Thornton" literary themes and their implications for our understanding of writerly methods and motives. Mary Michele Poellinger examines how the various narratives of Christ's Passion in both manuscripts deploy an imagery of violence that can inform our reading of the alliterative *Morte Arthure*, and irrespective of generic assumptions of difference, accounts for the integration of varying styles of religious and romance and "mixed" reading material in the collection. This is followed by perhaps the most convincing study of Thornton's intentionality in the volume, Michael Johnston's account of what he terms "Constantinian Christianity" in the London Thornton manuscript, perhaps the apogee of the Thornton scribe's career as book compiler. Next, Julie Nelson Couch examines the vernacular apocryphal renderings of the childhood of Christ in the London Thornton manuscript, taking issue with those, including myself, who have questioned the propriety of pairing one such narrative (characterized in its "Thornton" heading as "the Romance of the childhode/ of Ihesu Criste") with the grotesque and cannibalistic "Romance of Kyng Richerd" that immediately precedes it in the collection. I now perhaps have to stand corrected on the grounds advanced by Crouch, namely that "like *Richard, Childhood* presents a series of adventurous episodes, all forwarding the idea of the inimitable greatness of the Christ(ian) hero" (212). This is hardly too great a concession, however, since such shared features are merely indicators of a literary sensibility partly governed by a fondness for sensationalized incidents and racy storytelling.

The remaining essay, by Julie Orlemanski, turns to the practices of what might broadly be described as medical reading. The essay focuses specifically on the nature and context of the self-styled *Liber de diversis medicinis*, comprising a remedy collection and the fragments of a herbal, as the final large item in the Lincoln Thornton manuscript and its possible points of connection with the text of John Lydgate's *Dietary* found in the London Thornton manuscript. Orlemanski explains that Thornton's difficulties in copying the *Liber* are matched by evidence of similar discomfort experienced by fifteenth-century copyists of similar types of material elsewhere. She sensibly concludes that this seems to be an occupational hazard of transmitting medical knowledge in written vernacular forms where medicine is not maintained as "an autonomous, stable, or professional discourse" (255).

An instructive afterword on "Robert Thornton country" by Rosalind Field with Dav Smith closes the volume. Their contribution reminds us of the invaluable networks of association one can easily lose sight of by not having a geographically precise sense of the importance of place. Field and Smith highlight in particular what was lost in the Victorian rebuilding of Stonegrave Minster in the 1860s. Part of that irrecoverable loss almost certainly includes the site marking the final resting place of the Thornton scribe. On a happier note, the essay is usefully illustrated by images of the Thornton family tomb (preserving effigies of the scribe's parents; his father died ca. 1418) that is still extant because it was relocated to the north wall of the church as part of the restoration. The essay also reproduces two remarkable photographs, dating from 1862, that show the Victorian restoration at Stonegrave in progress, at the stage when the demolition and rebuilding of the twelfth-century north aisle housing the Thornton family burials was proceeding apace. The point is well made that this work was taking place and these photographs were being taken around the same time as the Early English Text Society commissioned George Perry, Dean of Lincoln, to produce his editions of the alliterative *Morte Arthure* (EETS OS 8; London, 1865); *English Prose Treatises of Richard Rolle de Hampole edited from Robert Thornton's MS. In the Library of Lincoln Cathedral* (EETS OS 20; London, 1866), and *Religious Pieces in Prose and Verse, from R. Thornton's MS* (EETS OS 26; 1867).

John J. Thompson, Queen's University, Belfast

SIMON HOROBIN AND LINNE R. MOONEY, EDS.
Middle English Texts in Transition: A Festschrift Dedicated to Toshiyuki Takamiya on his 70th Birthday.
Rochester, NY: York Medieval Press and The Boydell Press, 2014.
xix + 335 pp. + 18 color and 21 B&W figures.

At the end of her essay on book collectors in the current volume, contributor Carrie Griffin says of Professor Toshiyuki Takamiya and his renowned collection, "The Takamiya library is a private collection in name only; like the library of Pepys it is [*sic*] has regularly been a locus for sociability and scholarly work, and many readers will have experienced the hospitality and generosity of the collector" (240). Any scholar of Middle English literature who has worked for a time in the field of manuscript studies has at some point benefited from the kindness of Professor Takamiya through his willingness to provide from his collection references, microfilms, digital images, or the books themselves to junior and senior scholars alike. The present volume, a Festschrift in honor of Toshi Takamiya on his seventieth birthday, provides testimony of this: many of the contributors include notes at the beginning of their essays to thank Professor Takamiya for his help with their research.

The first section of the volume focuses on the main authors, Chaucer, Gower, and Langland. Richard Firth Green explores the "Common Paper" of Adam Pinkhurst's Scriveners' Company in London and offers a careful codicological examination of its contents and what it tells us about the "political" lives of its members. He also provides a useful transcription and translation of documents related to scriveners conducting business on Sundays, a dispute at the center of his analysis. Simon Horobin's essay on the B version of *Piers Plowman* in Oxford, Corpus Christi College, MS 201 (F) follows. Horobin reclaims the often dismissed idiosyncratic F, scrutinizing the scribe's response to the text and his heavy handling of the exemplars, which, Horobin asserts, included copies of the A and C versions. Terry Jones's essay on Gower's dedication to Henry IV in his *Confessio Amantis* questions the accepted chronology of events that lead to Gower's supposed change of allegiance from Richard II to Henry IV. After a close examination of Huntington Library, MS Ellesmere 26 A.17, Jones asserts that Gower remained loyal to Richard, in spite of a well-oiled Lancastrian propaganda machine. The last article in this section is Robert Yeager's brief but persuasive argument that John Gower was not the author of the short verse French dream-vision *Le Songe Vert*.

The next section deals with lyrics and romances in manuscripts, beginning with Phillipa Hardman's painstakingly thorough discussion of the unique copy of *Sir Fyrumbras* in Oxford, Bodleian Library, MS Ashmole 33. Hardman explores the author's process of drafting, revising, and reorganizing, and encourages her audience to reconsider the assumption that later copies of texts that survive were always copied from perfect exemplars. This is followed by a short and interesting piece by John Hirsh on a leaf in Oxford, Bodleian Library MS Rawlinson D.913, which, he argues, was at one point a "performance" copy for the various lyrics in Middle English and French that it preserves. Another short essay follows in which Gareth Griffith and Ad Putter introduce a new international collaborative project, *The Dynamics of the Medieval Manuscript*. Putter and Griffith's part of the project focuses on manuscripts containing Middle English romances, and their essay contends that in spite of the multilingualism of medieval England, manuscripts that preserve only Middle English romances are surprisingly the rule. This section ends with a brief essay by Eric Stanley on six lyrics in British Library MS Harley 2253 that are unusually written as prose in the manuscript; he reaches no specific conclusion but ponders a variety of possibilities.

The section on devotional writings opens with Susan Powell's fascinating comparison of the earlier years of Arundel's Constitutions with the later decades, just before the Reformation, when the Church handed over more authority to an efficient secular arm. This comparison leads Powell to conclude that while there is little physical evidence that the Constitutions were vigorously enforced, Arundel's legislation seems instead to have created a "climate of awareness" in its early years (146). This essay is followed by Michael Sargent's extensive reconsideration of the manuscript evidence for the very popular works by Walter Hilton and Nicholas Love, their circulation and provenance, to argue strongly that these men were not closely associated to Archbishop Thomas Arundel, as Jonathan Hughes has previously suggested. Mayumi Taguchi's exhaustive examination of Cambridge, Magdalene College, MS Pepys 2125 in the next essay provides a study of this miscellany of Middle English devotional literature and the unique circumstances of its compilation. This section concludes with a fascinating study by Mary Morse of one of the oldest birth girdles to survive in England. While Morse mainly deals with Takamiya MS 56, a roll of prayers that served as a devotional text as well as a protective charm for women in labor, she also provides more general information about the less familiar tradition of birthing girdles.

The final section examines collectors and later scholars. To understand more about the post-medieval popularity of *The Wise Book*, Carrie Griffin follows the trail of some early copies to several later collectors, Samuel Pepys, John Dee, and the present honoree, Toshiyuki Takamiya. Next, James Murphy explores the only surviving manuscript of Laurentius Traversagnus's *Margarita eloquentiae* in Rome, Vatican Library, Vat. Cod. Lat. 11441, the author's personal copy which was used by Caxton and preserves the original printer's marks. While most studies in the volume have centered on multiple or single codices, Natalia Petrovskaia's essay on Oxford, Bodleian Library, MS Rawlinson B 484 draws attention to the fundamental and often overlooked unit of the quire and how the later history of this earliest known fragment of the *Imago Mundi* in Rawlinson B 484 can tell us much about the interests of and relationships between antiquarian collectors. The last article, by Timothy Graham, describes the curious lives of the "Oxford Saxonist" team of William and Elizabeth Elstob and the manuscript, Takamiya MS 129, which contains their collaborative efforts to collate a series of Old English law codes.

The Festschrift closes with a heartfelt tribute to Professor Takamiya by his former students Takako Kato and Satoko Tokunaga, in an essay about the remarkable contribution Professor Takamiya has made to the rapidly growing field of digital facsimiles through his creation of the very successful and internationally acclaimed Humanities Media Interface (HUMI) Project. This is followed by a recently updated and comprehensive bibliography of Takamiya's scholarly work, including work published in Japanese.

All of the essays here, as Linne Mooney explains in her Preface, "offer new readings of texts, or new evidence... [or] offer new insights into medieval books, their producers, readers and collectors" (xv). This collection, as well as the scholar it honors, provides persuasive testimony for the importance of studying these medieval books and the lives behind the words on the page. The editors have presented here a fine collection of essays that cover an impressive range of topics and all fit neatly together in a volume with the history of the book at its heart, a fitting tribute to Professor Takamiya.

Jill C. Havens, Texas Christian University

MICHAEL JOHNSTON
Romance and the Gentry in Late Medieval England.
Oxford: Oxford University Press, 2014. pp. xvi + 301.

In this valuable study, Michael Johnston argues for the existence of a distinct genre of "gentry romance" appealing to a class that grew rapidly in importance in the late Middle Ages, confirming their sense of identity, expressing their interests, giving attention to their ambitions and concerns, and providing fanciful solutions to their problems. The gentry are defined as the group of knights, squires, and gentlemen lying at the bottom of the aristocratic pile, gentlemen just above yeomen. This was the decisive division in English society: between those who were "gentle" and those who were not. The manuscripts containing these romances are localized in the north Midlands.

In *Sir Degrevaunt*, the classic of the genre, the knight-landowner is threatened by the depredations of a neighboring earl upon his estates; this was a familiar reality for the gentry, who were always subordinate to the lords, subject to their intimidation and encroachment and unable to invoke the law without years of wrangling and harassment. The resolution is pure fantasy: Degrevaunt defeats the earl in chivalric combat and marries his daughter, so becoming an earl. *Sir Gawain and the Carle of Carlisle* and the *Avowing of Arthur* have vaguely similar plots, in which a member of the gentry faces up to the Arthurian court and proves his equality or even superiority (the carle turns out to be himself an aristocrat).

As Johnston says, such romances "mediate gentry economic fantasies" (67). *Octavian, Sir Isumbras,* and *Sir Eglamour* all have gentry heroes whose wives and children are snatched away by wild animals. This was not a common problem for the gentry, but what Johnston emphasizes here is the special importance of families in the life of the gentry, the disturbance if they fell out or were broken up, the importance of secure inheritance, and the difficulties of marrying daughters successfully on a limited income. The reuniting of the families in the romances after heroic endurance and battles removes such problems into fantasy land. A final group of romances, *Sir Cleges, Sir Amadace*, and *Sir Launfal*, take up the problem of the "spendthrift knight," always a worry for gentry families with their limited estates. As a concern, it is not addressed—that is not the business of romance—but swept aside in fantasy restorations to wealth. The heroes just strike lucky because they are loyal to their nature as gentlemen and do not descend to account-keeping.

The book is really in two parts, an introduction and three chapters in the first and then three further chapters in the second. In the first part, the gentry are defined and described with admirable specificity, even to the jobs they performed in society as sheriffs, escheators, justices of the peace, tax collectors, parish officials, and administrators of the manorial courts. Their interest in books is dealt with in detail, with illustration from gentry families in general, such as the Pastons. The role of the gentry romances in appealing to their primary audience is given close attention, and a number of prevalent motifs are identified. In Chapter 3, building upon the foundations established by scholars in the last twenty years, Johnston examines the nine manuscripts in which the nine gentry romances appear, sometimes in more than one copy. All are very familiar to scholars, among them Aberystwyth, National Library of Wales, MS Brogyntyn II. I (formerly Porkington 10); the Findern MS (Cambridge University Library MS Ff.i.6); the Heege MS (Edinburgh, National Library of Scotland, MS Adv. 19. 3.1); Thornton's MS Lincoln 91; Oxford, Bodleian Library, MS Ashmole 61; and Princeton University Library MS Taylor 9 (formerly the Ireland MS).

Provincial origin is demonstrated in analysis of dialect, of nonstandardized production features, and of other aspects of mostly noncommercial production. Seven of the manuscripts have internal evidence of provenance. In identifying the likely household scribes, Johnston is imaginatively specific in his guesswork: not just "household clerks" (the usual suspects), but stewards, bailiffs, keepers of manor records, secretaries, chaplains, and even the gentle owner himself.

The last three chapters deal with four manuscripts in turn: the Findern MS (containing *Degrevaunt*) and Heege MS (*Isumbras, Amadace*), both from Derbyshire; Thornton's Lincoln MS, with four gentry romances (*Octavian, Isumbras, Degrevaunt,* and *Eglamour*); and the Ireland MS (*Amadace, the Avowing of Arthur*). The Findern MS suggests an aspirant gentry audience (it includes poems by Chaucer) happy to see a knight defeat an earl in a fantasy of social ascent. The Heege MS is of yeoman household origin, the romances representing the yeoman class "looking in" (like Heathcliff) at the gentry. The Thornton chapter gives an excellent analysis of the construction of the manuscript and how it reflects Thornton's compilatorial ambitions, particularly in grouping together its four gentry romances. There is excellent new work on the Thornton family and its connections. The Ireland MS is associated with the middling gentry and contains a stirring account of a minor success in a land dispute between the Thorntons and the Stanleys, a much higher-ranking gentry family. The romances are the usual mix of recognizable allusion to the hero's gentry status alongside chivalric fantasies of ascent. The Ireland manuscript also contains manorial records of the family, which make a nice counterpoint to the romances in showing how the reality of gentry business involved collecting dues and rents, settling tenants' disputes, imposing fines, writing up accounts, and squeezing every last penny out of their tenants.

The last three chapters as a whole tell us about the gentry romances in these manuscripts, but they are chiefly remarkable for the enormous amount of hard graft that has gone into tracing the histories and affiliations of the different families. There has been heroic work in the Victoria County History and the old county histories and among the records of pleas, writs, wills, charters, inquisitions post mortem, the Calendars of the Patent, Close and Fine Rolls, and the local court rolls.

One of the minor problems with the book is that its argument rests on an unknowable reality: romance reading (or listening) may have been popular among the gentry, but there can be no certainty that the romances themselves mirrored the gentry's own lives. Another problem is that the contents of the miscellanies are not often the product of careful selection. There is always the reality of "exemplar poverty": gentry romances may be included because the scribe-compiler happened to come across them in the exemplars that he had access to. Another problem with the book is repetitiveness. Some of it is avoidable, such as repetition in the same words of the same ideas and information: the idea of the gentry romances "doing ideological work" is repeated over and over again. Once would have been enough. But some of the repetition is unavoidable because of the structure of the book, which begins with a sweep through the whole subject in the Introduction, followed by approaches to the gentry romances from different points of view, and concluding with three chapters in which most of them are treated again and at length. Since so much of the argument depends on the content of the stories and their relation to gentry life and expectations, their plots have to be rehearsed two or three times, sometimes in the same words.

But the book as a whole is a success and achieves its purpose of identifying a group of romances and analyzing its special relation to the realities of provincial gentry life. In the course of the study, an expert demonstration is given of the value of the study of manuscripts in relation to such a subject, and valuable new information is provided about the families who owned them. We get a lively sense that we *know* these families, their preoccupations, and their tastes.

Derek A. Pearsall, Harvard University

**KATHRYN KERBY-FULTON, JOHN T. THOMPSON,
AND SARAH BAECHLE, EDS.**
*New Directions in Medieval Manuscript Studies and Reading Practices:
Essays in Honor of Derek Pearsall.*
Notre Dame: University of Notre Dame Press, 2014.

At least one organizing principle of a festschrift is the work of the person to whom it is dedicated. For this reason alone, the editors of *New Directions in Medieval Manuscript Studies and Reading Practices: Essays in Honor of Derek Pearsall* no doubt faced a challenge: how to celebrate the career of a scholar who has advanced Middle English studies in so many roles—as close reader and general critic, textual editor, biographer, bibliographer, anthologizer. Drawn from a 2011 conference in honor of Pearsall's eightieth birthday, the twenty-five essays in this volume do, like their namesake, offer God's Plenty. Yet, as the title of the volume suggests, the editors give pride of place to Pearsall's advocacy of manuscript study for understanding late-medieval literary culture, particularly reading and compositional practices. The resurgence of manuscript studies can be conveniently traced to the 1981 conference he hosted at the University of York and the resulting edited collection, *Manuscripts and Readers in Fifteenth-Century England*. But his influence has been ongoing, and the essays in this volume, published more than thirty years after *Manuscripts and Readers*, testify to the vitality of a legacy that now extends to a second generation of scholars.

While manuscript studies is central to *New Directions*, the first third of the volume actually evokes features of Pearsall's earlier criticism. Part I, "Celebrating Pearsallian Reading Practices," focuses on close reading and questions of literary value. A. C. Spearing draws on the work of contemporary theorist Gary Saul Morson to offer a sensitive account of narrative freedom in *Troilus and Criseyde*, especially as expressed in an "I" that he argues is best understood as "a means of introducing proximity, experimentality, and a literary openness" (13) in a work characterized by "many different centres of consciousness" (23). Oliver Pickering assesses the value of the quite different, didactic voice of the anonymous Outspoken Poet of the *South English Legendary*, while Martha Driver reveals an important source of Pearsall's sense of literary value through a study of his references to Shakespeare.

Much of Part II, "England and International," reflects Pearsall's highly productive collaboration with Elizabeth Salter at York. Jocelyn Wogan-Browne's detailed account of two passion narratives—the thirteenth-century *Rossignos* and the fifteenth-century *Nightingale*—reveals not only the multilingual context of late-medieval writing in England but also changing stylistic trends and political uses of such poetry. Susan Powell draws on Salter's work more directly in a fine piece on *Wynnere and Wastoure*; arguing for Salter's claim that the heraldic device of the unnamed Second Knight of the poem denotes the Wingfield family, Powell further identifies the figure as Sir John Wingfield, chief administrator to the Black Prince. Sarah McNamer contributes an essay on the early Italian version of a truly international work also associated with Salter, the *Meditations on the Life of Christ*, which was translated into English in the early fifteenth century by Nicholas Love, prior of the Carthusian house of Mount Grace. Through a series of careful deductions, McNamer claims that Author A of the Italian version was likely a Poor Clare and yet more tentatively suggests that her name may have been Cecilia. Katie Ann-Marie Bugyis examines the theological and devotional significance of the glossing provided by another writer associated with Mount Grace, the anonymous Red Ink Annotator of *The Book of Margery Kempe*.

The eighteen essays that comprise the rest of the volume more consistently explore what individual manuscripts can tell us about the production, dissemination, and reception of literary writing in late-medieval England and Ireland. The four contributors in Part III attended the first York conference in 1981. In a somewhat retrospective essay, Julia Boffey turns to Huntington MS 136 to reflect on her growing sense of context as "a fluid thing that changes over time" (172) and the value of considering the known circulation patterns of all individual elements in a manuscript. A. S. G. Edwards examines Lydgate's literary fortunes in the twentieth century as reflected in the prices that the poet's manuscripts fetched at auction. A. I. Doyle's study of marginalia in several Bristol books serves as a model for what manuscript study can reveal about specific centers of literary production, while Carol Meale draws on a different kind of evidence—a 1526 monition list from Bishop Tunstall—to shed light on the career and milieu of the London mercer and bookseller John Colyns.

Several essays in the next two sections, mostly by emerging scholars, are likewise concerned with identifying and localizing literary networks. In

Part IV, Hannah Zdansky suggests that we turn to French and even Welsh manuscripts to understand peculiarities in the hand of the scribe of Cotton Nero A.x. Hilary Fox and Theresa O'Byrne offer insight into literary production in early fifteenth-century Dublin: Fox on the Langlandian inflections in the social and political criticism of Irish colonial rule offered by James Yonge's *Gouernaunce*; O'Byrne on the career, output, and scribal community of Yonge's apprentice Nicholas Bellewe, to whom she also attributes the English *Mirror of St. Edmund*.

The essays in Part V are devoted to what manuscripts can reveal about audience and reception. For Nicole Eddy, the marginalia in Lambeth Palace MS 491 indicate a need to expand our conception of the audience for medieval romance to include children and young adults. Karrie Fuller likewise focuses on the household as locus for reception in her account of the scribe-annotator dialogues in the copy of *Piers Plowman* made in the early sixteenth century by Sir Adrian Fortescue. Identifying at least three distinct annotators—Fortescue, his second wife, Anne Rede, and a third figure who may be another family member—Fuller underscores the diversity of views that *Piers* could elicit, even within a small circle, as well as the difficulty of pinpointing the precise religious sympathies of the annotators. Maura Giles-Watson assesses women's agency in a quite different context as she ponders how the humanist cult of literacy may have contributed to their exclusion from the early-modern stage.

The essays of the final two sections, while rooted in manuscript studies, also cohere around two main poles of vernacular literary activity in later medieval England: Chaucer and his followers and *Piers Plowman*. Part VI opens with Elizabeth Scala's thoughtful treatment of quotation and self-quotation in the *Nun's Priest's Tale*, practices that she claims effectively inaugurate the Chaucerian tradition by at once emptying out authority and engaging in self-authorization. Sarah Baechle surveys commentaries in some literary manuscripts from the Continent as prelude to her account of glosses in two manuscripts of the *Wife of Bath's Prologue*, marginalia that may be designed to limit interpretation by pointing the reader away from (or perhaps through) Jerome's *Adversus Jovinianum* and toward less virulently antifeminist scriptural sources. Peter Brown challenges us to consider at what point a different copy may be a different work, in this case how the putatively "corrupt" Canterbury manuscript of Hoccleve's *Male Regle* is in fact a "balade," which Brown suggests may have circulated in a monastic coterie. Stephen Partridge's study of Houghton MS Eng. 530 examines the challenges of identifying and enumerating scribal hands in a compilation and how the number of hands in turn affects our sense of the production of such a book.

The complex manuscript tradition of *Piers Plowman* has made it fertile ground for manuscript studies. Part VII opens with Jill Mann's trenchant critique of the Kane-Donaldson edition's argument that the C revision of *Piers* was made from a highly corrupt manuscript of the B Text—an argument she sees rooted foremost in an attempt to defend Kane's A Text against shared BC readings. Melinda Nielsen applies the accretive model of writing associated with *Piers*, or what she calls "an ongoing multistage composition process" (471), to Thomas Usk's *Testament of Love*, and in doing so builds on Anne Middleton's reconstructed manuscript description of the work. The volume concludes with Kathryn Kerby-Fulton's provocative and exemplary study of MS Bodley 851. Best known for containing the disputed Z Text of *Piers*, the manuscript is, for Kerby-Fulton, a vehicle for a revaluation of scribal agency. Arguing for a highly skilled scribe-maker with mercantile sympathies, she presents Z as an important lesson in how "scribal redactors can rise to poetic and intellectual heights we can *at moments* mistake for a great poet" (510).

The later essays in *New Directions* amply demonstrate the critical riches that have accrued since the publication of *Manuscripts and Readers in Fifteenth-Century England*. Because of this work, we simply know much more that we did thirty years ago about individual scribes, readers, and literary networks. Yet it is also fitting that Kerby-Fulton returns to the question of literary value, in this case by challenging the assumption that only authors produce literary value while scribes can at best merely preserve it. Most of the contributors in the volume approach individual manuscripts with the conviction that doing so will complicate the picture of agency in late-medieval literary culture, and that increased knowledge of individual agents and localized communities will reveal a greater range of interpretive possibilities and even (to borrow Spearing's term) freedom. If such work is at times speculative—as several contributors claim it must be—even the questions posed and alternatives raised serve a valuable purpose, if only to spur further research. This is a legacy of which Derek Pearsall should be proud.

Kevin Gustafson, University of Texas at Arlington

KATHLEEN E. KENNEDY
The Courtly and Commercial Art of the Wycliffite Bible.
Medieval Church Studies 35.
Turnhout, Belgium: Brepols, 2014. xiv + 230 pp. + 58 B&W illustrations.

In the last ten years a number of seminal works have been published on Wycliffite manuscripts. Kathleen Kennedy's book is the most recent. Her title is slightly misleading; nothing revisionist is suggested by *The Courtly and Commercial Art of the Wycliffite Bible*, its having long been accepted that Wycliffite Bibles were professionally produced and that that early copies were made for or owned by aristocrats. Yet the book is straightforwardly revisionist. In the first chapter Kennedy sets her sights on four commonplace beliefs that she rejects outright or significantly modifies: most copies of the Wycliffite Bible must have been made before the Arundel 1407–1409 Constitutions (rejected); copying began in Oxford and moved to London (qualified); "scruffy" copies postdating the Arundel ban were Lollard productions (largely rejected); Lollard antipathy for images explains why Wycliffite Bibles lacked images (rejected). Succeeding chapters support her rejections and qualifications.

Kennedy also uses a revisionist methodology, dating individual manuscripts by border style rather than paleography. Developing Kathleen Scott's anatomy of border motifs in *Dated and Dateable English Manuscript Borders*, Kennedy demonstrates that Wycliffite Bibles were openly copied throughout the fifteenth century, in the first quarter (Chapter 5), the second (Chapter 6), and the third and fourth (Chapter 7). She is not the first to have dated Wycliffite Bibles after 1409 (Forshall and Maddan also do so), but no one before has made so clear a case for consistent production by established scribes and border artists. In so doing, she also establishes visual criteria for quarter-century dating applicable to other manuscripts.

Because Kennedy addresses her work to a wide audience, she devotes Chapter 2 to terminology and basic principles of text hierarchy. She describes her book as "a sort of guidebook," but with only two illustrations in this chapter, a novice may find Scott's volume a useful supplement. Chapter 3 focuses on the professional production of individual books of the Bible in booklets, perhaps "on spec." Drawing on work by Anne Hudson, Ralph Hanna, and others, Kennedy addresses copies in scriptural anthologies, sometimes with non-Wycliffite translations, as well as in religious miscellanies. In the latter category, Kennedy diverges from analysis to speculation about reader motivation for biblical selection. Chapters 4 through 6 comprise the heart of the book. Chapter 4 begins with early illustrated Wycliffite Bibles. Because she includes the Glossed Gospels, excluded from Mary Dove's *The First English Bible*, the elaborately illustrated non-Wycliffite glossed Gospels (Corpus Christi College, Cambridge, MS 32) deserve a footnote, in particular because the manuscript is a major exception to Kennedy's contention that Bibles were largely aniconic in England. Chapter 5 is devoted to the border styles of artists working with Herman Scheerre, Chapter 6 to followers of the Corpus Master. The final chapter deals with the reuse of Wycliffite translations. The 259 copies of the Wycliffite Bible are cited in Appendix 2.

Generous illustration supports the detailed analysis of borders and figural images. To supplement the fifty-eight black-and-white figures, Kennedy typically selects images that are digitally accessible; footnotes direct the reader to the list of URLs (Appendix 1). Such access allows the reader to appreciate comments about color as well as to magnify tiny features of border design, sometimes difficult to perceive in the reproductions. In a few instances the argument is poorly served by the figures. For example, there are no heart-shaped leaves in Figures 4.11 or 4.12; neither are they illustrated in the cross-referenced *Dated and Dateable Manuscript Borders*. Similarly, there are no tiles in the historiation of Psalm 1 in Harley 1896 (Fig. 4.14), nor in the corresponding initial for *Beatus vir* in the Ranworth Antiphoner (URL not accessible, September 2014). There are tiles in the Ranworth initials for Psalms 26, 38, and 52, but they are not identical with the design used on the Norfolk rood screens that Kennedy cites. The orientation of elements is radically different. This is a minor point that in no way affects Kennedy's thesis, but an interrelationship between rood screen and manuscript illuminations, first queried by M. R. James, in no way clarifies the point at issue. Like border decoration, panel painting deserves meticulous attention to detail.

I also take exception to Kennedy's use of the label "Man of Sorrows." In the Mercy Seat Trinity in Harley 1896 (Fig. 4.15), she contends that Christ displaying his wounds is borrowed from the Man of Sorrows tradition, but such Trinities in England predate the introduction of that image. She identifies the manuscript as third-quarter Norwich work, but by mid-century this standard Trinity with Christ so represented was already in the repertoire of Norwich glass painters. Kennedy also calls the idiosyncratic Crucifixion in Douce 140 (Fig. 7.7) a Man of Sorrows. Admittedly, the label might be used for a variety of scenes, Christ shown with the instruments of the Passion, Christ with the Cross alone, Christ displaying his wounds, but never, to my knowledge, for the crucified Christ.

Kennedy's book is significant both for its contribution to Wycliffite studies and its anatomy of the border styles, but it is also an exciting book because it suggests research paths yet to be explored. To what extent can her observations about ink flourishing, *littera partita*, and twisted-scroll catchwords in Wycliffite Bibles be extended to other manuscript genres? Kennedy addresses statute collections, but evidence amassed by scholars in the *Index of Images* fascicles, edited by Kathleen L. Scott (not cited in Kennedy's bibliography), suggests that elaborate catchwords were used in university reference texts as well. The Cambridge fascicles record twisted scrolls, some shaded, four citations in Cambridge I (2008), and six (excluding Wycliffite Bibles) in the files for Cambridge II (in preparation). All but two are dated to the period Kennedy assigns to the Twisted-Ribbon Scribe. It remains to be seen whether the same scribe or workshop produced these manuscripts. A more careful attention paid to the humble catchword may document a scribal tradition of twisted scrolls.

Ann Eljenholm Nichols, Winona State University

PETER J. LUCAS AND ANGELA M. LUCAS
The Medieval Manuscripts at Maynooth: Explorations in the Unknown.
Dublin: Four Courts, 2014. xxvii + 276 pp. + 77 color plates.

This small collection of medieval manuscripts at the National University of Ireland, Maynooth, is little known, and there is no existing catalogue, a deficiency now admirably rectified by the present volume, which has been diligently assembled by Peter Lucas and Angela Lucas. They provide very detailed descriptive entries for each of the sixteen manuscripts, three single-leaf fragments, and a number of manuscript fragments in the bindings of nineteen early printed books. All the manuscripts are of Continental origin, and the majority are written in Latin; there is nothing in English or Irish. Most relate to the Church: there is a Bible, biblical commentaries, theological works, works on Church history and canon law, a missal, a breviary, two psalters, a benedictional, and three Books of Hours. The entries are supported by a bibliography and a number of indexes (of former owners, incipits, contents, general index). An appendix prints an extract from the will of Laurence Renehan, a significant donor, and the introduction surveys how and when this small collection might have been brought together, noting the paucity of information available beyond the books themselves. The volume is prefaced by a warmly written foreword by Hugh Connolly, the college president, and Cathal McCauley, the college librarian.

Unusually, the catalogue entries themselves are not listed chronologically by shelfmark but are arranged thematically. Types of manuscripts (liturgical; doctrinal) are grouped together, as are manuscripts that share a place of origin (five are from Liège). The entries are comprehensively informative, with detailed codicological descriptions of features such as quire signatures, the arrangement of hair and flesh sides, prickings, and variations in the numbers of lines on particular leaves. This intense level of detail would be unfeasible with a larger collection but is welcome here, and these manuscript descriptions might be used as models for students unfamiliar with codicological conventions.

The most intriguing section is that devoted to manuscript fragments still in situ in the bindings of incunabula and sixteenth- and seventeenth-century printed books. Here the entries are brief summaries that are richly illustrated, the photographs also offering much of interest to anyone interested in bindings and binding techniques. Essentially, this is a treasure trove of material laid out for future researchers to make new discoveries, since all of these manuscript fragments await identification; a similar generosity is evident elsewhere in the volume (xv–xvi), where the authors outline other possible avenues for scholarship among the Maynooth collections (in legal documents, Renehan's papers, the early printed books themselves).

The generosity of the publisher also deserves comment: there are seventy-seven color illustrations of excellent quality, and the volume as a whole is produced to a high specification. This small collection of medieval manuscripts is fortunately served by both the scholarly expertise of its editors and the skills of its publisher, and I am left wishing that Four Courts Press would extend its range to other manuscript catalogues.

Margaret Connolly, University of St. Andrews

WILLIAM MARX, ED.
The Middle English Liber Aureus and Gospel of Nicodemus.
Middle English Texts 48.
Heidelberg, Germany: Universitätsverlag Winter, 2013. xci + 143 pp.

NIAMH PATTWELL, ED.
Exornatorium Curatorum. Middle English Texts 49.
Heidelberg, Germany: Universitätsverlag Winter, 2013. xliv + 60 pp.

FRANCISCO ALONSO ALMEIDA, ED.
A Middle English Medical Remedy Book. Middle English Texts 50.
Heidelberg, Germany: Universitätsverlag Winter, 2014. 143 pp.

There is much variety in the latest group of Middle English Texts editions. The fact that the editors are working with material either unknown or inadequately studied places a heavy burden of editorial responsibility on them while also affording an exciting opportunity for introducing the works to a new readership. Each editor rises gamely to the occasion, and none more so than William Marx, whose edition of the *Liber Aureus and Gospel of Nicodemus* (almost as long as the other two Middle English Texts editions combined) should be required reading for anyone who wants to learn—or be reminded—how to produce a scholarly edition of a medieval text with clarity, intelligence, and wisdom. This prose text based on the Latin pseudo-Bonaventuran *Meditaciones vite Christi*, the apocryphal *Evangelium Nicodemi*, and the Gospels, survives in three manuscripts and partly in a fourth, all from the middle of the fifteenth century. As Marx notes, "The compiler was a learned individual who treated his sources critically and with a profound sense of purpose, and refashioned the narrative of the *MVC* in a way that produced a distinctive Middle English version of the Latin text" (xi). This work is now dealt with here by a learned editor with his own firm intention to elucidate the text for us.

Marx begins with a very ordered description of the four manuscripts, a method of laying out descriptions learned by many of us in our youth. This is followed by a discriminating analysis of the language. Not content with merely providing a linguistic profile for one of his four manuscripts not covered in the *Linguistic Atlas of Late Mediaeval English*, London, British Library, MS Egerton 2658, Marx also produces a linguistic profile for Dublin, Trinity College, MS 71, a copy of *Rolle's English Psalter Commentary* said to be in the same hand as Egerton and as the main one in another of his manuscripts, Manchester, John Rylands Library, MS Eng. 895.

This careful analysis allows him to explore various dialectal imponderables and to conclude that both the Egerton and Manchester manuscripts were produced in the same region as that of four Wycliffite manuscripts discussed here, the Central Midlands. He further notes that the scribe responsible for the Egerton, Manchester, and Trinity texts "was able to adopt specific forms or usages for particular assignments" (xxxi). Summarizing the convoluted history of the *Meditaciones vite Christi* and the *Evangelium Nicodemi* in a few telling sentences, he then explains precisely which parts of these texts are used by the compiler and to what effect. He cogently demonstrates how, rather than presenting two separate works, the translator brought together these texts to provide a historic narrative of the Passion and Resurrection of Christ. As the text is much supplemented by biblical material, various questions are also raised about the use or otherwise of the Wycliffite Bible. Very subtly Marx shows how this text "probably derives from a culture of interest in Lollard ideas while at the same time it is not a product of a strictly Wycliffite school of thought either before or after 1409" (lxxi).

If Marx's text may be discussed in relation to the supposed influence of Thomas Arundel's 1409 Constitutions, Niamh Pattwell's edition of around 1516 is in a direct line from their "predecessor," Archbishop Pecham's Syllabus of 1281, with which the *Exornatorium curatorum* opens. Pattwell begins with a very neat discussion of the sources. She shows how her text is "a combination of both the English Pechamite tradition and the French *Opus Tripartitum*" (xii) that originated with Jean Gerson (1363–1421). She worries away in an intriguing fashion about the meaning of the words "Exornatorium Curatorum," ultimately suggesting that it could be either [*Liber*] *Exornatorium Curatorum* "[The book] of those who adorn or embellish or provide for the care of souls," or *Liber Exoneratorium Curatorum* "[The book] of those who discharge or are responsible for the care of souls" (xiii).

In many ways, Pattwell's eleven printed editions are less interesting than Marx's four manuscripts to the extent that early printed texts are usually more standardized. There is therefore an unavoidable degree of repetition in her descriptions. Yet there are ways in which she could have expanded on some of these, particularly London, British Library, MS Lansdowne 379, which is part print and part manuscript (and has been described elsewhere by the present reviewer, who is undertaking a study of this manuscript, and by the *JEBS* reviews editor). It might have been helpful, too, had the editions been set out printer by printer, as this would have given more substance to Pattwell's strong argument about popularity. It is striking that over a period of almost forty years, all the major printers published the text: de Worde (1516?, 1518? with manuscript additions from another edition, 1520?, 1521?), Notary (1519), Pynson (1520?), Pepwell (1525?), anonymous (1530?), Treveris (1531?), Godfray (1532?), and Wyer (1552).

It is in the arguments about the text's genesis and usability that Pattwell's edition is at its most interesting, though perhaps she overemphasizes the degree to which it might have been made for lay reading, especially given the clerical connections that she draws out so well (for instance, in 1528 the bishop of Ely, Nicholas West, stipulated its delivery at parish level at least four times a year). It clearly must have been something of a best seller if the Oxford bookseller John Dorne could record in his ledger the sale of thirty copies in 1520 alone; it may be presumed that many of the buyers were interested clerics. Such readers would have encountered a text that opened with an almost "literal translation of Pecham's brief exposition on the fourteen articles and ten commandments" (xxii) and then moved on to the sacraments, confession, deadly sins, and dying.

The concentration on these same areas: the Ten Commandments, an examination of conscience, and preparation for death are all found as a compilation of three tracts in the *Opus tripartitum*. This work, which may have been written originally in Latin or French (or both) by Gerson, circulated in innumerable manuscripts throughout Europe and was printed as early as 1467 in Cologne. The three tracts would seem to have been a single compilation by 1414, when Gerson was an influential figure at the Council of Constance, from where the text's fame spread among various archbishops who recognized its usefulness. Having explored this context thoughtfully, Pattwell demonstrates that there is textual evidence that the compiler of the *Exornatorium curatorum* may have been influenced by the later French "translations of the Latin *Opus Tripartitum* rather than reproductions of the original Gersonian French tracts" (xli). For this reason she usefully includes for comparative purposes the 1506 edition of the *Instructions des curez* commissioned by the bishop of Le Mans.

With Francisco Alonso Almeida's edition, we move from religion to medicine. Yet it is obvious throughout his rigorous tour of this area that there was a narrow dividing line between the two, most memorably perhaps in the use of the term *"noli me tangere"* for an ulceration on the face. In the introduction, Alonso Almeida broadly categorizes research on medieval medical material and notes that "recipes can be excerpted, deleted, added, reordered and modified in a remedy book without necessarily affecting its meaning and utility" (10), unlike the academic treatises that are normally organized in logical sequence.

The single manuscript edited here, Glasgow, University Library, MS Hunter 185, in Latin, English, and French, is an attempt by the compiler to bring independent material together; it consists of five parts: a list of plant names; a list of ingredients for medicinal purposes; medical notes; a Middle English herbarium; and medical recipes, prognostic texts, and charms. Alonso Almeida describes the manuscript thoroughly with particular emphasis on the contents, language, and dialectal affinities of the two scribes, whom he localizes in Gloucestershire and Kent and for whom he provides two linguistic profiles. Especially useful is the chart of almost three hundred items in the fifth section of the manuscript (28–34). In this edition, much is done to demystify the different aspects of research on medical manuscripts in terms of indexing methods (by contents or intended audience) and categorization (by academic treatise or popular remedy book). Using Manfred Görlach's 1992 methodology for the study of cookery recipe texts, the editor analyzes the medical recipes in a streamlined way for his readership.

The glossary is probably the only real bone of contention I would have with this edition. The editor takes the unusual step of glossing "all the words contained in the text of H whose spellings and/or meanings differ in any aspect from PDE [present-day English]" (121). While harmless in its way, it results in clogging up the glossary with words that anyone with a modicum of understanding could easily decipher ("aboue," "afore," and so on) and with numerous cross-references (there are four slightly different spellings of "uenym"). It might have been better to have had a glossary shorn of common words so that a new readership could clearly see the sort of specialized words found in medical texts, something that the editor so usefully discusses in his sections on medical etymology.

However, like the other editors here, overall Alonso Almeida has discharged his responsibilities well. The three volumes here are part of an important editorial series, currently celebrating its fortieth year of publication since its institution by Manfred Görlach and Oliver Pickering. Given the many volumes produced since 1975, it would be extremely useful if the publishers could be encouraged to provide at the end of each volume a list of the previous published editions in the Middle English Texts series; its light should not be hidden under a bushel.

Veronica O'Mara, University of Hull

CAROL M. MEALE AND DEREK PEARSALL, EDS.
Makers and Users of Medieval Books: Essays in Honour of A. S. G. Edwards.
Woodbridge: Boydell and Brewer in association with D. S. Brewer, 2014.
259 pp. plus xvi.

There is probably no scholar to whom fellow medievalists across a wide range of subject areas owe more than Tony Edwards, for his vast and detailed knowledge and the energy and industry, over nearly five decades, of his researches and publications. He is a pioneer (like this festschrift's two editors) in that modern history of the book that has revolutionized criticism and bibliography, and one of the pioneers, too, in investigating what, at the outset of Edwards' career, many still dismissed as C. S. Lewis's "drab" period: the transition between medieval and Renaissance and between manuscript and print; Edwards's early publications, on Lydgate, Skelton, and Cavendish, among others, were centered on the fifteenth and earlier sixteenth centuries. A cornucopia of studies and editions of individual authors and manuscripts plus major reference and critical compendia on Middle English verse and Middle English prose followed, and this essay collection, with aptly matching characteristics of abundance, multiplicity, and meticulous innovative scholarship, is both an expression of appreciation and an important research publication in its own right.

New work on manuscript miscellanies is a major component. Orietta Da Rold argues both generally for attention to evidence from the physical makeup of manuscripts and specifically, in the case of Oxford Bodleian MS Laud Misc. 108, for the clues in its twelve-leaf quiring system, inter alia, to the likelihood of Oxford production, which she suggests could be extended to other thirteenth-century manuscripts containing English items. Susanna Fein's "The Fillers of the Auchinleck Manuscript and the Literary Culture of the West Midlands" is a complex inquiry into how far a group of vernacular moralizing and eschatological items in Auchinleck and certain other anthologies represents both a specifically West Midland literary canon and the channels of influence between the circles within which Auchinleck, British Library MS Harley 2253, Bodleian MS Digby 86, and some other miscellanies were produced. John Scattergood shows Trinity College Dublin MS 516 to be a personal compilation by a mid-fifteenth-century Bedfordshire vicar, John Benet, whose tastes tended toward history, politics, and political prophecies; the Latin and English texts convey Benet's "utilitarian" cast of mind in his preference for factual over entertaining, his literary or even spiritual reading, and his efficient organization of some sections.

At the extreme end of the scale for manuscript and data organization, the reference work with more than fifteen hundred items created by another fifteenth-century English cleric, John Whethamstede's *Granarium*, is, Alfred Hiatt shows, without parallel before or since: in its comprehensiveness and taxonomic complexity and its combination of classical and humanist knowledge with the medieval encyclopedic tradition. Rich multiplicity in quite different respects marks Martha Driver's exposition of the dazzling range of meanings, contexts, and purposes of the many things termed "pageants" in the late-medieval period. This paper will be illuminating for scholars in many areas. "Pageant" proves a multivalent concept and practice and one remarkably attuned to many aspects of fifteenth-century culture and society.

Carol M. Meale argues persuasively for Katherine de la Pole as a hitherto unrecognized patron of the fifteenth-century East Anglian book trade. If Katherine commissioned both some texts in Princeton MS Garrett 141 and Tokyo MS Takamiya 38 and those manuscripts' production, this demonstrates a woman playing a distinctive part in codicological and literary history. Kathleen L. Scott furnishes an annotated conspectus, packed with potential value for developing research, of 182 merchant owners of both manuscripts and printed books (with evidence of financial backing for printing from this class, too), derived from book inscriptions and allusions in other sources. Toshiyuki Takamiya and Richard Linenthal, on early printed Continental books owned in Britain, offer detailed accounts of five out of forty in the Takamiya collection: four with evidence of pre-Reformation monastic ownership (Fountains and Hailes abbeys, the Ashridge College of Good Men, and an unidentified Scottish house) and a fifth bound by Wynkyn de Worde, whose printed pastedowns reveal unique evidence of a compositor's work.

A. I. Doyle unpicks a tangled web arising from his discovery of an earlier version of More's 1523 response to Luther, printed by Pynson, involving international political conflict, pseudonymous literary disguises, insults, elaborate fictitious backstories, and serious religious controversy, all at the highest level of international drama conceivable within a study of Henrician printing. Following another complex trail in "From Poggio to Caxton: Early

Translations of some of Poggio's Latin *Facetiae*," Lotte Hellinga uncovers, among other things, how Poggio's often bawdy and anticlerical fables stimulated Caxton to some unusually lively writing. Analogous detective work leads Nicolas Barker to speculate about the story behind the replacement by the Scales Binder of an earlier yellow-silk and silver-clasped binding for Bodleian MS Tanner 190; clues point to the originally Italian volume having been "liberated" from the French Royal collection, among other adventures, and reaching England as war booty—perhaps consequently somewhat the worse for wear and in need of rebinding

John J. Thompson examines the afterlife of Nicholas Love's *Mirror* from the fourteenth to the sixteenth century, asking how the type of reading experience it inculcates may have fared amid a period of religious reformations and counterreformations. The repackaging of Love in the 1530s as part of guided meditational reading as an orthodox counter to Tyndale's English Bible leads Thompson to speculate whether the practice of interiorized spiritual reading and meditation might have offered a comforting retreat for the soul in a society buffeted by religious change and hostilities. John Burrow, exploring whether *Winner and Waster* perhaps influenced Langland, concludes that if so, *Piers Plowman* eschews the earlier poem's provocatively subtly ambivalent approach to winning and wasting.

Jane Griffiths shows Crowley's 1550 editions presenting *Piers Plowman* diversely, encouraging readers' own interpretations: his paratextual additions package it for sixteenth-century readers as both a national literary classic and reformist polemic, but Crowley also insists that it is no simple, triumphalist prophecy of Catholicism's downfall. Yet one reader's annotations show strong resistance to Crowley's approach. Chaucer's editorial afterlife appears in Simon Horobin's investigation into the collation and annotation by the early eighteenth-century antiquarian Beaupré Bell of several Chaucer texts. Horobin locates these in the context of widespread contemporary dissatisfaction with Urry's 1721 edition, arguing both that Bell contemplated an edition and that his methods, including his blunders, testify to contemporary attitudes and assumptions toward editing.

Powerful manifestation of how texts and interpretations over time are subject to *mouvance* and cultural, credal, or physical refashioning is just one welcome element in this excellent volume full of new research that will be widely valued.

Helen Phillips, Cardiff University

RICHARD J. MOLL, ED.
William Caxton: The Book of Ovyde Named Methamorphose.
Studies and Texts 182.
British Writers of the Middle Ages and the Early Modern Period 4.
Toronto, Canada: PIMS and Bodleian Library, 2013. 652 pp.

It was William Caxton who first produced an English translation of Ovid's *Metamorphoses*, no doubt one of the most influential classical texts in the English literary world. Caxton—a merchant, diplomat, and publisher-printer—was also a prolific translator. He translated and published twenty-one works in English, mainly from French but also from Latin and Dutch. According to Wynkyn de Worde, Caxton's successor, Caxton was a diligent translator who "fynysshed" translating *Lives of the Fathers* from French into English "at the laste daye of hys lyff," a project de Worde completed by publishing and printing his master's translation (7).

Caxton's translation of *The Booke of Ovyde Named Methamorphose*, however, does not exist as a printed edition. Only part of it, Books 10 to 15, was known to have survived for almost five hundred years, until 1966, when a manuscript containing Books 1 to 9 of his translation was rediscovered. The English literary world then had to wait almost another half a century before Richard J. Moll's eagerly awaited edition appeared in 2013.

Moll's introduction opens with an account of the reunion of the two volumes of the single manuscript. Caxton's translation of Books 10 to 15, Cambridge, Magdalene College, Pepys Library 2124, has been known to be in the Pepys library since 1688, while the copy that contains Books 1 to 9 had been long lost as "the very rubbish of the Thomas Phillipps collection" (2). The rediscovered Phillipps manuscript was put up for an auction in London in 1966 and initially sold to an American collector. Public appeals in the United Kingdom managed to raise only 22 percent of the necessary matching funds needed to keep it in Britain, and the Phillipps manuscript was about to be separated from the other half of the manuscript by the Atlantic Ocean. Then George Braziller came up with an idea to publish and sell facsimiles of the manuscript as a way to raise the funds. The first half of the manuscript is now Cambridge, Magdalene College, Old Library F.4.32, and it sits "together in a display case" with the Pepys manuscript (2).

Moll's edition is the first critical edition of Caxton's entire translation. The text of the single extant manuscript is "presented with a minimum of editorial interventions" (48). Hence cases of Caxton's mistranslation, such as Daedalion to be transformed into an "ostrich" rather than a "goshawk," are allowed to stand as they are (note to 11.732). The text, which was produced "with a wide range of readers in mind" (2), has modern capitalization and punctuation and hence is easy to read, particularly with the aid of an extensive glossary (577–609), a useful index of proper names, which gives both Middle English and modern forms (610–652), and an introduction to the grammatical features of Caxton's language (36–41).

The extensive introduction also invites further scholarly investigation into hitherto understudied areas. For example, Moll untangles some of the complicated textual tradition of Ovid's works before Caxton. Caxton used the French *Ovide moralisé* in prose as the source text of his translation. This prose *Ovide moralisé* was itself an adaptation of the French verse *Ovide moralisé*. The verse version contained multiple layers of interpretation and explanation of Ovid's original poem, but the anonymous author of the prose version reproduced "only the historical and moral interpretations of its verse source" and removed the "Christian allegorizations" (21). Three manuscripts of the French prose version survive, although none of them was used by Caxton as a base text for his translation (22). The analysis of textual errors suggests that Caxton's text and the London manuscript both derived from a now-lost common source (α), while manuscripts now in Paris and Saint Petersburg derived from a different copy (β).

Moll's central interest, of course, lies in Caxton's text; hence Moll does not discuss the textual relationships between the three manuscripts further and only occasionally cites, in his Explanatory Notes, readings of the French source, primarily using the Saint Petersburg manuscript (50–51). In the absence of a critical edition of the French *Ovide moralisé* in prose, readers are left to speculate about the reasons behind Moll's choice of the Saint Petersburg manuscript as his main source.

According to Moll, Caxton mostly translated his base text closely and conformed to the style of its source. On very rare occasions, however, Caxton "added some rhetorical colour" (29) and his own comments to his translation (35). Caxton's translation techniques would be worth further investigation. Moll's appendices, which offer only short extracts of the French source, are useful and yet tantalizing. The unknown origin of the manuscript inevitably stirs our further interests, too. There is no scholarly consensus as to whether Caxton printed his *Methamorphose*. Some scholars argue that Caxton never printed the book, whereas Moll takes the stance that the extant manuscript was a presentation copy made from Caxton's printed copy.[1] Moll examines unusual errors in the manuscript, as "typographical errors are very different from paleographical errors," but he identifies only nineteen unusual errors, out of which only one might be a typical typographical error. This is "scant evidence" for unusual errors as he admits (43–45).

Caxton himself says that he finished his translation in 1480 (498), while Caxton's *Methamorphose* was written on the paper also used in Caxton's printed edition of Gower's *Confessio amantis*, completed in 1483 (42). The paper evidence, however, does not necessarily mean that Caxton commissioned the production of the manuscript in Westminster. Other evidence indicates the manuscript's strong connection with Bruges. We know that Caxton's source, the French *Ovide moralisé* in prose, was probably written in Bruges in the 1470s (22), and it is suggested that the manuscript of it now in London was written for Edward IV (20). The script of the manuscript of Caxton's *Methamorphose* is also in a Flemish style that according to Lotte Hellinga, "fits in with some of the manuscripts produced for Edward IV at this time," and three out of four pictures in the manuscript are attributed to a Dutch artist, probably in Bruges (27).[2] The French *moralisé* was also printed by Colard Mansion in 1484 in Bruges (20), and it had long been thought that Caxton published a series of books in Bruges in collaboration with Mansion before he moved to Westminster.[3]

Recent scholarship, however, suggests that several of Caxton's books were published in Ghent rather in Bruges.[4] Does this make it less likely that Caxton was directly involved with the making of this Dutch-style manuscript of *The Booke of Ovyde Named Methamorphose*? Moll's introduction thus provokes intriguing questions. His edition of the entire text of Caxton's translation will no doubt "renew interest in Caxton's text" and "encourage study of it in its own right" (2) as well as inspiring more work on the production of manuscripts and printed books in the fifteenth century both in Flanders and England.

Takako Kato, De Montfort University

NOTES

1. William Kuskin, *Symbolic Caxton: Literary Culture and Print Capitalism* (Notre Dame, IN: University of Notre Dame Press, 2007), 241; Lotte Hellinga, *William Caxton and Early Printing in England* (London: British

Library, 2010), 74; Karen Cherewatuk, "Malory's Thighs and Launcelot's Buttock: Ignoble Wounds and Moral Transgression in the *Morte Darthur*," in *Arthurian Literature XXXI*, ed. Elizabeth Archibald and David F. Johnson (Cambridge, UK: Brewer, 2014), 35–60, at 58.
2. Hellinga, William Caxton, 73.
3. For example, Moll discusses the publication of the *Recuyell of the Historyes of Troye* in Bruges (5).
4. The Incunabula Short Title Catalogue (ISTC) record of the *Recuyell* suggests it may have been published in Ghent; see ISTC number il00117000 at http://www.bl.uk/catalogues/istc/index.html. See also Hellinga, *William Caxton*, 51.

ED POTTEN AND SATOKO TOKUNAGA, EDS.
Incunabula on the Move: The Production, Circulation and Collection of Early Printed Books.
Transactions of the Cambridge Bibliographical Society XV, Part 1 (2012). Cambridge, UK: Cambridge Bibliographical Society, 2015. 175 pp.

This important book contains the proceedings of a day-long conference held at Clare College Cambridge on March 6, 2012. The conference (with the same title as the volume) was held to commemorate the birth in 1912 of J. C. T. Oates and was sponsored by two important current incunable projects, Cambridge University Library's Incunabula Cataloguing Project (funded by the Andrew W. Mellon Foundation) and the Early Illustrated Book Research Initiative (funded by Keio University).The aims and achievements of the conference are explained in a succinct Introduction by the editors (each of whom is allied to one of the projects) with the subtitle, "The Current State and Future Direction of Incunabula Studies."

In "Ulrich Zel's Early Quartos Revisited," Paul Needham offers an important overview and valuable new analysis of Cologne's first printer. He first reviews the opinions of Robert Proctor (1898), Ernst Voulliéme (1903), A. W. Pollard (1908), Francis Jenkinson (1908/1926), and Severin Corsten (2007) on the sequence of the early quartos. As he says, "It is worth the effort to understand the bases of their reasonings, and to consider whether other approaches can test and extend their results" (11). A table compares the chronological orders of Proctor, Voulliéme, Jenkinson, and Corsten in relation to the printing type, lines per page, and pinholes. However, it is in Needham's specialist area, paper stocks, that he is able to argue that these "provide a promising new approach to the challenge of finding relative chronologies within Zel's Type-1 quartos" (27), and in doing so, he reinforces Jenkinson's chronology, drawn up as preparation for his 1908 Sandars lecture, which was not published until 1926, after his death. Appendix 1 offers "Notes on Tract Volumes Containing Zel and Other Early Cologne Quartos," and Appendix 2 provides "Francis Jenkinson's List of Early Zel quartos." There are seven color plates.

Satoko Tokunaga, the author of the next essay, is working with Takako Kato to create an online database of copy-specific features. The preliminary results of this research are presented as "Rubrication in Caxton's Early English Books, c.1476–1478." Rubrication can appear in many forms, but for the purpose of comparative analysis, initial letters, paragraph marks, underlinings, and initial strokes are considered in Caxton's six folio and fifteen quarto editions issued between 1476 and 1478, of which sixty-one of the seventy-five recorded copies have so far been examined, thirty-eight of which contain rubrication. In the quartos, rubrication of initials was only minimally intended and almost never executed, it seems, whereas rubrication was an important element of the folios, particularly in *The Canterbury Tales*, *The History of Jason*, and *The Dictes and Sayings of the Philosophers* (1476–1477) when compared with the 1478 folios. Strikingly, although the research is still at an early stage, "the diverse but regular appearance of rubrication across multiple copies supports the hypothesis that the books were rubricated soon after printing," perhaps in or around the printing house (70). Eight color plates support the argument.

The remaining essays are more discursive and of a later period than the first two, with the exception of the sixth essay, "The Woodcut as Exemplar: Sources of Inspiration for the Decoration of a Venetian Incunabulum," by Laura Nuvoloni. This essay, which was commissioned after the conference, might have been better last in the volume, since it deals with a recent purchase (in the same month as the conference) by Cambridge University Library of a copy of the second volume of a Latin Bible printed in Venice in 1482 to 1483 by Franciscus Renner of Heilbronn, one of the first German printers to settle in Venice. (The final essay in the volume, by Emily Dourish and William Hale, also freshly commissioned, ends with mention of this purchase.) With the aid of six color plates, the essay identifies Anton Koberger's 1481 edition of Nicholas of Lyra's *Postilla* or one of his four editions of the *Biblia latina cum postillis Nicholai de Lyra* as the source of inspiration of the rare hand-drawn illustrations of the Book of Ezekiel (devised by Nicholas to accompany his commentary on the Bible) found in the Cambridge purchase.

The remaining essays are broadly chronological (1789 to the present day) and of interest to the general bibliophile as well as the academic. The third essay provides important new information on fifteen copies of Gutenberg's 42-Line Bible, printed in Mainz around 1455. In "Gutenberg Bibles on the Move in England, 1789–1834," Eric Marshall White reveals how

British bibliophiles benefited from the Napoleonic monastic depredations and uncovers new, extra, and corrective material about these copies, all in England or Scotland during this period (but only six remaining in the British Isles today). Of particular interest (in a particularly interesting essay) are White's new provenances for three copies, the vellum copy in the British Library, Lord Spencer's copy in the John Rylands Library, Manchester (although the clinching inscription is unreadable in the plate, 100), and the Huntington Library copy. A table lists the provenances and sources with the present locations.

As White says, "Research into book provenances ... is a marriage of bibliography and biography that offers a powerful tool for answering larger historical questions" (79). This is true of both White's essay and the following one, by John Goldfinch. Its plain title, "Movements of Incunabula between the Former British Museum Library and the University Library in Cambridge," conceals a fascinating and sometimes horrifying story of when, how, and why incunables were sold and exchanged between these two and other libraries and even individual book collectors. Sometimes no money or exchange was required. One can applaud the spirit in which duplicate copies were sent to the new municipal reference libraries in the late nineteenth and early twentieth centuries while worrying whether these libraries now, in more philistine times, still guard and cherish their important donations or are even aware that they were gifts of the British Museum (which kept no systematic list of the books that were sent). The latest book exchange on the British Museum's part would appear to have been in 1957, when fifteen British Museum duplicate incunables were sent to Cambridge University Library, four of them from Hans Sloane's library. Goldfinch writes dryly and tellingly, ending with the rather shocking breaking up at Cambridge University Library in 1960 of the British Museum Library's second Royal Library copy of the *Recuyell of the historyes of Troye* (1473–1474) in order to exchange it for a Caxton *Vocabulary* (1480). The appendix consists of "Lists of Incunabula Included in the Donations and Exchanges between the British Museum Library and Cambridge University Library, in 1889, 1948, and 1957."

Perhaps next in terms of subject matter should be the last essay in the volume, "Incunabula on the Increase: The Development of Cambridge University Library's Incunabula Collections after 1954," by Emily Dourish and William Hale. Indeed, the essay sheds a little more light on Goldfinch's *Recuyell* story: the exchange was with H. P. Kraus. Dourish and Hale were involved in the Incunabula Cataloguing Project, which lists online the university's incunables and supplements Oates's catalogue information by additional copy-specific details. They use the evidence of the 277 incunables obtained since 1954 (140 bought and the rest donated) to study patterns of acquisition, taste, and practice over the intervening sixty years, ending with the purchase of the Lyra Bible discussed by Nuvoloni. Finally, although not final in the volume, in "Bibliophiles in Cambridge, 1975–1978: A Reminiscence," Toshiyuki Takamiya recalls his three years as a graduate student in Cambridge, the scholars he met, and the lifetime habits and knowledge he imbibed, along with the friendships.

This is an important book, packed with valuable information, and a worthy tribute to the memory of Oates, university librarian, past president of the Cambridge Bibliographical Society, and author of *A Catalogue of the Fifteenth-Century Printed Books in the University Library Cambridge* (Cambridge, 1954).

Susan Powell, University of Salford

**ROBERT R. RAYMO AND JUDITH G. RAYMO, COMPILERS;
SHARI PERKINS AND JARED CAMINS-ESAKOV, EDS.**
The Chaucer Collection of Robert R. Raymo.
New York: privately printed, 2015.

Robert Raymo, a scholar of dignity and distinction in the field of medieval English, died in 2009, and his wife, Judith, who was always party to his enterprises, has brought out in his memory a catalogue of their Chaucer collection. It harks back to an exhibition of part of the collection in 2000, on the six-hundredth anniversary of Chaucer's death, and the centenary of the similar Grolier Club exhibition in 1900. The present little book is a work of some dedication, but it is also fascinating in its own right. It contains all kinds of Chaucer materials, not only books, but the prize of the collection is undoubtedly an almost uninterrupted sequence of the great editions of the complete works of Chaucer—and of course, "complete" in the first two centuries meant more than complete.

The sequence begins with William Thynne's edition of 1532, continues with a revised reprint of the same (1548–1550), the edition of 1561 by John Stow, the two editions by Thomas Speght (1598 and 1602), and the revised reprint of 1687, and concludes with the highly original edition by Thomas Urry (1721), the first in roman type (all those preceding were in black letter), with its interesting but disastrously innovative spelling. Many editions and reprints followed; the "modern" era began with the return to the manuscripts in Thomas Tyrwhitt's edition of the *Canterbury Tales* (1775–1778) and Thomas Wright's edition of 1847 to 1851 and truly came into its own with the monumental edition by W. W. Skeat (1894–1897). The collection continues up to the present day, the only significant omission being the first edition of F. N. Robinson (1933), which could have been picked up at any secondhand bookshop (or from me, though my copy is much disfigured by enthusiastic undergraduate scribblings). There are also the magnificent art editions from the Kelmscott Press (1896), the Golden Cockerel Press (1927), the Shakespeare Head Press (1928) and the Basilisk Press (1975): all are here.

With the long procession of modern editions of the *Works* or of single or selected poems, the interest shifts to items of more particular interest, especially for reception studies—translations, for instance, not only into modern English verse and prose (with "impurities expunged" in Cowden-Clarke, 1835), but also into many foreign languages, some of them unexpected, like Swedish (1938), Czech (1956), Welsh (1976), Georgian (1977), and Hebrew (1980). Then there are eighty versions with pictures, including nearly twenty written for children, and perhaps to be added to that number is a version of the Miller's Tale with "cheering drawings" (1961); dramatic versions, the first in 1903, one of the most recent (1994) a pantomime; and editions of special interest to collectors, with owners' inscriptions, or reader's marginalia, or fine bindings, or fine paper. There are many oddities that one would like to see, though most will be able to do without a version of the Reeve's Tale prepared by J. R. R. Tolkien for recitation at a "summer diversion" and privately printed (1939); or excerpts from the *Canterbury Tales* presented as "an evening's entertainment" by the Little Red Schoolhouse (1964); or the Wife of Bath's Prologue presented as "a liberated woman's great story," profusely illustrated (1973); or a version of the Franklin's Tale by Suky Best, a photorealist, called "Photo-Love No. 3: Dorigen's Promise" (1998).

Interest sags in the long listings of familiar critical studies, biographies, anthologies, and literary histories that follow, even though some are old and valuable in themselves, like Richard Braithwaite's commentary on two of the *Tales* (1665), Warton's *History of English Poetry* (1774–1781), Godwin's *Life of Chaucer* (1804), and Todd's *Illustrations of Gower and Chaucer* (1810). Oddities abound, both of inclusion and categorization, such as the address on the occasion of the installation of the incised carving "Alleluia" by Eric Gill, illustrator of the Golden Cockerel edition, in the gallery of the Bridwell Library at Southern Methodist University in 1980, or the book by Irving Ungar, *Justice Illuminated; The Art of Arthur Szyk*, an artist who produced a series of pilgrim portraits, published in Berkeley by Frog (1999). "The Wife of Beith's [*sic*] Reception at the Gates of Hell" (1777) is more promising (the devil would not let her in). There are some famous old engravings, such as the Pilgrims on their way to Canterbury by William Blake (1810/1860) and Thomas Stothard (1817), and portraits of Chaucer, like that of George Vertue (1717) and another, new to me, supposed to have been found in 1803 in the house where Oliver Cromwell was born.

The rest is for fun alone: a collection of "Imitations and Parodies" with a graphic novel by Seymour Chwast, the cover showing the Wife of Bath on a bicycle (2011); a board game called "Hazard" based on the *Tales* (1995); miniature books, including one with the *Tales* pictured on a front cover half an inch by three-quarters but blank pages for the rest, and another, only a little larger, containing a selection of the *Tales*, supposed to have been carried into space by an astronaut. There are recordings of readings, including one by Raymo himself on radio on the occasion of the publication of the *Riverside Chaucer* in 1987; figurines, a jug, a mug, a magnet, all with Chaucer subjects; and finally, to ensure that no barrel remains unscraped, some "ephemera"—cigarette cards, postage stamps (from St. Vincent in the West Indies), and "Chaucer's magnetic quip kit." Eccentric as much of this stuff is, it does testify to the ubiquity of Chaucer, at least a certain version of him, in the modern cultural imagination.

Derek A. Pearsall, Harvard University

RICHARD H. ROUSE AND MARY A. ROUSE
Bound Fast with Letters: Medieval Writers, Readers, and Texts.
Foreword by Robert Somerville.
Notre Dame, IN: University of Notre Dame Press, 2013. xvi + 570 pp.,
incl. many col. figs.

This is the second collection of reprints or revisions of previously published essays and lectures (the first entitled *Authentic Witnesses*, also from Notre Dame Press, 1991) by what is a remarkable and perhaps unique scholarly partnership. The book contains eighteen chapters and is divided into four parts: I. "Writing It Down, Practicalities and Images 500–1200"; II. "Patrons and the Use of Books, 1250–1400"; III. "Commercial Book-Makers, French and Italian, 1290–1410"; IV. "Epilogue, Archives in the Service of Manuscript Study, Nicolas Flamel." After the Foreword and the authors' general Introduction, each part has its own introduction and each of the chapters a few preliminary lines explaining its significance.

For the readers of this *Journal* it will be Parts II–IV, Chapters 6–18 which will have most relevance, but they would be unwise to ignore Chapter 1, on the vocabulary of wax tablets, for its applicability throughout the Middle Ages. One only misses any references to the survival of physical specimens, some of the most striking being in France, the focus of most of the volume. Readers might also be interested in Chapter 4, "From Flax to Parchment," in which I must confess personal involvement, for its general interest.

The Rouses' early major achievements within the scope of our Society were discovery of the actual identity of the compiler at Bury St. Edmunds of the mid-fourteenth-century union catalogue of books in English monastic libraries and its immediate predecessor from the Oxford Franciscans, and the indexing of patristic commentators on Holy Scripture, both of which they edited for the Corpus of British Medieval Library Catalogues (CBMLC II and XI). They then moved on to fascinating studies in detail of the personnel of the Parisian book trade, which, as they remark in their last chapter, no one, surprisingly, had done before (for all the work done on illuminators in the same period). The majority of the chapters here are by-products of those researches, concerning French texts and some Latin, running into the fifteenth century. They lament how few historians absorbed with archives and those engaged with manuscript books look into the other resources. One might also notice how few archivists have paid attention to the hands that occur in both, only quite recently (if sometimes arguably) undertaken in England.

    A. I. Doyle, University of Durham

FIONA SOMERSET AND NICHOLAS WATSON, EDS.
Truth and Tales: Cultural Mobility and Medieval Media.
Columbus: Ohio State University Press, 2015.

This book, edited by Fiona Somerset and Nicholas Watson, brings together fourteen essays, many by well-known names in Middle English literary studies, related by their central concern with law and ethics, truth and falsehood, nobility, social class, and social mobility, as played out in Middle English literature. Throughout Richard Firth Green's career, these have been concerns central to his research and publications, and while his is the first essay in the book, the remainder is in effect a festschrift for him: the editors and other eleven authors dedicate the book to him as "friend, colleague, teacher, mentor, model." Since the fourteen essays are so tightly related to the central topic, this is a model for the kind of festschrift that both scholars and publishers must welcome.

The book's contents are divided into five sections; the first on "The Truth of Tales," contains only Green's essay on two medieval urban legends about truth. The second section, on "The Claims of History," contains chapters by Thomas Hahn, Stephen Yeager, M. J. Toswell, and Fiona Somerset; the third, on "Cultural Divides and Their Common Grounds," contains chapters by Alastair Minnis, Michael Johnston, Lisa J. Kiser, and Barbara A. Hanawalt; while the fourth, on "New Media and the Literate Laity," contains chapters by Nicholas Watson, Robyn Malo, Kathleen E. Kennedy, and Michael Van Dussen. A final section, "The Truth of Tales 2," contains a single chapter by Andrew Taylor to mirror Green's at the beginning. Many of these names will be familiar to scholars of Middle English literature, and other contributors represent the new generation of scholars in the subject trained or mentored by Green. It is a blockbuster collection, an excellent tribute to Richard Firth Green. Only a few of the articles in the book deal with issues of manuscript and early print production and dissemination, the central concern of most readers of *JEBS*, so I just focus on those in the remainder of this review.

Michael Johnston's essay (135–150) on "Mercantile Gentility in Cambridge, University Library MS Ff.3.38" is more about the close social status of franklins on the lowest rung of the rural landed class and that of merchants on the highest of the urban bourgeoisie than it is about the Cambridge manuscript. The portion of the argument of greatest interest to manuscript scholars comes when Johnston argues that CUL Ff.3.38 can be identified as having been produced in Leicester or its surrounds as an urban household book, and thus its inclusion of the unique copy of "A Good Matter of the Merchant and His Son," which illustrates the noble generosity of a merchant in contrast to the rapacity of a franklin, seems appropriate to this milieu (141–142). For *JEBS* readers, the argument for Leicester provenance based not only on *LALME* but also on the manuscript's connections with Oxford, Bodleian Library, Ashmole 61, which is linked to Leicester by several of the texts it contains (and Johnston's having shown elsewhere that these two manuscripts share a paper stock; *JEBS* 15, 85–100), may be of greatest interest.

The argument about the question of gentility, synonymous with generosity, is further developed by contrast with the romance of *Octavian*, which comes only thirty folios later in the Cambridge manuscript, because the romance illustrates the opposite argument: that gentility (generosity) is innate and is revealed even when the subject (Octavian) is himself unaware of his status. Johnston concludes that the story of "A Good Matter of the Merchant and His Son" in CUL Ff.3.38 "marks an incipient attempt to carve out a place for urban socioeconomics within literary culture" but that "its inclusion alongside *Octavian* reminds us that this was a premature effort" (150).

Nicholas Watson's chapter, "The Ignorance of the Laity: *Twelve Tracts on Bible Translation*" (187–205), relates to the titular Middle English tract(s) that survive in their fullest version uniquely in Cambridge University Library MS Ii.6.26. The argument for dating the *Twelve Tracts* and relating them to other texts advocating translations of the Bible is of course superb, well worth reading, but does not deal much, if at all, with the manuscript context.

Robyn Malo, "York Merchants at Prayer: The Confessional Formula of the Bolton Hours" (206–222), has a stronger focus on its manuscript, York Minster Library MS Add. 2, than most chapters in this book. After an excellent review of previous scholarship establishing ownership of the manuscript by the Blakburn and Bolton families, wealthy mercantile families from the Mickelgate area of York, Malo dissects the confessional formula added to folios 1 to 4 and 209 to 210 at the beginning and end of the volume by a hand of the mid-fifteenth century. She finds that the confessional deviates from standard language for confessing the Seven Deadly Sins or breaking the Ten Commandments and concludes that these anomalies are not born out of ignorance but are deliberate modifications to suit members of these families who recognized their status in the community, recognized the need to maintain good relations with other families of similar status, and made allowances for activity that helped to maintain the family business and the family's status. In this respect, she argues, the Bolton Hours confessional formula is similar to other lay-produced penitential literature such as Peter Idley's *Instructions to His Son*, in that both adapted standard texts (*summae confessorum* or manuals such as John Mirk's *Instructions for Parish Priests* or Robert Mannyng of Brunne's *Handlyng Synne*) "to better suit their [Boltons' or Idley's] environments" (222). She concludes:

> We need to develop a more radical way of thinking about devotional literature that acknowledges the possibility that lay readers did not always mirror clerical interests and concerns—an approach that might encompass the worldview of the Bolton Hours' confessional formula, which explores how virtuous, moneymaking participants in the active life might achieve salvation too. (222)

Finally, among chapters relating to manuscripts and print, Kathleen E. Kennedy writes on "A London Legal Miscellany, Popular Law, and Medieval Print Culture" (223–237), with a focus on the printing of Richard Arnold's book on London antiquities by Adriaen van Berghenin 1502 and its subsequent printing history. Kennedy describes Arnold's professional life and personal connections in relation to the kinds of legal and civic documents he collected in his Book, comparing his collection (presumed to have existed in manuscript before it was printed) with others such as the books of customs compiled by city officials and other anthologies collected by the London fishmonger who owned BL Egerton 2885 and the compiler of BL Additional 38131, but in particular with Sir Thomas Cook's legal miscellany, Cambridge, Trinity College O.3.11. She writes, "Though we cannot know why or how Arnold's own manuscript came to this fate, Arnold's Book happened to be the version of this popular form of manuscript miscellany that ended up in print" (232).

The remainder of the article considers the several printed editions of Arnold's Book and re-editions, extracts, and summaries of the book that were subsequently printed by Treveris, Rastell, Wyer, and Redman. Kennedy considers why there was a flourish of such printings particularly in the 1540s and why the content of Arnold's Book continued to appeal to London book-buyers for more than a century. She concludes, "Arnold's Book stands at the very beginning of this process [of publishing legal materials for the popular market], and facilitated the development of this popular publishing trend until the professional law printers like Redman took over" (237).

These articles of particular interest to *JEBS* readers are only a few in this interesting and informative collection, well worth a perusal or purchase to grace the shelves of any institutional or personal library.

Linne R. Mooney, University of York

JOHN SCATTERGOOD
John Skelton: The Career of an Early Tudor Poet.
Dublin: Four Courts Press, 2014. 432 pp. + 5 illustrations.

Skelton was in his own time a challenging writer, one who both leveled and prompted criticism, and his reputation since his death in 1529 has been an uneven one. John Scattergood's very substantial new study aims to "describe the shape and details of this extraordinary career with all its contradictions and inconsistencies." To this end it offers a richly detailed account of Skelton's various affiliations—at court, as a parish priest, as a member of a London circle of scholars and ecclesiasts—and explores in revealing depth the conventions and modes that informed the works he produced. Although Skelton's oeuvre obstinately resists easy categorization, its impulses are broadly those of praise or blame, and a persuasive case is made here for his cultivation of an ethical poetic. Working with biographical and much other historical detail, Scattergood constructs a series of contexts significant to Skelton's creative practice and explores the variety of ways in which these were likely to have been influential on Skelton's decisions about what and how to write.

These contexts situate Skelton first at the court of Henry VII, serving as tutor to the princes Arthur and Henry, and while producing works in both prose and verse relevant to the exercise of rule, also writing in *The Bowge of Court* about the precariousness of court life and exploring the potentialities of elegy and different forms of lyric verse. His years at Diss, from 1503 to 1512, are seen to have prompted experiments with a poetic informed by confessional and liturgical modes. Skelton's return to London and Westminster, and his new role as *orator regis,* meant the cultivation of a more obviously public voice, exercised in poems celebrating events such as the English victory at Flodden. Not all the writing of these years was celebratory, however, and the chapters on this part of his career deal successively with the variously open and subversive kinds of critique launched by Skelton against an assortment of scholars, grammarians, and statesmen. It is by no means easy to delineate a clear trajectory here, but Scattergood confronts and clarifies the various contradictions apparent in Skelton's writing (his changing views about Wolsey, for example), and interprets them as the inevitable results of his strong, often irascible, engagement with events taking place around him.

The special intensity of this engagement is likely to account in some part for another of the challenges of Skelton scholarship: his evident tendency to rewrite and revise his works, to the extent that accurate definition of the canon of his writings remains difficult. Scattergood acknowledges this briefly in his introductory chapter and returns to it intermittently in discussion of individual works; his focus in the book is not primarily on textual matters, however, but rather on the elucidation of the traditions and contexts informing Skelton's practice.

These traditions—the forms of Latin, English, and sometimes French writing that Skelton knew and worked with—are unfolded across the book in generous and learned but always accessible detail. Forms explored include vituperative exchange, "alewife" poems, allegory, Juvenalian and Menippean satire, elegy, epitaph, and household ordinances; the traditions of Chaucerian and post-Chaucerian verse are also usefully mined. All of these are richly illustrated with a tissue of quotation that brings aspects of Skelton's own practice (in both Latin and English) sharply into relief. The contexts in which and for which Skelton wrote are constructed in equally expansive detail, too, authoritatively informed by Scattergood's extensive knowledge of fifteenth- and sixteenth-century history and its written sources. Chronicles, letters, ambassadorial reports, and sermons are just a few of the forms of writing drawn on here to give some sense of the tide of events to which Skelton responded.

Readers of *JEBS* will be particularly interested in the parts of the book that deal with the transmission and circulation of Skelton's works. The introductory chapter and chapter 3 (on "Songs and Lyrics") make specific use of two early-sixteenth-century manuscript collections, British Library, Harley MS 2252 (John Colyns's book) and Bodleian Library, Rawlinson MS C. 813 (the Welles anthology), to suggest both the social contexts in which Skelton's works were copied and the textual problems inherent in processes of scribal transmission. Other manuscripts such as British Library, Royal MS 18 D ii (a Percy household collection) and Additional MS 26787 (Skelton's *Speculum principis*, seemingly repurposed some years after its production) are discussed and illustrated. The nature of Skelton's contacts with the printers Wynkyn de Worde, Richard Pynson, and Richard Faques is treated in relation to particular works and is seen as especially relevant to the publication of propaganda poems and to his intervention in the so-called "Grammarians' War" of 1519 to 1521.

As the author notes in the preface, this book has had a long gestation. It is also a long book, running to more than four hundred pages. It is a timely companion to John Scattergood's revised edition of *The Complete English Poems of John Skelton*, recently published by Liverpool University Press in the Exeter Medieval Texts and Studies series, and it offers readers much food for thought as well as copious amounts of information and persuasive readings of individual poems. As an historian, a literary scholar widely read both inside and outside the late-medieval and early-modern periods, and an acute and sensitive critic, Scattergood is concerned to understand how and why Skelton wrote "in order to make something happen" (416). In its scope and depth, this book offers a rewardingly comprehensive study of Skelton's life and writings. It is at the same time a compelling study of the business of being a late-medieval or early-modern author.

Julia Boffey, Queen Mary University, London

DANIEL WAKELIN
Scribal Correction and Literary Craft: English Manuscripts 1375–1510.
Cambridge: Cambridge University Press, 2014. xviii + 345 pp.

While I am interested in scribal assertions that religious texts have been scrutinized and corrected and intrigued by Chaucer's (ironic?) request for such correction in *Troilus and Criseyde*, I would not have thought a whole book might be written on the subject. And I fear that if Daniel Wakelin had expressed surprise to me at the vast number of scribal corrections one encounters in manuscripts, my response might have been a milder version of Joel Harris's: "So what?" (xi). This book demonstrates how wrong I would have been.

In a perceptive and stimulating Chapter 1, Wakelin explains the two halves of the book: the first suggests "that scribes strove to do a good job," the second that "the craft of correcting becomes a little like literary criticism" (8). Both are suggestions that the editor and critic of medieval texts may want to challenge (and this is a book that invites engagement and argument), but Wakelin is careful in arguing his case. "Certainly not" may change to "Well, if you put it like that" in the reader's responses to the sometimes counterintuitive statements made here.

The methodology (10–11) depends on a corpus of all the manuscripts with English in the Huntington Library: fifty-two once-separate books with primarily English content, plus fragments of English in twenty-eight volumes largely in Latin and French, all dating from the second half of the fourteenth century to the turn of the sixteenth century. The sample serves for tabular and statistical purposes, but Wakelin has also used manuscripts from libraries in Britain and the United States that are direct or cognate copies of other manuscripts (there is an index of manuscripts at 335–337). He has also read widely in sometimes surprising works on criticism, poetry, and craftsmanship.

There are four parts: Part I, "Contexts," Part II, "Craft," Part III, "Literary Criticism," and Part IV, "Implications." Part I begins with Chapter 2 ("Inviting Correction"), which is discursive and even playful at times. Chapter 3 ("Copying, Varying and Correcting") introduces the first of several tables with which the book is furnished. Table 3.1 cites the percentages of divergence in direct copies of the prose *Brut* and its continuation and in the *Gilte Legende* and the *Canterbury Tales*, while Table 3.2 does the same with cognate copies of the *Canterbury Tales* and *Piers Plowman*. Tables are not to everyone's taste (and Wakelin does not ultimately make many claims for his), but one can see that the empirical work is necessary (whatever its inherent shortcomings) in the amorphous subject he has chosen to study. What these tables show is the small percentage of divergences (never more than 4 percent) and the variable (but never high) numbers of corrections that remove the divergences. Most of the variation that exists seems to be mechanical error, and, although Wakelin notes (perhaps ruefully) that some English manuscripts show deliberate variation, there is very little evidence of this in his samples (Table 3.3 lists those that do occur in two cognate copies of the *Canterbury Tales*).

Chapter 3 also considers the case of gaps rather than corrections. Wakelin's Huntington Library sample has examples of this in only ten manuscripts, one of which, a *Canterbury Tales* finished by Geoffrey Spirleng in 1476, has twenty gaps which can be compared with the exemplar (Table 3.4) to reveal a particularly conscientious and indeed timid scribe. The conclusions are that most scribes do not diverge from the text and that most corrections remove divergences (but only a fraction of a percent of divergence in the direct copies and only 3-4 percent in the cognate copies).

I describe Chapter 3 at some length in order to explain Wakelin's commendably painstaking methodology. Chapter 4 ("People and Institutions") offers a sensible overview of who scribes and correctors might be. Wakelin is disarmingly honest; in assessing who might correct scribes' work, he admits that a scribe correcting himself may not look very different (or at all different) from another scribe correcting him. However, he attempts to assess the respective work of "scribe" and "collaborator" in his Huntington sample (Table 4.1), with what may be a decisive result: 62 percent overall were corrected by the scribe of the manuscript and only 16 percent by another (the "collaborator"), who seems to be involved very seldom in any scribal stint. According to Wakelin, "This engagement in correcting is what allows the scribes to become skilful readers of what they copy" (76). The chapter ends with "prompts," marginal indications that correction is needed (but rarely supplied, it seems).

Part II ("Craft") consists of three chapters developing Wakelin's belief that scribes were craftsmen, since their "Techniques" (the title of Chapter 5) "foster their agency and intelligence" (101). This first chapter of Part II deals with erasure and overwriting, crossing out, subpuncting, interlineation, and marginal insertions. It also, interestingly, deals with the fact that some corrections are clearly meant to be seen, that is, obvious signs (some as obvious as rubrication) are used to indicate false word order, transposition of words or phrases, omissions, and the like (the term *signes de renvoie* is used). This is an informative discussion, again accompanied by a table and (like Figure 1) far too pale a figure (one longs for the old days of clear glossy plates, especially when reading about the care with which books were once produced).

Chapter 6 ("Accuracy") deals with what Wakelin contends is the first impulse of the scribe: to correct the text before him, even to the extent of collating exemplars (although not mentioned here, this brings to mind James Grenehalgh and Carthusian scribal habits). Of course, "not all the errors are corrected, nor indeed are the corrections all correct" (129). Table 6.1 is presented with many caveats but does at least demonstrate that correction was frequent; of the fifty-two Huntington manuscripts, only two had few (one in ten pages) and only three had many (three in a page). Generally, paper copies and presentation copies are corrected less often, paper being ephemeral and presentation copies having to look good. "Works of religious reflection or instruction" (135) are corrected more than secular works (whether one of the texts, *Piers Plowman*, is really such a work is arguable). In this chapter, it may seem brave of Wakelin to deal with "the quality of correcting" (141), and his methodology (comparing texts with modern editions) may seem precarious, if not foolhardy, but it achieves an interesting result, demonstrating that 84 percent of the corrections accord with the text presented in modern editions.

Chapter 7 ("Writing Well") moves the reader toward the topic of Part III ("Literary Criticism") by perhaps an odd route: the attention scribes pay to what seem to us as readers and scholars minutiae and trivialities (the spelling or the shape of a word) and the concomitant neglect of what we think is important. Wakelin invites us to realize that we look at a page to know what is in it, whereas scribes are trained to look at what is on it. (Editors of medieval texts have to combine the two, of course, as some scribes did). Some of these changes are of interest, such as corrections to archaic verb forms, pronouns, phrases, and the like, but toward the end of the chapter, Wakelin himself appears to have lost patience: the words "needless," "fuss(y)"/"fussiness," and "persnickety" start to appear, and one scribe is even called "this meddler" (180). What I think Wakelin does not consider is the psychology of copying material in which one has no active involvement. By an imperfect analogy, the reading of student essays is alleviated only by having a red pen in one's hand to intervene: I would suggest that for the intelligent scribe, the tedium of copying might only be relieved by personal interventions, however small and ultimately meaningless.

At any rate, the subject matter of Chapter 7, where we reach the depths of scribal correction, is immediately relieved by Chapter 8 ("Diction, Tone and Style"), which, with Part III, introduces the second part of the book's title. Chapter 8 looks at corrections that involve synonyms, doublets, and alternative adjectives and adverbs, in the (forlorn, it seems) hope that they may show more literary engagement with the text than editors have given them credit for. Commendably thorough and impartial as Wakelin is, and aware that the editor and the paleographer approach a text with different mind-sets, nevertheless, in this chapter and later, his statistical approach seemed to me to limit his responses. I regretted the fact that the personality of the individual scribe is not taken into account—Wakelin would probably say "cannot be taken into account" in a study of this sort. Scribes have different personalities, training, attention spans, dexterity, intelligence, contexts, material, and probably much more. Editors come to know these things and to know the scribes of the manuscripts they edit.

Wakelin does indeed offer case studies to balance the tabular method. In one of these, a copy of *The Fall of Princes* with prompts offering alternative words, sixty-eight unerased words and prompts are extant. Only ten of these prompts are given (Table 8.2), some of which correct semantic or eyeskip errors, which Wakelin discusses from a literary-critical perspective but rarely justifies from this perspective. The words of the poem are "tedious" (191), and its "dull wording" (194) might be preferable to the corrections, but what the corrections show, Wakelin suggests, is "the notion that the words they correct are worth such close attention" (195). It seems to me that some of these prompts (iv, vi, viii) offer synonyms with an extra syllable where a line has been mismetered.

This matter of rhyme (together with page layout) is dealt with in Chapter 9 ("Form"). Here Wakelin seems to me visually rather than aurally focused (as he argues his scribes are). The percentage of corrections in verse as opposed to prose is significant: ninety-one to sixty eight (although Wakelin calls the difference "only moderately" corrected, 218, and "only a little more frequently corrected," 226). In his interesting case studies he seems surprised that scribes should worry about rhyme as much as they clearly do. Although at the end of the chapter he comments of one scribe that "he pursues visual regularity remorselessly yet is completely deaf to the sound-patterning" (243), nevertheless he overstresses the "needlessness" (222) of "pointless" (226) corrections to bad rhymes. Those of us who were brought up reciting poetry throughout our school lives cannot help but balk at a lost syllable or a false rhyme. As Wakelin says of one scribe: "The rhyme seems to wake him up at the line's end"; indeed it does, and it implies that reading poetry aloud and learning it by heart were to some extent pleasurable activities for schoolchildren in a now-lost age of much-condemned rote learning. As Wakelin notes, scribes writing verse work faster than those writing prose—it must be more enjoyable to be rushed along by verse than to labor through prose.

Finally, in Part III, Chapter 10 investigates "Completeness," "the negative recognition, born from their practical experience as craftsmen, of the problems of the material texts they make and use" (246). In order to complete texts, scribes either add (marginal annotations and marginal/interlinear addition) or delete (as with an Austin canon scribe from Leicester who, instead of noting gaps or filling them in, deletes what is there). Although rhyme is not particularly foregrounded here, Wakelin's case studies are rhymed texts (other than a brief mention of the "Tale of Melibee"), a fact that tends to confirm my response to the previous chapter: that rhyme is important to scribes not only because it "encourages an 'oculocentric' perception of the text" (252) but because of auditory and oral enactments of the text (however muted or mumbled).

The final part of the book, Part IV, deals with "Implications" in two chapters. Chapter 11 ("Authorship") looks at corrections made by the author rather than the scribe, although there are serious difficulties in some assertions on holographs, as Wakelin's first example shows, where he notes Kari-Anne Rand's forthcoming identification of the hand of *The Equatorie of the Planetis* (not Chaucer's). In looking at Chaucer (?), Capgrave, Hoccleve, and the Franciscan friar James Ryman, Wakelin considers the successive stages of authorship through drafts, final copies, and corrected final copies, raising the question of authorial or scribal revision, when it occurs and why, and pondering what it might amount to. (There is a section on metrical corrections in relation to Hoccleve which I was pleased to see.) The conclusion is somewhat downbeat: "In their corrections, authorial composition and scribal revision look alike, for they share the qualities of responsible attention and critical judgement which this practice nurtures" (301). That is probably a wise conclusion, given that paleography is a very inexact science (or is perhaps an art).

Art is what Wakelin suggests it might be in the final chapter ("Conclusion: Varying, Correcting and Critical Thinking"). As he says, "Distinguishing correction from variance is not easy" (302), but might we be able to think of scribes as authors? Is what they do "wilful creativity" (305)? Well, no, he concludes (although what they do might be the ancestor of what was to become "literary criticism"), but why should we want it to? Perhaps the time for praising variance is past, and now that we have quite enough digital and other forms of variance, "it might be worth praising invariance" (306) and giving credit to scribes as men with "an interest in their own craftsmanship" who paid "close attention to the texts they copied" and had a "consciousness of value" (308–309).

Wakelin's book has been very well planned, with painstakingly collected data, and it demonstrates reading of a wide range of manuscripts and secondary criticism of many different types. This is a learned, provocative, sometimes wrong (I think), but overall stimulating book that I found a pleasure to read and which will affect my reading of the next manuscript I see (and perhaps all the rest, too).

Susan Powell, University of Salford

About the Authors

Julia Boffey is Professor of Medieval Studies in the Department of English at Queen Mary, University of London. Her most recent book *Manuscript and Print in London c. 1475-1530* (British Library, 2012) was reviewed in *JEBS* 16.

Joyce Boro is Professor of English literature at the Université de Montréal. Her work focuses on the English reception of Spanish literature. She is the editor of John Bourchier, *Lord Berners's Castell of Love* (MRTS 2007) and Margaret Tyler's *Mirror of Princely Deeds and Knighthood* (2014), and the author of articles and essays on romance, translation, Lord Berners, John Fletcher, and book history.

Nicole Clifton is Associate Professor of English at Northern Illinois University, where she teaches Middle English literature and language. Her research focuses on Middle English romances and their manuscripts.

Margaret Connolly teaches palaeography and medieval literature at the University of St. Andrews and is a general editor of the Middle English Texts series. Her most recent publication is a collection of essays, *Insular Books: Vernacular Manuscript Miscellanies in Late Medieval Britain* (2015), which she edited jointly with Raluca Radulescu. She has also published a volume for the *Index of Middle English Prose* series, editions of Middle English religious prose texts, and the monograph *John Shirley: Book Production and the Noble Household in Fifteenth-Century England* (1998).

A.I. Doyle is Honorary Reader in Bibliography at Durham University and formerly (for many decades) Keeper of Rare Books at Durham. His areas of expertise range widely around the production and dissemination of manuscripts in northern Europe from 1300 to 1700. Author of many articles on these subjects, he notably supplied masterly introductions to facsimiles of the Vernon Manuscript (1987) and the verse manuscripts of Hoccleve (2002). Doyle is the most widely-cited expert in the field of medieval English paleography.

Martha W. Driver is Distinguished Professor of English and Women's and Gender Studies at Pace University in New York City. A co-founder of the Early Book Society for the study of manuscripts and printing history, she writes about illustration from manuscript to print, book production, and the early history of publishing. In addition to publishing some 55 articles in these areas, she has edited twenty journals over eighteen years, including *Film &*

History: Medieval Period in Film and the *Journal of the Early Book Society*. Her books about pictures (from manuscript miniatures to woodcuts to film) include *The Image in Print: Book Illustration in Late Medieval England* (British Library Publications and University of Toronto), *An Index of Images in English MSS*, fascicle four, with Michael Orr (Brepols), and *The Medieval Hero on Screen* and *Shakespeare and the Middle Ages*, with Sid Ray (McFarland). She contributed to and edited *Preaching the Word in Manuscript and Print in Late Medieval England: Essays in Honour of Susan Powell* with Veronica O'Mara (Brepols, 2013).

Mimi Ensley is a PhD student in English at the University of Notre Dame, specializing in Middle English literature. Her research interests include history of the book, reception history, and the reading of medieval texts in the early stages of the printing press.

Alexandra Gillespie is an Associate Professor of English and Medieval Studies at the University of Toronto. Her research interests are in medieval manuscript production and the advent of printing. She is currently finishing a study of Chaucer's books and exhibits of annotated manuscripts and printed books that belonged to the Tudor antiquaries Matthew Parker and John Stow.

Carrie Griffin is currently lecturer in Early Modern English Literature at the University of Limerick, Ireland. She has also served as a Research Associate of the English Department, University of Bristol, and was formerly Marie Curie Postdoctoral Fellow at Queen Mary, University of London. Her edition of the *Wise Book of Philosophy and Astronomy* was published by Middle English Texts in 2013, and she is the editor, with Mary C. Flannery, of *Spaces for Reading in Later Medieval England*, forthcoming with Palgrave Macmillan.

Kevin Gustafson is Associate Professor of English and Associate Dean of the Honors College at the University of Texas at Arlington. He has published on a range of late-medieval and early modern writers and is currently working on a critical edition of the original version of Richard Rolle's English Psalter.

Ralph Hanna is Professor of Palaeography emeritus and emeritus fellow of Keble College, Oxford. His most recent major publication is *Editing Medieval Texts* (Liverpool, 2015). Other publications include editions for the Early English Text Society, *Richard Rolle: Uncollected Verse and Prose, with Related Northern Texts* (o.s. 329, 2007) and *Speculum Vitae: A Reading, Editions I and II* (o.s. 331-2, 2008).

ABOUT THE AUTHORS

Jill C. Havens is an Instructor II in the English Department at Texas Christian University. She is currently preparing an edition of Richard Rolle's English Psalter with Kevin Gustafson for the Early English Text Society.

Takako Kato is Senior Lecturer in English and Digital Humanities at De Montfort University. With Satako Tokunaga, she is currently working on the Caxton and Beyond Project (http://www.caxtonandbeyond.dmu.ac.uk/), funded by the Katharine F. Pantzer Research Fellowship by the Bibliographical Society. She co-authored *The Production and Use of English Manuscripts 1060 to 1220* (Leicester, http://www.le.ac.uk/ee/em1060to1220/, 2010; 2013), and her other publications include articles in *Middle English Texts in Transition*, edited by Simon Horobin and Linne R. Mooney (York, 2014) and *New Medieval Literatures* 13 (2012 for 2011).

Michael P. Kuczynski is Associate Professor and Chair of English at Tulane University, New Orleans. His research interests include manuscripts and early printed books, especially psalters, and recently have been concentrated on the marginal glosses of the Wycliffite Bible.

Michael Madrinkian is a doctoral candidate at the University of Oxford and lecturer in Middle English at Christ Church, Oxford. His research focuses primarily on manuscript circulation and textual criticism of religious literature in the fourteenth and fifteenth centuries. His current doctoral work examines the textual, geographical, and literary contexts of the *Piers Plowman* manuscripts.

J. R. Mattison is a second year M.Phil. student in English at Jesus College, University of Oxford. Her research focuses primarily on book use in late medieval England.

Linne Mooney is Professor of Medieval English Palaeography at the University of York (UK). She writes on late medieval English scribes, late medieval English manuscripts, Middle English authors, circulation, provenance, and patrons. She is also still acting as co-treasurer for European members of the Early Book Society.

Ann Eljenholm Nichols is preparing the second Cambridge fascicle for *An Index of Images in English Manuscripts from the Time of Chaucer to Henry VIII*.

Veronica O'Mara is a Professor in the Department of English at the University of Hull. Her main research areas are Middle English religious literature, female literacy, preaching, and the relationship between manuscript and print. She has recently edited (with Martha W. Driver) *Preaching the Word* *in Manuscript and Print in Late Medieval England: Essays in Honour of Susan Powell*, Sermo 11 (Turnhout: Brepols, 2013) and (with Virginia Blanton and Patricia Stoop) *Nuns' Literacies in Medieval Europe: The Hull Dialogue*, Medieval Women: Texts and Contexts, 26 (Turnhout: Brepols, 2013), and *Nuns' Literacies in Medieval Europe: The Kansas City Dialogue*, Medieval Women: Texts and Contexts, 27 (Turnhout: Brepols, 2015).

Derek Pearsall is Professor Emeritus of English at Harvard University, having retired in 2000. He has written extensively on Chaucer, Langland, Lydgate, and medieval English literature generally.

Helen Phillips is a retired Professor of English at Cardiff University. Her research interests are broad: political and cultural implications of late-medieval writings and their afterlife, Chaucer, Robin Hood studies, dream poetry, romances, nineteenth-century medievalism. Her most recent edited book is *Chaucer and Religion* (Cambridge: Brewer, 2010), to which she contributed chapters on "The Matter of Chaucer: Chaucer and the Boundaries of Romance" and "Morality in the *Canterbury Tales*, Chaucer's Lyrics and the *Legend of Good Women*."

Oliver Pickering is Honorary Fellow in the School of English, University of Leeds, and a Fellow of the English Association. He has published widely in the field of medieval English texts and manuscripts (often on aspects of the *South English Legendary* collection), and he has been co-editor of the Middle English Texts series and editor of *The Library*. His book-length publications include two volumes of the *Index of Middle English Prose* series (with Susan Powell and Veronica O'Mara, respectively). He was formerly Deputy Head of Special Collections in Leeds University Library.

Susan (Sue) Powell is Professor Emeritus of Medieval Texts and Culture (University of Salford) and a Research Associate at the Centre for Medieval Studies, University of York. She is currently a Visiting Research Fellow at the Institute of English Studies, University of London. She is an editor of manuscripts and early printed books, and her research focuses on religious and devotional texts and institutions. Her latest book, co-edited with Vincent Gillespie, is *A Companion to the Early Printed Book in Britain 1476-1558* (Cambridge: Brewer, 2014), and she is currently preparing an edition of the household papers of Lady Margaret Beaufort for the British Academy (Records of Social and Economic History).

Alexandra Reider is a Ph.D. student in the English Department at Yale. Her research interests include medieval multilingualism and the wisdom tradition in Old and Middle English literature. She has also published on the intersection of heroic terminology and tribal identity in *Beowulf*.

Anneliese Pollock Renck is a Visiting Assistant Professor of French at Bucknell University. She has previously published on female patronage and translation in fifteenth-century manuscript production, and is currently working on a book on the development of female reading and authorship in fifteenth and sixteenth-century France, forthcoming from Brepols.

Olivia Robinson is Stipendiary Lecturer in Medieval English at Brasenose College, Oxford, and works on translations between English and French in the late Middle Ages.

Nicholas Shangler is a Visiting Assistant Professor of French at Xavier University. He is refining his doctoral work on language and meaning in the French Renaissance for publication as a book while beginning research on a new project examining language politics in the early French colonial empire.

John Thompson is Chair of English Textual Cultures at Queen's University, Belfast, where he is also Director of the Institute for Collaborative Research in the Humanities. He has been a member of the Early Book Society since its inception and is currently interested in the textual afterlives of late medieval English religious literature. Together with Kathryn Kerby-Fulton and Sarah Baechle, he has recently edited *New Directions in Medieval Manuscript Studies and Reading Practices, Essays in Honour of Derek Pearsall* (Notre Dame, Indiana, 2014).

Deborah Thorpe is a Research Fellow at the Centre for Chronic Diseases and Disorders (C2D2) at the University of York. Her current research explores evidence for aging and age-related neurological conditions in the handwriting of medieval scribes and the impact of disease and disorder on scribes' working lives.

Livia Visser-Fuchs is an independent scholar, who worked and published for many years on the library of Richard III, especially his Book of Hours, and a variety of related subjects, with her co-author, Anne Sutton. At the same time she has been studying the life and work of Jean de Wavrin (1400 to after 1476), the Burgundian composer of a collection of chronicles of England. His career, his own book, his extensive library, and his patronage of an unusual illustrator have made this project a major one, but it is now approaching its completion.

Daniel Wakelin is Jeremy Griffiths Professor of Medieval English Palaeography in the University of Oxford and a Fellow of St. Hilda's College. He has recently been appointed as a co-editor of *JEBS* and has worked with Linne Mooney on the Nota Bene section of this issue. His recent publications include *Scribal Corrections and Literary Craft: English Manuscripts 1375-1510* (Cambridge University Press, 2014) and "When Scribes Won't Write: Gaps in Middle English Books," *Studies in the Age of Chaucer*, 36 (2014), 249-78. He has also contributed essays to *Probable Truth: Editing Medieval Texts from Britain*, edited by Vincent Gillespie and Anne Hudson (Brepols, 2013) and to *A Companion to the Early Printed Book in Britain*, edited by Susan Powell and Vincent Gillespie (D. S. Brewer, 2013), both of which are reviewed in this issue.

Kathryn Walls is Professor of English at the Victoria University of Wellington. She is the editor (with Marguerite Stobo) of William Baspoole's *The Pilgrime* (ACMRS 2008) and author of *God's Only Daughter: Spenser's Una as the Invisible Church* (Manchester UP 2013).

The eighteenth edition of the *Journal of the Early Book Society*
was published in Fall 2015
by Pace University Press

Cover Design by Mary Katherine Cornfield
Interior Design by Angela Taldone
The journal was typeset in Arno Pro
and printed by Lightning Source in La Vergne, Tennessee

Pace University Press

Director: Sherman Raskin
Associate Director: Manuela Soares
Graduate Assistants: Mary Katherine Cornfield and Angela Taldone
Student Aide: Kelsey O'Brien-Enders